AENEAS SILVIUS PICCOLOMINI

EUROPE

(c. 1400–1458)

TRANSLATED BY ROBERT BROWN

INTRODUCED AND ANNOTATED
BY NANCY BISAHA

THE CATHOLIC UNIVERSITY OF AMERICA PRESS
WASHINGTON, D.C.

Translation, introduction, and annotations
Copyright © 2013
The Catholic University of America Press
All rights reserved

Library of Congress Cataloging-in-Publication Data
Pius II, Pope, 1405–1464.
[Historia rerum Friderici Tertii imperatoris. English.]
Europe (c. 1400–1458) / Aeneas Silvius Piccolomini ; translated by Robert Brown; introduced and annotated by Nancy Bisaha.
pages cm
Includes bibliographical references and index.
ISBN 978-0-8132-3263-8 (pbk)
1. Europe—History—476–1492—Early works to 1800.
2. Holy Roman Empire—History—Frederick III, 1440–1493.
3. Frederick III, Holy Roman Emperor, 1415–1493.
I. Brown, Robert D. (Robert Duncan), 1950– translator.
II. Bisaha, Nancy, editor.   III. Title.
DD173.P5813 2014
943'.028—dc23   2013024763

To Diana, Dave, and Jocelyn

CONTENTS

List of Illustrations   xi
Acknowledgments   xiii

Introduction   3
The Author, 5   The Concept of Europe, 10
De Europa (Europe), 16   Notes on the Text,
Translation, and Apparatus, 36

EUROPE

Dedication Letter   49
1. Hungary   51
2. Transylvania, Valachia   64
3. Thrace, Romania, Constantinople   69
4. Origin and History of the Turks   72
5. The Battle of Varna   79
6. The Battle of Kosovo   90
7. The Fall of Constantinople   93
8. The Battle of Belgrade   101
9. Macedonia, Thessaly   103
10. Boeotia   106
11. Attica   107
12. The Peloponnese, the Isthmus, Achaea   108
13. Acarnania   111
14. Epirus   111

15.	Albania	113
16.	The Illyrian Nations, Bosnia	115
17.	Dalmatia, Croatia, Liburnia	116
18.	Istria	117
19.	Carniola	119
20.	Carinthia	120
21.	Styria	124
22.	Austria	127
23.	Moravia	135
24.	Silesia	136
25.	Poland	138
26.	Lithuania	141
27.	Ruthenia	147
28.	Livonia	147
29.	Prussia: The Teutonic Brothers	148
30.	The Saxon Nation, Pomerania	156
31.	Thuringia, Halberstadt	158
32.	Brunswick, Saxony	160
33.	Denmark, Norway, Sweden	165
34.	Bohemia	170
35.	Frisia	171
36.	Holland, Utrecht, Dordrecht, Westphalia	173
37.	Hesse	179
38.	The Franks	180
39.	Franconia	186
40.	Bavaria, the Palatinate, Swabia	191
41.	The Margravate of Baden, the Tyrol, Switzerland	196
42.	Alsace, the Vogtland, Savoy, Arles	197
43.	France	201
44.	Ghent	208
45.	England	209
46.	Scotland, Ireland	211

Contents

47. Spain, Castile, Navarre, Portugal	212
48. Italy: Genoa	216
49. Italy: Milan	219
50. Italy: Venice	231
51. Italy: Mantua	234
52. Italy: Ferrara	235
53. Italy: Bologna	237
54. Italy: Florence, Lucca, San Casciano	241
55. Italy: Siena	251
56. Italy: Piombino	255
57. Italy: Viterbo	258
58. Italy: Rome	259
59. Italy: Umbria, the Marches	274
60. Italy: Ascoli Piceno	283
61. Italy: Urbino	284
62. Italy: Rimini	285
63. Italy: Faenza, Fabriano	286
64. Italy: Aquila	287
65. Italy: Naples	288
Appendix: Reigns of Selected Rulers	311
Bibliography	317
Index	335

ILLUSTRATIONS

All illustrations are courtesy of the Archives & Special Collections Library, Vassar College

Pope Pius II and Emperor Frederick III	xvii
Sixteenth-Century Map of Europe	xviii
Sixteenth-Century Map of Prussia	xix
Constantinople	xx

ACKNOWLEDGMENTS

ONE OF THE MOST REWARDING aspects of this project has been to witness again and again the generosity of colleagues around the world. Many of the individuals who kindly assisted us were scholars we had met or knew well, but just as many were strangers to us before the project began—known only by their fine work and reputation. We gratefully acknowledge the alacrity and care with which they responded to our queries and read portions of the manuscript. Some of them effortlessly produced an answer to an identification or translation question with which we had struggled for months; others confirmed that an educated guess, in fact, made good sense. Sometimes they replied with a good natured "I have no idea," reassuring us that we were not overlooking the obvious. These scholars as a group became our "Republic of Letters," reminding us on many occasions of the camaraderie Aeneas shared with all the humanists he named as his narrative traveled across Europe. Their expertise saved us from numerous errors and helped fill in many lacunae. All errors and omissions are completely our own.

Several individuals read the manuscript in full or large portions of it. We especially wish to thank Tom Izbicki for his suggestions, corrections, and encouragement as well as his quick answers to many little questions throughout the process. John Monfasani also offered helpful comments on the manuscript and aided us on a number of details. John V. A. Fine read several sections on the Balkans, lending his expertise and friendly support early in the project. Thomas Brady read several portions of the work pertaining to Germany, generously offering specific suggestions as well as useful guidelines for dealing with tricky titles and personal and place names. William Urban helped us with several challenging passages on Eastern Europe and the Teutonic Knights and was a ready correspondent on numerous questions. Patrick Geary came to the rescue on a handful of puzzling medieval identifications, on which Aeneas's vague descriptions gave us few leads. Bill Caffero was very helpful on several passages dealing with obscure battles and military leaders. Colin Imber helped us navigate questions on the Ottoman Empire and key battles in Eastern Europe. Erika Harlitz generously helped us untangle the mysteries of the reigns of Scandinavian leaders, which we hope we have not since re-tangled. Steven Epstein, Kenneth Gouwens, and Charles Stinger all provided helpful insights on passages dealing with Italy. Catherine Castner came to our aid on some unusual place names and helped us think through a number of issues. John Najemy and Carol Helstosky offered much-appreciated advice and support at a critical juncture. Finally, we thank the anonymous reader for the press who pushed us to clarify our interpretations, saved us from several errors, and increased our resolve to polish this project and see it through.

Other scholars kindly assisted on critical interpretive points. Our warm thanks to Jane Black, Robert Black, Sarah Brooks, Chris Celenza, Niels Gaul, Norman Housley, Andrea Marza, David Peterson, Marios Philippides, Tom Scott, Michael Shank, John Tolan, and Zsombor Toth. Jessica Pigza at the New York Public Library also kindly assisted us in finding a rare book in electronic form after many failed attempts to secure a microfilm.

We turn now with equal pleasure to friends, colleagues, and students at Vassar. From the History Department, Jim Merrell read and offered insightful comments on an early draft of the introduction to this book; the final version does not do justice to his compelling remarks. Both Jim and Rebecca Edwards were a great sup-

Acknowledgments

port on this project at several key points in its development, and their friendship sustained us amidst the challenges. Thanks also go to Miriam Cohen and Bob Brigham for their faith in this project, which they read in an early stage. Librarian and historian Ron Patkus was a tremendous help on several tricky points and cheerfully lent his prodigious research skills. Zoltan Markus from the English Department also helped with some interpretive questions and put us in touch with specialists who sought to answer our arcane queries. We also wish to thank the determined and resourceful specialists at the Vassar Library who helped us acquire important books and microfilms, including librarian Deb Bucher and the staff of the Interlibrary Loan and Acquisitions Departments. For all their help in securing a map and other images for this volume, we thank, again, Ron Patkus, as well as Mary Ann Cunningham, Gretchen Lieb, and Stephanie La Rose. For general moral support, we warmly thank Mark Seidl and Leslie Offutt, with special thanks to Michelle Whalen for her unflagging good cheer and technical assistance on matters great and small. Last, but by no means least, we thank our student research assistants who lightened our burdens at many steps along the way: Michael Greene, Gwendolyn Collaco, and Sarah Hutcheson. A special thanks to Michael for double-checking the appendix of rulers.

At the Catholic University of America Press we are very pleased to thank the director, Trevor Lipscombe, who supported this project and helped us navigate the review and submission process at several important stages. We also wish to thank David McGonagle, his predecessor, who warmly welcomed us to the press and encouraged our work in the early stages. Managing editor Theresa Walker offered sound advice and kindly answered a good many questions related to editing and the submission process. We are also grateful to copy editor Nicole Pfeifer for helping us polish the final version and for bringing some thoughtful questions to our attention, and Anne Kachergis for assistance with images and graphics.

Acknowledgments

Finally, we wish to thank our families, who generously made room in their lives for extended visits from Aeneas and his wonderful text. To our spouses, Diana Brown, who, together with providing constant encouragement, improved the translation in several places, and David Bieler, who helped with countless formatting questions and technical challenges, educating us both in the wonderful world of file-sharing technology, we could not have completed this project without your support, understanding, and unlimited patience at every turn. To Jocelyn Bieler, who patiently bore with her mother's frequent disappearances to her office, a hearty thanks for immeasurably brightening her breaks from the ongoing task. We dedicate this book to the three of you.

Nancy Bisaha and Robert Brown
Vassar College

Pope Pius II and Emperor Frederick III. Hartmann Schedel, Liber chronicarum (Nuremberg, 1493), fol. cclxvii(r).

2. Sixteenth-Century Map of Europe. Aeneas Silvius Piccolomini (Pope Pius II), *Opera quae extant omnia* (Basel, 1571), 387.

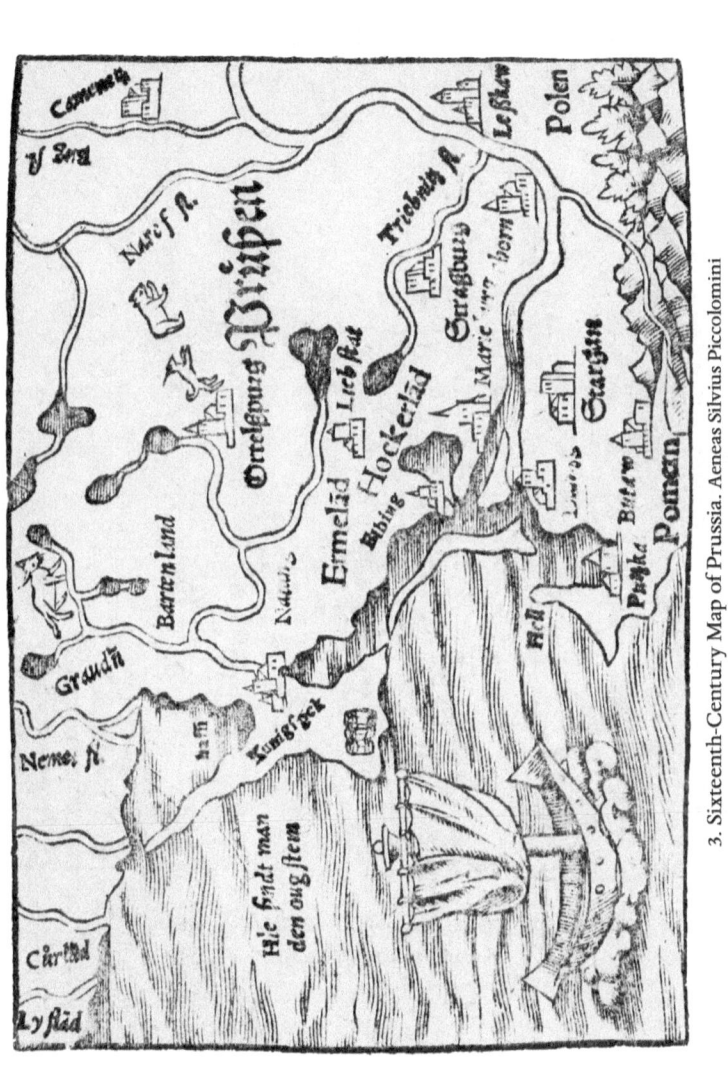

3. Sixteenth-Century Map of Prussia. Aeneas Silvius Piccolomini (Pope Pius II), Opera quae extant omnia (Basel, 1571), 420.

4. Constantinople. Hartmann Schedel, Liber chronicarum (Nuremberg, 1493), fol. ccxlix(r).

INTRODUCTION

INTRODUCTION

Few words are as powerful or as controversial as "Europe." It signifies a continent, a historical phenomenon, an economic or political force, and an ideological concept with vast cultural influence. Moreover, within each of these categories, a multitude of interpretations and definitions exist. Despite the lack of agreement on its meaning, "Europe" is a surprisingly solid and weighty term.[1] Much of this substance, at least from a historical point of view, may be attributed to the creation of the European Economic Community (EEC) in 1957 and the European Union (EU) in 1993. But for many, the EEC and the EU merely standardized the workings of an entity that had functioned as a unit for centuries, despite frequent internal disputes and violent confrontations. This is not to say that the boundaries of Europe are or ever have been fixed. The creation of the EU, in particular, has renewed debates about which countries or peoples can or should be called "European." How far east the boundaries should extend or whether a Muslim country like Turkey may belong, are questions of particular interest to many. Simultaneously celebrated and vili-

---

1. Recent studies on the concept of Europe include Anthony Pagden, ed., *The Idea of Europe from Antiquity to the European Union* (Cambridge: Cambridge University Press, 2002); Evlyn Gould and George J. Sheridan Jr., eds., *Engaging Europe: Rethinking a Changing Continent* (New York: Rowman and Littlefield, 2005); Gerard Delanty, *Inventing Europe: Idea, Identity, Reality* (London: Palgrave Macmillan, 1995). See also Peter Rietbergen, *Europe: A Cultural History* (London: Routledge, 1998).

fied, Europe is both a place and an idea whose existence is simply taken for granted. This was not always the case.

Aeneas Silvius Piccolomini's *Europe* (1458), presented here for the first time in English, was written when the modern concept of Europe as a cultural or political unit was just beginning to take shape. Before his time, it was a word used by relatively few writers and with far less consensus than it is today; "Christendom," in fact, was the standard designation. A century later, however, "Europe" was a commonly used term and topic of interest.[2] Many factors surely brought about this shift: exploration and colonization of Africa, the Americas, and Asia, which vastly expanded the science of geography; the Protestant Reformation which complicated the more familiar notion of "Christendom"; and Ottoman domination of Eastern Europe, which made terms like "Christian" and "European" less stable than they had once been.[3] But amidst all these significant developments, one must consider what "Europeans" were reading—especially about themselves. The timing alone of *Europe*, even if it remained one little-known manuscript, makes it well worth the attention. This work, however, immediately found a broad and eager audience and was widely circulated in both manuscript and print; it was even translated within a century into two modern languages.[4] Thus, it is a very important text for anyone interested in the origins of the modern notion of Europe. Not only did Aeneas compose it when concepts of Europe were changing

---

2. John Hale, "The Discovery of Europe," chap. 1 of *The Civilization of Europe in the Renaissance* (New York: Atheneum, 1994). Denys Hay also notes a marked increase in the use of "Europe" instead of "Christendom" in the sixteenth century; see *Europe: The Emergence of an Idea* (Edinburgh: Edinburgh University Press, 1957), 101. The concept of Europe is treated later in the introduction.

3. Hale, *Civilization*, 4–5; Hay, *Europe*, chaps. 5–6; Delanty, *Inventing Europe*, chap. 4.

4. The circulation of *Europe* is discussed later in the introduction. For more on the text itself, see the following two very helpful articles: Nicola Casella, "Pio II tra geografia e storia: la 'Cosmographia,'" *Archivio della Società romana di storia patria* 95 (1972): 35–112; Barbara Baldi, "Enea Silvio Piccolomini e il *De Europa*: umanesimo, religion, e politica," *Archivio storico italiano* 161 (2003): 619–83.

but he was a well-known writer who helped influence that very change.

THE AUTHOR

Aeneas Silvius Piccolomini was born in 1405 in Corsignano, a small suburb of Siena; after he became Pope Pius II in 1458, he rebuilt the town and named it Pienza.[5] The youngest of eighteen children, Aeneas was raised in a noble but poor family with a small patrimony; the once-prominent Piccolomini had fallen on hard times following their exile from Siena in 1385. Despite their straitened circumstances, Aeneas's parents were able to secure a good education for their son, with help from an aunt and uncle who took

5. On Aeneas's life, two of the best primary sources are his autobiography, *The Commentaries*, and his letters. The former is in the process of being edited and translated by Margaret Meserve and Marcello Simonetta: *The Commentaries* (Cambridge, Mass.: Harvard University Press, vol. 1, 2003; vol. 2, 2007). A full translated version may be found in *The Commentaries of Pius II*, trans. Florence A. Gragg, ed. Leona C. Gabel (Northampton, Mass.: Smith College, 1951), vols. 1–5. The majority of Aeneas's letters were edited by Rudolph Wolkan in *Der Briefwechsel des Eneas Silvius Piccolomini* in *Fontes rerum austriacarum*, vols. 61, 62, 67, 68 (Vienna: Alfred Holder, 1909–18). A fine selection of over seventy of Aeneas's letters has recently been translated with welcome critical commentary; see *Reject Aeneas, Accept Pius: Selected Letters of Aeneas Sylvius Piccolomini (Pope Pius II)*, intr. and trans. Thomas M. Izbicki, Gerald Christianson, and Philip Krey (Washington: The Catholic University of America Press, 2006). Among the modern studies on Pius, see R. J. Mitchell, *The Laurels and the Tiara: Pope Pius II 1458–64* (London: Harvill Press, 1962); Cecilia M. Ady, *Pius II (Aeneas Silvius Piccolomini) the Humanist Pope* (London: Methuen and Co., 1913); Giacchino Paparelli, *Enea Silvio Piccolomini: L'Umanesimo sul Soglio di Pietro* (Ravenna: Longo, 1978). See also Berthe Widmer, *Enea Silvio Piccolomini, Papst Pius II* (Basel: Benno Schwabe and Co., 1960), which includes selections of Aeneas's works. Useful essays on Pius can be found in Eugenio Garin, *Portraits from the Quattrocento* (New York: Harper and Row, 1963) and Robert Schwoebel, *Renaissance Men and Ideas* (New York: St. Martin's Press, 1971). Among the collections of essays on Pius, see Zweder von Martels and Arjo Vanderjagt, eds., *Pius II, 'El Più Expeditivo Pontifice': Selected Studies on Aeneas Silvius Piccolomini (1405–1464)* (Leiden: Brill, 2003); Luisa Rotondi Secchi Tarugi, ed., *Pio II e la cultura del suo tempo* (Milan: Guerini e Associati, 1991); Arturo Calzona et al., eds., *Il sogno di Pio II e il viaggio da Roma a Mantova* (Mantua: Leo S. Olschki, 2003); Manlio Sodi and Arianna Antoniutti, eds., *Enea Silvio Piccolomini Pius Secundus Poeta Laureatus Pontifex Maximus* (Rome: Libreria Editrice Vaticana, 2007); Fabrizio Nevola, ed., *Pio II Piccolomini il Papa del Rinascimento a Siena* (Siena: Protagon Editore, 2009). See also the older but excellent collection of essays edited by Domenico Maffei, *Enea Silvio Piccolomini Papa Pio II* (Siena: Varese, 1968).

Aeneas in while he studied in Siena. After learning grammar, rhetoric, and law in Siena, he spent some years as an itinerant scholar in Florence, Padua, Bologna, and Ferrara. There he met and studied with prominent humanists like Francesco Filelfo, Guarino da Verona, and Giovanni Aurispa.

In 1431 Aeneas landed his first job, as a secretary in the service of Cardinal Domenico Capranica. He accompanied the cardinal to Switzerland in the spring of 1432 to attend the Council of Basel and remained with the council for the next ten years working for various prelates. This was an exciting period in church history. The gathering at Basel was the first major council following the resolution of the Papal Schism (1378–1417), which was reached at the Council of Constance; the plan established at Constance was for general councils to be called at regular intervals in order to address problems within the church. Basel, therefore, represents the highpoint of political and ecclesiastical influence in the conciliar movement, with its members laboring to initiate reform and to bring the pope under their jurisdiction. Meanwhile, Pope Eugenius IV (r. 1431–47) endeavored to resist many of the directives of Basel. These battles culminated with the council deposing Eugenius and electing Amedeo of Savoy as anti-pope Felix V (r. 1440–49). Had Aeneas silently witnessed these events, his future path toward clerical preferment might have been smoother, but to his later embarrassment, he penned dozens of passionate letters, an oration, and three treatises defending conciliarist positions. To be sure, it was his job to argue his employers' views as persuasively as possible, but there is much to suggest that Aeneas personally agreed with many of the council's goals.[6]

Despite these later difficulties, Basel proved fruitful for Aeneas's intellectual development and political advancement. As he obtained

6. See Izbicki et al., *Reject Aeneas*, specifically 117–20, 137–49, 154–56. Aeneas's pro-conciliar writings and later retractions are analyzed by Emily O'Brien in *The Anatomy of an Apology: The War against Conciliarism and the Politicization of Papal Authority in the Commentarii of Pope Pius II (1458–64)*, Ph.D. diss., Brown University, 2005.

positions of greater importance, Aeneas found increasing opportunities to address the council and became known for his rhetorical prowess. He was appointed master of ceremonies in the conclave that elected Felix V, and went on to serve the anti-pope as secretary. The Basel years, moreover, afforded Aeneas numerous chances to travel in France, Germany, Switzerland, and Italy, either with his employers or on embassies for them. He went as far as England and Scotland in 1435/36 on a covert mission for Cardinal Niccolò Albergati to King James I of Scotland to help negotiate assistance for the French in the Hundred Years' War. Aeneas's fascination for the societies and cultures he visited and his keen observations would contribute significantly to his material for composing *Europe*.

By 1442, it was clear that few European powers would support Basel's deposition of Eugenius and election of Felix. In that year, Aeneas accepted a position in the chancery of Holy Roman Emperor Frederick III (r. 1440–93)—a post that acquainted him well with Germany, Austria, and Bohemia. Aeneas spent much of the next thirteen years in the imperial court, rising through the ranks to become Frederick's trusted adviser and agent. These were life-altering years for Aeneas in two ways. In 1445 he left his conciliar sympathies behind and swore an oath of loyalty to the pope, and in 1446 he entered the priesthood. Both shifts also had serious consequences for Frederick, who was reconciled with the pope in 1447 thanks to Aeneas's persistence and finesse. Thus ended Frederick's neutrality between Basel and Rome, and the council was left more powerless than before. Meanwhile, Aeneas's star continued to rise.

Aeneas's entry into holy orders and his rapid path to preferment, however, led some contemporaries and later scholars to question these sudden changes and doubt his sincerity.[7] For years Aeneas had been known for his love poetry, which he began circulating at Basel, and for his racy comedic works. In 1444, a mere two years

---

[7]. The boldest modern argument was made by Georg Voigt in *Enea Silvio de' Piccolomini als Papst Pius II und sein Zeitalter*, 3 vols. (Berlin: De Gruyter, 1856–63).

before his conversion, he completed his famous novel *The Tale of Two Lovers*, the bawdy play *Chrysis*, and a sardonic treatise titled *On the Miseries of Courtiers*. His letters up to this point, moreover, reveal a man who warmly jested about the love affairs of others and engaged in his own, fathering two children out of wedlock who died in infancy. Yet there is much to support the view that Aeneas entered the church with gravity and resolve. He had considered taking holy orders during his student years in Siena after hearing the sermons of San Bernardino, but decided to put off such a move until he was ready to accept the demands of religious life wholeheartedly. Indeed, he took sacred vows very seriously, fulfilling them even at great risk to his health. While journeying to Scotland in 1435, Aeneas's ship was tossed for days by gales, prompting him to swear that if he arrived safely, he would walk barefoot to the nearest shrine to the Virgin. Although it was winter and the distance was ten miles, Aeneas fulfilled his pledge, resulting in a lifelong battle with an affliction which was commonly described as the gout, but more likely frostbite arthritis.[8] Further evidence of a change of heart can be found in his letters of 1445–46, which show growing austerity and sense of his own mortality.[9] Unlike many clergymen of his day—including the scandalous cardinal Rodrigo Borgia (later, Pope Alexander VI)—when Aeneas took holy orders in late 1446, by all accounts he firmly put the sins of the flesh behind him.[10]

Shortly after his ordination, Aeneas became bishop of Trieste (1447) and Siena (1450). In the meantime, he remained in Freder-

---

8. This condition, which leads to cartilage attrition and osteoarthritis, makes more sense than gout although the symptoms are very similar; see W. W. Buchanan, "Frostbite Arthritis Consequence of First Papal Visit to Scotland?" *Clinical Rheumatology* 6, no. 3 (1987): 436–38. See also Pius's *Commentaries*, book I, for his account of the journey (Meserve and Simonetta, vol. 1: 20–29; Gragg and Gabel, vol. 1: 16–20).

9. See Izbicki et al., *Reject Aeneas*, 204–5, 231–33, 235–38.

10. For a discussion of Aeneas's complicated personal shifts, see Thomas Izbicki, "'Reject Aeneas!' Pius II on the Errors of his Youth" in *Pius II*, ed. von Martels and Vanderjagt, 187–203.

Introduction 9

ick's service, where he was anything but idle. In 1453 the Ottoman Turks captured Constantinople, and the threat they posed to Europe became an obsession for Aeneas. Upon hearing the news, he immediately wrote impassioned letters to Pope Nicholas V (r. 1447–55) and other rulers and prelates lamenting the loss of the city and calling for common Christian action.[11] Aeneas played a key role in three imperial diets where the prospect of a crusade was discussed: Regensburg, Frankfurt (both in 1454), and Wiener-Neustadt (1455). Frederick could not rouse himself to attend any of these diets, but Aeneas delivered stirring orations in his absence, at least one of which received wide circulation.[12] The Turkish advance would also feature prominently in Aeneas's growing concept of Europe and its need for a united front.

Aeneas was created cardinal by Pope Calixtus III (r. 1455–58) in late 1456; it was during his cardinalate, in 1458, that he wrote *Europe*. A few months later, he was elected pope and took steps to plan a crusade against the Turks.[13] He convoked the Congress at Mantua (1459) in the hopes of organizing a large-scale, multinational offensive. The bickering of European powers and their mistrust of the papacy, however, presented a host of obstacles. Pius's dismay at the failure of Mantua, among other challenges, led to his issuing the controversial papal bull, *Execrabilis* (1460), which condemned the calling of councils without papal consent—a complete reversal of his youthful conciliarism. During his pontificate, Aeneas also spent considerable time restoring order to the Papal States and pacifying warring factions in Italy. In addition, he faced unrelenting

11. Wolkan, *Briefwechsel*, vol. 68, 188–215; Izbicki et al., *Reject Aeneas*, 306–18. Aeneas had also expressed concern about the Turkish advance before 1453, such as his reaction to the Christian defeat at Varna (1444).
12. See Johannes Helmrath, "The German *Reichstage* and the Crusade," in *Crusading in the Fifteenth Century: Message and Impact*, ed. Norman Housley (New York: Palgrave Macmillan, 2004), 53–69.
13. Specific details of Aeneas's election to the papacy are humorously portrayed in his autobiography, the *Commentaries*, book I (Meserve and Simonetta, vol. 1: 176–201; Gragg and Gabel, vol. 1: 93–104).

pressure from France to support its claim to the throne of Naples. In spite of all these preoccupations, Pius found time to write several works including, in 1461, *Asia* and his controversial letter to Mehmed II, ostensibly offering his enemy a peaceful alliance in exchange for his conversion to Christianity.[14] Also during his pontificate, Pius composed his fascinating autobiography, the *Commentaries*. The crusade, however, remained his ultimate goal. Pius's last dramatic act as pope was an attempt to lead the crusade personally, but illness overtook him before it left Italy. He died at the port of Ancona on August 14, 1464.[15] Viewed as a whole, Aeneas's extraordinary career—with his direct experience of many countries, his unparalleled political connections, and his commitment to protect Europe against the Turks—explains both his interest in and profound knowledge of the European continent.

THE CONCEPT OF EUROPE

Seeking the "true" origins of the notion of Europe is a task scholars take on at their own peril. In the past few decades, some claims have been made for different moments in the premodern era as the birthplace of this monumental idea.[16] Most scholars, including our-

14. *Asia* is printed in the *Opera omnia*, 281–386; for a recent edition see *Descripción de Asia*, ed. and trans. Domingo F. Sanz (Madrid: Consejo Superior de Investigaciones Centíficas, 2010). For analyses of this work, see Casella, "Pio II tra geografia e storia"; also Margaret Meserve, "From Samarkand to Scythia: Reinventions of Asia in Renaissance Geography and Political Thought" and Konrad Vollman, "Aeneas Silvius Piccolomini as a Historiographer: *Asia*," both in *Pius II*, ed. von Martels and Vanderjagt. Pius's letter to Mehmed II is edited and translated by Albert Baca, *Epistola ad Mahomatem II (Epistle to Mohammed II)* (New York: Peter Lang, 1990); see Nancy Bisaha, "Pope Pius II's Letter to Sultan Mehmed II: A Reexamination" *Crusades* 1 (2002): 183–200, for an analysis of the work and Pius's intentions.

15. On Pius II and crusade, see Norman Housley, "Pope Pius II and Crusading," *Crusades* 11 (2012): 209–47. See also Kenneth Setton, *The Papacy and the Levant (1204–1571)* (Philadelphia: American Philosophical Society, 1978), vol. 2; Nancy Bisaha, "Pope Pius II and the Crusade," in *Crusading in the Fifteenth Century*, ed. Housley.

16. One of the more recent studies which focuses on the Carolingian era is found in Michael Mitterauer, *Why Europe: The Medieval Origins of its Special Path*, trans. Gerard Chappel (Chicago: University of Chicago Press, 2010), originally published in German in

selves, see not one formative moment, but a series of moments that built upon each other over the centuries.¹⁷ The Renaissance was a major milestone in this development, but there were many important precedents.

The ancient Greeks played a significant role, as they introduced the earliest concepts of Europe; Roman writers, in turn, continued to shape the idea. Herodotus, Strabo, Pliny, and others found Εὐρώπη, or *Europa*, a convenient label as their narratives surveyed the continents. It was also used from time to time in a geopolitical sense; Greek writers employed "Europe" and "Asia" to denote the seriousness of the Persian threat to the Hellenes or to distinguish Greeks from "barbaric" neighbors. Though the term was not common in the Middle Ages, it was occasionally applied to Muslim or Mongol threats to Christendom.¹⁸

While Renaissance thinkers inherited some of their ideas about Europe from predecessors, two very important changes took place regarding their use of "Europe." First, and most apparent, was a surge in frequency, which has already been noted; for various reasons, Renaissance writers found the term far more applicable and meaningful than previous generations. Second, and equally important, is the way in which the term was used. Arguably, it is not

---

2003. See William Caferro's thoughtful review in the BMCR, July 15, 2011. For an earlier claim, see *The Birth of the European Identity: The Europe-Asia Contrast in Greek Thought, 490–322 B.C.*, ed. H. A. Khan (Nottingham: Nottingham Classical Literature Studies, vol. 2, 1993).

17. See, for instance, Hay, *Europe*; Delanty, *Inventing Europe*; Rietbergen, *Europe*; Pagden, *The Idea of Europe*.

18. See Khan, *The Birth of the European Identity*, especially Jan Ziolkowski's essay, "National and Other Contrasts in the Athenian Funeral Orations." On medieval usages, see Urban II's sermon at Clermont in 1095, or at least William of Malmesbury's version of it, calling for the First Crusade; Hay, *Europe*, 32. See also Alexander of Roes' thirteenth-century reference in Felicitas Schmieder, "Der mongolische Augenblick in der Weltgeschichte oder: Als Europa aus der Wiege wuchs," in: *Produktive Kulturkonflikte*, ed. Felicitas Schmieder, Das Mittelalter 10, no. 2 (Berlin: Akademie Verlag, 2005), 63–73. As Hay has noted, "up to and including the thirteenth [century] the word Europe itself is thus rarely met in passages other than those descriptive of geographical situation"; see *Europe*, 51.

until the Renaissance that large numbers of the inhabitants of the continent of Europe began to imagine and describe themselves as "European"—to embrace a common cultural and, to some extent, political, identity and destiny. While the roots of European identity can be traced to antiquity, we would do well to ask if Greeks, Romans, or medieval Christians saw themselves as part of a reasonably coherent "European" culture before the Renaissance. Scholarship on this topic has strongly suggested they did not.[19]

Unlike early modern Europeans, the ancient Greeks commonly thought of their larger community as being their individual city-states or, in moments of confrontation with a greater external enemy like Persia, Macedon, or Rome, "Hellas" might be invoked. Romans also viewed their towns or provinces as their broader community, or if they were looking to describe their broader collective, the "Roman Empire." Hence, while ancients used the term Εὐρώπη or *Europa*, it appeared less frequently in their writings than "Asia," suggesting that one's grander sense of "self" was more elusive and variable than the two-dimensional, monolithic "other."[20] In the Middle Ages—when Florentines, Castilians, or Scots wished to define themselves more broadly—they preferred the name "Chris-

---

19. In addition to studies cited previously, a recent article shows that ancient Greeks clearly perceived Western European peoples as outsiders, or "multiple others, each hinting at some desire or dread." See Paul T. Keyser, "Greek Geography of the Western Barbarians," in *The Barbarians of Ancient Europe, Realities and Interactions*, ed. Larissa Bonfante (Cambridge: Cambridge University Press, 2011), 37–70.

20. "Asia" was not always used in the same way, for that matter. While it could refer to the entire continent of Asia, it usually stood for Asia Minor. Alexander the Great and the Romans, of course, conquered parts of Asia, not to mention Africa, which further complicated the self-other dichotomy. Indeed while the Romans originated in Europe, they became lords of the world, as they saw it, and tended to view themselves as culturally more like the cosmopolitan peoples of North Africa and Asia than the Germans and Celts. See Hay, *Europe*, 3–5; Anthony Pagden, "Europe: Conceptualizing a Continent," in Pagden, *The Idea of Europe*, 33–42; Delanty, *Inventing Europe*, 16–23; see also *Roman Europe*, ed. Edward Bispham (Oxford: Oxford University Press, 2008), which discusses the empire's experience in Europe but does not support the notion of Rome as self-identified with Europe; see especially Benet Salway, "The Roman Empire from Augustus to Diocletian," 72–78, and Bispham's introduction, 1–7.

Introduction 13

tian" to "European." Indeed, Christendom (*Christianitas*) was the term of choice for the area that takes in (but is not limited to) Europe. The identities that mattered most to medieval thinkers were religious faith, social status or trade, and citizenship or residence on the smallest scale, such as village or town.[21] What held Christendom together was allegiance to the pope and, perhaps, a loose concept of fealty to the Germanic Roman Emperors, titled "Holy Roman Emperors" from the twelfth century onward.[22] Finally, patriotism or proto-nationalism, if either can be said to have existed at this stage, were only vague ideas in the later Middle Ages; terms like "German" or "French" were more commonly used to identify foreigners than oneself.[23]

What conditions, then, prepared Renaissance society to embrace a common European identity, and what inspired Aeneas to write a history not of the world, or Christendom, or Italy, but of recent events "among the Europeans" (*apud Europeos*)? To some extent, this shift in thinking may be attributed to the degradation of two institutions with claims to universal power: papacy and empire. Papal authority, which had long defined Latin Christendom, was compromised in three ways: first, by the move to Avignon (1305–77); then by the Schism (1378–1417) in which two, then three, popes claimed the title; and finally by the conciliar movement, which threatened to decentralize church powers and policy. As for the Holy Roman Empire, the growing autonomy of city-states

---

21. See William C. Jordan, "'Europe' in the Middle Ages," in Pagden, *The Idea of Europe*, 72–90; Suzanne Conklin Akbari, "From Due East to True North: Orientalism and Orientation," in *The Postcolonial Middle Ages*, ed. Jeffrey Jerome Cohen (New York: St. Martin's Press, 2000), 19–34. See also Akbari's recent *Idols in the East: European Representations of Islam and the Orient, 1100–1450* (Ithaca, N.Y.: Cornell University Press, 2009) for her discussion of how medieval Christianity and Islam were by no means viewed as synonymous with Europe and Asia.

22. Hay, *Europe*, 72.

23. Concepts of foreigners and barbarians in the ancient and medieval period are also discussed in Nancy Bisaha, *Creating East and West: Renaissance Humanists and the Ottoman Turks* (Philadelphia: University of Pennsylvania Press, 2004), 43–50.

and local lords forced emperors to accept the loss of their authority over non-German and even German states. The role of emperors in the fourteenth and fifteenth centuries became ever more limited and weak.[24] At the same time, parochial forces began to compete with and challenge the supranational powers of empire and church. This may be seen in the growing use of vernacular languages in official, scholarly, and literary circles and the increasing power of locally born clergymen as opposed to foreigners appointed by Rome.[25]

While papal and imperial authority dwindled, the Ottoman Empire grew stronger in the East. Founded by Osman (d. ca. 1326), the Ottoman Dynasty expanded beyond its origins in northwest Anatolia, spread into the Balkans, defeated the crusades of Nicopolis (1396) and Varna (1444), and captured Constantinople (1453). The conquest of Constantinople came as a particular shock to many Christians, including Aeneas, who lamented it as a devastating loss to faith and learning as well as a blow to European security. On hearing the news he wrote, "The nearby house has been burned; now we await the fire. Who now lies between us and the Turks? ... The leader of the Turks chose an opportune time for himself. He safely invaded the Greeks while the Latins accepted divisions among themselves."[26] For a time, however, it seemed as if Christians might overcome their differences. Italian powers negotiated a truce, the Peace of Lodi in 1454; Frederick III called diets to discuss a crusade; and Philip of Burgundy swore an oath to lead a crusade.

24. Hay, *Europe*, 63–72; Jordan, "'Europe' in the Middle Ages," 82–83; 88.
25. Jordan, "'Europe' in the Middle Ages," 84–87. See also Hay's discussion of Petrarch's frequent use of the term "Europe," demonstrating its growing appeal in scholarly circles; *Europe*, 59–60.
26. Letter to Nicholas of Cusa, in Izbicki et al., *Reject Aeneas*, 315. On European reactions to the fall of Constantinople, see Robert Schwoebel, *The Shadow of the Crescent: The Renaissance Image of the Turk (1453–1517)* (New York: St. Martin's Press, 1967); see also Bisaha, *Creating East and West*. For an overview of some of Aeneas's writings on the Turks, see Johannes Helmrath, "Pius II und die Türken," in *Europa und die Türken in der Renaissance*, eds. Bodo Guthmüller and Wilhelm Kühlmann (Tübingen: Max Niemayer Verlag, 2000), 79–137.

In addition, Hungarian forces won a surprising victory against Mehmed II's army at Belgrade in 1456. Pope Calixtus III (r. 1455–58) made crusading his top priority, and his forces won some victories of their own against the Turks. But by 1458, few Christians had made good on their promises to further the cause of holy war and, worse, they returned to the same petty quarrels, decried by Aeneas in 1453.[27]

Against the backdrop of the Ottoman advance and Christian apathy, Aeneas's *Europe* could be read as an exhortation to Christians to view themselves as part of a cultural, religious, and geographical collective, even as it acknowledges the diversity among its peoples.[28] It is tempting to imagine unity was Aeneas's goal, given his impassioned pleas to defend Europe during his papacy and his evocation of a common European culture in other writings.[29] It is not clear, however, if this was Aeneas's conscious intention in writing *Europe*, nor should we underestimate the much simpler aim, which he himself states, of recording recent events for the sake of their preservation. Indeed, while Aeneas may have hoped all Christians would show greater deference to both pope and emperor, his history subtly suggests that complete political harmony in Europe was not essential to defeating the Turks, nor was it likely to occur in the near future. What Western Christians most urgently needed to do

27. Hay and Delanty discuss Aeneas's writings specifically vis-à-vis the Ottomans, and Hale notes the importance of the Ottoman advance in the fifteenth and sixteenth centuries to the evolving definitions of the boundaries and culture of Europe; see Hay, *Europe*, 83–87; Delanty, *Inventing Europe*, 35–38; Hale, *Civilization of Europe*, chap. 1. See also Rietbergen, *Europe*, chap. 7.

28. Casella sees this message more fully articulated in the *Commentaries*, but still present in the earlier *Europe*; see "Pio II," 35. Baldi argues persuasively that Aeneas was taken up with reflections on the current state of Europe during the period from August 1457 to August 1458 as can be seen by examining not just *Europe* but also his *Germania* and *Historia Bohemica*; see *Pio II e le trasformazioni dell'Europa Cristiana (1457–1464)* (Milan: Edizioni Unicopli, 2006), 29–30. See also Baldi's arguments in "Enea Silvio Piccolomini e il *De Europa*," 619–20, 678.

29. See, for instance, his letter to Mehmed II (1461) in which he ostensibly invites the sultan to convert to Christianity, but spends a great deal of time lavishing praise on the achievements and power of European nations.

was unite well enough (and long enough) to defend their common boundaries—a strikingly modern message. Whatever Aeneas's goal in writing *Europe* may have been, the narrative certainly gave readers much to contemplate about their shared interests and future.

Without claiming too much for Aeneas, it is reasonable to argue that this widely disseminated work played a significant role in shaping early modern perceptions and definitions of Europe. To underscore the uniqueness and influence of Aeneas's vision of Europe, one should note that it was Aeneas who took the little-used classical adjective "European" (*Europaeus*) and reintroduced it to his generation[30]—infusing it with a host of cultural associations that we have come to identify with a collective Western identity.

DE EUROPA (EUROPE)

"As briefly as I can, I wish to record for posterity what, to my knowledge, were the most memorable deeds accomplished among the Europeans and the islanders who are counted as Christian during the reign of Emperor Frederick III. I will also include earlier material from time to time, when the explanation of places and events seems to demand it."

Thus begins the text known today as Aeneas Silvius Piccolomini's *Europe*. Early manuscripts and editions designated it *De gestis sub Friderico III*, or some variation, but by about 1490 *Europa* or *De Europa* was the preferred title.[31] What prompted Aeneas to write this ambitious work? In his dedication letter to Cardinal Antonio de la Cerda, he states that the idea came to him while writing a continuation of the *Augustalis libellus* by Benvenuto da Imola (d. 1387/88), which was a list of Roman emperors accompanied by very brief notices of the years of their reigns, number of battles, and genealo-

---

30. Hay, *Europe*, 87.
31. *De Europa*, ed. Adrian van Heck (Vatican City: Biblioteca Apostolica Vaticana, 2001), 4; Casella, "Pio II," 106–12. Aeneas does not appear to have assigned a title to this text.

gies.³² Upon completing this task, Aeneas resolved to compose a different piece that would vastly expand upon the model, since so much had happened in Frederick III's reign alone; a timely attack of the gout, as his dedication claims, afforded Aeneas the opportunity to complete the work.

However, Aeneas's interest in Europe as a collective was more than a casual foray into recent history to occupy his convalescence. He had completed or begun other regional histories before this point (on Germany in 1457 and Bohemia in 1458); wrestled with the concept of universal government in his treatise, *On the Origins and Authority of the Roman Empire* (1446); and had directly and repeatedly mentioned "Europe" in his letters and orations, particularly those responding to the fall of Constantinople in 1453. We must also recall the richness of his experiences as a scholar, traveler, and diplomat that enabled him to undertake such a daunting project.³³ Europe, then, had long been a subject of fascination for Aeneas, and his goals were probably more complex than he states in this brief preface.

The text was composed quickly, if not fully completed, within the forty days of Lent, as Aeneas suggests in his dedication letter of March 29, 1458. Developments in Greece and Austria that took place later in the year appear in *Europe*, as do references to his *History of Bohemia*, which was not completed until June of 1458 or later. Nor is it likely that the work was composed all at once; the portion on Italy was probably conceived separately and written first.³⁴ This helps to explain the uneven nature of the work. Not every region

---

32. Casella, "Pio II," 43. For more on Benvenuto and Aeneas's use of him, see Paul Kunzle, "Enea Silvio Piccolominis Fortsetzung zum Liber Augustalis von Benvenuto Rambaldi aus Imola und ein ähnlicher zeitgenössicher Aufholversuch," *La Bibliofilia* 60 (1958): 166–79.
33. On Aeneas's preoccupation with Europe and discussions of it in his other works, see Hay, *Europe*, 83–87; Baldi, "Piccolomini e il *De Europa*," 619–20. See also Bisaha, *Creating East and West*, passim, for a discussion of Aeneas's vision of European civilization threatened by Ottoman "barbarism."
34. Casella, "Pio II," 40–43; Baldi, "Piccolomini e il *De Europa*," 644–45; Baldi, *Pio II e le trasformazioni*, 50, n. 18; van Heck, *De Europa*, 6.

receives the same amount of attention; Scotland, for example, receives two paragraphs while Italy takes up roughly one third of the work. Geographical descriptions also vary considerably, with more than half the work containing rich topographical detail whereas sections on Italy, England, Scotland, Spain, and Portugal have almost none. In addition, historical depth differs from section to section. Despite Aeneas's stated focus on the reign of Frederick III (beginning in 1440), in some sections he looks back to the late fourteenth century or the ancient and medieval periods, while sticking closely to the last few decades in chapters on England, Spain, and Italy. *Europe*, then, is not the most unified or polished of Aeneas's works, but given the changes that took place in the author's life in 1458 with his duties as a cardinal and his election to the papacy, one can understand his lack of time to hone and edit the work.

Despite its occasional unevenness, *Europe* found a large audience because there were so few Renaissance works like it, and readers were hungry for the richness and breadth of information it offered in one convenient package. Scholars and students today are much more familiar with Aeneas's majestic and engaging autobiography, the *Commentaries*, which reproduces and expands much of the material found in *Europe*. But if we want to gain insight into what people were reading by Aeneas and about Europe in the fifteenth and sixteenth centuries, we cannot look to the *Commentaries*; it was kept hidden from all but a handful of readers until its publication in 1584.[35] This oft-quoted work, then, was practically unknown until the Renaissance was nearly over. For at least a century, by contrast, *Europe* was viewed as an unsurpassed general history of quattrocento society.

---

35. See O'Brien, *Anatomy of an Apology*, 19.

The Nature of the Text and Its Precedents

Europe is first and foremost a history of recent deeds or events, as Aeneas asserts in the first sentences of the text. So much geography appears along the way, however, that he soon interjects: "Although it is not my design to publish a geography, the history that I am writing may occasionally require some representation of places. For this makes it clearer" (para. 17). Given all his attention to the physical space of Europe, it is easy to understand why several scholars have chosen to ignore Aeneas's disclaimer and describe the text as a geography or a chorography, as well as a history.[36] For Eugenio Garin, history and geography do not compete, but complement each other, revealing Aeneas's interest in "the conjunction between man and earth, in the link between history and environment, between towns and their inhabitants, between places and the life that went on in them."[37] If the content is mostly historical, the organization is decidedly geographical—not chronological. As Casella has argued, this innovative approach to history reflects Aeneas's "personal intuition of the new reality of affairs" and his sense that traditional imperial history was no longer suitable to the times.[38]

While Aeneas's interest in marrying history with geography was unusual among humanist historians, at least one other notable contemporary, Flavio Biondo, demonstrated the same passion in his *Italy Illuminated* (first published in 1453). Like Aeneas, Biondo takes a broader approach to history than most contemporaries who tended to write about a specific person, state, or province.[39] One can also point to similarities like the use of classical place names

---

36. See Margaret Meserve, *Empires of Islam in Renaissance Historical Thought* (Cambridge, Mass.: Harvard University Press, 2008); Baldi, "Piccolomini e il *De Europa*"; Casella, "Pio II"; Eugenio Garin, *Portraits from the Quattrocento* (New York: Harper and Row, 1963).
37. Garin, *Portraits*, 38.
38. Casella, "Pio II," 43.
39. Eric Cochrane, *Historians and Historiography in the Italian Renaissance* (Chicago:

(or Latinized postclassical names) rather than modern vernacular designations. However, there are several differences between the two works. Aeneas focuses more heavily on recent history and does so in a sustained fashion, even as he moves from place to place; Biondo's style, by contrast, is less fluid and more anecdotal.[40] It is possible that Aeneas drew on this work in writing *Europe*; he was certainly aware of it and refers to it in paragraph 235. But scholars have not regarded Biondo as a direct source for inspiration, so much as a kindred spirit who read many of the same sources as Aeneas.[41]

One cannot claim complete originality for Aeneas, however. He employed numerous sources, including classical authorities, medieval chronicles, and contemporary texts; his use of them ranged from inspiration in form and style to direct quotations. His borrowing, moreover, is so free and sometimes unacknowledged that it may surprise modern readers accustomed to strict notions of intellectual property. A contemporary source that Aeneas essentially mined is Bartolomeo Facio's humanist history of King Alfonso I of Naples, *Rerum gestarum Alfonsi regis libri*.[42] Aeneas does not credit

---

University of Chicago Press, 1981), xv. Biondo's expansive *Decades* (i.e., *Historiarum ab inclinatione romani imperii decades*, which he began to circulate in 1443) may also have influenced Aeneas. It does not have the same geographical approach, but it, too, brought history up to the present era and covered all of Italy; see Gary Ianziti, *Writing History in Renaissance Italy: Leonardo Bruni and the Uses of the Past* (Cambridge, Mass.: Harvard University Press, 2012), 260–62, 282.

40. See Jeffrey White's comments on Aeneas and Biondo in *Italy Illuminated* (Cambridge, Mass.: Harvard University Press, 2005), vol. 1: xviii.

41. Cochrane regards *Italy Illustrated* and *Europe* as independently conceived; see *Historians*, 45. Recent studies and translations of Biondo by Pellegrino, Castner, and White note Biondo's influence in the genre, but not on Aeneas. See Nicoletta Pellegrino, "From the Roman Empire to Christian Imperialism: The Work of Flavio Biondo," in *Chronicling History: Chroniclers and Historians in Medieval and Renaissance Italy*, ed. Sharon Dale, Alison Williams Lewin, and Duane Osheim (University Park: Pennsylvania State Press, 2007), 281. See also Baldi, "Piccolomini e il *De Europa*," 658, n. 129. On Biondo's sources, see White, *Italy Illuminated*, xvii; and *Italia Illustrata*, ed. and trans. Catherine J. Castner (Binghamton, N.Y.: Global Academic Publishing, 2005), xxvii–xxviii.

42. The official date of the text is 1457, but Pietragalla and Kristeller show that it was completed and circulated as early as 1455. See Paul Oskar Kristeller, "The Humanist Bartolomeo Facio and his Unknown Correspondence," in *Studies in Renaissance Thought*

Introduction   21

this source at any point in *Europe* nor has his debt to Facio been noted before now, to the best of our knowledge.[43] Yet a close comparison of the two texts reveals frequent borrowing by Aeneas, in some passages quoting Facio almost verbatim.[44]

Why Aeneas used this contemporary source so extensively but failed to cite it, as he did John Jerome of Prague or Niccolò Sagundino, is hard to say. It is also puzzling that Aeneas avoids all mention of Facio in *Europe*—not even taking the opportunity to name him (or any humanist) at the court of Naples, in contrast to his descriptions of so many other cities and their scholars. Such borrowing from Facio raises legitimate questions about Aeneas's originality. What other contemporary sources might he have used without any reference to them? Was Aeneas's own experience, as Baldi contends (and as we were once inclined to agree), his "privileged and principal source"[45] or will additional research reveal a good deal more wholesale, uncredited borrowing?[46]

Our recent discovery of Facio as a key source unfortunately takes us well beyond the parameters of this introduction, but it invites further examination of Aeneas's writings against an exciting

---

and Letters II (Rome: Edizioni di Storia e Letteratura, 1985), 274; Daniela Pietragalla, ed., *Rerum gestarum Alfonsi regis libri* (Alessandria: Edizione dell'Orso, 2004), xx.

43. Emily O'Brien discusses the parallels between Facio's history and Aeneas's later work, the *Commentaries*. She describes Aeneas's acquaintance with Facio and his access to Facio's text but states that it is impossible to know if Aeneas deliberately imitated him or if they were rather similarly influenced by Caesar's writings; see "Arms and Letters: Julius Caesar, the *Commentaries* of Pope Pius II, and the Politicization of Papal Imagery," *Renaissance Quarterly* 62, no. 4 (Winter 2009): 1080–89.

44. Aeneas met Facio (d. 1457) while he was visiting Naples in 1456 and corresponded with him the following year. He may have obtained a copy of the *Res Gestae* at this point or borrowed a copy belonging to his former employer and fellow cardinal Domenico Capranica in Rome. See Pietragalla, ed., *Rerum gestarum*, 596, n. 121; Kristeller, "The Humanist Bartolomeo Facio," 271.

45. Barbara Baldi, *Pio II e le trasformazioni*, 52.

46. Franco Gaeta has shown how freely Aeneas, writing as Pius II, made use of Juan de Torquemada's work (without mentioning it) in his "Letter to Mehmed II"; see "Sulla 'Lettera a Maometto II' di Pio II," *Bulletino dell'Istituto storico italiano per il medioevo e archivio muratoriano* 77 (1965): 127–227.

body of growing scholarly work on premodern authorship.[47] For now, it is helpful to step back and note three points. First, our sense of authorship today differs significantly from that of premodern writers, many of whom valued the work of compiling as much as original composition.[48] Second, the footnote is a fairly recent invention; a great many early writers did not feel obliged to mention all (or any) sources.[49] Third, many Renaissance historians used texts, especially recent ones, without naming them.[50] In short, Aeneas was not alone in his practices, and to be fair, most of his borrowing from Facio was no simple cut and paste. He summarizes a vast amount of detail, rewords most passages that he does copy, and substantially reorders events to conform to his geographical plan. He also adds details from other sources and relies on his own judgment of various individuals and occurrences rather than uncritically repeating Facio's views.[51] Aeneas exported elements from Facio's text to his own, but he was not seeking to mimic him.

47. Some recently published collected essays include Slavica Ranković, ed., *Modes of Authorship in the Middle Ages* (Toronto: Pontifical Institute of Medieval Studies, 2012); Hall Bjørnstad, ed., *Borrowed Feathers: Plagiarism and the Limits of Imitation in Early Modern Europe* (Oslo: Unipub, 2008); Guillemette Bolens and Lukas Erne, eds., *Medieval and Early Modern Authorship* (Tübingen: Narr Verlag, 2011). Thanks to Ron Patkus for help on this subject.

48. As Sigbjørn Olsen Sønnesyn has argued, William of Malmesbury took as much pride in his collections of extracts from other authors as he did in his own monumental history of the kings of England; see "Obedient Creativity and Idiosyncratic Copying: Tradition and Individuality in the Works of William of Malmesbury and John of Salisbury," in Ranković, *Modes of Authorship*, 113–14. See also Andrea Carlino's comments on the sixteenth-century scientific compilations, "*Kunstbüchlein* and *Imagines Contrafactae*: A Challenge to the Notion of Plagiarism," in Bjørnstad, *Borrowed Feathers*, 87–108.

49. Anthony Grafton, *The Footnote: A Curious History* (Cambridge, Mass.: Harvard University Press, 1997).

50. Mark Phillips's article on historical sources used by Bruni, Machiavelli, and Guicciardini reminds us of their debt to texts that they, too, did not name; see "Machiavelli, Guicciardini, and the Tradition of Vernacular Historiography in Florence," *American Historical Review* 84 (1979): 86–105.

51. See, for instance, his discussion of Giovanni Ventimiglia (para. 55) in which he repeats Facio's error on Ventimiglia's relationship to Tocco, but goes on to add other details. He also does not share Facio's harsh opinion of Cardinal Vitelleschi (Facio, *Rerum gestarum*, 5.45), even though he uses details of his account (para. 228) of the cardinal's downfall.

Moving from contemporary sources to earlier ones, classical texts were Aeneas's most obvious influence as shown by his eager citation of them. Geographical and encyclopedic treatises by Strabo, Pliny, and Ptolemy feature prominently, and Aeneas repeatedly quotes from them; Pomponius Mela was also used, if less extensively. Of these, only Pliny had been well known to Latin readers before the Renaissance.[52] Aeneas reflects their impact on his narrative by mixing geography with other subject matter. He appears to have drawn special inspiration from Strabo, who saw geography as a key to understanding ethics, politics, and particularly the course of war—a subject of great interest to Aeneas. Strabo believed that one could not understand battles won and lost without also comprehending the territory armies were fighting for.[53] Strabo's *Geography*, moreover, with its assertions of the superiority of Europe in terms of climate, topography, and resources, may also have provided confirmation of Aeneas's own sense of Europe's preeminence.[54] But *Europe* cannot be called a mere imitation of any of these classical sources; Aeneas's bolder emphasis on history and his sustained narration of major events and the lives of key figures set his work apart from them.[55]

Less expected in a humanist history like *Europe* are the medieval influences. Not only does Aeneas draw content from chroniclers

---

52. See Marcia Milanesi, "La rinàscita della geografia dell'Europa, 1350–1480," in *Europa e Mediterraneo tra medioevo e prima età moderna: l'osservatorio italiano*, ed. Sergio Gensini (San Miniato: Pacini Editore, 1992), 35–59. Pomponius Mela's work circulated in some manuscripts north of the Alps, but only became known in Italy through the circulation of Petrarch's copy of it; see Mary Ella Milham, "Pomponius Mela," in *Catologus Translationum*, ed. Paul Oskar Kristeller (Washington: The Catholic University of America Press, 1984), vol. 5: 258. For a list of other sources cited by Aeneas, see van Heck, *De Europa*, 7. For more on Aeneas's use of classical geographers, see Casella, "Pio II"; see also van Heck passim, who meticulously notes classical references in his edition of *De Europa*.

53. Strabo, *Geography*, 1.1.17–18.

54. Hale, *Civilization of Europe*, 14; Hay, *Europe*, 3. Strabo had recently been translated from the Greek by Guarino da Verona and Gregorio Tifernate.

55. Strabo's influence is much more pronounced in Aeneas's *Asia*; see Casella, "Pio II," 60.

such as Otto of Freising and Ekkehard of Aura but he even shares certain stylistic qualities.[56] Like many of his predecessors, Aeneas attempts a more universal approach to history—in his case, covering a broad expanse of territory rather than several centuries. There are also glimmers of the medieval worldview in Aeneas's attributions of calamity or good fortune to the hand of God, although he was by no means alone among devout Renaissance historians in making these occasional pronouncements. At the same time, the direct style of *Europe* is reminiscent of the lively "political realism" of Italian late medieval (vernacular) chroniclers, whose interests and experiences were intensely local.[57] They could also be unabashedly biased: "Chroniclers were not modern detached historians. They were opinionated, often deeply partisan, and intensely personal ... [but] it is precisely this mix of the anecdotal and the historic, of portents and politics, that makes these writings so engaging to read."[58] Like its medieval forebears, *Europe* is indeed colorful and reveals much about the personal interests and leanings of its author.

While Aeneas, consciously or unconsciously, took some cues from the medieval chronicle tradition, it is by no means out of place among contemporary Renaissance histories—his use of classical models being one of the surest tests. Granted, Aeneas is not generally claimed as a paragon of humanist historiography.[59] Yet, recent

---

56. For more on humanist interest in medieval history, see Robert Black, *Benedetto Accolti and the Florentine Renaissance* (Cambridge: Cambridge University Press, 1985), 317–29.

57. Later vernacular historians Machiavelli and Guicciardini also wrote in this vein and intentionally avoided many of the constraints of humanist rhetoric, but, like Aeneas, they took a broader geographical purview; see Dale et al., *Chronicling History*, xiv.

58. Dale, et al., *Chronicling History*, ix. Aeneas may have also been influenced by medieval encyclopedias, such as the works of Isidore of Seville and Vincent of Beauvais. For an introduction to this genre, see Gregory Guzman, "Encyclopedias," in *Medieval Latin: An Introduction and Bibliographical Guide*, ed. F. A. C. Mantello and A. G. Rigg (Washington: The Catholic University of America Press, 1996), 702–7.

59. Two fairly recent encyclopedia entries on historical writers suggest Aeneas's deficiencies: Nicholas Terpstra describes his historical works as "largely polemical";

scholarship has also shown that Renaissance historians were not as objective, rational, or critical with their sources as they (and later interpreters) have claimed. A more critical approach to history was certainly inaugurated in the quattrocento, but these high-minded goals were not reached overnight.[60] For that matter, Renaissance historiography was not a fully established field until the sixteenth century. As Margaret Meserve has pointed out, "there was no such thing as a professional historian in the quattrocento"; writers held a variety of jobs, primarily as civil servants, and fit the writing of history in among their many other duties.[61] Aeneas, then, was in very good company among the many notaries, secretaries, and chancellors who turned their attentions to the study of the past—none of these men had any formal training in, nor devoted their full attention to, what we could call the science of history.

To say that Aeneas did not always achieve the highest standard of objectivity and reason—to be fair, even Leonardo Bruni fell short at times—does not imply that these principles were unimportant to him. For example, after criticizing John Hunyadi's flight from the battlefield of Varna, he notes his own limits and prejudices by stating, "Perhaps in the eyes of a military expert the battle seemed unsalvageable, and he preferred to save a few than lose everyone" (para. 31). In other crucial ways, Aeneas reflects the impact of the new model of history. Like Bruni's influential *History of the Florentine People* (completed in 1449), *Europe* imposes a narrative that explores the man-made reasons behind events, the consequences of human choices, and the lessons they provide. His account of Francesco Sforza's incredible rise from condottiere to

---

see *A Global Encyclopedia of Historical Writing*, ed. D. R. Woolf (New York: Garland Publishing, Inc., 1998), vol. 2: 713; Lucian Boia commented on his "direct and personal style that was far from humanist canons"; see *Great Historians From Antiquity to 1800: An International Dictionary* (New York: Greenwood Press, 1989), 269.

60. See the useful and concise overview of trends in the field of Renaissance historiography by Meserve in *Empires*, 6–9.

61. Meserve, *Empires*, 7.

duke of Milan, for example, shows his subject wrestling with adversity and opportunity, patiently awaiting the right moment to move, and judiciously choosing peace or compromise when victory was unlikely. Finally, although Aeneas prefers pithy quotations to lengthy addresses in *Europe*, one sees hints of the typical humanist use or invention of speeches by key characters.[62] Aeneas's attention to rhetoric, then, distinguishes him from medieval compilers or encyclopedic writers and provides some continuity as he moves from nation to nation.[63]

In sum, as the previous examples of direct borrowings and subtler imitations have shown, Aeneas's *Europe* was heavily indebted to the work of others. At the same time, no single text that he used offered a clear blueprint, which gives *Europe* a distinctly fresh and innovative quality. The creative way he reworks and weaves all these pieces together and weds them to his own unique life experience and point of view should not be minimized. A traveler, poet, politician, clergyman, and scholar, Aeneas developed passionate opinions about the past and present. Much as he admired his classical models, much as he drew upon medieval and contemporary authors, he broke free of them so that his own voice richly rings through the text. As Vollman has put it, "he successfully blends the knowledge he has gathered into his personality, his thinking and his feeling."[64] In the end, the very eclecticism of his approach shows him to be an extremely learned, well-read, and curious man, capable of bringing an enormous amount of far-flung material together in a compelling and highly readable narrative.

---

62. On speeches in humanist histories, see Cochrane, *Historians*, 4; lengthier and more florid speeches appear in Aeneas's *Commentaries*, which uses much of the same material as *Europe*. For more on Bruni's new approach, see Gary Ianziti, "Challenging Chronicles: Leonardo Bruni's *History of the Florentine People*," in Dale et al., *Chronicling History*, 249–72.

63. See Vollman, "*Enkyklios Paideia* in the Work of Aeneas Silvius Piccolomini," in *Pius II*, ed. von Martels and Vanderjagt, 11.

64. Vollman, "*Enkyklios Paideia*," 12. See also Baldi's comments on how Aeneas's experiences and voice shape the text: "Piccolomini e il *De Europa*," 677–78.

Content: Some Observations on the Narrative

The main focus of *Europe* is unquestionably political history—the most common and respected subject matter among Renaissance historians.[65] As such, *Europe* places Aeneas in what we would call his comfort zone. To quote Casella, "The writer and the political man combined as one in him; his two activities, literature and politics, were always in close rapport."[66] To clarify, for Aeneas, as for most of his contemporaries, "politics" was not confined to what we would call the secular state but often blended seamlessly with the purview of the church.

Few writers were as well placed as Aeneas to relate such a broad range of events from all over Europe, given his extensive travels and access to both diplomatic exchanges and recent written works like Facio's history. Scholars of military history will also find his text a treasure trove of information on famous and lesser-known battles and generals.[67] *Europe*, moreover, edifies and entertains with its frequent glances beyond the worlds of war and policy. Aeneas pauses to take note of the surprising quirks of rulers, colorful dynastic marriages and struggles, and curious local customs. We learn, for instance, that Filippo Maria Visconti of Milan, in addition to being lavish in spending and impatient of repose, was "reluctant to allow people dressed in mourning to approach him, unwilling to hear talk about death, and astonishingly fearful of thunder and lightning" (para. 181). Or in his section on Lithuania, we read of kings keeping bears as pets or attack animals (para. 89). Aeneas's gift for storytelling also comes out in his vivid accounts of battles, speeches, and descriptions of miracles. In short, *Europe* is no dry list of facts but an engaging set of stories that shrank the vast borders of the continent

---

65. Cochrane, *Historians*, 9; Pellegrino, "From the Roman Empire to Christian Imperialism," 277; Meserve, *Empires*, 7.
66. Casella, "Pio II," 35.
67. D. S. Chambers has specifically remarked on Aeneas's "fascination or even positive zest for war"; see *Popes, Cardinals and War* (London: I. B. Tauris & Co., 2006), 55.

and familiarized readers far and wide with information once foreign and hard to come by. Aeneas's chosen focus within each region tells a tale of its own that merits our interest as it projected a sense of each region's importance, as Aeneas saw it, to generations of readers who would absorb, repeat, and develop his interpretations. He simultaneously helped forge enduring stereotypes about regional identities while enabling Europeans to think of themselves as part of a powerful community with many similarities and common interests.

Geography, while secondary, remains a powerful motif that brings continuity and narrative flow to this lengthy composite work. The way in which Aeneas moves from one end of Europe to another provides subtle, plot-like drama and surprising twists. Judging from previous models, it does not appear that Aeneas was following any conventional order when he chose to begin his narrative in Eastern Europe.[68] He commences specifically in Hungary, at the epicenter of battles against the Ottoman Turks, then proceeds along winding, circuitous paths through central and Northern Europe, on to England, Scotland, and Spain, before concluding with a lengthy discussion of Italy. In a sense, *Europe*'s beginning and end define three dominant themes: the Turkish advance, the papacy, and King Alfonso of Naples—the first as an illegitimate aggression, the latter two as rightful authorities in Italy and Europe. Emperor Frederick III, of course, occupies much of the narrative, albeit as an arbiter rather than a forceful actor among stronger personalities and vibrant city governments. Central and Eastern Europe, in general, receive much attention from Aeneas, reflecting his wealth of firsthand knowledge and interest. English readers who are more accustomed to Renaissance studies on Italy or England, or ones on Germany that only begin during Martin Luther and Charles V's

---

68. Classical writers like Strabo and Pliny, for instance, begin their descriptions in the West. Aeneas, it might be noted, repeated the tactic of opening in the East in his *Asia* (1461).

Introduction   29

time, will come away with a much better sense of fascinating key figures and issues in Frederick's reign.[69]

The Ottoman Turks appear early in the text and are paradoxically portrayed as both outsiders and key players in the fate of Eastern Europe. After several references to the Ottomans in the first two chapters, Aeneas devotes an entire section to the origins of the Turks and the rise of the Ottoman Dynasty in chapter 4, with the following preface: "The Turkish race is Scythian and uncivilized. Although I may seem to be digressing from my plan, I think it not irrelevant to describe their origin and expansion. For in our era, this race of people has grown so great that it controls Asia [Minor] and Greece and instills terror throughout Latin Christendom" (para. 20). With this brief, almost apologetic statement, one sees Aeneas wrestling with the question of whether the Turks deserve a place in this work. Could they be considered as part of Europe? Despite Aeneas's hesitation to include the Turks, he devotes a great deal of narrative space to them. They deal a crushing blow to the Crusade of Varna in 1444 (dramatically told in paragraphs 30–32); they stage a brilliant siege and inflict suffering on the Greeks in the fall of Constantinople (paras. 36–43); and they haunt chapters 3–16 where Aeneas describes region after region of glorious ancient Greece and the Balkans, now held captive by the "barbarians."[70]

By prominently featuring the Ottoman advance in a treatise on Europe, Aeneas sent a message to his contemporaries: the Turks were a European problem. The eastern nations were most exposed,

---

69. See Casella, "Pio II," 36–37; Baldi, "Piccolomini e *De Europa*," 660–61, 669. For Aeneas's half-hearted defense of the German imperial seat, see para. 134; Baldi, "Piccolomini e il *De Europa*," 679.

70. See, for example, in para. 48: "In Thessaly, they say there was a king called Graecus, after whom Greece was named; also, that Helenus reigned here, from whom Helen acquired her name. Homer referred to the Thessalians with three names: Myrmidons, Hellenes, and Achaeans. Here are the narrows of Thermopylae, renowned for the slaughter of the Persians. Although they once withstood the attack of Xerxes, they failed completely to obstruct the passage of the Turkish army." For more on Aeneas's attitudes toward the Turks, see Meserve, *Empires*; Bisaha, *Creating East and West*.

but unless all Europeans stood together, they would fall, one by one, before the onslaught. This goal, perhaps, led Aeneas to overplay his rhetorical hand at times by overemphasizing rare crusading victories, like that of Belgrade (1456), and exaggerating the papacy's influence in affairs like the Peace of Lodi and the growing stability of the Italian peninsula.[71] But Aeneas would not allow himself to stray from the facts, however dismal, for long. As much as he believed in the necessity of crusade, in *Europe* he exposes the crusaders' divisions and mutual deceptions. John Hunyadi, the highly regarded Hungarian general who won many battles against the Turks, is shown recklessly committing his outnumbered troops to battle at Varna and then fleeing the field (paras. 30–31). King Wladyslaw of Hungary and Poland is depicted more heroically in the story of Varna but is also accused of seizing the throne of Hungary from the rightful heir (para. 29). Even Cardinal Cesarini and the Hungarian crusaders, whom Aeneas generally admired, come under scrutiny for painting early victories as more impressive than they were (para. 28).[72] Aeneas also grimly notes the shameful lack of aid the Hungarians and Greeks received from fellow Christians and the collusion of both the Genoese (para. 29) and the despot of Serbia George Branković (para. 26) with the Turks. Even countries like Albania and Bosnia, which were managing to hold their own, come across as precariously close to defeat—which, indeed, they were (paras. 57–59).

Ironically, one can imagine readers taking a very different message away from the text regarding the Turks. Despite Aeneas's efforts to portray the Turks as interlopers in Europe, his descriptions inadvertently reveal them to be firmly grounded in the landscape; they were enemies but also allies, and some of their rulers, like Murad II, could be noble and reflective. In many ways, they

---

71. Casella, "Pio II," 36–37; Baldi, "Piccolomini e *De Europa*," 660–61, 670; Baldi, *Pio II e le trasformazioni*, 54–59.

72. On Cesarini's exaggerations, see Imber, *Crusade of Varna*, 17.

appear no worse than the Christian peoples of Europe, whose stories in *Europe* are by no means consistently heroic or honorable. Meserve's observations on the ambivalence of fifteenth-century historians are especially helpful in understanding this dichotomy: "The larger implications of the new historiography could be risky, sometimes downright threatening, to deep-seated European views on the nature and order of the world, the direction and purposefulness of human history, and the role that the Christian faith had to play in its unfolding."[73] Aeneas's *Europe* offers a prime example of the quattrocento historian's tension between objectively reporting and the need to make sense of the greater (i.e., Christian) purpose of human affairs.

It is perhaps Aeneas's belief in humanity's greater purpose that explains the positive spin we see at other points in *Europe*. For all the political division the text reveals, it also shows the continent at the height of its cultural achievements, progressing toward religious unity. Ironically, for Aeneas the very threat of annihilation by the Asiatic forces of "barbarism" thrust Europe's sophistication and piety into sharp relief. He sustains the theme of the achievements of European learning by mentioning centers of education and prominent scholars across the continent. Aeneas also presents developments in church history in largely optimistic terms. The core of European civilization, the Christian faith, was shared in varying degrees by all of the countries he treats.[74] The conversions of kings like Clovis and entire peoples like the Saxons feature prominently. Nor is the triumphant progress of the Catholic Church shown as a thing of the distant past. The conversion of Wladyslaw II Jagiello of Lithuania, who was given the throne of Poland in exchange for embracing Christianity, was less than a century old when Aeneas wrote *Europe* (para. 87). The Livonians had also recently converted and were feeling the civilizing effects

---

73. Meserve, *Empires*, 9.
74. Baldi, "Piccolomini e *De Europa*," 673–74.

of Christianity: "The Christian religion opened up this part of the world to our generation, cleansed it of its barbarism and revealed a gentler way of life to its ferocious tribes" (para. 95). True, Aeneas could not avoid addressing the serious problems which recently plagued the church, like the papal schism, conciliarism, and the revolt of Hussite heretics in Bohemia, but taken as a whole, his text reveals a great deal of recovery and hope—of Christendom coming together more than it was coming apart. The mid fifteenth-century papacy, as described by Aeneas, was stronger than it had been in many years and more spiritually committed to its role as arbiter and leader of European nations. The Peace of Lodi (1454) had recently been concluded in Italy between the major powers, and the reign of Alfonso of Naples seemed to promise even greater stability and prosperity for the peninsula. In the end, Aeneas sought not to dismantle the idea of Christendom but to present it, for the first time, in all its complexity, as identical to the current boundaries of Europe.[75]

Despite the grand scope of these themes and the tendency to focus on rulers and popes, *Europe* is more than a history of elites. In his quest to capture the distinctive character of each region, Aeneas includes topics more often found in eclectic chronicles than orderly humanist histories. The overall effect is an engaging and variegated account with fascinating discussions of middling classes and peasantry, women and children, dissidents and non-Catholic sects, and of such topics as local foods, industry, and culture. In paragraphs 91–93 on Lithuania, for example, Aeneas pauses to provide details about the diverse beliefs of Slavic pagans converted by John Jerome of Prague. Some worshipped snakes, others fire, others the sun, and others a sacred wood. On the subject of Scotland, Aeneas includes a folk legend about a tree that reputedly produced fruits which turned into ducks. "When I eagerly investigated this

---

75. Hay, *Europe*; 84, Baldi, "Piccolomini e *De Europa*," 637.

matter," he wryly adds, "I learned that miracles always recede further into the distance and that the famous tree was to be found not in Scotland but in the Orkney islands" (para. 167). Aeneas puts little stock in tales of the fabulous. He does, however, include without commentary or challenge several stories of strange occurrences interpreted as portents, and his careful scrutiny of sources also seems to ebb when it comes to imaginative tales of Lithuanian rulers and their amusements with bears (para. 89).

Even the section on Italy, heavy with blow-by-blow accounts of recent wars and tangled alliances, is lightened by intriguing details on the life and landscape of the people. We read that Pope Calixtus III "built shipyards in Rome, a thing previously unheard of, and on the bank of the Tiber in the Leonine City he constructed and armed a great many galleys which he launched against the Turks" (para. 240). Where most chroniclers simply comment on the number of ships Calixtus commissioned, Aeneas provides that bit of detail that enables us to appreciate the direct impact this made on the artisans, economy, and environment of Rome. When discussing Florence, Aeneas not only describes the powerful leader Cosimo de' Medici but pauses to comment on the state's method of taxation and its crushing effect on the poor before a system of assessment (the *catasto*) was reinstituted (para. 214). Similarly, in Saxony the salt-works of Lüneburg and the silver mines of Goslar receive special mention.

Women of all stations also appear regularly. While they are often described as pawns in arranged marriages, Aeneas delights in relating examples of strong, intelligent women who surpassed their husbands and male counterparts, like the formidable Margaret I of Denmark, Sweden, and Norway, who united Scandinavian kingdoms under her rule (para. 116). In his section on France, Aeneas marvels at Jeanne d'Arc's success in leading the troops and adds, without a hint of scorn, that she is believed to have received instructions from God (para. 156). Another woman is introduced in a humorous passage on the slovenly, boorish Count Henry of Gorizia: "His Hungarian wife, a woman of outstanding beauty and more than a man's audacity, had him imprisoned. He was soon freed through the help of Count Ulrich of Cilli and drove his wife from home. He died not long afterwards, leaving his sons as heirs—young men of good character who resembled their mother more than him" (para. 67).

Rounding out Aeneas's range of topics is a subject dear to his heart: recent scholarship. Poland is described as an undeveloped country for the most part, but Kraków is set apart, namely for its impressive university. Almost every region of Italy is accompanied by mentions of its most prominent humanists. We hear of Francesco Filelfo writing epic poetry in Milan and Francesco Barbaro's demise in Venice. Rivalry between Greek and Latin scholars is conveyed in his description of a debate on Plato versus Aristotle led by Ugo da Siena at the Council of Ferrara/Florence (1438–39): "The debate went on for many hours. Finally, when Ugo, the host of the banquet, had defeated one after another of the Greek philosophers with his eloquent arguments and forced them into silence, it became clear that the Latins, who had long ago surpassed Greece in the arts of war and military glory, were in our time also outstripping them in literature and every branch of learning" (para. 196). In such passages, one senses how many of these scholars Aeneas had met and knew well. Quite a few were men of small means like himself, who had risen to great heights in their profession and in the realm of politics. Some met tragic deaths in purges due to their connections with the mighty, like Giacomino Bossi in Milan under the Ambrosian Republic (para. 186) or Adam de Moleyns in England during the feuds preceding the Wars of the Roses (para. 165).

Aeneas's closeness to many of his subjects invites questions regarding his impartiality. To be sure, Aeneas shows his sympathies very clearly in places. He inclines heavily, for instance, toward Alfonso of Naples (chap. 65). He gladly takes aim at the government of Siena, which had treated his family poorly in recent generations and rebuffed his many efforts at friendship. But it is his proximity to people like the enigmatic Frederick III that enabled Aeneas to capture his strengths, weaknesses, and bizarre passions: "[Frederick] values every person's particular virtue and deems it worthy of reward. He puts up magnificent buildings, though his admiration and passion for gardens and gemstones is excessive. And in the conduct of affairs, he is rather slow and easy-going" (para. 82). Aeneas's knowledge of (and often friendship with) so many figures in his story poses critical challenges to modern readers, but it also provides his narrative with marvelous details.

In sum, *Europe* provides rich material on a vast assortment of people, places, and events. It was read by many contemporaries and remained a popular work for over a century. Above all, it influenced the way Aeneas's contemporaries and later generations in Europe would think of themselves; it has also led at least one scholar to call Aeneas a father of the modern concept of Europe.[76] But this heritage is a complex one, indeed. On the one hand, *Europe* (especially when read in tandem with *Asia*) helped shape an ideology of cultural unity and superiority to the East—a notion that would rally contemporaries in the short term, but lead to long-term, unforeseen cross-cultural tensions. In a sense, one could say Aeneas's treatise did a more effective job of marginalizing the Turks than his crusade ever did. On the other hand, the treatise helped fashion a sense of cultural unity and achievement that enabled Europeans to consider the ties that bound them in peaceful, productive ways. *Europe*, like humanism itself, has left us with a complex and often conflicting legacy.

---

76. Baldi, "Piccolomini e *De Europa*," 621.

NOTES ON THE TEXT, TRANSLATION, AND APPARATUS

Europe was once thought to be part of a larger work called the *Cosmographia*, which paired it with Pius's *De Asia* (1461). This tradition dates back to 1509, when a French printer by the name of Geofroy de Tory published the two works as one treatise. Most printings of *Europe* after 1509 followed Tory's innovation, but Nicola Casella has effectively proven that the two works were written separately by Aeneas and share few structural and stylistic similarities.[77]

Soon after it was completed, *Europe* began to draw a wide audience. At least nine manuscripts of the work survive, but it found its largest audience via the printing press.[78] The work was printed on thirteen separate occasions in Germany, Italy, and France between 1490 and 1707, on its own, as part of the *Cosmographia*, or as part of Aeneas's sixteenth-century *Opera omnia*.[79] *Europe* was printed at least twice more as an appendix to Hartmann Schedel's popular 1493 "Nuremberg Chronicle" (*Liber Chronicarum*). The Chronicle, with the addition of *Europe*, was soon translated into German, giving Aeneas's text a boost in vernacular readership north of the Alps.[80] *Europe*—along with *Asia*—was also translated into Italian in 1544 by Fausto da Longiano. The Italian edition is noteworthy because the translator added new sections on Africa and some recently discovered areas—showing that Aeneas's text was still read and appreciated a century after its composition as an authoritative work needing only minor updates and additions.[81]

Until recently, scholars commonly used the version found in

---

77. See Casella, "Pio II."
78. For a description of the manuscripts, see van Heck, *De Europa*, 8–11.
79. For a list of the printed editions, see Casella, "Pio II," 108–12.
80. Casella, "Pio II," 103–12. This German version did not include the long section on Italy.
81. See *La Discrittione de l'Asia et Europa di Papa Pio II*, trans. Sebastiano Fausto (Venice, 1544); Casella, "Pio II," 49. An electronic version of this text is currently available on Google Books

sixteenth-century printings of Pius's *Opera omnia*, which contains many errors. Adrian van Heck's recent Latin edition, based on a careful analysis of manuscripts, is the most authoritative version of the Latin text. The present translation is based almost entirely on van Heck's version, supplemented by two Vatican Library manuscripts.[82] We have also maintained van Heck's division of the text into 275 paragraphs, which makes for easier reading and cross-referencing. In recent years, *Europe* has been edited and translated into Spanish by Francisco Socas and German by Günter Frank, Paul Metzger, and Albrecht Hartmann.[83] In making our own version, we have consulted these works frequently and gratefully acknowledge our many debts to our predecessors in the interpretation of the Latin, the identification of names, and the phrasing of the translation. Van Heck's edition (which Frank, Metzger, and Hartmann translated, notes and all, while adding a few notes of their own) offers a wealth of information to the scholar. Van Heck's notes include most classical and medieval textual references and thorough cross-references on persons, places, and events found in other works by Aeneas. We did not attempt to reproduce all of van Heck's notes, although we cite many of the references he has identified—particularly when Aeneas calls attention to those works in his text. Serious scholars will, no doubt, consult his version or the German translation for a full list of references. What our edition has done that the others have not is to provide the first English translation of *Europe* along with a much fuller introduction, explanatory footnotes, and other supporting materials.

82. Urbinas Latinus 885 and Vaticanus Latinus 3888, which exemplify the two main families of manuscripts identified by van Heck (*De Europa*, 8–9). We consulted these (on microfilm) when van Heck's text seemed problematic. In several instances, which are recorded in the notes, we have followed their readings or offered our own emendations in preference to the text of van Heck.

83. *La Europa de mi Tiempo*, ed. and trans. Francisco Socas (Seville: Universidad de Sevilla Publicaciones, 1998); *Enea Silvio Piccolomini, Europa*, ed. Günter Frank and Paul Metzger, trans. Albrecht Hartmann (Heidelberg: Verlag Regionalkultur, 2005).

Aeneas's Style

The best introduction to Aeneas's Latin style is his own appraisal, written in response to Cardinal Zbigniew Olesnicki's praise of his letters: "I realize that I have but a small ability in speaking and that my vocabulary is lacking and colorless; in this regard I have to abide by my own self-evaluation. I will own to the fact, however, that I speak directly and clearly since I reject purple prose. I do not strain to express myself because I do not handle matters beyond my reach. I know what I know and feel that the man who understands himself well can make others understand what he has to say. It is impossible for someone in the dark to enlighten someone else. I avoid a knotty style and long periodic sentences. If I use elegant words I try to make them fit in their context; in any case, I do not ransack my dictionary for elegant words but use those that come to mind. My one goal is to be understood and I am not annoyed that my simple and unadorned style does not meet the approval of the learned."[84]

Aeneas is over-modest and exaggerates the extent to which he eschews ornament and intricacy (*Europe* contains many complex periodic sentences), but his self-assessment is basically sound. In *Europe*, he refers to Cicero as the greatest orator (para. 136) and, along with Quintilian, the best teacher of eloquence (para. 213). For Cicero, the ideal orator commands the full range of stylistic registers, from the relatively unadorned "plain style" (*genus tenue*), which is appropriate for explication and proof, to the fuller, more varied "middle style" (*genus medium*), suitable for entertainment, to the copious and ornate "grand style" (*genus grande*), whose function it is to move and persuade.[85] Which style is appropriate for any given subject is a matter of decorum and taste. It would be wrong to

---

84. *Selected Letters of Aeneas Silvius Piccolomini*, trans. Albert R. Baca (Northridge, Calif.: San Fernando Valley State College, 1969), 47–48, 116.
85. Cicero, *Orator*, 61–101.

Introduction 39

suggest that Aeneas's style can be defined purely in terms of Ciceronian theory. Many models, including post-classical authors (who are not discussed here), contributed to its formation. Nevertheless, Cicero's schema provides a useful, if imprecise, tool for outlining its general character.

To begin, it is clear that Aeneas's own description of his style in the letter to Olesnicki invokes the *genus tenue* as defined by Cicero and that the bulk of *Europe* is composed in a straightforward and unpretentious style. For the most part, Aeneas uses few figures of speech and pays no systematic attention to rhythm, the overall quality being less fluent and euphonious than that of Cicero's style in general and closer in some ways to that of Caesar. In the quotation cited previously, Aeneas says, literally, that he is "naked" (*nudus*) and "reject[s] all clothing" (*vestem omnem rejicio*), which, as noticed by van Heck,[86] is an allusion to Cicero's description of Caesar's simple and yet elegant style as "naked, upright, and attractive, with all stylistic ornament stripped off like clothing."[87] Aeneas cannot rival the smoothness and regularity of Caesar's style but, by the same token, he is freer and more animated. Even the plainest passages are enlivened by variety in word order, striking phraseology, word-plays, and a sprinkling of proverbial expressions, personal remarks, and aphoristic or witty sayings in the tradition of the classical *sententia*. Sentence length is also nicely varied. Though typically of medium length and little complication, his sentences run the gamut from the terse to the elaborate, the latter sometimes overflowing with so much information that it is hard for the reader to digest it all.[88]

---

86. Van Heck, *De Europa*, 5.
87. Cicero, *Brutus*, 262: *nudi enim sunt, recti et venusti, omni ornatu orationis tamquam veste detracta.*
88. Cf. Meserve and Simonetta, *Commentaries*, vol. 1, xx: "In matters of style, his generic debt to Caesar notwithstanding, Aeneas strives to imitate the rhetorical fullness of Ciceronian prose. In those passages where he was able to edit the *Commentaries* to his satisfaction, his periods are long, heavily subordinated—and occasionally unwieldy. One sometimes senses the author struggling to marshal the many details of time, place,

Though the *genus tenue* is foundational, it frequently blossoms into a fuller, more diversified and consciously artistic manner, which may be loosely classified as the *genus medium*. This is marked by greater elaboration in sentence structure; rhetorical figures such as alliteration, anaphora, antithesis, asyndeton, chiasmus, and ellipse; and dramatic snatches of direct speech. Many of the delightful anecdotes and digressions that adorn the work are composed in this more studied manner.[89] Aeneas's character sketches and potted biographies are also carefully composed, with a Sallustian brevity and incisiveness that is calculated to stimulate and please as well as to enlighten.[90] The grand style is absent, as one would expect in a work that is largely factual, non-polemical, and unembellished with long speeches, though aspects of it are briefly glimpsed at times, for instance, when Aeneas waxes passionate on the subject of religion (e.g., paras. 37, 42) or describes an especially impressive scene, event, or personality (e.g., paras. 150, 216, 275).

On the whole, the stylistic quality of *Europe*, like its historical coverage, is a little uneven, conveying the impression of a work that was written in haste and without much revision. But what it may lack in polish, it makes up for in vigor. Its great merit is that it seems to be driven by enthusiasm for the material rather than the

---

personality, motivation, cause and effect which his remarkable memory had stored up over the long decades of an eventful career." Note that these comments apply to the *Commentaries*, which is more stylistically ambitious and highly polished than *Europe*.

89. For example, the investiture of Carinthian rulers (paras. 64–65), the suicidal nobleman of Styria (para. 70), Conrad von Kaufungen's abduction of the princes (para. 110), the trickery of Otto of Mainz (para. 136), the miraculous tree of Scotland (para. 167), the battle of ants and the battle of falcons and ravens (paras. 202–3), the tornado of San Casciano (para. 216), the mistress of Francesco Sforza (para. 247); his descriptions of battles and sieges, though conventional in some respects, are also memorable (e.g., Varna (paras. 30–32), Constantinople (paras. 36–43), Tannenberg (para. 99), and Naples (paras. 266–68).

90. For example, the portraits of Henry, the count of Gorizia (para. 67); Emperor Frederick III and Albert (paras. 82–83); Filippo Maria Visconti (para. 181); Francesco Foscari (para. 192); Galeotto Baldassino (para. 224); Eugenius IV (paras. 232–33); Nicholas V (paras. 234–36); Calixtus III (paras. 240–44); Niccolò Piccinino (para. 250); Francesco Sforza (para. 251); and Alfonso (paras. 272–75).

demands of rhetorical invention. Not that Aeneas is incapable of conventional embellishment, but he is sparing in its use and never allows it to distract from the essence of what he has to say. One has the sense of a writer who is not "working up" his material to satisfy a literary ideal but intent upon reproducing it as directly as possible, with a freshness and immediacy that is faithful to its intrinsic interest. When the material most engages him (as in the aforementioned anecdotes and digressions, battle descriptions, and biographies), he shows a fine eye for detail, a well-paced and varied narrative technique, and a droll sense of humor. Whatever else may be said, Aeneas's style meets the most important test: it is never boring.

The English Translation

The translation presented here is modest in its literary ambition, its primary aim being to provide a clear and faithful version of Aeneas's words for the non-Latinist. To that end, we have tried to maintain a balance between literal accuracy and readability and to retain Aeneas's own voice as much as possible. We remain close to his sometimes elaborate sentence structures and bookish phraseology, without reducing them to bland colloquial English, though it was often necessary to divide an unwieldy period into two or more English sentences and to trim some redundancy. If the result can be clearly understood and enjoyed and convey to the reader a sense of Aeneas's idiosyncratic personality, it will have served its purpose.

The translation of personal and geographical names also presented some choices and challenges. Almost all of Aeneas's proper names are either in classical or medieval Latin, or a Latinized version of a more recent vernacular name. Some of these names were translated by van Heck, Socas, or Frank, Metzger, and Hartmann, but many were left in their original Latin form. In these cases, studies on the period provided much-needed context and corroborating description to help match these lesser-known figures to their more commonly used vernacular names. Pietragalla's edition of Facio's *Rerum gestarum Alfonsi regis libri* also helped with identifications. In addition, several scholars, whom we gratefully note in our acknowledgments, came to the rescue when our research had failed to find the answer.

Oftentimes even when it was clear to us whom Aeneas was talking about, we still faced concerns about clarity and readability. For many individuals, for instance, Aeneas uses only first names and titles, such as "Julianus, cardinal of Sant' Angelo," or simply "the cardinal of Sant' Angelo." It would have been more faithful to the text to preserve these names as they appear or to footnote every variation, but rather than double our footnotes, we usually opted to use surnames or titles where Aeneas does not—the aforementioned case, for example, we simply translated as "Cardinal Giuliano Cesarini." We did, however, maintain Aeneas's tendency, like that of his contemporaries, to avoid assigning numbers within the text to most rulers (such as Henry VI of England), although he uses them on rare occasions. Finally, we opted to follow the practice of most current historians by preserving a sense of local variations of first names—for instance Giovanni, Jean, or Juan, rather than John in all cases. We made exceptions for very well-known figures like kings, emperors, popes, and certain individuals like John Hunyadi, for whom most scholars use an Anglicized version. While we endeavored to be as consistent as possible, there were times when we had to go by what "sounded right" to our ears, knowing that some readers may take issue with our decisions. Above all, we hope that we have been clear, for clarity was our greatest goal.

Place names were easier with the help of geographical dictionaries like the *Orbis Latinus*. Van Heck was also helpful on modern names of many places; Frank, Metzger, and Hartmann helped especially with several Germanic ones. In addition, two recent editions of Biondo's *Italia Illustrata*, by Castner and White, along with

Introduction   43

Pietragalla's edition of Facio's history, provided clues on several lesser-known Italian towns and landmarks. And, as with personal names, historical studies were indispensable. A handful of place names remain uncertain, and we have noted these for the reader so that our researches and educated guesses will not obscure the original name for readers who may immediately recognize the Latin form.

Yet another decision involved which geographical names or spellings to use in many cases, and we are indebted to several readers who shared invaluable tips.[91] Where we encountered some variation, we generally used the most preferable English form or spelling found in the *Merriam Webster Geographical Dictionary*. In cases where the Renaissance name was quite different from the modern (e.g., "Ragusa" versus "Dubrovnik"), but the older version is still well known to scholars and students, we chose to preserve it. Finally, at several points Aeneas uses classical names for peoples in ways that are imprecise to modern readers; in these cases we left "Illyrians" and other names in the text and footnoted the fifteenth-century group or groups to whom he was most likely referring, be it the Bosnians, Croats, or others. Where Aeneas is speaking of places in a purely classical sense, such as narrating Strabo's description of ancient cities, we left them in their classical form rather than updating them to modern versions.

Apparatus: Footnotes

Like the translation, researching and preparing the supporting apparatus also involved certain choices. There are two basic ways to annotate this work: historically and geographically. Without underestimating the potential interest and importance of this work to geographers, we opted to focus on the historical aspects—a choice that we think would not have displeased Aeneas, given his

---

91. We especially wish to thank Tom Izbicki, Tom Brady, John Fine, and the anonymous reader for the press.

previously mentioned insistence that this is primarily a history.[92] Deconstructing and testing Aeneas's sense of geography is a noble task, and one that we will leave to the experts in that field.[93]

Next came the decision of how to annotate the historical details. Given that no existing edition or translation has provided more than a few proper names and dates, much work needed to be done. Our goal was to identify and explain, for the general reader as well as the specialist, the events, persons, and phenomena that Aeneas discusses. Some of these particulars are well known to scholars and students; we annotated them nonetheless to flesh out the details and to help all readers get a better grasp of the intricacies of Aeneas's world. Many of these specifics, we imagine, are far from general knowledge, even for specialists. Hence, while we have prepared the translation and notes for a broad audience, it is our belief that even Latinists and scholars of Aeneas will find something of value in the notes from time to time. An appendix of rulers is also included in this volume to aid readers in understanding the text.

The footnotes aim to be informative and explanatory but not overwhelming to Aeneas's text. This is, to be clear, not a critical edition that claims to present the last word on scholarly debates or the most recent research; nor did we survey a broad range of contemporary primary sources. Instead, we strove to shed light on little-known details and to explain them to the extent that was needed to facilitate an understanding of Aeneas's text. Scholars will, no doubt, think of studies that they would have used or at least cited when perusing our sources, but our selections were often determined by how fully and how well a scholar delves into minute historical context. As such, many excellent recent studies were not used and many excellent older studies were. Thorough

92. Casella notes the preponderance of history over geography in *Europe*, as opposed to *Asia*, where the opposite is true; see "Pio II tra geografia e storia," 50.
93. For a fine example of a recent edition that does examine the author's sense of geography, and a work that may have influenced Aeneas, or at least can be read as a contemporary parallel, see Castner's edition of Biondo's *Italia Illustrata*.

Introduction   45

scholars like Cecilia Ady still remain authorities on the movements and lives of key historical figures, and we are indebted to studies like hers. On the other end of the spectrum, a few recent websites provided some helpful information as well. Although we made every effort to check information from them and to use them as a jumping-off point, two websites on condottieri and cardinals of the church contained reliable information and we were grateful to have had access to them.[94]

The sources we used are all noted in the bibliography and many are cited in the footnotes. Because much of the information presented in the footnotes is considered generally accepted and encyclopedic, we do not provide citations for every reference. We hope that readers and scholars will use our work in combination with their own research and writings, and we look forward to seeing what light this text may shed on various fields of Renaissance and European studies. We also hope that specialists will forgive us the details that we were unable to identify or some that they would have explained or dated differently. On dates alone, we sometimes found more variation than we expected and had to use our best judgment.

Despite the choices and challenges, it has been a great pleasure to have worked so closely with Aeneas, as it were. Our labors were sustained by the richness of his words and the liveliness of his mind. Through translating and researching his portrait of Europe and its peoples, we learned much about him and found him to be *un buon compagno*.

94. For the Cardinals of the Holy Roman Church, created by Salvador Miranda and hosted at Florida International University, see http://www2.fiu.edu/~mirandas/cardinals.htm. For the Condottieri di Ventura website, created by Roberto Damiani, see http://www.condottieridiventura.it/. The cardinal website provides a bibliography after each entry; the condottieri site generally does not but has an extensive bibliography at the end. Judging from our own cross-checking and consultations with other scholars, it seems a well-researched and reliable aid. It was very helpful in making basic identifications of the many obscure military figures Aeneas mentions, often only by first name.

EUROPE

DEDICATION LETTER

To ANTONIO, called Lérida, presbyter cardinal of the Holy Roman Church and his most reverend father, Aeneas, cardinal of Siena, a man of equal rank but unequal merit, sends warmest greetings.¹

When I had an attack of the gout recently and was suffering from my customary joint pains,² a German bookseller³ came to me with a small book containing not so much the deeds as the names—and a little about the characters—of the Roman emperors up to Wenceslas, son of Charles IV.⁴ Since four emperors seemed to be missing from the work⁵ (for its author, Benvenuto da Imola,⁶ had died under

---

1. Aeneas's other writings shed little light on his relationship with Spanish cardinal Antonio de la Cerda or Cerdá y Lloscos (1390–1459). In the *Commentaries*, for instance, de la Cerda appears a decent but somewhat self-interested figure who helps elect Aeneas pope in the conclave of 1458. We can glean some sense, however, of Aeneas's interest in de la Cerda from his biographical details. Trained in theology at Lérida, he became a high-ranking official in the papal curia and was elevated to the cardinalate in 1448, making him the first and only cardinal created by Nicholas V on that date. He also had the strong support of Alfonso V of Aragon, who pushed for his election as bishop and cardinal. Like Aeneas, de la Cerda traveled extensively, visiting monasteries in England, Scotland, and Ireland. Finally, he was viewed as a friend and supporter of humanists and helped Aeneas with many theological questions; see *Dizionario biografico degli italiani* (Rome: Istituto della Enciclopedia, 1979), vol. 23; hereafter, *DBI*. Thanks to Ron Patkus for help on this question.

2. Aeneas's problems with arthritis or gout began in 1435 on a diplomatic voyage to Scotland; see the introduction for further discussion of his illness.

3. The term *librarius* can also mean copyist or librarian.

4. Emperor Wenceslas (r. 1378–1400); Emperor Charles IV (r. 1346–78).

5. Emperors Rupert (r. 1400–10); Jobst (1410–11); Sigismund (1411–37); Albert II (1438–39).

6. Benvenuto da Imola (c. 1330–87/88), author of the *Augustalis libellus*, a list of Ro-

Wenceslas), the bookseller asked me to add to the book what was lacking. I was unwilling to disappoint the man and completed the succession of emperors up to our own era, imitating the brevity of my predecessor.

But when I considered the many great achievements within the Christian world from the time when Frederick[7] received power to this day, I decided to compose a separate work, in which I would commit to posterity a concise account of some notable events belonging to this era. I have therefore published a short history and dedicated it to you. Since you suffer from the same disease as I do, you will easily have time to read and appraise my writings during an attack of gout.

It would have been worthwhile, I confess, to compose a history of events from the beginning of our era up until the present, as I have often intended. But that project would have required more than a single attack of gout—especially one occurring during the fast of Lent. The gout loves my residence and no sooner departs than it happily returns. Perhaps, then, it will one day serve this purpose.

Farewell, and if you stumble upon a criticism of someone that is overly harsh, ascribe it not so much to my nature as to the torments of gout. And if anything strikes you as ignorant, foolish, or ridiculous, take up your pen and delete it.

Rome, March 29, 1458[8]

---

man emperors accompanied by brief notices of the years of their reigns, battles, and genealogies.

7. Frederick III (1415–93), Holy Roman Emperor from 1440–93.

8. Despite the date of this letter, Aeneas continued to write or add to the work through the summer, possibly as late as August 1458; see the introduction for more on this.

AS BRIEFLY AS I CAN, *I wish to record for posterity what, to my knowledge, were the most memorable deeds accomplished among the Europeans and the islanders who are counted as Christian during the reign of Emperor Frederick III. I will also include earlier material from time to time, when the explanation of places and events seems to demand it.*

1 HUNGARY

1. HUNGARY, which lies next to Frederick's native land of Austria and stretches eastward, will furnish the starting point of my narrative. Some call this country Pannonia, as though the Hungarians succeeded the Pannonians. But Hungary does not occupy the boundaries of Pannonia, nor was Pannonia ever so extensive as Hungary is today. For Pannonia was confined between the Danube and the Alps which face Italy and the Adriatic Sea, while to the west it bordered Noricum and the Inn River and to the east the Mysians, Triballians, and the Sava River. These borders include a large part of Austria, inhabited by Germans; Styria too, which was once called Valeria, is contained within the same boundaries. But Hungary, though it embraces lower Pannonia from the Leitha River to the Sava, extends beyond the Danube River toward Poland and occupies the lands once held by the Gepids and Dacians. The empire of the Hungarian nation is much broader than Hungary itself. For the Dalmatians whom they call Slavs; the Illyrians known as Bosnians; the Triballians or Mysians, who are called both Serbi-

ans and Rascians; and the Getes, of whom some are named Vlachs and others Transylvanians, submitted to the rule of the Hungarians. Some, however, have defected in our time after suffering defeat by the forces of the Turks. The Romans first acquired this province, up to the Danube River, under Caesar Octavian, when they subdued Bato, king of the Pannonians, and laid low the Amantians between the Sava and the Drava. Across the Danube, the Emperor Trajan conquered Dacia, which is now part of Hungary, and created a province on barbarian soil; it was lost under Gallienus and recovered by Aurelian.[9] After the Romans, the Huns (a Scythian race) and the Goths (people who came from the islands of the Baltic Sea) occupied Pannonia at different times, and then the Lombards, who originated in Germany. Finally, the race of Hungarians flooded in from the farthest regions of Scythia. They have held sway until this day and exercise sovereignty far and wide on both sides of the Danube.

Not far from the source of the Don River there still exists another Hungary, the mother of that Hungary of ours of which I am speaking. It is quite similar in language and customs, although ours, which worships Christ, is more civilized; the other one observes a barbaric way of life and bows down to idols.[10]

2. In Hungary, through which flows the Danube, Sigismund, the son of the Roman Emperor Charles IV, a Bohemian native of German descent, reigned in our time with mixed success for over fifty

---

9. Augustus Caesar (63 BCE–14 CE). He assumed control of the Roman Empire in 31 BCE; Bato was the name of two leaders of the Pannonian-Dalmatian revolt of 6–9 CE; see *The Oxford Classical Dictionary*, ed. 4 (Oxford: Oxford University Press, 2012), 226. Emperor Trajan, r. 98–117 CE; Emperor Gallienus, r. 260–68 CE; Emperor Aurelian, r. 270–75 CE.

10. Possibly a reference to the mysterious "eastern" Hungarians of *Magna Hungaria* described in a thirteenth-century account by Friar Julian; see Pál Engel, *The Realm of St. Stephen: A History of Medieval Hungary 895–1526* (London: I. B. Taurus, 2005), 99. Aeneas refers to this region and conversion efforts under Pope Eugenius IV in his *Commentaries*, Bk XII; see *The Commentaries of Pius II*, trans. Florence A. Gragg, ed. Leona C. Gabel (Northampton, Mass.: Smith College, 1951), vol. 5: 795.

years.[11] He was a prince of remarkable wisdom and magnanimity, renowned for his beneficence and liberality. He was a man, too, of striking physical majesty and good looks but was thoroughly unlucky in war. Not only the Turks but also the Bohemians often routed him in battle. His first wife was Maria, daughter of King Louis, and along with her he received the kingdom.[12] For her sake, he put to the sword thirty-two leading Hungarian chieftains who had rebelled at some time previously.[13] This led soon after to his being cast into prison himself, when the queen passed away. He was entrusted to the safekeeping of a widow whose husband he had killed, until the nobles of the kingdom should decide upon his punishment. But Providence did not fail him, even as a prisoner in desperate straits; and through his powerful eloquence he proved to the woman that it was better to preserve royal blood than to shed it. When she had released him, he married Barbara, daughter of Count Herman of Cilli, and not long afterward he raised a supporting force, won back the kingdom, and punished his betrayers. In the presence of the foremost nobles of the kingdom, he heaped honors and riches upon the sons of the widow. The son of one of them is still alive—Ladislas Garai, count palatine of the realm.[14]

3. Many illustrious deeds of this Sigismund have been entrusted to memory. The most glorious was his restoration of the unity of

---

11. Sigismund of Luxembourg (1368–1437) reigned as king of Hungary from 1387–1437. He was elected king of Germany and Holy Roman Emperor in 1410, along with two other candidates (he claimed the title in 1411), and king of Bohemia in 1419.

12. Louis I of Hungary (r. 1342–82) and Poland (r. 1370–82). Upon his death in 1382, his daughter Maria (1370–95) was crowned queen of Hungary; Sigismund, Maria's husband, was crowned king consort in 1387.

13. Hungarian chronicler János Thuróczy also mentions this story, which the editor dismisses as a folk legend; see *Chronicle of the Hungarians*, trans. Frank Mantello, ed. Pál Engel (Bloomington: Indiana University Press, 1991), 49–52.

14. Barbara Cilli (c. 1390–1451). Sigismund was imprisoned by his own party of nobles in 1401. As part of the negotiations for his release, he married the powerful count of Cilli's daughter. The story of the widow was another popular fiction; the Garai brothers were among Sigismund's earliest and most consistent supporters. See Engel's note in Thuróczy, *Chronicle*, 62, n. 110.

the Catholic Church, then split into three parts, at the general council which he convened in Constance;[15] to achieve this, he traveled throughout Italy, France, Spain, and England. He indulged Duke Vytautus of Lithuania by sending him a crown so that he could call himself king; however, Vytautus died before celebrating the coronation ceremony.[16] He ordered the restoration of Prussia, which the king of Poland had taken from the Brothers of St. Mary with German arms.[17] With Pippo of Florence in command, he waged fierce wars with the Venetians.[18] He imprisoned his brother, Wenceslas, king of Bohemia, because he was unfit to rule; he was carelessly guarded, however, and some Bohemians smuggled him out of prison, to the great detriment of the state.[19] Sigismund received the imperial crown from Pope Eugenius IV in Rome. After many misfortunes, he finally took possession of Bohemia. He bestowed the margravate of Brandenburg upon Frederick, burgrave of Nuremberg.[20] His daughter Elizabeth, whose mother was Barbara, was joined in marriage by him to Duke Albert of Austria,[21] and, as his last wish, while he lay dying in the Moravian city of Znojmo, he bequeathed to Albert the kingdoms which he had ruled. His bones lie in Varád.

15. The Council of Constance (1414–18) ended the Great Schism (1378–1417) with the deposition of three rival popes and the election of Pope Martin V.

16. Vytautus or Witold, Grand Duke of Lithuania (r. 1401–30); see also para. 89.

17. A reference to the Battle of Tannenberg (1410) in which combined forces of Poles and Lithuanians defeated the Teutonic Knights, or Brothers of St. Mary, as Aeneas calls them. Sigismund attempted to rule in the knights' favor. See paras. 99–100.

18. Filippo Scolari or Pippo Spano, a Florentine patrician who travelled at age thirteen to Hungary as a merchant's apprentice and soon showed talent as an administrator and soldier. He led Hungarian troops against the Venetians in 1411–12. See Michael Mallett, *Mercenaries and their Masters: Warfare in Renaissance Italy* (Totowa, NJ: Rowman and Littlefield, 1974), 64–65.

19. Sigismund deposed his half brother, Wenceslas IV of Bohemia, in 1402, but he was reinstated by the royal council after agreeing to major concessions.

20. Sigismund took power in Bohemia after Wenceslas's death in 1419; he was crowned emperor by Eugenius in 1433. Sigismund awarded Brandenburg to Frederick in 1417; see Thomas A. Brady Jr., *German Histories in the Age of Reformations, 1400–1650* (Cambridge: Cambridge University Press, 2009), 87.

21. Duke Albert V of Austria (1397–1439) married Elizabeth in 1421, thereby establishing the Austro-Hungarian Habsburg line.

Hungary

4. When Albert was crowned with his wife at Székesfehérvár, he also received the crown of Bohemia. Marveling at his success, the leaders of Germany also decided to elevate their own flesh and blood by entrusting him with the Roman Empire.[22] Albert was not permitted to assume this position unless the lords of Hungary acquiesced, and to them it seemed disadvantageous for their king to rule the Germans; they had therefore bound Albert by oath not to accept the empire without their approval. However, after being summoned to the king, who was then in Vienna, they were overcome by his pleas and granted their consent. Promoted to emperor, he returned to Hungary with the intention of marching against the Turks, who had then invaded Serbia. But while he paused at Buda (which is where the kings reside), a German-born judge of that city had a certain Hungarian drowned in the river for a crime he had committed. The Hungarians, who hate the German race, took great exception to this and immediately provoked a riot, seizing arms and indiscriminately slaughtering any Germans in their path. There was a flight to the castle, where the king was keeping himself confined. The houses of merchants, the majority of whom were Germans, were ransacked.[23]

At that time, Jacopo della Marca, a Minorite friar famous for his erudition and piety, was preaching the Gospel to the people of Buda.[24] In order to quell the riot, he faced the armed and raging populace with an image of the crucified Savior in his hand and begged them humbly to refrain from slaughter, cease pillaging, and lay down their arms. Not in the least understanding his words

22. Albert became king of Bohemia, Holy Roman Emperor, and king of Hungary in 1438.
23. Thuróczy identifies the man who was executed as John Otvos, adding that he was tortured to death before his body was thrown into the river; see *Chronicle*, 98. The riot, which occurred in May 1439, has been attributed to social and ethnic tensions between the Germans, who possessed municipal power as well as considerable wealth in the town, and the Magyars; ibid., 99, n. 225.
24. Franciscan preacher Jacopo della Marca (1391–1476) was an inquisitor in Hungary at the time pursuing Hussite heretics.

(for the occasion did not allow for an interpreter)[25] and thinking that the leadership of Christ would benefit their undertaking, they raised Jacopo and his Crucifix aloft in their arms and rampaged through the city plundering one house after another. However, the spoliation was reduced and the bloodshed mitigated to some extent by the presence of Jacopo, who, now with pleas, now with tears, attempted to allay the frenzy of the inflamed mob.

After the suppression of this riot, the death of George de Palocz—the bishop of Esztergom[26] and custodian of the kingdom's precious treasure—occurred. Together, the king and queen headed for Esztergom. In the presence of the queen and selected barons of the realm, the coffers were opened and the treasure was observed. The queen secretly removed the crown which they call "holy" and, after entrusting it to a faithful old woman,[27] closed the coffers and sealed them.

5. A little later, Albert marched up to the Tisza River. There he encamped and waited for larger forces with which he could attack the Turks besieging Smederevo. However, the town was taken by storm before reinforcements arrived.[28] Upon returning to Buda, he fell ill with dysentery and decided to head back to Vienna, either to die among his own people or because he hoped that the air in which he had been nurtured would contribute something toward his recovery. But on the journey, he grew sicker and sicker and, after sealing his will, he died at Neszmély on the 27th of October, survived by his pregnant wife. He was a God-fearing prince and a man excelling in both liberality and justice. He was a bold and decisive warrior, too: he subjugated the Moravians and Bohemians by force of arms and confined the Poles inside their own kingdom

---

25. Or "for no interpreter was available."

26. Reigned 1423–39.

27. Helene Kottaner, who left behind a written account; see *The Memoirs of Helene Kottaner*, trans. Maya Bijvoet Williamson (Rochester, N.Y.: D. S. Brewer, 1998).

28. Sultan Murad II captured the fortress of Smederevo on August 18, 1439, after a two-month siege.

when they roamed abroad.²⁹ He seemed to hold out great prospects for Christendom, and the people expected no less of his valor. The shortness of his life prevented the fulfillment of his splendid promise. His power, which so rapidly had reached its summit, collapsed in an instant, for he reigned as emperor for not even two full years. His stature was tall, his body muscular and strong, his face awe-inspiring, his beard shaved in the fashion of his race, his upper lip unshorn. His modest clothing was cinched at the waist by a heavy golden belt, and he always had a sword at his side. His body was buried in Székesfehérvár.

6. When they learned of the king's death, the Hungarians in assembly deemed it shameful and dangerous for so great a kingdom to lie beneath a woman's jurisdiction. With fervent pleas, they urged the queen to take as her husband King Wladyslaw of Poland, who could protect the people with his army.³⁰ The woman agreed on the condition that the rights of her son would not be compromised if she bore a male. Prelates of the churches and the eldest and most prestigious leaders of the realm were sent as ambassadors to Poland. While they were on their way, Albert's posthumous son Ladislas was born. At Székesfehérvár, on the same day that he made his appearance, he received his baptism, which is the seal of Christian faith, the belt of knighthood, and the holy crown of Hungary, which his mother held in her possession.³¹

---

29. While Albert was elected king of Bohemia by a majority of the Bohemian Estates, a minority party of Hussites, which included George Podiebrad, offered the crown to Casimir of Poland. Albert succeeded in driving the Poles back to Silesia and Moravia in 1438; see Jonathan Zophy, ed., *The Holy Roman Empire: A Dictionary Handbook* (Westport, Conn.: Greenwood Press, 1980), 12.

30. Born in 1424, he is known as Wladyslaw III of Poland (r. 1434–44); Vladislas IV of Hungary (r. 1439–44).

31. Aeneas's chronology is slightly off. Ladislas Postumus was born in what is now Komarno, Slovakia, on February 22, 1440. Queen Elizabeth arranged his coronation with the Holy Crown of St. Stephen at Székesfehérvár on May 5. A civil war resulted, with the majority of nobles supporting Wladyslaw the Pole. See János Bak, "The Late Medieval Period, 1382–1526," in *A History of Hungary*, ed. Peter F. Sugar and Péter Hanák (Bloomington: Indiana University Press, 1990), 63.

Taken away from there, he remained for almost twelve years under the guardianship of Emperor Frederick III, to whom his mother entrusted both him and the crown.³² Despite the queen's prohibition, the ambassadors approached Wladyslaw and after overwhelming him with generous promises brought him to Hungary, where they crowned him and hailed him king.³³ For a long time, and with varying fortune, the mother of Ladislas fought against him, and the Hungarians were divided into two factions. Ulrich, count of Cilli, while supporting his cousin [the queen] and defending the right of Ladislas to the throne, was captured by the Poles and long tormented in prison.³⁴ Dénes, archbishop of Esztergom,³⁵ who was later granted the honor of a cardinalate, a man of illustrious family and character, crowned both kings, one voluntarily, the other by compulsion. For he was summoned to the Pole [Wladyslaw] and, although he had journeyed to Buda under an official guarantee, was not set free until he crowned him in Székesfehérvár. Returning home as soon as he could, he opposed the efforts of the Poles with the utmost zeal.

7. Cardinal Giuliano Cesarini was sent to Hungary by Pope Eugenius. He was a man of the highest intelligence, remarkable eloquence, and outstanding erudition.³⁶ Although he arranged a temporary truce in the war between Wladyslaw and Elizabeth, he was unable to secure peace. When the queen died, almost all the nobles of Hungary defected to the Poles.³⁷ Only Jiškra the Bohemian, a skillful and effective warrior, defended the side of Ladislas [Postu-

---

32. Frederick, then duke of Styria, later Emperor Frederick III, was Ladislas Postumus's second cousin.

33. Wladyslaw's coronation took place on July 17, 1440.

34. Count Ulrich of Cilli (1406–56), first cousin of Elizabeth, led the Habsburg party against Wladyslaw and his baronial supporters.

35. Dénes Szécsi, cardinal of San Ciriaco (r. 1439–65) and cardinal archbishop of Esztergom (r. 1440–65).

36. Preacher and scholar Giuliano Cesarini (1398–1444), created cardinal in 1426. He was sent as papal legate to mediate peace between Wladyslaw and Elizabeth.

37. Elizabeth died on December 17, 1442.

Hungary

mus] in Hungary.[38] With a small band of soldiers, he often defeated, put to flight, and destroyed huge forces of Hungarians and Poles and twice robbed John Hunyadi of his camp when Hunyadi was surrounded by great armies.

This John was a Vlach by birth—not highly born, but a man of supple intelligence and lofty spirit who loved virtue.[39] He fought many successful battles with the Turks and enriched the churches of Hungary with the enemy's spoils. He was the first of all the Hungarians to show that the armies of the Turks could be broken and vanquished. Inspired by these deeds, Wladyslaw himself also ventured into battle with Murad, the commander of the Turks. I will speak of this later in its proper place.[40]

8. Cardinal Giuliano Cesarini arranged a treaty between Emperor Frederick and Wladyslaw, who called himself king of Hungary, stipulating that the emperor had permission to restrain the Hungarians if they inflicted any injury on Austria or Styria; the same license was granted to Wladyslaw against the subjects of Frederick who were harassing Hungary.[41] The town of Günz is in Hungary, very close to Styria and Austria. This place and many surrounding castles were seized by brigands, who forayed from them into Austria and drove off a large quantity of livestock and people. Disturbed by this, Frederick rapidly put together an army and crossed into Hungary, where he sacked the strongholds and hanged eighty of the brigands on the gallows.[42]

---

38. Jan Jiškra (or Giskra) of Brandýs (d. c. 1470), a former Hussite captain and mercenary leader in Sigismund's army. He supported Elizabeth's claim in North Hungary (Slovakia) and controlled the region until King Matthias's reign; see Anton Špiesz and Dušan Čaplovic, *Illustrated Slovak History* (Wauconda, Ill.: Bolchazy-Carducci, 2006), 54–55.

39. John Hunyadi (c. 1400–56), governor or voivode of Transylvania, was the leading general in the Hungarian royal service and later became regent for Ladislas (Postumus) V.

40. Ottoman Sultan Murad II (r. 1421–51); see paras. 29–32.

41. The treaty was probably concluded in December 1442.

42. Aeneas describes this campaign in a letter dated May 21, 1445; see Rudolph Wolkan, ed., *Der Briefwechsel des Aeneas Silvius Piccolomini* in *Fontes rerum austriacarum*, vol. 61 (Vienna: Alfred Holder, 1909–18), 499.

9. After Wladyslaw had fallen in battle, an assembly of the Hungarians was held in Pest. This place faces Buda across the Danube. It is neither encircled with walls nor adorned with fine houses but has the look of a village. Here Ladislas, the son of Albert, was appointed king by general consensus of the nobles and at once began to war against the Turks on his own authority. However, his battles were no more successful than those of Wladyslaw.[43]

John Hunyadi was chosen as governor of the kingdom in the absence of the king.[44] He governed the country with an iron rod, as they say, and while the king was away he was regarded as his equal. After routing the Turks at Belgrade (as I will relate when I come to the affairs of Serbia), he survived for a brief time before dying of disease.[45] When he was ill, they say that he forbade the Body of Our Lord to be brought to him, declaring that it was unworthy for a king to enter the house of a servant. Although his strength was failing, he ordered himself to be carried into church, where he made his confession in the Christian way, received the divine Eucharist, and surrendered his soul to God in the arms of the priests. Fortunate soul to have arrived in Heaven as both herald and author of the heroic action at Belgrade!

10. Ladislas, who for some time had been released from the guardianship of the emperor and taken back into his father's kingdoms, had retreated from Hungary into Austria out of fear of the Turks. When he heard of the Turks' destruction and the death of the governor, for whom the count of Cilli bore an open hatred, he returned again to Hungary at the insistence of the count himself, who had heard this news with joy, as if celebrating the elimination

---

43. Ladislas was kept under close guard by Frederick III despite the Hungarian proclamation of his kingship in 1445. He was only released in 1452 after the Austrian Estates had rebelled and under great pressure from Ulrich Cilli, John Hunyadi, and the Czech nobility. See paras 74–75.

44. He was named governor in June 1446.

45. Belgrade was successfully relieved on July 22, 1456; Hunyadi died on August 11. See paras. 44–46.

Hungary 61

of a rival. But while he was inspecting the Turkish spoils and the corpses of the slain enemy at Belgrade, the count himself—whose person was second only to the king and who, as the king's uncle, was now the sole lawgiver for the Hungarians—was murdered in the royal senate by László, son of Hunyadi, finding death where he had hoped to find power.[46] Although this profoundly shook the king's emotions, he suppressed his grief and freely admitted that his uncle had been justly killed. The corpse of the deceased was sent to Cilli. The king took refuge in Buda, where he ordered the sons of Hunyadi who had followed the court to be imprisoned and the eldest, László, who had assassinated the count, to be put to death.[47] He took Matthias as a captive to Austria and ordered him to follow on behind when he set out for Bohemia.[48] After staying a few days in Prague, he met his death, either from a virulent illness, as most have reported, or by poison, as others claim.[49] He was a man of the noblest blood, descended from emperors on both his father's and his mother's side. On the same day that the king closed his eyes, Matthias arrived in Prague and was taken into custody by the governor George.[50] The body of Ladislas was buried in the fortress of Prague next to his great-grandfather Charles IV, Emperor of the Romans, in the shrine of St. Vitus.

11. Following the death of King Ladislas, the Hungarians arranged to pick a successor on the first of January. The nobles assembled en masse at Buda, including Michael Szilágyi, thronged by a large troop of soldiers; he is said to have been accompanied by thirteen thousand cavalry and seven thousand infantry which were garrisoned in Pest. Michael was Hunyadi's brother-in-law and uncle

---

46. Ulrich Cilli was murdered on Nov. 9, 1456.
47. Ladislas was coerced first to pardon Hunyadi while essentially his prisoner, and second, by the opposition, to arrest and punish both him and his brother.
48. Matthias Corvinus (c. 1443–1490); later crowned king of Hungary in 1458.
49. Ladislas died on November 23, 1457, at the age of seventeen. His body was exhumed in the 1980s and it was determined that he died of leukemia.
50. George Podiebrad (1420–71), elected king of Bohemia on March 2, 1458.

of Matthias.⁵¹ Owing to the execution of his nephew László, he held a vehement animosity toward many of the barons of the kingdom. His power filled them with great terror, and the fear-stricken assembly was now doubtful that the election of a king would be conducted freely. But when Michael approached the gathering, he said that he had not brought armed men to impose force on the congregants but to deter any who might try to interfere with the freedom of the lords and the people in choosing a king. His only advice to them, as an inhabitant of the kingdom, was to recall the services of John Hunyadi. He alone had driven the armies of the Turks from the kingdom of Hungary and won glorious victories for the nation. His reward was not what he deserved: of his sons, one had been cruelly put to death, another was being held captive in Bohemia. It was in the power of the barons to exalt the memory of John, to deliver Matthias from captivity and place him at the head of the kingdom which his father had saved by his courage. It was insupportable that this power be conferred upon outsiders. For his part, he pardoned all who had plotted against his nephew and had his eyes fixed upon the welfare of the realm. If they thought anyone else more useful to the country, he would in no way block the election of a superior candidate.

The matter remained in doubt for a while, since each of the barons feared for himself. Finally, a reconciliation was achieved among the nobles, reportedly through the initiative of Juan Carvajal, cardinal of Sant' Angelo, a man of exceptional learning and character, who at that time was acting as an apostolic legate.⁵² On January 24 [1458], surrounded by forty thousand men who were waiting in the middle of the frozen Danube for the result of the election, impa-

---

51. Michael Szilágyi (c. 1410–61), Hungarian commander and vice-bailiff of Belgrade. He briefly served as Matthias's regent before Matthias sent him to the Serbian front where he died.

52. Juan Carvajal (c. 1400–69) became cardinal in 1446. He spent six years in Hungary (1455–61) preaching and supporting the cause of crusade and reconciling some of the divisions between competing parties. Aeneas knew him from the Council of Basel. See Kenneth Setton, *The Papacy and the Levant (1205–1571)* (Philadelphia: American Philosophical Society, 1978), vol. 2, chap. 6.

tient to hear the great secret, the eighteen-year-old Matthias was proclaimed king.⁵³

12. Whoever you are reading this, try now to predict the future! Here is a truly remarkable proof of the fickleness of human affairs. Of two young men almost identical in age and character, one was carried from the throne to his tomb while preparing a bedchamber for his new bride;⁵⁴ the other, while anxiously awaiting a death sentence, was summoned from prison to become king. His freedom is said to have been purchased from the governor of Bohemia by a betrothal and other agreements.⁵⁵ It is amazing that his mother did not drop dead from joy, when, after suffering so many calamities, she heard that her son had been named king before she even learned of his release from captivity.

13. In the part of Hungary which stretches north beyond the Danube and which they now call Sepusium (the Gepids once settled there), a famous brigand called Aksamit, a native Bohemian infected with the deadly taint of the Hussites, extended a warm welcome to soldiers who flocked to him from all quarters in the desire for plunder, calling them "Brethren."⁵⁶ He made the entire region pay tax to him and built strongholds at strategic locations from which he could move quickly in one direction or another. At the end of each month, he distributed the booty individually, and a man who had been in the camp a whole month received no more

53. Matthias's birthdate is not certain; some sources claim it was 1443 rather than 1440, which would have made him not yet fifteen. He was formally crowned at Székesfehervár in 1464—after Frederick III finally returned the crown of St. Stephen and the two were at peace.

54. Ladislas was betrothed to Madeleine, the daughter of Charles VII of France.

55. Matthias married George Podiebrad's daughter Katerina in 1461. She died in 1464 at age fifteen.

56. Bohemian noble and mercenary leader Peter Aksamit of Kosov (d. 1458) helped Jiškra govern a large part of Slovakia from 1438–57. The "Brethren," or Czech mercenary companies under Jiškra's leadership, turned increasingly to plunder and intimidation as their numbers grew. See Spiesz, *History of Slovakia*, 55. Aeneas makes numerous references to Aksamit's activities in his letters during his service to Frederick III. See Wolkan, *Briefwechsel*, vol. 68: 171 ff.

than one who had been enrolled in the brotherhood a single day before the distribution. In this, he asserted he was following the teaching of the Gospel, which promises equal compensation to laborers in the Lord's vineyard, whether they arrive at the first or the eleventh hour.[57] This society was engaging in widespread plunder, already numbered five thousand armed men, and was growing larger day by day. It could only be abolished by inviting its leader Aksamit to serve in the army of King Ladislas.

2 TRANSYLVANIA, VALACHIA

14. THE REGION of Transylvania is situated beyond the Danube and was once inhabited by the Dacians—a fierce people, famous for many defeats inflicted on the Romans. It is inhabited in our time by three races: the Germans, Székelys, and Vlachs.

The Germans stem from Saxony. They are brave men, well versed in war, who are called Siebenbürger in their native language from the seven cities in which they dwell.

The Székelys are believed to be oldest of the Hungarians and the first who emigrated from ancient Hungary into this region. For this reason, although they cultivate the fields with their hands and live in the country rearing herds of cattle, they are called nobles and, when they meet one another, they exchange the greeting of "noble master." They pay no tribute except in the year when a king of Hungary is crowned; at that time they deliver to the king as many cows as there are heads of households, whose number is said to exceed sixty thousand. But if they are ordered to go to war and disobey, they are subject to capital punishment and their belongings are attached to the treasury.[58]

57. Matthew 20:1–16.
58. The Székelys moved into Transylvania in the thirteenth century and became the largest Hungarian-speaking ethnic group in the region. They were cattle breeders who maintained their military function by performing service in the royal army as

Transylvania, Valachia

The Vlachs are an Italian race, as I will explain a little later.[59] However, you would find few trained men among the Transylvanians who do not know the Hungarian language. In this country, there was a town called Beszterce, which was subject to the Crown. While he was in Vienna, King Ladislas presented it to John Hunyadi. The townspeople resented this and long resisted, but, under compulsion, they obeyed his orders.[60] But when John died and his son László was killed at Buda, they shamefully rebuffed Michael Szilágyi, who was seeking to obtain the throne for John's other son Matthias. Michael was outraged and, upon learning of the death of King Ladislas, returned there with an army, stormed the town, plucked out the eyes of some rebellious citizens, amputated the hands of others, put others to the sword, and destroyed the town with fire.[61]

Not long after this, about three thousand Turks invaded Transylvania and plundered large numbers of cattle and men. They were pursued by the people of Sibenik, and the Germans too, who wiped them out in a massacre and returned home in triumph with the recovered booty. They had scarcely entered the city when Michael appeared from another direction at the head of a large force, planning the city's destruction in revenge for its aiding the people of Beszterce against him. But when the people of Sibenik stayed inside their well-fortified city, he was frustrated in his desire and retreated full of threats.

15. Among the Hungarians, Paolo Vergerio of Capodistria died in our time—a man highly versed in Greek and Latin literature, many of whose works are extant and praised by scholars.[62] He

---

light horsemen. As Aeneas notes, they paid no taxes but branded oxen for the king at each coronation; see Engel, *Realm of St. Stephen*, 115.

59. Valachia roughly corresponds to modern day Romania, once the Roman province of Dacia; see para. 16 for further discussion of the Italian question.

60. Hunyadi was named perpetual count of Beszterce in 1453.

61. The citizens of Beszterce revolted in 1458 against Szilágyi when he failed to uphold the privileges guaranteed under Hunyadi and treated them as serfs; see Gabor Barta et al., *History of Transylvania* (Budapest: Akadémiai Kiadó, 1994), 228.

62. Pier Paolo Vergerio (c. 1369–1444), an influential humanist and teacher in early

translated Arrian's *The Deeds of Alexander the Great* from Greek into Latin at the instigation of Emperor Sigismund. He wrote *On Noble Manners*, made friendships with Greeks and foreigners,[63] and published a famous invective against Malatesta, who had ordered the statue of Virgil to be removed from the marketplace of Mantua.

Of the Hungarians who distinguished themselves in the humanities during our era, I am familiar with two: John Vitéz, bishop of Varád, who obtained the chancery of the realm, and another John—John Pannonius—his nephew on his sister's side,[64] who studied Greek and Latin literature under Guarino da Verona[65] and who shows equal proficiency in verse and prose. However, they say these men were of Slavonic origin.[66]

A large number of men practiced as jurists. Outstanding among them was Dénes, born of a family of Nagykanizsa, who was awarded the bishopric of Esztergom and also earned the honor of a cardinalate, as I mentioned before.[67]

In military affairs, Nicholas, voivode of Transylvania; Michael Ország; and Pancrace, who invaded Kalocsa, acquired renown.[68]

---

fifteenth-century Italy, who counted Salutati and Bruni among his friends. He served Emperor Sigismund from 1418 until the ruler's death in 1437, then retired and spent his last years in Buda. Aeneas and other humanists were critical of Vergerio's translation of Arrian. See John M. McManamon, *Pierpaolo Vergerio the Elder: The Humanist as Orator* (Tempe, Ariz.: Medieval and Renaissance Texts and Studies, 1996).

63. Literally "Greeks and barbarians" (*grecas ac barbaras amicitias comparavit*). This is probably a reference to Greeks like Manuel Chrysoloras, whom he met in Florence, and "barbarians" to his years in Germany and Hungary in the service of Sigismund.

64. John Vitéz of Sredna (c. 1408–72), humanist, bishop of Varád (1445), and archbishop of Esztergom (1465). He served Emperors Sigismund and Albert as well as John Hunyadi and Matthias. John Pannonius (1424–72), humanist and accomplished Neo-Latin poet. Both he and his uncle rebelled against King Matthias in 1471; see Maria Birnbaum, "Humanism in Hungary," in *Renaissance Humanism*, ed. Albert R. Rabil (Philadelphia: University of Pennsylvania Press, 1988), vol. 2: 293–334.

65. Guarino da Verona (1374–1460), perhaps the most highly regarded humanist educator in the early quattrocento. See para. 198 for more on him.

66. Vitéz was born in Sredna in modern day Croatia.

67. Dénes Szécsi; see para. 6.

68. Nicholas Ujlaki, ban of Mačva and voivode (governor) of Transylvania. Ország and Pancrace of Liptov were two of the seven captains elected at the Hungarian diet of 1445 to restore order after King Wladyslaw's death; see Engel, *Realm of St. Stephen*, 288.

Michael Szilágyi, who became great through another's ruin, now enjoys an illustrious reputation. John Hunyadi, whose name overshadows the rest, enhanced the glory not so much of the Hungarians as the Vlachs, from whom he was descended.

16. Valachia is a very broad region which extends all the way from Transylvania to the Black Sea. It is almost entirely flat and lacking in water. In the south, it is bordered by the Danube. The north is occupied by Roxanians, known in our time as Ruthenians, and, in the direction of the Dniester River, a Scythian tribe of nomads whom today we call Tartars. This land was once inhabited by the Getes, who repulsed and shamefully routed Darius, the son of Hystaspes,[69] captured King Lysimachus[70] alive, and inflicted many defeats upon Thrace. They were finally subjugated and destroyed by Roman arms. To keep the Dacians in check, a colony of Romans was founded under the leadership of a certain Flaccus,[71] after whom it was named Flaccia. When the name was corrupted by the long lapse of time, as tends to happen, it became known as Valachia, and the inhabitants were called Vlachs instead of Flaccians. This people still uses the language of Rome, though it is greatly altered and scarcely intelligible to an Italian.[72]

Among the Vlachs, there were two factions in our time, one of Danians and the other of Dragulans.[73] Since they were unequal to the Danians and frequently oppressed by them, the Dragulans called in the Turks for assistance. With the aid of their arms, they destroyed the Danians almost to the point of annihilation. John Hunyadi, relying upon the power of the Hungarians, brought help to the Danians but did less to reestablish them than to garner re-

---

69. Darius the Great (550–486 BCE); the battle took place in 513/12 BCE.

70. Lysimachus (c. 360–281 BCE), Macedonian general and one of the successors (diadochoi) to Alexander the Great; this battle took place in 292 BCE.

71. Probably Pomponius Flaccus, appointed governor of Moesia in 19 CE.

72. For more on Aeneas's theory of Romano-Dacian ancestry and the views of his contemporaries, see Gábor Vékony, *Dacians-Romans-Romanians* (Budapest: Matthias Corvinus Publishing, 2000), chap. 1.

73. The rival houses of Dăneşti and Drăculeşti.

nown and riches for himself, for he appropriated the lands of the Danians which he rescued from the control of the Turks for the perpetual benefit of himself and his descendants.

The Vlachs also inhabit the islands of the Danube, including Peuce, which was known by report to the ancients, and have settlements in Thrace as well. Some of the Vlachs are subject to the Turks, some to the Hungarians.

17. I am well aware that the description of countries is fraught with difficulty, since the authors whom one is obliged to follow prove to be not only divergent but also contradictory and substantially in disagreement with one another. The boundaries of the countries, too, have often shifted in proportion to the influence and power of their rulers. For a country which was once extensive has, in our time, either vanished or shrunk to a modest size. On the other hand, one which was nonexistent or tiny appears to us now very large and prosperous. The ancients did not know of Lombardy and Romagna, while the modern era is completely ignorant of Insubria, Emilia, and Flaminia. In the reign of King Emathio (from whom Emathia was named),[74] Macedonia was confined within narrow borders. Later, the valor of its kings and the perseverance of its people expanded it considerably through the subjugation of neighboring populations. I therefore think it fair that readers should make allowances if the territorial boundaries identified in my work are not what they themselves have imagined or found in other authors. I report what I have derived from others, whether the ancients or modern authors, without tampering with it. Although it is not my design to publish a geography, the history that I am writing may occasionally require some representation of places. For this makes it clearer.

---

74. According to Isidore of Seville (*Etymologies*, 9.2.78), the Macedonians were originally named Emathians after King Emathio; cf. Pliny, *Natural History*, 4.33.

3 THRACE, ROMANIA, CONSTANTINOPLE

18. NOW THAT I have discussed the Vlachs and Hungarians, I turn my attention to the Thracians and their affairs. Thrace, according to most authors, including the more distinguished, is a spacious country which extends over a broad area. It is bordered by the Black Sea and the Propontis in the east; the Aegean Sea, the Strymon River, and the land of Macedonia in the south; the Danube in the north; and, on its western margin, not only by the mountains of Paeonia but Pannonia and the Sava River. I observe that Pliny of Verona held this opinion and also Strabo,[75] who affirms that the ridges of Mount Haemus divide Thrace in the middle; he is also certain that the Dardanians, Triballians, and Mysians inhabited Thrace. No one, however, who matches the writings of the ancients with the present situation, will deny that the Triballians inhabited the plains in which either the Rascians or Serbians now have their homes. Beyond the Triballians, the Mysians, who settled between the Danube and Mount Haemus,[76] stretch eastward all the way to the Black Sea. Today they call these people Bulgarians. Next to them, the maritime region extending south to the Hellespont is Romania—a Greek nation, though once it was barbarian, and it is returning to barbarism in our own time, now that the empire of the Greeks has been destroyed and the Turks hold sway.[77]

The capital city of this country [Thrace] is Byzantium, formerly called Agios. The Spartans founded it under the leadership of Pausanias.[78] When they consulted Apollo as to where they should seek

---

75. Pliny, *Natural History*, 4.42; Strabo, *Geography*, 7.5.1.
76. In other words, the Balkan Mountains.
77. "Romania" here and for many authors of the medieval and Renaissance periods was used to designate areas ruled by the Byzantine (i.e., Eastern Roman) Empire.
78. Spartan general and allied hero of Plataea, Pausanias captured Byzantium from the Persians c. 477 BCE but was later accused of treason and died in 469.

a home, history records that the oracle commanded them to locate their habitation "opposite the Blind." By the Blind he meant the people of Megara, who founded Chalcedon. When they had first sailed to Thrace and seen the site where Byzantium was later built, they had passed over this fertile shore and chosen a poorer one in Asia [Minor] directly opposite. This is according to Strabo.[79] But according to ecclesiastical authors, the emperor Constantine the Great,[80] having decided to transfer the seat of empire from the city of Rome to the east in order to curb more easily the inroads of the Parthians, headed for the Troad and there laid the foundations of a royal city, where Agamemnon and the other Greek chieftains had once pitched their tents against King Priam. But when he was prompted in a dream by Christ our Savior, who designated another place, he left unfinished the work he had begun (traces of which long remained), sailed to Thrace, and sought out Byzantium, declaring that God had revealed this place to him. He soon enlarged the city, erected new walls, raised lofty towers, adorned it with the most magnificent private and public buildings, and so greatly enhanced its beauty that it could worthily be called a Second Rome.[81] The old writers who saw it in its prime considered it the home on earth of the gods rather than emperors. The emperor bestowed on the city the name of New Rome, but the obstinacy of the people succeeded in having it called Constantinople instead, after its founder.

19. Under the emperors, many episcopal councils were held in this city, many heresies which arose in Christianity were suppressed, and many were invented, among which the most durable was that concerning the procession of the Holy Spirit.[82] Although it was at-

---

79. Strabo, *Geography*, 7.6.29–30.

80. Constantine (c. 272–337) began ruling in the Western Roman Empire as tetrarch in 306. He became sole ruler in the West in 312 and of the entire empire in 324.

81. Much of the building of the city actually took place after Constantine's death. In the fifth century, Theodosius II built a massive land wall, which protected the city for centuries; see Jonathan Harris, *Constantinople: Capital of Byzantium* (London: Hambledon Continuum, 2007).

82. During the ninth century, it became common practice for Latin Christians,

tacked and rejected in several councils, it persisted until our own time, when, as I will relate in due course, it was finally condemned and cast out under Pope Eugenius IV at the Synod of Florence,[83] not only by the Latins but also the Greeks. But although Joseph, the patriarch of that nation, and John, its emperor, recited the creed in unanimity with the Latin Church, the Church of Constantinople considered it virtually sacrilege to believe what the Roman Church believed. The patriarch, who had agreed to unification, had died in Florence, and the emperor had not survived for long after returning home.[84] His successor Constantine, whether as the result of others' deception or his own madness, seemed in no way favorable to union. He had already driven Gregory, the newly appointed patriarch, from his home and seized the church's property because he was turning to the true faith.[85] Pope Nicholas had dispatched Isidore of Kiev, the bishop of Sabina and a cardinal of the universal church, an industrious man who had long governed the church of the Ruthenians, to inquire why the Greek nation was rejecting the pacts

---

even the pope, to add the term *filioque* to the Nicene Creed. This altered the original (fourth century) concept of the procession of the Holy Spirit from the Father alone, to procession from the Father and the Son. This issue among others led to the Schism between the Greek and Latin churches in 1054. See Sir Steven Runciman, *The Eastern Schism* (Oxford: Clarendon Press, 1955), chap. 2.

83. The Council of Ferrara-Florence, 1438–39, was attended by seven hundred Greek delegates, including the emperor and the patriarch, to work out the terms of a union. The Byzantine delegation, driven by mounting losses to the Ottomans and the promise of Western military aid in exchange for submission, reunited with the Roman Catholic Church on July 6, 1439. The agreement was decisively rejected by the inhabitants of Greece and the majority of the Orthodox clergy; see Deno Geanakoplos, *Constantinople and the West* (Madison: University of Wisconsin Press, 1989), chap. 11.

84. Patriarch Joseph of Constantinople died in Florence on June 10, 1439, before he was able to sign the declaration of Union. Emperor John VIII Paleologus (d. 1448) lived several more years after the Union but was unable to convince the majority of the Greek population to accept it.

85. Constantine XI Dragases Paleologus (r. 1448–53), John VIII's brother, was neither pro- nor anti-Union. He likely avoided implementing the terms of the union to preserve morale among the Orthodox populace. Patriarch Gregory III, despairing of his recalcitrant flock, returned to Rome of his own accord in 1451. See Donald Nicol, *The Immortal Emperor: The Life and Legend of Constantine Palaiologos, Last Emperor of the Romans* (Cambridge: Cambridge University Press, 1992).

which its own envoys had concluded with the Latins in Florence.[86] He had just coaxed the emperor and his senate onto the right path when war with the Turks, under the leadership and provocation of Mehmed II, burst upon the people of Constantinople like a sudden storm. I will describe this a little later in its proper place.[87]

4 ORIGIN AND HISTORY OF THE TURKS

20. I NOTE that many writers of our time, not only orators or poets but even historians, are ensnared in the error of referring to the Turks as "Trojans."[88] I believe they are influenced by the fact that the Turks occupy Troy, which was inhabited by the Trojans. But the Trojans originated in Crete and Italy. The Turkish race is Scythian and uncivilized.[89] Although I may seem to be digressing from my plan, I think it not irrelevant to describe their origin and expansion. For in our era, this race of people has grown so great that it controls Asia [Minor] and Greece and instills terror throughout Latin Christendom. My narrative will also extend the account of Thracian affairs with which I commenced.

21. According to the report of the philosopher Ethicus,[90] the an-

---

86. Isidore (c. 1385–1463) was appointed metropolitan of Kiev in 1437 and participated in the Council of Florence. Shortly thereafter, he became a cardinal and was deposed from his episcopal position in 1444 by the Russian clergy. Isidore was later sent by the pope to Constantinople to affirm the union in 1452, accompanied by a paltry two hundred soldiers to help with the city's defense.

87. See paras. 36–43.

88. Lat. *Teucri*.

89. Here Aeneas refers to a contemporary debate on the origins of the Turks. See Michael J. Heath, "Renaissance Scholars and the Origins of the Turks," *Bibliothèque d'humanisme et renaissance* 41 (1979): 453–71; Margaret Meserve, *Empires of Islam in Renaissance Historical Thought* (Cambridge, Mass.: Harvard University Press, 2008), chap. 1.

90. Ethicus or Aethicus Ister (fl. seventh century), author of the *Cosmographia*, was thought to be a late classical authority in Aeneas's time. What follows hews closely to his account. For more on Aeneas's use of Aethicus, see Meserve, *Empires of Islam*, 99–104. See Otto Prinz, ed., *Die Kosmographie des Aethicus* (Munich: Monumenta Germaniae Historica, 1993), for a recent edition.

Origin and History of the Turks   73

cestral home of the Turks lay beyond the Pyrrichean Mountains[91] and the Taracontan islands opposite the "Breasts of the North."[92] They were a ferocious and shameless race, given to fornication with whores and every kind of illicit intercourse. They ate what other people abominate—the flesh of beasts of burden, wolves, and vultures—and even partook of human fetuses. They observed no religious festival except the Saturnalia in August. They heard about rather than experienced the power of the Romans, though they paid tribute to Octavian Augustus in gold from the coast[93]—and that, in fact, on their own initiative. For when they noticed that neighboring regions all around them paid him annual tribute, they concluded that a new god of the days and seasons had appeared and sent him gifts every year.

This race, according to Otto of Freising, the historian and uncle of Emperor Frederick I Barbarossa, emerged from the Caspian Gates during Pepin's reign over the Franks and clashed in a fierce battle with the Avars (who are called Hungarians in our time), with many losses on both sides. Then, after crossing Pontus and Cappadocia, they gradually infiltrated the other adjoining populations and built up their strength through clandestine raids in the manner of brigands.[94] By occupying strategic mountains and passes from which they could easily launch assaults when opportunity offered,

91. A mountain range in Georgia.

92. The term *aquilonis ubera* refers to two legendary mountains, behind which Alexander the Great was said to have driven the Northern peoples of Gog and Magog and built a gate to contain them.

93. "They heard about rather than experienced the power of the Romans" is a paraphrase of Pompeius Trogus (Justin, *Epitome*, 2.3.5); the tribute story derives from Aethicus. See Meserve, *Empires*, 101. This may also be a reference to a visit from emissaries of the Scythians to Augustus (Augustus, *Res Gestae*, 31). The phrase *in auro littorico* is of uncertain meaning but possibly alludes to gold-mining in the Caucasus. See David Braund, *Georgia in Antiquity: A History of Colchis and Transcaucasian Iberia, 550 BC–AD 562* (Oxford: Clarendon Press, 1994), 24–25, 61–62.

94. Otto (c. 1111–58), bishop of Freising, was related to Frederick I (r. 1152–90) by marriage. Otto dates these events to 756; see *The Two Cities: A Chronicle of Universal History*, trans. and ed. Charles Mierow et al. (New York: Octagon Books, 1966), Bk V.

they rose so high and became so confident that they now vied openly and on equal terms with their neighbors for the possession of land. As time went on, they finally occupied not only Pontus and Cappadocia but Galatia, Bithynia, Pamphylia, Pisidia, the two Phrygias, Cilicia, Caria, and so-called Asia Minor, right up to the coast of Ionia and the shores of the Greek sea. They recognized no single chief in particular but varied in their allegiances, like factions, some following one leader, others another.

22. About one hundred and twenty years ago, as Niccolò Sagundino,[95] a distinguished expert in Greek and Latin history, has informed me by letter, a man of this race called Osman,[96] who at that time possessed little and was virtually unknown among the common people, conspired to amass a large body of soldiers from various sources and began to roam abroad, not only harassing whatever Christians had survived but also attacking and subjugating people of his own race. His efforts were facilitated by the outbreak of internal strife among the leaders of the Turks. For while they were tearing one another apart, he attracted from all quarters those who had a natural lust for pillaging and spoils, and, having quickly acquired power and reputation, took control of many towns, partly through force and partly through their capitulation.[97]

23. Osman was succeeded by his son Orhan, who aptly pursued his father's project and greatly advanced it.[98] He was followed by his

95. Sagundino or Sekoundinos (c. 1402–63) was a Greek scholar who was captured in Venetian Thessalonica in 1430 by the Ottomans. After thirteen months, he was released and served the Venetian government on various diplomatic missions. He wrote an account of the Ottomans, *Liber de familia Automanorum id est Turchorum*, in 1456 and dedicated it to Aeneas. See *Mehmed II the Conqueror and the Fall of the Franco-Byzantine Levant to the Ottoman Turks*, ed. and trans. Marios Philippides (Tempe, Ariz.: ACMRS, 2007) for the text and notes.

96. Osman (d. ca. 1326) founded the Ottoman dynasty in northwest Anatolia.

97. Aeneas's description is similar to recent scholarly interpretations of ghazi warfare and the early Ottomans' rise to power. See Linda Darling, "Contested Territory: Ottoman Holy War in Comparative Context," *Studia Islamica* 91 (2000): 133–63 for an overview.

98. Under Orhan's leadership (r. 1326–62), Bursa was captured (1326) and became

son Murad.⁹⁹ Murad was the first of the Turks to cross into Greece, at a time when two men were disputing the Greek empire, and one of them, who feared defeat, called him in for assistance. Once there, he deliberately protracted the war and, having observed that the strength of the two had been sapped and squandered, leaving both men in a weakened and exhausted state, he changed course,¹⁰⁰ as the saying goes, and turned his arms upon them indiscriminately, as opportunity offered. Having occupied Gallipoli, a city strategically situated by the straits of the Hellespont in the Chersonese, he openly attacked the other Greek cities, brazenly laying claim to the Greek empire for himself and his heirs. He brought beneath his sway a large part of Thrace with almost no one daring to oppose him.¹⁰¹ When he died, he left two sons, Suleyman¹⁰² and Bayezid. Suleyman soon passed away, and the whole enterprise fell to Bayezid, who was favored by the winds of good fortune. He so far extended the boundaries of the new kingdom as to occupy almost all of Thrace (with the exception of Constantinople and Pera), Thessaly, Macedonia, Phocis, Boeotia, and the greater part of Attica; he also weakened the Mysians and Triballians¹⁰³ and Illyrians¹⁰⁴ by frequent expeditions.¹⁰⁵ As for Constantinople, having

---

the first Ottoman capital. Other important conquests include Nicaea (1331) and Nicomedia (1337).

99. Murad I (r. 1362–89).

100. Literally "turned prows," quoting Sagundino.

101. It was actually during Orhan's reign in 1352 that the Ottomans first entered Europe as Byzantine auxiliaries, assisting Emperor John VI Cantacuzenus against his rival for the Byzantine throne, John V Paleologus. Orhan's son Suleyman (d. 1357) led most of the military maneuvers in Thrace. When an earthquake destroyed the walls of Gallipoli and other towns in 1354, Suleyman occupied them. After his death, his younger brother Murad, who later became sultan, took over operations in Europe and expanded Ottoman dominion over Greece and much of the Balkans. See Colin Imber, *The Ottoman Empire 1300–1650: The Structure of Power* (Hampshire: Palgrave Macmillan, 2002), 9–10.

102. His name was actually Jakub, and he was executed when his brother Bayezid ascended the throne; see Philippides, *Mehmed II the Conqueror*, 63n6.

103. Here, Aeneas probably means the Serbians; see para. 1.

104. Probably the Bosnians, but Aeneas uses the term broadly for modern peoples; see paras. 1 and 58.

105. Bayezid I "The Thunderbolt" (r. 1389–1402) led the Ottomans to victory at the

stripped it of all its countryside and places of recreation close to the city, Bayezid oppressed it with so long and arduous a siege that the citizens despaired of their safety and began to discuss surrender.[106] Without doubt they would have perished and fallen into the hands of a most savage enemy had it not been for Tamerlane, the mighty king of the Scythians, who toppled and demolished everything in his path like a torrential river. When Bayezid tried to stand in his way and resist him, Tamerlane defeated and captured him in Asia after a great and bloody battle.[107]

This is the Tamerlane who is known as "the terror of nations" and said to have had an army of 1,200,000 men—a greater number than Xerxes and Darius, whose forces are reported to have drunk the rivers dry. He called himself "the wrath of god," and his cruelty was worthy of the name. He destroyed many splendid cities of Asia and butchered people like cattle, with no respect for age or sex. He sacked and burned Damascus, the most famous city of Syria. At dinner, he ordered Bayezid to be chained and fed beneath his table like a dog. To mount a horse, he used him like a footstool.[108]

24. After Bayezid's defeat, his sons, who were many, fell into the hands of the Greeks when they tried to cross into Thrace to escape danger.[109] However, the eldest, Suleyman, was released by the

---

Battle of Kosovo (1389) against rebellious Balkan lords; his father Murad I was killed in this battle. Bayezid spent much of his reign breaking Balkan resistance and strengthening Ottoman control over the region; John V. A. Fine, *The Late Medieval Balkans* (Ann Arbor: University of Michigan Press, 1987), 410–11; 425–30. Hereafter, *LMB*.

106. Bayezid's forces blockaded Constantinople from 1394–1402.

107. The Battle of Ankara (1402).

108. Timur Lenk or "Timur the lame" (1336–1405) carved a central Asian empire from Mongol successor states, Turkish emirates, and Ottoman territories. Bayezid died in captivity in 1403. Other sources also contain the stories of Timur's wretched treatment of his prisoner, but they may be apocryphal. For more on this, see Meserve, *Empires*, 204–5.

109. Sultan Bayezid's sons—Suleyman, Musa, Isa, and Mehmed—fought each other for the throne, with the assistance of various Christian rulers, who took advantage of the chaos. Only Suleyman and his family and Musa, however, were active in Europe; Imber, *Ottoman Empire*, 17.

Origin and History of the Turks 77

Greeks and took possession of his father's kingdom. When King Sigismund of Hungary faced Suleyman in a pitched battle, he suffered a tumultuous rout and abandoned his camp and baggage. A great slaughter of Christians took place; Duke John of Burgundy was captured in the battle and purchased his freedom with a large quantity of gold.[110]

When Suleyman died, his son Orhan, a youth of tender age, was robbed of both his kingdom and his life by his uncle Musa. A little later, Musa was lost in battle without a son, leaving his brother Mehmed as his heir.[111] After grinding them down in war, Mehmed imposed heavy taxes on the fierce and warlike tribes of Vlachs, who, as I stated previously, control a large region across the Danube. He also crushed some Turkish princes in Asia and entirely robbed them of their kingdoms.[112] He persecuted the Christians who lived beneath his rule with extreme severity.

25. When Mehmed died, his son Murad,[113] who was staying in Asia at that time, attempted to cross into Thrace when he heard of his father's death. But the Greek emperor long prevented him and released Mustafa, the remaining son of Bayezid, to seize power, lending him his full support.[114] But when Mustafa was defeated and killed in battle, the victorious Murad acquired the whole kingdom and proceeded to assault, capture, and ransack Thessalonica, an illustrious city of Greece which at that time was held by the Venetians. Strengthened by that success, he added Epirus and Aetolia—

---

110. A reference to the Crusade of Nicopolis (1396), where Bayezid, not Suleyman, directed operations. John the Fearless of Burgundy (r. 1404–19) was one of the many captives taken at this battle.

111. After years of fighting and intrigue, Mehmed I (r. 1413–21) emerged as sole ruler of the Ottoman Empire.

112. Mehmed led several expeditions into Anatolia, mostly against the emir of Karaman.

113. Murad II (r. 1421–51).

114. Mustafa, Murad II's uncle, was released from custody by the Byzantines in 1421 to challenge Murad's claim to the throne. Yet another Mustafa, Murad's younger brother, also challenged Murad's claim in 1422; see Imber, *Ottoman Empire*, 22.

by no means obscure regions—to the rest of his kingdom.[115] He ravaged the lands of the Illyrians,[116] took many towns by force, and sacked and burned them. Following the custom of his race, he entered into marriage with a great many wives, including the daughter of George, despot of Serbia.[117] Not long afterward, he led an army against George, heedless of their familial bond. George, who could not match the power of his son-in-law and feared the fury of the enemy, left one of his sons to guard Smederevo with a garrison and fled to Hungary with his wife and other children together with the priests of his nation. However, Smederevo was stormed and pillaged, and the despot's son was robbed of his eyesight.[118] Driven from his country, George spent a long exile in Hungary. John Hunyadi, who was already famous for his feats in arms, often led his army into Serbia, where he inflicted numerous defeats on the Turks and crushed their commanders in battle.[119] But although he recovered a large part of Serbia, he did not restore it all to George; much he kept for himself and much he gave to his friends—not without justification, since he had repelled the enemy through his own valor, and the loyalty of George was questionable. Squeezed between the Hungarians and the Turks, he had deceived now one side, now the other, and in matters of religion he neither heeded the Roman Church nor obeyed the law of Muhammad.

---

115. Byzantium ceded Thessalonica to Venice in 1423. Murad II's troops conquered the city in 1430. Epirus and Aetolia were captured in 1431.

116. Probably Croatia here, judging by the context; see paras. 1 and 58.

117. Murad II married Mara Branković in 1435; she was the daughter of George Branković (r. 1427–56).

118. George's son, Gregory, surrendered the fortress in 1439, and Murad II let him rule southern Serbia as his vassal. But in 1441, both Gregory and his brother Stephen were accused of treason and blinded; see Fine, *LMB*, 530–31.

119. Hunyadi won victories against the Turks in Serbia in 1441–42 and in 1448 before the Second Battle of Kosovo.

5 THE BATTLE OF VARNA (THE TURKISH WARS [5-8])

26. HAVING come this far, I would like to trace the activities of this man to their conclusion. When the fighting ended badly at the Battle of Varna, which I will describe a little later,[120] Hunyadi fled and retreated into Serbia. Learning of his arrival, George went to meet him, intercepted him en route, and, as if he were an enemy, imprisoned him and would not release him until he retrieved the towns within his jurisdiction which Hunyadi had formerly occupied.[121] Not long afterward, when John was leading his forces toward Sofia and seemed poised to inflict significant losses upon the Turks, George revealed to Murad all the plans of the Hungarians; thanks to this warning, Murad dealt the Christians a massive defeat, as I will relate in due course. But when the Turks had conquered Constantinople and were threatening to march into Serbia, he crossed over to Hungary for a second time in search of help and, after traveling all the way to Austria, approached King Ladislas. George was now advanced in age—a man worthy of respect, if only his religious beliefs had been correct: such was the authority of his speech, such the majesty of his appearance.

George was approached by the Minorite friar Giovanni da Capistrano, a man renowned for his pure life and famous in our time among the preachers of the Gospel.[122] Giovanni asked whether he

---

120. See paras. 28–32.
121. It was Vlad Drakul "the Impaler," ruler of Valachia, who captured Hunyadi after Varna. George Branković captured Hunyadi after the Second Battle of Kosovo in 1448.
122. Capistrano (1385–1456), a Franciscan friar, spent the last years of his life in Eastern and central Europe (1451–56) preaching against the Hussite heresy and working to support crusade. He accompanied John Hunyadi during his final campaign against the Ottomans and was present at the Christian victory of Belgrade (1456); see para. 44. He died shortly thereafter of the plague. The following conversation between him and Branković probably took place in 1455 when Giovanni was attending the Hungarian

was willing to listen to him. When George consented, he expounded to him the beliefs and doctrines of the Roman Church. Through an interpreter, he discussed the Scriptures with him at length and ardently exhorted him to abandon the error of his nation. Finally, George gave the following response: "I have lived for ninety years and know no other religion than the one I received from my forefathers. Up until now my countrymen have considered me wise, though unlucky. But now, as people often do, you want to make an old man lose his mind.[123] I would rather end my life with a noose than abandon the traditions of my ancestors."[124] And with these words, he departed from his sight. So dangerous it is to have been steeped in a damned religion![125]

27. Returning home, George learned that Michael Szilágyi, who was then commanding the garrison in Belgrade, and his brother László had left the city in carriages, and he sent soldiers to catch or kill them. When Michael noticed the approach of enemies, he leaped from his carriage and mounted a horse that was being led behind it, thus saving himself by swiftly taking flight. László was discovered in his carriage and died after being stabbed and torn apart with many wounds. But George did not get away with this scot-free. When Michael found out a few days later that he was traveling near the bank of the Danube, he attacked him with an armed

---

Diet to lobby for a crusade. See Joseph Held, *Hunyadi: Legend and Reality* (Boulder, Colo.: East European Monographs, 1985), 153.

123. Reading *senem* (as in the 1571 edition) for mss. *senes*; the translation is indebted to Socas. Van Heck follows the mss.: *tu nunc, quod sepe agitant senes, delyrum efficere cupis*. This might mean, "But now, as old men often do, you want to make me lose my mind." But in this context, the "old man" ought to be the *grandevus senex* and self-proclaimed nonagenarian, George (born 1377), rather than Giovanni (born 1385). With *senem*, the phrase *quod sepe agitant*, "as people often do," might refer to previous attempts to convert George. However, the correction is tentative; text and interpretation both remain uncertain.

124. "Traditions of my ancestors" may refer to the independent Serbian Church, established in the thirteenth century, or Orthodoxy in general.

125. This seems to be the required sense, but, if so, the Latin is ungrammatical. Perhaps *imbuisse* is a corruption of *imbibisse*, "to have imbibed."

The Battle of Varna 81

band and carried him off in captivity. When George defended himself with a sword, Michael cut off two fingers of his right hand. He was ransomed for a great weight of gold but did not survive for long, for the bleeding of his mutilated hand could not be stanched. Such was the end of this treacherous man.[126]

George's son Lazarus took up the reins of government after him, excluding his brother Gregory, whom Murad had formerly blinded. He and his sister, Mara (who, as I mentioned, was married to Murad), fled to Mehmed for protection and begged in vain for his assistance.[127] Then Lazarus died, and no small quarrel arose over his succession.[128] Gregory strove to win back his father's kingdom with the aid of the Turks. The widow of Lazarus[129] begged the Hungarians for help, and Cantacuzina, the former wife of Count Ulrich of Cilli, and George's daughter, remained hopeful of obtaining a portion of the inheritance.[130] At the invitation of the Hungarians, Cardinal Juan Carvajal traveled there to recover the strongholds of Serbia, which block the Turks' entry into Hungary, in the name of the Apostolic See or to see that they were handed over to the Hungarians. Without achieving his purpose, and not without grave danger (for he barely escaped the clutches of the Turks), he returned to Buda.

28. Let me continue now with the exploits of Murad, which I left in mid-course. This was a great man in peace and war, as beloved

---

126. These events took place in 1457. George's attack might have been revenge for the death of Ulrich of Cilli, George's son-in-law, who was murdered by László Hunyadi (Szilágyi's nephew), but there had long been tension and battles between the two families; see para. 10.

127. Mara was childless but had a cordial relationship with Mehmed II and his son Bayezid II, which enabled her to act as an intermediary and negotiator in Serbian and other European affairs; see Franz Babinger, *Mehmed the Conqueror and His Time*, trans. Ralph Manheim (1953. Rev. ed. Princeton, N.J.: Princeton University Press, 1978), 162–64.

128. January 1458.

129. Helen Paleologus.

130. For an explanation of these complex alliances and intrigues and the eventual Ottoman takeover of Serbia, see Fine, *LMB*, 570–76.

by his own people as he was hated by ours. He entered Hungary with a hundred thousand warriors[131] and plundered the country far and wide, but a barren year prevented him from gaining possession of the kingdom; compelled by the dearth of supplies, he returned home.[132] Cardinal Giuliano Cesarini, who was sent to confront him by Pope Eugenius, raised the spirits of the Hungarians and persuaded them to take up arms. A Christian army advanced to Sofia as far as the Great Arch[133] and fought several successful battles with the Turks, to the great glory of John Hunyadi, who then commanded their forces. His name struck such fear into the enemy that, when their children cried, mothers made them be quiet by threatening that John would come. The Turks, however, mustered in large numbers and ventured to engage the Christians, but their success in battle failed to match their courage; overcome by the valor of the Hungarians, they took to flight after suffering many losses.

The Hungarians who took part in the fighting exaggerated their exploits out of a desire for glory and, turning something great into something even greater, wrote to Emperor Frederick that thirty thousand of the enemy had been killed and many more captured in the Turkish defeat. Cardinal Cesarini maintained in his own letter that no more than six thousand of the enemy had fallen in that battle and that nine military standards had been captured; furthermore, that John Hunyadi had shown remarkable courage both as a general and a soldier, too—and he was believed. This victory of the Christians caused the Turks more panic than loss, since they thought that the military strength of not only Hungary but also Germany had been mobilized against them. Dismayed and stricken with fear, as if the whole West had formed a league, they therefore

---

131. A possible exaggeration. On the varying reports of numbers, see Held, *Hunyadi*, 86, 88.

132. Autumn and winter of 1443.

133. Probably the Zlatitsa Pass in the Balkan Mountains, which was the farthest extent of the campaign. See Colin Imber, ed. and trans., *The Crusade of Varna, 1443–1445* (Aldershot: Ashgate, 2006), 17.

sued for peace. The Hungarians, who had no illusions about their strength and ascribed their victory more to chance than to their own power, thought it dangerous to try their luck further and accepted the terms of peace which the Turks proposed on their own initiative. A truce of ten years was declared.[134]

Both sides swore an oath in conformity with their own rituals, and what the despot of Serbia had lost in the war was returned to him.[135] The outcome was galling to Cardinal Cesarini, who thought that the victory should be exploited. To Pope Eugenius, too, no news could have been more distressing, since nothing concerned him more than the propagation of the Christian faith. He therefore wrote to the cardinal that a treaty struck with the enemies of religion without his consultation held no validity. He ordered King Wladyslaw of Poland, who at that time was occupying Hungary, to dissolve the accord, while he himself annulled the oaths and, using threats as well as pleas, demanded the undertaking of a new war.[136] He sought reinforcements from Christian rulers, but except for Duke Philip of Burgundy, no one was stirred to action by zeal for the Christian faith. All by himself, Philip equipped a fleet that sailed to the Hellespont and tried to prevent the Turks crossing from Asia into Europe.[137] Francesco, cardinal of Venice, who was

---

134. Having lost much in the war, both sides were interested in negotiations, if only to buy time before the next attack. Murad, moreover, needed to mobilize in Asia Minor against the Grand Karaman, Ibrahim Beg. Murad and Wladyslaw concluded a ten-year peace treaty on June 12, 1444.

135. Murad and George Branković reached an agreement by which George regained his lands and the Danube fortresses of Golubac and Smederevo, and his sons were returned to him. Murad secured the release of his brother-in-law, Mahmud Pasha, who was captured the previous December; see Imber, *Crusade of Varna*, 23.

136. Cesarini and the Byzantines also put pressure on Wladyslaw to break the treaty as it had done nothing to ensure their safety or return any of their lost possessions. Moreover, Burgundian forces and the papal fleet had already begun to mobilize. For more on the treaty and various debates surrounding it, see Setton, *Papacy and Levant*, vol. 2: 77–81; Imber, *Crusade of Varna*, 20–25.

137. On Philip's interest in crusading, see Jacques Paviot, "Burgundy and the Crusade," in *Crusading in the Fifteenth Century: Message and Impact*, ed. Norman Housley (New York: Palgrave Macmillan, 2004), 70–80.

Eugenius's nephew, was sent there with a large number of galleys and took command of the fleet.[138]

29. Wladyslaw, who had invaded a foreign kingdom [Hungary], thought it would serve his interests for the inhabitants to be preoccupied with war.[139] He therefore summoned reinforcements from Poland, Bohemia, and the other neighboring nations; recruited troops in Hungary; and resolved to invade the territories of the Turks, entrusting command of the campaign to John Hunyadi. There are said to have been about forty thousand horsemen, though many have recorded a figure less than half of that. The lords of Hungary and a multitude of priests took part, and Cardinal Giuliano Cesarini brought with him a large number of crusaders. They set off through Valachia, forded the Danube, and came to Mysia,[140] in order to cross its level plains into Romania. Learning of the enemy's arrival and lacking confidence in the Greeks and Turks who remained in Europe, Murad assembled an army of Asian soldiers. But the crossing of the straits afflicted his mind with considerable anxiety, for he was well aware that the papal fleet controlled the sea. While he fretted, so they say, and turned the matter over in his mind, some men of Genoa dispelled his worries by promising to carry his troops on their own ships for a price. There is a place between the Propontis and the Black Sea where the width of the straits is no more than five stades[141]—such is the distance that separates Europe and Asia. The ancients called it the Thracian Bosphorus, and it is about forty stades from the Horn of Byzantium. Here the army of Murad was transported for a carrier's fee of one gold coin per head, and, if the report is accurate, the total was one hundred thousand.[142]

---

138. Francesco Condulmer (c. 1410–53); cardinal of San Clemente from 1431 and admiral of the crusader fleet. The pope and Venice also supplied galleys for this expedition.
139. Aeneas discusses the contest over the throne of Hungary in paras. 6–9.
140. Here, Mysia corresponds to modern day Bulgaria.
141. A stade is roughly equivalent to 660 feet or 180 meters.
142. Allies of the Ottomans since the early 1350s, the Genoese provided ships for the

The Battle of Varna

30. The Christians had reached the place called Varna when they received news that the forces of the enemy were approaching in countless numbers. Wladyslaw and the cardinal thought they should retreat and seek a fortified position in the mountains, to avoid being surrounded by the enemy. Hunyadi opposed this and argued against it. He said that he knew the strength of the Turks and that rumor always exceeds the truth. But even if all the Turks were present, they would still be no match for the Hungarians. The Turks, he said, glittered with golden and parti-colored garments, the Hungarians with iron and bronze. The Christian army was prepared to stand firm and to pursue, untrammeled as it was by a mass of people and belongings and with its gaze fixed upon its commander's signals—or mere nod.[143] On the other hand, if one examined the character of the Turks, they ought to be considered women rather than men. If a Christian army led by the king of Hungary, attended by an apostolic legate, and holding within its ranks so many illustrious nobles should take to flight, then never again would the Hungarians have the heart to take on the Turks. Hunyadi's opinion prevailed.

They waited for the enemy, who, when they appeared on the following day, seemed to have an even larger army than rumor had reported, either because, to the fearful, all things seem bigger than they really are or because rumor had by no means exaggerated the extent of Murad's recruitment. Terrified by the sight, Hunyadi began for the first time to reflect on the magnitude of the danger and warned the king to flee. The king criticized the tardiness of his advice and said that it would do more harm to flee than to fight. In a pitched battle they could hope for victory, for larger armies had often yielded to smaller, and it was not so much the number of sol-

---

ferrying of Murad's army in 1444. The Ottoman army was likely only 30,000-40,000 when it crossed the Bosphorus, but swelled to 60,000 by the time it met the crusaders at Varna; the Christian army was probably no larger than 20,000; see Setton, *Papacy and Levant*, vol. 2: 89–90.

143. Cf. Quintus Curtius, *History of Alexander*, 3.3.26–27.

diers as their bravery and discipline which brought about victory. Moreover, God esteemed the better cause and was readier to help the few, if only they were bold. If they fled, they would hand victory to the enemy, offering up their backs to be stabbed and their comrades to be slaughtered with impunity. Bursting with anger, he also reproached John for his boastful words on the previous day and, after ordering everyone to take up arms, awaited battle.[144]

Murad had taken up position on a nearby hill from which he could view his own men as well as the enemy. When he gave the signal for attack, fifteen thousand horsemen formed up en masse and charged the Christians to provoke battle. They all had white capes over their breastplates, which looked like wings when they were blown by the wind. They were followed by an equal number of men clad in green cloaks. The reins of many of their horses appeared golden, and their helmets gleamed brightly with silver and precious stones. Even the scabbards of their swords were decorated with huge pearls.[145]

The Christians accepted battle and entered into the fray with defiant hearts. Our vanguard routed the Turks after felling a large number in the initial onslaught. This struck great fear into Murad, who was expecting no such outcome, and he would have abandoned his army and fled forthwith if the satraps who surrounded him had not grasped the bridle of his horse, rebuked him for his cowardice, and threatened him with death if he fled. He therefore stood his ground, albeit unwillingly, and, after ordering his bravest men to take up arms, resumed the battle.[146] The fighting con-

---

144. The Battle of Varna took place on November 10, 1444. Sources differ on how the Christian army came to take up its position at Varna, although it is likely that the king deferred to Hunyadi on most strategic decisions. Like Aeneas, the Anonymous Ottoman Chronicle depicts Hunyadi as brash and arrogant before the battle; see Imber, *Crusade of Varna*, 94–95. Other sources, like Thuróczy's chronicle, show him to be coolheaded and cautious.

145. Aeneas is likely invoking a classical commonplace about Asian dress. See J. P. V. D. Balsdon, *Romans and Aliens* (London: Duckworth & Co. 1979), 61–62.

146. The sources also disagree on Murad's resolve in battle, following patriotic lines

The Battle of Varna

tinued with full intensity for several hours, during which victory seemed to lean at one moment toward the Christians, at another to the Turks. On both sides men fell in droves, though more on the side of the Turks, whose ill-protected bodies were easily pierced with arrows and swords. But in the end, as from hour to hour a new enemy marched forward and the unscathed replaced the wounded, the Hungarians were overwhelmed, more by sheer numbers than by valor, and gradually began to fall back.

31. It was then that Wladyslaw, with a squadron of his own men whom he had brought from Poland—men no less brave than they were loyal—made an attack upon the hill occupied by Murad (as I mentioned before) and the wagons encircling it, in order to detach the victorious enemy from the battle and restore the Christians' morale. A new battle was joined there, striking new terror into Murad. Throughout the camp, men panicked and lost the heart to resist. If Hunyadi had equaled the king's valor and followed fortune when she smiled upon him, there is no doubt that this day would have deprived Murad of his life and his descendants of the Greek empire. But as soon as he saw the Christian standards giving ground, he extricated himself from the line of battle with ten thousand Hungarians and Vlachs and beat a hasty retreat, without taking leave of the king and with victory still in the balance. Perhaps in the eyes of a military expert the battle seemed unsalvageable, and he preferred to save a few than lose everyone. The Poles attributed their catastrophic defeat in this battle to Hunyadi's folly and cowardice; for his part, Hunyadi complained that his recommendations had been spurned. Abandoned to his fate, Wladyslaw was unhorsed and butchered while fighting bravely on the perimeter of the enemy's defense works.[147] His head was impaled on a spear and

---

as in the case of Hunyadi. Thuróczy, too, portrays Murad as terrified; see *Chronicle*, 144. The Ottoman Anonymous shows him as a brave and aggressive warrior; see Imber, *Crusade of Varna*, 98–99.

147. Aeneas glosses over the recklessness of Wladyslaw's charge into the center of the field in an effort to strike Murad. Even Polish chronicler Jan Długosz portrays the king

displayed to populations throughout Greece and Asia as a token of victory. The Poles were wiped out, their camp ransacked, and those guarding the barricade of wagons killed. The bishops and Hungarian nobles who were present were overtaken by the same fate.

Cardinal Cesarini fled when the battle was lost, but although he escaped the enemy, he could not escape the treachery of the Hungarians. While he was watering his horse at a pool, some brigands chanced upon him and recognized him. Thinking that he possessed money, they pulled him from his horse, killed him, removed his clothes, and abandoned his naked corpse to the wild animals and birds. Such was the end of that indisputably great and admirable man, in whom it was hard to decide which was superior, his erudition or his eloquence. He was a person of agreeable presence, charming character, pure conduct in every stage of his life, and religious fervor, which moved him to endure anything for the sake of Christ, including death itself.[148]

32. While fleeing, Hunyadi was taken prisoner by the despot of Serbia (as I described previously).[149] For several years after the end of this war, the Poles believed their king to be alive and thought he had been captured, not killed. The blame for the disaster fell to a large extent on Cardinal Condulmer of Venice for not having guarded the straits properly or reported the crossing of the enemy to the Christian leaders, which had been his second duty.[150] There

---

as rash and criticized by both his own knights and Hunyadi; see *The Annals of Jan Długosz*, trans. and abridged by Maurice Michael (West Sussex: IM Publications, 1997), 496.

148. Contemporary reports on the exact manner of Cesarini's death varied greatly, and many, including Aeneas, who knew the cardinal well, hoped he survived the battle for months afterward; see Piccolomini, *Reject Aeneas, Accept Pius: Selected Letters of Aeneas Sylvius Piccolomini (Pope Pius II)*, intr. and trans. Thomas M. Izbicki, Gerald Christianson, and Philip Krey (Washington: The Catholic University of America Press, 2006), 200–21; Imber, *Crusade of Varna*, 31.

149. See para. 26. Vlad Drakul captured Hunyadi in 1444 after the Battle of Varna; George Branković captured him in 1448.

150. The fleet's efforts to prevent the crossing were hampered by Murad's use of artillery, fired from both shores, and a rising storm; see Imber, *Crusade of Varna*, 30. Długosz claims the cardinal did send word of the crossing to Cesarini before the battle; see *Annals*, 494.

The Battle of Varna

is little agreement on the number of the slain. It is known for certain that more fell on the Turkish side, but in proportion to the number of their forces the loss inflicted on the Christians was far greater.

The victor Murad did not pursue the fleeing enemy, nor did he swagger and speak boastfully among his men or hold a cheerful expression, as he had in the past. When asked why he was so dejected and not reveling in the enemy's defeat, he said: "I would prefer not to win more victories like this." Having ordered the surviving troops to pack up their kits, he sent them home, while he returned to Adrianople and fulfilled the vows for victory which he had made to his god. And then, after pondering the fact that the responsibilities of kingship preclude true happiness and fearing, too, the fickleness of fortune, which favors no one forever, he summoned the leaders of his provinces and appointed his oldest son Mehmed to replace him as king. Choosing instead a private life, he himself set out for Asia with a few companions to share his retirement and devoted himself to some solitary form of religious observance.[151]

Halil Pasha, who surpassed the other Turkish satraps in wealth and influence, was assigned as regent for Mehmed, who was not yet fit for rule on account of his youth.[152] The other sons of the king were put to death according to the custom of that race, to prevent them from causing unrest in the kingdom.[153] Among the Turks, it is luckier to be born the child of a commoner than a king.

---

151. This was actually Murad's second retirement. He first abdicated in the summer of 1444 and retired to Manisa after concluding his treaty with Wladyslaw. He was recalled that autumn to meet the Hungarian advance, which culminated in the Battle of Varna. After the battle, Murad retired again but was recalled in 1446 to deal with a janissary revolt; see Imber, *Ottoman Empire*, 26–27.

152. Halil Pasha (d. 1453) served as grand vizier under Murad II and Mehmed II. Mehmed was only fourteen in 1446.

153. See also para. 35. Mehmed II has often been regarded as the legislator of royal fratricide, but it did not become a formal practice until the sixteenth century. The custom was abandoned in the late sixteenth century after the accession of Mehmed III led to nineteen such executions; see Imber, *Ottoman Empire*, 108–9.

6 THE BATTLE OF KOSOVO

33. A LONG period of time then elapsed in which neither the Hungarians nor the Turks took it upon themselves to challenge the other in combat; the calamity each had experienced kept them at home in a state of shock. The bloody battle of Varna had shattered the strength of both sides, and neither the Turks nor the Hungarians had a king who was ready for war. Hunyadi governed the latter, Halil Pasha the former, in another's name.[154] Hunyadi, the more aggressive and militarily experienced of the two, could not forget the shame he had incurred at Varna and pondered day and night on how to erase the infamy and repair his losses. The inactivity of the Turks, who for a long time had shown no sign of preparing for war, gave him hope of success. Convinced that they lacked both strength and resolution, he considered that the time was ripe for recovering his former glory and destroying the Turks. Even if they had armies, he thought they would lack a commander-in-chief and that an army without a leader was worth no more than a leader without an army. At once, therefore, he mustered troops from Hungary, summoned reinforcements from Bohemia, and assembled a sizable force of mercenaries, whom he resolved to lead against the Turks in the belief that he could attack them and destroy them before they received the news that he had left Hungary: such was the skill and dispatch he brought to all his undertakings.[155]

As I mentioned before, George, the despot of Serbia, revealed his plans to the Turkish leaders and made out the great danger threatening their people to be greater than it really was. The Turks were dismayed by the news and were at a loss for what to do. Murad was now an elderly man devoted to religion and had relinquished

---

154. Hunyadi was elected governor at the annual diet of Hungarian nobles in 1446.
155. Hunyadi's troops marched through Serbia, burning and pillaging, in September and October of 1448; see Setton, *Papacy and Levant*, vol. 2: 99.

The Battle of Kosovo

the cares of government.[156] Mehmed, who was still a young man, was thought unable to sustain the burden of such a major war. As for Halil Pasha, they considered him incapable of commanding the obedience which is essential in war. And so they trembled and seethed with anxiety, turning their minds this way and that but finding no plan satisfactory. Bogged down in their deliberations, the satraps finally decided the safest course was to recall Murad from retirement, for they believed that the veterans would refuse to serve under anyone else and reckoned that the fortunes of war should be tested under no other leader than one who had made a habit of winning. Halil Pasha was the author of this proposal and thereby thoroughly offended the feelings of Mehmed, who was eager to prove himself a man in this campaign and feared that he would lose power if his father resumed the throne: such is the fickleness of human wishes. Ambassadors were therefore sent to recall Murad, who promptly assembled an army and marched against the enemy. The soldiers followed him as eagerly as if they were going on a plundering expedition.

34. Hunyadi had now crossed over to Sofia with his forces. After overthrowing local governors who had confronted him and ravaging a broad swath of the enemy's territory, he had just encamped in the region called Basilsa[157] when the approach of Murad's forces was announced. Hunyadi did not wait to be challenged but initiated the fight himself.[158] When battle was commenced, the outcome of the struggle long remained uncertain. Where Hunyadi fought, the enemy was routed and turned tail, and a great slaughter was carried out. In the same way, Murad was victorious on his own wing, where he overwhelmed and routed the Hungarians. Finally, when

---

156. Aeneas is mistaken. Murad had abdicated and left governing of the empire to Mehmed and his adviser shortly after the Battle of Varna, but returned two years later to quell a janissary revolt; in late 1448 he was in control of the government in Edirne. See Babinger, *Mehmed the Conqueror*, 51–53.

157. Van Heck's trans.: Pelitza.

158. The Second Battle of Kosovo (October 17–19, 1448).

the two victors came head to head, the Christians were unable to withstand the onslaught of the Turks. Although they were superior in courage, they were surpassed in numbers and compelled to give way out of exhaustion rather than defeat. When Hunyadi could no longer keep his men in position through threats and pleas, he fled from the battle with a few companions. Many Hungarian nobles and some bishops fell in that engagement; the rank and file was massacred. However, just as many of the Turks perished. Murad took home a victory purchased with copious bloodshed and died soon afterward, leaving the throne to Mehmed as he had previously intended.[159] According to the custom of his ancestors, his body was buried in Bursa, a city of Bithynia and the capital of the Asiatic kingdom.

35. Shortly before Murad died, he had married the daughter of Isfendiyaroglu, a noble satrap in Sinop. She gave birth to a son called Ahmed Celebi, who was six months old when Murad entrusted him to Halil Pasha as he was dying. Halil betrayed both the mother and her child to Mehmed to curry his favor. Mehmed summoned thirty matrons, so they say, to identify the boy, and once he had confirmed that he was an offspring of Murad, he had him strangled and, after returning the son to his mother, held a royal funeral for his brother, thus inaugurating his reign with fratricide.[160] Some say that Halil substituted another boy called Ahmed Celebi, and that he was killed instead of Murad's son, while Ahmed Celebi was secretly raised in Constantinople. But after the capture of the city, he was removed and taken to Venice, and it was he whom Pope Calixtus ordered to be kept under guard in the palace as the brother of Mehmed.[161] I, for my part, leave the truth of the matter to the

---

159. Murad actually died over two years later, on February 3, 1451.
160. On Ottoman royal fratricide, see para. 32.
161. An alleged half-brother of Mehmed, Bayezid Osman, was baptized by Pope Calixtus III and renamed Calixtus Ottomanus in 1456. He later joined Pius II on his journey to Ancona, from which a crusade was planned, served Paul II, and became attached to the Habsburg court. See Babinger, *Mehmed the Conqueror*, 238, 324–25.

Greeks, though I am well aware that circumstances such as these give rise to many fictions, and I have often seen a barber's son perform the office of a king.

7 THE FALL OF CONSTANTINOPLE

36. THUS it transpired that, after the death of Murad, Mehmed took up the helm of state as he had desired. He reformed the institutions of his ancestors to suit his temperament, proclaimed his own laws at home and abroad, enriched the treasury, contrived new taxes, increased the size of his forces, and began to vent his rage and insults upon the nobles and courtiers.[162] As I noted previously, this is the Mehmed who waged war on the people of Constantinople, and now would seem to be an appropriate time to report what I have learned about him.

Mehmed had long meditated on how to bring Constantinople beneath his sway. He thought it incompatible with his glory that there was a city situated in the midst of the Turks which did not obey his authority. Furthermore, the honor which would accrue to his reputation if he captured the city would be all the greater in proportion to the disgrace of his forebears, who had abandoned their efforts after making the same attempt. And so, with amazing rapidity, having shared his plan with a few others and concealing his real purpose, he built and fortified a castle on the coast at the mouth of the Bosphorus, a little way distant from the city.[163] Thereupon, he simultaneously declared and waged war on the city by launching an attack, contrary to his oath and the agreements into which he had entered.[164]

---

162. On Mehmed's new policies, including his marginalization of Muslim noble families in favor of slaves he promoted, see Norman Itzkowitz, *Ottoman Empire and the Islamic Tradition* (Chicago: University of Chicago Press, 1972), 25–26.

163. Rumeli Hisari, located about six miles north of Constantinople on the European side of the Bosphorus, was completed in less than five months in 1452.

164. When he assumed the throne in 1451, Mehmed renewed the treaty that his father had made with the Byzantine Empire.

37. The Greeks had perceived his intention and, because they lacked confidence in their own strength, had turned for help to the Latins, whom they begged for assistance with tears and lamentation. For shame! The ears of our leaders were deaf, their eyes blind. They failed to see that if Greece fell, the rest of Christendom would collapse—though I tend to believe it was their preoccupation with private enmities or interests which caused them all to neglect the public welfare.[165] Meanwhile, Mehmed mustered forces from all quarters and attacked the imperial city by land and sea with impressive armaments and formidable vigor.[166] He excavated tunnels and hidden ditches of great depth; raised a broad ramp; rapidly erected a pontoon bridge, extending for two miles of the city's length, where the sea laps the walls on the side facing the town of Pera; built wooden siege towers of such a height that they topped the city walls, though these were very high; and installed a variety of siege-engines and artillery. For many days, the city was attacked and defended by both sides with the greatest vigor. Finally, a proclamation was made throughout the camp by a herald that all the soldiers should observe a religious fast on May 28,[167] and

---

165. For theories on why so little western aid came to Constantinople, see Kelly De Vries, "The Lack of a Western European Military Response to the Ottoman Invasions of Eastern Europe from Nicopolis (1396) to Mohács (1526)," in *Guns and Men in Medieval Europe, 1200–1500* (Aldershot: Ashgate, 2002), 539–59.

166. Ottoman troops began their attacks on or around April 7, 1453; their forces are estimated to have been about 80,000 strong. The population within the city was some 50,000—only 7,000 of whom were fighting men. The entire operation was concluded in only seven weeks. For more on the siege and sack of Constantinople, see Sir Steven Runciman, *The Fall of Constantinople 1453* (Cambridge: Cambridge University Press, 1965); for primary sources, see Philippides, *Mehmed II the Conqueror*, and J. R. Melville Jones, trans. and ed., *The Siege of Constantinople 1453: Seven Contemporary Accounts* (Amsterdam: Adolf M. Hakkert, 1972). One of Aeneas's main sources is Leonard of Chios; see Marios Philippides, "The Fall of Constantinople 1453: Bishop Leonardo Giustiniani and his Italian Followers," *Viator* 29 (1998): 206.

167. The text has the date as April 27 (*quinto Kal. Maii*), which seems a scribal error given the more accurate dates Aeneas provides in previous works like his letters. Wolkan, for instance, has *pridie calendas junias* (May 31) as the date of the attack; see *Briefwechsel*, vol. 68: 207.

The Fall of Constantinople

that on the next day after that they should be armed and ready to attack the city in full force and could plunder it for three days.[168] On the appointed day, a fast was kept until nightfall. As soon as the stars began to shine, invitations were issued and banquets held throughout the camp. Each man feasted cheerfully with whatever friend, relative, or acquaintance he had, and, when they had drunk enough, they embraced, exchanged kisses, and said a final farewell, as if they would never see each other again.

In Constantinople, however, the priests, with the people following in their wake, carried sacred images in procession through the city, calling upon Heaven for help and prostrating themselves, and the citizens all applied themselves to fasting and prayer. As night came on, each returned to the place he was assigned to defend. The main walls of the city were famous throughout the world for their height and thickness, but owing to their age and the Greeks' neglect they were devoid of battlements and ramparts; the outer walls, however, were appropriately fortified. On these, the Greeks staked their salvation, and the armed soldiers decided to make their stand between the main and the outer walls. They say that the shape of the city was roughly triangular: two sides were washed by the sea and equipped with walls suitable for repelling naval assaults, while the remaining side, which faced the land, was enclosed by an enormous ditch outside the high walls and the outer walls just mentioned.

38. The battle commenced a little before dawn [May 29], since the Turkish soldier was more tolerant of danger than delay and weighed the risk of wounds and bloodshed against the sweet prospect of plunder. While they fought in darkness, the Turks, who had weapons aimed at them from above, suffered greater destruction. But when it grew light, and the signal was given, they commenced

---

168. Mehmed and his generals were eager to take the city by storm before reinforcements from the west could arrive. A fleet was on its way from Venice, armed with help from the pope; see Runciman, *Fall of Constantinople*, 161.

a general assault, not only on Constantinople but also Pera, to prevent it from offering assistance to the Greeks. Each unit was assigned its own section of the walls and gates, so that the brave would be distinguished from the cowardly by the division of labor, and the soldiers' courage be fired to ever greater heights by the competition for glory;[169] the naval forces were ordered to attack assigned sections in the same way. Wooden towers were moved up to the city, and the soldiers brought picks, grappling hooks, and ladders. Then, raising their shields over their heads, they advanced in a dense *testudo*.[170] The Greeks rolled heavy rocks on top of them, and when the *testudo* came apart and faltered, they probed it with spears and pikes until they loosened the latticework of shields and strewed the ground with lifeless and mutilated soldiers. It was a massacre, and, as their spirits waned, the Turks began to fight more feebly. But Mehmed stood by, calling upon all the bravest soldiers by name and exhorting them to return to battle: some he enticed with rewards, others he intimidated with threats. The struggle began afresh. Once again, the Turks undermined the wall and battered the gates. Reforming the *testudo*, they mounted one another's shoulders and climbed atop it, where they strained to catch hold of the enemy's weapons and arms. Once again, the uninjured and the wounded, the half-dead and the dying were rolled together in a heap. Every manner of dying could be seen, and many an image of death.[171]

39. Giovanni Giustiniani, a man of noble birth from Genoa, the capital of the Ligurians, who in the days preceding seemed to have defended the city single-handedly, was wounded in this struggle.[172] When he saw he was bleeding, he secretly removed himself from

---

169. This, together with the following description of a *testudo* and certain other details, derives from Tacitus's account of the battle of Cremona (*Histories* 3.27–28).

170. "Tortoise"—a Roman formation consisting of soldiers screened by a roof and side-wall of shields.

171. A conflation of Tacitus, *Histories*, 3.28 and Virgil, *Aeneid*, 2.369.

172. Giovanni Giustiniani-Longo arrived in Constantinople with seven hundred soldiers and archers in late January 1453 and was given command of the landward walls.

The Fall of Constantinople 97

the battle in search of a doctor so as not to discourage the others. But when the emperor learned that Giustiniani was absent, he asked where he had gone and, after finding him, begged him not to desert the battle. Undeterred, Giovanni ordered a door to be opened through which he could return into the city to tend his wound. For the gates of the city, through which lay the way to the outer walls, were barred, so that a soldier would have no means of flight and therefore resist the enemy more stoutly. Meanwhile, the defense slackened. Noticing this, the Turks bore down more fiercely and, since a part of the wall had been shattered by bronze cannon and filled up most of the ditch, they climbed over the debris, scaled the outer wall, and dislodged the Greeks. The door which had been opened for Giovanni was now open to everyone and caused a wilder stampede. It was then that the emperor died, not fighting in a manner befitting a king but taking flight, when he was overwhelmed and trampled after falling in the gate's narrow passageway.[173]

40. Amidst so great a throng of soldiers there were only two—one Greek, the other Dalmatian—who proved themselves to be men: Theophilus Paleologus and John Sclavus.[174] Considering it disgraceful to flee, they held off the Turks' attack for a long time and slaughtered many of them, until they finally fell among the corpses of the foe—not so much vanquished as exhausted by victory. Giustiniani escaped to Pera and sailed from there to Chios,

173. Other writers, such as Doukas and even Aeneas's key source, Leonard of Chios, describe the emperor nobly hurling himself at the attackers rather than fleeing. It is impossible to determine how he met his end as no one who took part in the final stand appears to have survived to give a report. See Philippides, *Mehmed II the Conqueror*, 109, n. 11.

174. A kinsman of the emperor, Theophilus, and one of his companions, John Sclavus or Dalmata, attempted to rally the Greeks and hold off the Turks at the gate opened by Giustiniani and his men. It hardly bears mentioning that far more than two Byzantine defenders remained at the walls to fight. On Aeneas's and other humanists' conflicting views of the Greeks, see Nancy Bisaha, *Creating East and West: Renaissance Humanists and the Ottoman Turks* (Philadelphia: University of Pennsylvania Press, 2004), chap. 3.

where he fell ill, either from his wound or from grief, and ended his life ingloriously—a fortunate man had he breathed his last on the walls of Byzantium. About eight hundred Greek and Latin soldiers perished in the gateway, some pierced in the back with wounds, some crushed by the mob. And now the enemy were occupying the higher wall and assisting the entrance of their comrades by rolling rocks onto the townspeople. As soon as they had captured the city and killed everyone who dared to resist, they took to pillaging. The victors, whose numbers were beyond count, showed utter depravity in their lust and cruelty: neither rank nor age nor sex protected anyone. Rape was mixed with butchery, and butchery with rape.[175] Old men of advanced age and women worthless as booty were dragged off just for sport. When a mature young woman or a male of conspicuous good looks fell into the hands of the looters, they were torn to pieces and finally drove the plunderers themselves to murder one another. Anyone who was hauling off money or heavy offerings from the churches was cut down by others of superior strength. And since this immense and ill-assorted army, comprised of native Turks,[176] allies, and foreigners, held such a diversity of languages, customs, and desires, and each man differed in his sense of right and wrong, for three full days there was nothing in Constantinople that was not permitted.[177]

41. The Church of Hagia Sophia, the world-famous work of Emperor Justinian, to which no other bears comparison, was stripped of its sacred furnishings and exposed to every kind of filthy behav-

---

175. Some details of the rape of Constantinople derive from Tacitus, *Histories*, 3.33.
176. Lit. "citizens" (*civibus*).
177. Western writers exaggerated the atrocities of 1453, and their accounts must be read with care. Nonetheless, modern scholars concur that thousands were killed and many more were captured and either sold into slavery or kept as booty. For further information on the sack, the aftermath, and Western reactions, see Philippides, *Mehmed II*; Runciman, *Fall of Constantinople*; Bisaha, *Creating East and West*; Robert Schwoebel, *The Shadow of the Crescent: The Renaissance Image of the Turk (1453–1517)* (New York: St. Martin's Press, 1967); and L. F. Smith, "Pope Pius II's Use of Turkish Atrocities," *Southwestern Social Science Quarterly* 46 (1966): 408–15.

The Fall of Constantinople

ior. The bones of the martyrs, which had been the most prized objects in the city, were thrown to the dogs and swine. The images of the saints were either defiled with mud or destroyed by sword; the altars were demolished. In the churches themselves, they installed either brothels for prostitutes or stables for horses.[178] Servants were forced by blows and torture to search out their masters' hidden possessions and dig up what they had buried. Many treasure troves were discovered, which the unlucky townsmen had stored underground at the beginning of the war. If they had used these for the defense of the city, perhaps they would have preserved their lives and the liberty of their native land; but a greedy man has no power over gold.[179] All captives were taken to the camp.

42. I am ashamed to speak of the Christians' disgrace. I will tell of it nonetheless and not shrink from recording it for posterity, since I am convinced that one day, and perhaps before I die, men will arise to avenge so great an outrage inflicted on our Savior. The image of the Crucified One, whom we worship and confess to be the true God, was seized by the enemy and carried in procession from the city to their tents with trumpets and drums leading the way. They defiled it with spittle and mud and nailed it again to a cross in mockery of our religion. Next, they placed on its head the cap which they call a *sarcula*,[180] formed a ring around it and proclaimed, "This is the God of the Christians." They then cast stones and mud at it and disrespected it in shocking ways. But these things cause no harm at all to our God who reigns in Heaven, nor can they

---

178. Many of the Christian churches, including Hagia Sophia, were converted into mosques and others were confiscated for secular uses, but several remained in Christian hands during Mehmed's reign. See Sir Steven Runciman, *The Great Church in Captivity: A Study of the Patriarchate of Constantinople from the Eve of the Turkish Conquest to the Greek War of Independence* (London: Cambridge University Press, 1968), 187–89.

179. Greed and hoarding, among other supposed failings, were common Western charges against the Byzantines; see Schwoebel, *Shadow of the Crescent*, 16–17.

180. Leonard of Chios describes it as a Turkish felt cap (*pileum Teucrale quod Zarchula vocant*), probably a janissary cap; see *Historia Constantinopolitanae urbis a Mahumete II captae*, ed. J. P. Migne, *Patrologia Graeca* (1866), vol. 159: 942.

in any way demean his majesty: such is his glory, such his grandeur, and such his perfect beatitude that neither can the praises of men exalt nor their slanders diminish him. It is we who are injured and put to shame by these things—we who, through our cowardice and sloth in allowing the worship of the true God to decay, are forfeiting our good name in this life and our hope of salvation in the next.

43. At the banquet following these events, Mehmed happened to drink more than usual and, in order to mix blood with wine, the cruel and bloodthirsty butcher ordered the captured leaders and noblemen of the city to be slaughtered in a vile and pitiful manner. Lucas Notaras, who had held great influence with the emperor, was beheaded after his older son had been killed before his eyes and the other one set aside for immoral purposes; two other of his sons had fallen in the war.[181] Cardinal Isidore, who had been captured in the turmoil, was not recognized owing to a change of clothes and ransomed himself for three hundred aspers—a coin of relatively little value. Many Venetians, Genoese, and other Latins were put to the sword; some were ransomed for large amounts of gold.

This year, the year of Christ our Savior, 1453, stood out for the capture of Constantinople—a year as shameful and distressing to the Christian people as it was fortunate and joyful to the nation of the Turks. The people of Pera (an old Genoese colony), who are also called Galatans, surrendered to Mehmed before they were asked to, when they learned of the disaster suffered by the Byzantines. Their city walls were demolished; the belongings of many were plundered, contrary to the treaty; women and children were treated as playthings.[182]

---

181. Notaras was a senior minister, or Megadux, in the imperial administration. The exact circumstances of his execution and the fate of his children are not certain. Aeneas follows Leonard of Chios's account; Doukas and Kritoboulos have slight variations on it.

182. The walls were demolished, but the Perans and their possessions were spared on the whole.

8 THE BATTLE OF BELGRADE

44. HALIL PASHA, who, much to Mehmed's displeasure had stayed alive until that day, was wretchedly tortured to death on the pretext of having betrayed the plans of the Turks to Emperor Constantine. The great wealth that he had amassed is said to have caused his destruction, together with his recall of Murad to the throne from private life after he had resigned his power.[183] Enriched by his money and elated by such great success, Mehmed began to prepare an expedition against the Hungarians.[184] He spent about three years planning this and, after summoning leaders from throughout the kingdom, he made his way into the mountains of Thrace and reached the Sava River with a huge and menacing force. His army is said to have contained one hundred and fifty thousand men, though a good many authors subtract a third from this total. Cardinal Juan Carvajal, a man of outstanding ability whom I have mentioned before, was sent as a legate to those parts by Calixtus III (who during this time had attained the papal throne) in order to rouse the Germans to arms and stem the power of the Turks. He promised the forgiveness of their sins to all who were willing to campaign against the Turks and, with the help of Giovanni da Capistrano, who at that time was preaching the Gospel to the Hungarians, he got together no small army of crusaders, not from the rich or the nobly born but the penurious and simple common people. The ears of the rich were deaf to the Gospel, and the leaders failed to hear the word of God. Content with the present state of affairs, the powerful seek for the coming kingdom of Christ only as they are dying, while the poor

---

183. Halil was imprisoned on June 1 and executed on July 10, 1453. His great fortune was confiscated by the royal treasury, but Kritoboulos claims Mehmed later restored it to Halil's sons; see Kritovoulos, *The History of Mehmed the Conqueror*, ed. and trans. Charles T. Riggs (Princeton, N.J.: Princeton University Press, 1954), 87.

184. Actually, Mehmed next turned his attention to Serbia, successfully seizing the southern portion in 1454–55.

are trustful and readily submit to the word of preachers. Over forty thousand received the sign of the cross—an army protected more by faith than the sword. Hunyadi, too, had substantial forces under arms.[185]

45. As he drew closer, Mehmed was full of hope and swollen with incredible pride, thinking that neither mountains nor rivers stood in his way. Bragging to his men, he claimed that Hungary was already all but conquered. The emperor of the Latins, he said, was close at hand, and, now that the empire of the Greeks had been destroyed, the end was near for that of the Latins, too; the whole world would be subject to the Turks. He promised them large spoils and offered up Germany and Italy for his soldiers to pillage. He boasted that every place lay open to Turkish arms. But the braggadocio of his arrival was equaled by the shame and dishonor of his retreat. When he assaulted Belgrade, a small city situated at the confluence of the Danube and Sava, he failed to capture it by any means. He shattered the front walls with siege-engines, his army burst into the city, and the battle continued by day and night. At one moment, the enemy seemed vanquished, at another victorious. Finally, Mehmed was wounded beneath a nipple, abandoned his baggage, and fled by night in trepidation.[186] I have covered the sequence of this battle in my *History of Bohemia*, so there is no reason to dwell on it further here.[187]

46. Three Johns were held to be the architects of this victory: the cardinal legate, under whose leadership the campaign had been waged, Hunyadi, and Capistrano, who both took part in the battle.

---

185. Aeneas is describing the beginnings of the Crusade of Belgrade—the most significant Christian victory against the Turks in the fifteenth century, where several thousand commoners answered Capistrano's call to help defend the city in 1456. See Norman Housley, "Capistrano and the Crusade of 1456," in *Crusading in the Fifteenth Century*, 94–115.

186. July 22, 1456. Mehmed was actually wounded in the leg; Setton, *Papacy and Levant*, vol. 2: 181.

187. See *Historia Bohemica*, ed. Joseph Hejnic and Hans Rothe (Cologne: Bohlau Verlag, 2005), vol. 1: book 5.

But neither Capistrano mentioned Hunyadi nor Hunyadi Capistrano in the letters which they wrote to the pope or their friends about the victory that had been won. Each affirmed that God had granted victory to the Christians through his own agency. The human mind is exceedingly greedy for honor and readier to share kingship and wealth than glory. Capistrano had the ability to disdain possessions, trample on pleasures, and subdue lust, but not to spurn glory. Someone may say, perhaps, that he was not concerned about his own honor but that of God, who wished to save Christendom through the poor and unarmed. I yield to this defense, though Hunyadi, too, claimed to be only the agent of victory, not its author.[188]

They say that from then onward Mehmed never recalled that defeat without stroking his chin and his beard, shaking his head, and cursing the day on which he had joined battle at Belgrade.

9 MACEDONIA, THESSALY

47. ADJOINING THRACE, and extending in a westerly and southern direction, is Macedonia, which once ruled the world. It lies between two seas, the Aegean and the Adriatic. Its southern flank is protected by the rear of Thessaly and Magnesia. Its northern part is bordered by Paeonia and Paphlagonia,[189] though those regions, too, later passed into the jurisdiction of the Macedonians and were added to Macedonia. Epirus and the land of Illyria[190] are also contiguous with Macedonia, one bordering it in the south, the other in the north. On the Adriatic coast lies the ancient city of Dyr-

188. The lack of cooperation between Hunyadi and Capistrano is well illustrated by Capistrano's spontaneous decision to lead an enormous procession/charge outside the city, shouting "Jesus! Jesus!"—in utter defiance of Hunyadi's orders that no one should advance beyond the walls. Hunyadi's troops rushed out to assist them and the Turks fled their encampments that day. For more on the Battle of Belgrade, see Setton, *Papacy and Levant*, vol. 2: 173–81.

189. Should read "Pelagonia"; see Pliny, *Natural History*, 4.33.

190. Illyria probably signifies Bosnia here.

rachium, which acquired its name from the peninsula on which it is situated; it was formerly called Epidamnus and had been founded long ago by the Corcyreans. Not far below its territory was Apollonia, a city endowed with excellent laws and noteworthy for the education of Augustus Caesar, who studied Greek literature there. On the other shore is Thessalonica, once a powerful city, made famous both by the epistles of the apostle Paul and by the impetuous and implacable anger of Theodosius the Great. In outrage at the murder of some magistrates there, this otherwise most merciful emperor ordered the entire population of the city to be slaughtered. Eleven thousand men are said to have been killed.[191] Ambrose, the bishop of Milan,[192] did not allow so savage a crime to escape rebuke. He barred the emperor from entering church and compelled him to do penance—nor did the mighty emperor refuse to comply with his pastor's judgment. As a result, a law was proclaimed that a sentence of death passed on anyone should not be carried out until thirty days had elapsed. Pliny reports that this city enjoyed free status.[193] Strabo asserts that its founder was Philip, the father of Alexander.[194] Both assign it to Macedonia. Andronicus, son of Manuel, the emperor of Constantinople, received it as part of his inheritance and finally handed it over to the Venetians out of hatred for his brother John [VIII], who succeeded his father as emperor. Murad, the aforementioned emperor of the Turks, snatched it away from the Venetians.[195] This man subjugated the rest of Macedonia up to the mountains of Paeonia, as well as what they now call Albania. How amazing is the

191. The massacre, a reprisal against sports fans who had killed a Roman garrison commander in a riot, took place in May 390; around 7,000 perished. Theodosius regretted his hasty command and sent orders, too late, to rescind it.
192. Bishop of Milan from 374–97, Ambrose was later canonized.
193. Pliny, *Natural History*, 4.36.
194. Strabo, *Geography*, 7.7.4.
195. Despot Andronicus Paleologus, son of Manuel II, offered Thessalonica to Venice to save it from Murad II's siege rather than out of fraternal spite; see Setton, *Papacy and Levant*, vol. 2: 19. Venice ruled the city from 1423–30. It was captured by Ottoman forces on March 29, 1430.

Macedonia, Thessaly

mutability of things and how fleeting the glory of human power! This is the same Macedonia which was renowned for two kings, subdued Greece and Thrace, and extended its empire into Asia, conquering Armenia, Iberia, Albania, Cappadocia, Syria, Egypt, Taurus, and the Caucasus. This is the same Macedonia which brought the whole of the east under its power and ruled the Bactrians, Medes, and Persians. This, too, was the conqueror of India, carrying its military standards in the footsteps of Father Liber and Hercules.[196] This is the same country which now has fallen subject to the filthy race of the Turks and is forced to pay them tribute and bear their most miserable yoke. The armies of the Turks also invaded Magnesia and Thessaly within our time. The celebrated mountains, Pierian Olympus and Ossa, together with Pindus and Othrys, formerly the home of the Lapiths (who once upon a time, according to Pliny, controlled seventy-five cities),[197] are subservient to Turkish rule. The Turks possess the whole Peneus, the most famous of Thessaly's rivers.[198] This river rises near Gomphi and flows down a wooded valley between Ossa and Olympus. It runs for nearly five hundred stades and is navigable for half its length. A five-mile stretch in its course is called Tempe, where the gently sloping hills to the left and right rise up beyond one's sight, and the valley is suffused with its own verdant light. Here the Peneus glides along, green with pebbles, adorned with grassy banks, and melodious with the song of birds. It picks up, without absorbing it, the river Orcus, which floats on its surface like oil (as Homer said), and which it rejects after carrying it for a short distance. For it refuses to mingle its own silvery waters with the waters of punishment, which were created for the Furies. This is what Pliny says

---

196. "Father Liber" was a Roman name for the god Dionysus, who, according to myth, invaded India with Hercules; see Pliny, *Natural History*, 4.39.

197. Pliny, *Natural History*, 4.30–31.

198. Mehmed II led an army through Macedonia, Thrace, and Thessaly in early 1458, but his main objective was the Morea or Achaea.

about the Peneus.¹⁹⁹ So many are the blessings which the arms of the Turks have wrested from Christians, although I would attach greater blame to our own laziness.

48. In Thessaly, they say there was a king called Graecus, after whom Greece was named; also, that Helenus reigned here, from whom Helen acquired her name. Homer referred to the Thessalians with three names: Myrmidons, Hellenes, and Achaeans.²⁰⁰ Here are the narrows of Thermopylae, renowned for the slaughter of the Persians.²⁰¹ Although they once withstood the attack of Xerxes, they failed completely to obstruct the passage of the Turkish army.

10 BOEOTIA

49. NEXT after Thessaly comes Boeotia, which stretches from east to west, touching both the Euboean Sea and the Gulf of Crisa. It is mentioned by almost all historians owing to the fame of Thebes. Here is the birthplace of the Muses in the grove of Helicon, here the glades of Cithaeron, the river Ismenus and the springs of Dirce, Arethusa, and Aganippe. This city, which was once the homeland of Father Liber and Hercules and which produced the brave Epaminondas²⁰²—a city not inferior to Athens in fame—is in our time the insignificant stronghold of Thebes, which in recent years has been occupied by the Turks together with the rest of Boeotia.²⁰³

---

199. Pliny, *Natural History*, 4.8.30–31; cf. Homer, *Iliad*, 2.751–55; Strabo, *Geography*, 9.5.20.
200. Homer, *Iliad*, 2.684.
201. Battle between the Persians and Greek allies, led by Spartan King Leonidas, in 480 BCE.
202. Theban leader and general (c. 410–362 BCE) who broke Spartan domination over Boeotia.
203. Thebes became a vassal state of the Ottoman Empire in 1446; see Babinger, *Mehmed the Conqueror*, 50.

11 ATTICA

50. NEXT comes Hellas, which our countrymen call Greece. The ancients called it Acte, which means "coast"; then, through an alteration of the name, they called it Attica.[204] Homer referred to all the inhabitants of Attica as Athenians, since Megara had not yet been built. However, the part of it which is called the Megarid makes Attica stretch from Boeotia all the way to the Isthmus of Corinth. Near the Isthmus, in fact, was a column, which contained the following inscription on the side facing the Peloponnese: "This is the Peloponnese, but not Ionia." And on the side looking toward Megara: "This is not the Peloponnese, but Ionia."[205] For the people of Attica and the Ionians were the same. Having frequently quarreled with the Peloponnesians over their borders, they finally reached a consensus and had this column erected. Although Attica is rocky and barren, most writers have praised it extravagantly, calling it the abode of the gods, who occupied these parts, and the ancestral heroes. In Attica, the city of Athens once enjoyed great distinction and needed no words of commendation: such was its surpassing fame. In our time, the same place looks like a small town. However, on the rock where the ancient temple of Minerva[206] stood is a citadel celebrated through all of Greece for its massive size and impregnability. A certain Florentine surrendered this to Mehmed after begging for reinforcements from the Latins and finding no one to help him. In reward for this, he was given a country estate on which to live out his life in ignominy.[207]

204. Strabo, *Geography*, 9.1.3
205. Strabo, *Geography*, 9.1.6.
206. The Parthenon (completed in 438 BCE).
207. After withstanding a siege of two years by one of Mehmed's generals, the last Florentine duke of Athens, Franco Acciaiuoli, surrendered the Acropolis in June 1458 and retired to Boeotia as a vassal of Mehmed; he was murdered four years later on Mehmed's orders; see Babinger, *Mehmed the Conqueror*, 159–60, 178.

12 THE PELOPONNESE, THE ISTHMUS, ACHAEA

51. THE PELOPONNESE is connected to Attica.[208] It was once called the acropolis of all Greece. For in addition to the distinction and power of the peoples who inhabit it, its very topography marks it out for hegemony and power. It contains many gulfs and many capes as well as large and remarkable peninsulas, which are delightful for their variety. Its shape has been said to resemble the leaf of a plane tree, being almost equal in length and breadth. From west to east, it measures one thousand four hundred stades; according to Polybius, its perimeter or circumference, if one omits the gulfs,[209] amounts to four thousand stades. Artemidorus adds four hundred more to this, and Pliny seems to agree with him, following the authority of Isidore.[210] The same writer says that the land is encircled by two seas: the Ionian and the Aegean.

52. The narrow neck of land where it begins is called the Isthmus, which is five miles wide. King Demetrius, the dictator Caesar, the emperor Gaius, and Domitius Nero attempted to dig a channel through this strip—an ill-starred enterprise, as the fate of them all revealed.[211] Here was located the famous colony of Corinth. After the power of the Turks penetrated into Europe, the Greek leaders ran a wall across the strip from sea to sea and sundered the Peloponnese from the rest of Greece; they called the wall the Hexamilion.[212] Today, the Latins call this country [i.e., the Peloponnese] the Morea. It includes Achaea, Messenia, Laconia, the Argolid, and

---

208. The following paragraph is a paraphrase of Strabo, *Geography*, 8.1.3–8.2.1.
209. Reading *sinibus* for van Heck's *finibus*.
210. Pliny, *Natural History*, 4.9.
211. Demetrius Poliorcetes (d. 283 BCE), son of Antigonus, the king of Macedonia, and Stratonice; Julius Caesar (d. 44 BCE); Gaius, also known as Caligula (r. 37–41 CE); Nero (Lucius Domitius Ahenobarbus) (r. 54–68 CE). See Pliny, *Natural History*, 4.9.
212. The Hexamilion ("Six Mile Wall") was built in 1415 by Emperor Manuel II Paleologus.

The Peloponnese, the Isthmus, Achaea 109

Arcadia, which occupies the center of the peninsula. When Murad had sacked Thessalonica and subdued Boeotia and Attica (except for Athens), he marched as far as the Hexamilion and, to the consternation of the Greeks, demolished the wall and imposed an annual tribute on the Peloponnesians when they surrendered.[213] But when the Hungarians were persuaded to take up arms against the Turks by Cardinal Giuliano Cesarini, and, having succeeded in a few battles, began to bring more pressure to bear on the enemy, Constantine, the despot of this country, who, as I described previously, later reigned as emperor in Constantinople and there met his death,[214] was emboldened to deny tribute to the Turks and to rebuild the Hexamilion. For this he was fined a large sum, and the Hexamilion was destroyed again.[215]

53. When Murad had defeated and destroyed the Hungarians at Varna and Constantinople had fallen, the Albanians, a large number of whom then inhabited the Peloponnese, took up arms and strove to depose Constantine's brothers—Demetrius and Thomas—and raise a minor Greek nobleman to the rank of king.[216] Both sides begged for the help of Mehmed, to whom the nobler side seemed more deserving; he therefore supplied Demetrius and his brother with reinforcements to use against the Albanians. The Albanians were suppressed, submitted to their former masters, and paid a tribute of fifteen thousand gold pieces to Mehmed.[217]

---

213. The first destruction of the Hexamilion and attacks in the Peloponnese took place in 1423; here Aeneas refers to Murad's second destruction of the wall in 1431; see Setton, *Papacy and Levant*, vol. 2: 96.

214. See paras. 36–39.

215. Constantine Paleologus rebuilt the Hexamilion in 1443 when he became Despot of the Morea; the wall was destroyed by Murad II's cannon in 1446 and the Morea was again ravaged. It is estimated that 60,000 people were carried off in the raids; see George Ostrogorsky, *History of the Byzantine State*, trans. Joan Hussey (New Brunswick, NJ: Rutgers University Press, Revised Edition, 1969), 567.

216. This revolt occurred in 1453 over a tax increase. Manuel Cantacuzenus, a great grandson of Emperor John VI, became their leader; see Fine, *LMB*, 564.

217. This occurred in 1454. Aeneas fails to mention that the despots' already substantial tribute due to Mehmed was also increased.

Although Thomas could call himself emperor by hereditary right, since a long succession of his ancestors had ruled the Greek race, he nevertheless abstained from that title through fear of Mehmed. When Pope Calixtus, at the beginning of his pontificate, incited the Christian leaders to fight the Turks, Thomas thought that the Turkish Empire was certain to collapse and refused to pay tribute to Mehmed. However, when he saw that actions proved less impressive than words, he settled his differences with Mehmed by paying the tribute and throwing in extra gifts. But now, if the news reported in recent days is true, he has been forced to incur a greater penalty for his breach of faith and made entirely subservient to Mehmed. The whole Peloponnese has been added to the Turkish Empire.[218]

54. As one leaves the Peloponnese through the neck of the Isthmus and enters the rest of Greece, Strabo and Pliny say one arrives in Attica,[219] but, according to Ptolemy,[220] in Achaea, whose boundaries he describes as follows. To its west he places Epirus, to its north, Macedonia and a portion of the Aegean Sea; its eastern border he defines as the shores of the same sea, all the way to Cape Sounion; to the south, the coast of the Adriatic Sea where the Achelous River floods into the Gulf of Corinth. If this is so, Achaea embraces Attica, Boeotia, Phocis, Thessaly, Magnesia, Aetolia, and Acarnania. However, the same Ptolemy, in another passage where he lists the inland cities of the Peloponnese, says that Helice, Bura, Helena, and Pherea[221] are in Achaea and asserts that, strictly speaking, Achaea is

218. Due to the despots' inability to pay their tribute for three years and Thomas's courting of both church union and Western aid, Mehmed led a large army into Greece in the spring of 1458. The Greeks made a heroic effort to save Corinth and other cities, but the force against them was overwhelming. By the end of the summer, the Ottomans had conquered about a third of the Peloponnese. Thomas continued to seek Western aid and would soon be encouraged, if not adequately supported, by Aeneas upon his election as pope. See Setton, *Papacy and Levant*, vol. 2: chaps. 6–7; Fine, *LMB*, 565.
219. Strabo, *Geography*, 9.1.1–6; Pliny, *Natural History*, 4.23.
220. Ptolemy, *Geography*, 3.14.1.
221. Ptolemy, *Geography*, 3.14.36 (the last two names are a mangled version of Ptolemy's Pellene and Pherae).

Acarnania and Epirus   111

situated inside the Peloponnese. For my part, now that I have briefly summarized the affairs of the Peloponnese and Attica in keeping with the plan of my work, I hasten on toward the west.

13   ACARNANIA

55. THE FIRST place one comes to is Acarnania, which lies between Epirus and Boeotia and seems to join or blend with Aetolia. Today it is called a duchy. Giovanni Ventimiglia, a native Sicilian, gave his daughter in marriage to the despot of Acarnania. When the Turks were harassing Acarnania and besieged his son-in-law, he crossed the sea with a small troop of horsemen, attacked the besiegers, and inflicted a slaughter that deserves to be remembered. For with only a small detachment he routed an enormous force and succeeded in saving his son-in-law. The latter, however, was captured in an ambush by the Turks soon after this and lost his kingdom, though they say that Epirus is still governed in his name.[222]

14   EPIRUS

56. ON ITS western frontier, Epirus begins at the Acroceraunian Mountains and extends eastward for one thousand three hundred stades to the Ambracian Gulf.[223] Ptolemy reports that in the north

---

222. A reference to the Tocco family, who were the lords of Arta. In 1444 Alfonso of Naples sent troops to the region under Giovanni Ventimiglia's command. The relationship between Ventimiglia, marquis of Gerace, and the despot of Arta, Carlo II Tocco (d. 1448), is unclear. Ryder describes Ventimiglia alternately as his son-in-law and brother-in-law in two different publications; either way, he does not appear to have been his father-in-law. Aeneas also conflates Carlo II and his son Leonardo, who was expelled by the Turks in 1449. See Alan Ryder, *Alfonso the Magnanimous, King of Aragon, Naples and Sicily, 1396–1458* (Oxford: Clarendon Press, 1990), 303; idem, *The Kingdom of Naples Under Alfonso the Magnanimous* (Oxford: Clarendon Press, 1976), 272; see also Fine, *LMB*, 544, 563.

223. This paragraph is a paraphrase of Strabo, *Geography*, 7.7.5–6.

it adjoins Macedonia, in the east, Achaea, as far as the mouth of the Achelous River; its western side, he states, is bordered by the Ionian Sea.[224] Strabo called this same sea the Ausonian Sea.[225] In Epirus, Theopompus[226] related that there were fourteen tribes, of whom the best known were the Chaonians and Molossians. For, once upon a time, first the Chaonians ruled the kingdom and later the Molossians, descendants of the Aeacidae through the lineage of their kings, who underwent an amazing expansion; the old and distinguished oracle of Dodona flourished under their control. The seaboard of this land is reportedly rich and fertile, and once there were many cities and well-fortified towns in Epirus. But owing to its peoples' revolts, which brought them into conflict with the Romans, the country was laid to waste. According to Polybius, seventy cities of the Epirotes were razed by the general Aemilius Paulus after he had conquered the Macedonians and defeated King Perseus.[227] The majority of these belonged to the Molossians, and one hundred and fifty thousand people were reduced to slavery.[228] Pliny of Verona assigns this calamity to the Macedonians and adds two cities to the number destroyed.[229] Since the Macedonians held sway over the Epirotes, I believe that Pliny subsumed both races under one name.

In Epirus there occurred the world-famous battle of Actium, in which Caesar Augustus defeated Mark Antony in a naval action, together with Cleopatra, queen of Egypt; for she, too, was present and took part in this engagement.[230] For this reason, the victorious Augustus founded a city in the Ambracian Gulf and named it Nicopolis, meaning the City of Victory. The mouth of the Ambracian Gulf is a little more than four stades in width, and its circum-

224. Ptolemy, *Geography*, 3.13.1.   225. Strabo, *Geography*, 7.7.5.
226. Theopompus of Chios, a historian of the fourth century BCE.
227. Polybius, *Histories*, 30.15.
228. Consul L. Aemilius Paulus conquered Perseus in 168 BCE and ordered his troops to pillage the Epirote towns as punishment for their alliance with Macedonia.
229. Pliny, *Natural History*, 4.39.
230. September 2, 31 BCE.

ference comprises three hundred stades; in every part of it there is fine anchorage. In the past, as one entered the gulf, one encountered the Greek Acarnanians, who dwelt on its right side, and the temple of Actian Apollo towering atop a hill near its mouth. Below this lay a plain with a sacred grove and a dockyard where Caesar laid up nineteen ships as a tithe offering,[231] arranging them in order of their oarage, from those having a single bank of oars to those with ten. On the left side are Nicopolis and Cassope, a colony of the Epirotes. In our day, Epirus is called Arta. A few years ago, the admiral of the royal fleet, Vilamari by name,[232] caught and burned some Venetian galleys after pursuing them along its coast. On the same coast, according to Strabo, a voyage on the Adriatic ends at the Acroceraunian Mountains and the Ionian Sea begins.[233] In Strabo, the Ausonian and Ionian Sea seem to be one and the same, since he states that the shore of Epirus is washed by the Ausonian Sea.

15 ALBANIA

57. WHAT IS now called Albania was once the part of Macedonia which faced west. As I have recorded, it was the site of Dyrrachium and Apollonia—cities not without fame in antiquity. The language of the nation is intelligible neither to the Greeks nor to the Illyrians. I believe that this race of people once came from the Albania which reportedly neighbors Colchis in Asiatic Scythia, for floods of barbarian tribes frequently occupied the provinces of Greece and Italy. In this land, Musa held power. Though born of Christian parents, he failed to hold fast to the Catholic faith and strayed toward the madness of Muhammad. But he spurned the rites of Muhammad as frivolously as he had deserted Christ, for he returned to the law of

---

231. An offering to a divinity of a tenth of the spoils.
232. Bernat de Vilamari (d. 1463), who served Alfonso of Naples.
233. Strabo, *Geography*, 7.5.8.

his ancestors and, although he scorned both religions and remained loyal to neither, preferred to die as a Christian rather than a Turk.[234] He died of disease shortly after the fall of Constantinople.

George Skanderbeg, a man of noble birth, received his inheritance. He spent almost his whole life in arms, fighting for the name of Christ, and defeated and destroyed many large Turkish squadrons. Somehow he singlehandedly kept that region faithful to the Christian Gospel, though today it is said to be largely deserted owing to so many enemy invasions.[235] King Alfonso often sent soldiers to Albania and, after taking control of the city of Krujë, defended it against the Turks.[236] When Skanderbeg's fraternal nephew sided with the Turks and hatched a plot against his uncle, he was captured by him, dispatched to Alfonso, and thrown into prison.[237] Pope Calixtus, too, sent Skanderbeg much monetary assistance.

Vlorë is an Albanian city of no great size, located at a seaport where the crossing to Italy is shortest. Bayezid was the first of the Turks to occupy it, and, when it rebelled, it was recovered by Murad.[238] I do not know what trouble is threatening Italy.

234. Skanderbeg's uncle, Moses (Musa) Komninos Golem. Skanderbeg defeated Komninos and his Turkish auxiliaries in March 1456 and took over his territory but later pardoned his uncle; see Babinger, *Mehmed the Conqueror*, 152.

235. George Castriot "Skanderbeg" (c. 1404–68). When his father John became an Ottoman vassal in 1423, George was sent to Edirne as a hostage and converted to Islam. In 1443 George (called by the Turkish name "Iskender") returned to Albania, where Ottoman officials were instituting direct annexation of his family's holdings. George seized control of the fortress of Krujë by stratagem and declared himself a Christian, going so far as to impale the Ottoman officials who refused to accept baptism; see Fine, *LMB*, 521–22, 556. For more on Skanderbeg, see *The Living Skanderbeg: The Albanian Hero Between Myth and History*, ed. Monica Genesin et al. (Hamburg: Kovac, 2010).

236. Skanderbeg became Alfonso's vassal by formal treaty in 1451, making Alfonso suzerain of Albania. Alfonso furnished some assistance in this relationship, as at Krujë, but Skanderbeg retained a good deal of independence. See Setton, *Papacy and Levant*, vol. 2: 102; Ryder, *Alfonso*, 304.

237. Hamza Castriot, a convert to Islam, was captured in the battle of Tomoritsa (September 2, 1457) and sent to Naples. See Babinger, *Mehmed the Conqueror*, 152; Fine, *LMB*, 596.

238. The city was first captured in 1417 during the reign of Mehmed I, not of Bayezid I, and again in 1435 under Murad II.

16 THE ILLYRIAN NATIONS, BOSNIA

58. AFTER Albania come the Illyrian nations, which look toward the west and the north. In our time, we refer to this race of people as Slavs. Some are called Bosnians, some Dalmatians, others Croatians, Istrians, and Carnians. Bosnia slopes inland toward Pannonia and looks to the north. The other peoples border on the sea, extending as far as the source of the Timavo and facing Ausonia [i.e., Italy] on one side and Pannonia on the other. The Timavo pours its waters into the innermost gulf of the Adriatic Sea; Strabo reported that its spring was called "the mother of the sea."[239]

59. In Bosnia, the king of that nation, called Stephen (for this is the name they traditionally give their kings), observed the Christian religion but for a long time refrained from the sacrament of baptism. But last year he sent for Cardinal Juan Carvajal, whom I have mentioned often, who washed him with the waters of baptism and duly initiated him into our sacred rites. He then declared war on the Turks, with whom he was allied by a treaty. Now he is said to be vacillating a little.[240]

In this region, the heretics known as Manichees, an abominable class of people, hold a great deal of influence. They assert that there are two principles of reality, one of good and one of evil. They do not recognize the primacy of the Roman Church nor do they admit that Christ is equal and consubstantial with the Father.[241] Their

---

239. Strabo, *Geography*, 5.1.8.

240. Stefan Tomas (r. 1443–61) was likely baptized in the Bosnian Church as an infant and rebaptized as a Catholic in 1457. As Fine argues, his status as a Bosnian Christian did not prevent him from being recognized as rightful king by Pope Nicholas V or seeking papal counsel in a Catholic annulment of his marriage early in his reign; see John V. A. Fine, *The Bosnian Church: A New Interpretation* (Boulder, Colo.: East European Quarterly, 1975), 301–3. Concerns that he was wavering probably had much to do with his overtures to make peace with the Ottomans.

241. Dualism or Manicheism, if a handful of Catholic sources can be believed, was practiced only by a very small sect in Bosnia; the Bosnian Church, while neither

monasteries are said to be located in hidden mountain valleys, where sick matrons vow to God that, if they recover, they will serve the holy men for a certain time; when they are restored to health, they fulfill their vows with their husbands' permission and live in common with the monks for the prescribed time.[242] No decrees of the Apostolic See, no Christian arms have sufficed to eradicate this stain. God permits the heretics to reign in order to test us.

17   DALMATIA, CROATIA, LIBURNIA

60. IN DALMATIA, Stephen, the ruler of a duchy between Bosnia and Dalmatia who had been infected with the poison of the Manichees, inflicted great casualties on the people of Ragusa. Although this man had often ambushed Christians and sold them to the Turks, he had the gall to send emissaries to Rome and seek assistance from the Apostolic See, petitioning Christians for the expenses of a war which he had waged against Christians.[243] And there was no lack of men ready to listen to such impious words.

In Croatia, there was an Austrian woman who, though humbly born, had been rewarded with marriage to a count for her excellent character and elegant beauty. She was riding from one castle to another for recreation when she was taken captive during a sudden raid of the Turks and detained by them for some time. Her husband finally became impatient and ransomed her for a large amount of gold.[244]

Catholic nor Orthodox, did accept the Trinity and shared many common beliefs and practices with the two churches. See Fine, *Bosnian Church*.

242. The source of Aeneas's information on this matter is unknown. This may be a convoluted reference to the monastic and rural quality of the Bosnian clergy.

243. Stefan Vukčić Kosača, Bosnian ruler or herceg of Hum, later called Hercegovina (r. 1435–66). He alternated between vassalage under the king of Bosnia and alliances with the Turks. He is said to have considered converting to Catholicism but never did; see Fine, *LMB*, 476–81; 577–79.

244. Aeneas mentions this event, without naming the woman or her husband, in a letter dated September 1448; see Wolkan, *Briefwechsel*, vol. 68: 69.

61. Perhaps someone will ask whither I have banished Liburnia, through which a famous poet relates that Antenor traveled on his way to Italy.[245] The boundaries of countries are unclear to a large extent and it is difficult to untangle modern problems, let alone solve ancient ones. Pliny said that Liburnia ended where Dalmatia began and that it contained Tragurium, a place well-known for its marble, and also the colony of Salona, which was 112 miles from Iadera, and that Iadera was 160 miles from Pola.[246] From this, it transpires that the Liburnians dwelt between the Croatians and the Dalmatians. It is also possible that the Croatians—this people's modern name—invaded the territory of the Liburnians. Let it suffice for me to have noted these points. If anyone wants more definite information, he should consult the ancient authors. Ptolemy lumped Liburnia and Dalmatia with Illyria and said that Illyria bordered on Pannonia in the north, upper Mysia in the east, Istria in the west, and Macedonia and the Adriatic coast in the south.[247]

18 ISTRIA

62. THE ANCIENTS assigned Istria to Italy. It contains Poreč, Pula, and Iustinopolis, which they call Capodistria.[248] However, to include it with Italy is inappropriate, since it is separated from it by a gulf of the Adriatic and, like a peninsula, surrounded by sea where it joins the mainland. To its rear is a rocky and mountainous region, which the ancients called Albia. Pliny said that Istria was contiguous to Liburnia,[249] which makes it clear that the Croatians replaced the Liburnians. They say that Istria was named from the Ister River, which was falsely believed to flow from the Danube into the Adriatic. Both Pomponius Mela and Nepos,[250] who came

---

245. Virgil, *Aeneid*, 1. 244.
246. Pliny, *Natural History*, 3.140–41.
247. Ptolemy, *Geography*, 2.16.1.
248. Modern day Koper.
249. Pliny, *Natural History*, 3.129.
250. Pomponius Mela, *Description of the World*, 2.63; Nepos fr. 19 Marshall.

from the vicinity of the Po, gave credence to this error. In fact, no river pours into the Adriatic from the Danube. They were misled by the story of the Argonauts, who were held by tradition to have sailed up the Ister [i.e., Danube] into Istria from the Black Sea. It is clear, however, that they sailed upstream from the Danube into the Sava and thence to the Nauportus River (which I suppose is what we call the Ljubljanica today), whose marshes Strabo calls Lugeum.[251] Their ship arrived at the Adriatic after being carried on their shoulders through the mountains from the Nauportus. Today, the Istrians are Slavs, though the coastal cities use the Italian language and are fluent in both tongues. The better part of the country is the coastal region, which is subject to the rule of the Venetians; the House of Austria controls its interior. The people of Wallsee own the town of St. Veit an der Glan, which is situated on the Tisza River. From there to Aquileia is one thousand stades, according to Tuditanus, who conquered the Istrians.[252] Tradition holds that the frontier of Italy is the Mursia River.

I have learned of nothing noteworthy that was done in this land during our time, though the Austrians and Venetians were engaged in a serious dispute over their frontiers, and the subjects of each side came into conflict. I was once sent by the emperor to settle this quarrel, but, although I arranged a truce and set new boundaries, I was unable to eradicate the dispute root and branch.[253]

---

251. Strabo, *Geography*, 7.5.2. Lake Cerknica or Kirknitz in Slovenia.
252. Gaius Sempronius Tuditanus. See Pliny, *Natural History*, 3.19.129.
253. This probably refers to events c. 1450–51; see Marija Wakounig, "Una duplice dipendenza. I conti di Gorizia, Venezia e il Sacro Romano Impero (1350–1500)," in *Da Ottone III a Massimiliano I: Gorizia e i conti di Gorizia nel medioevo*, ed. Silvano Cavazza (Gorizia: Edizioni della Laguna, 2004). This squares with Aeneas's mention of having recently returned from Istria in a letter of July 16, 1450; see Wolkan, *Briefwechsel*, vol. 67: 161.

19 CARNIOLA

63. NEXT after the Istrians come the Carnians, with whom the Iapidians are numbered. However, the Slavs, whose language dominates the region, divide the Carnians in half and say that Carniola has two parts.[254] One is dry and sparsely watered, and here they locate the Istrians and Carsians, who inhabit the mountains between Ljubljana and Trieste and range as far as the Timavo. The other, where the Sava River has its source, along with the Nauportus—whose modern name is the Ljubljanica—and very many other rivers, is well irrigated. In this country, while Emperor Frederick was seeking the crown of the German kingdom in the city of Aachen, Count Ulrich of Cilli and Albert, the emperor's brother, joined forces and laid siege to the famous city of Ljubljana, which is named after the river on whose banks it lies. For a long time, they assaulted it with siege-engines of every kind but lost their valuable equipment when they were bloodily repulsed by Frederick's soldiers and stripped of their camp.[255] The Slavs and Italians call this town Lubiana, taking the name from the marsh of Lugeum.

---

254. Reading a period after *sequuntur* and a comma after *obtinet* (reversing van Heck's punctuation).
255. Frederick was elected on Feb. 2, 1440, and crowned in Aachen on June 17, 1442. His brother Albert, who later became duke of Austria as Albert VI (r. 1446–63), attacked Ljubljana in the spring of 1442 in concert with Ulrich Cilli. After they were repulsed and their baggage seized by the townspeople, the troops took to raiding around Carniola until Frederick paid them their wages. The compromise he reached with his brother in March 1443 allowed Albert to administer some of the Habsburg lands and collect their revenues for six years. See William Coxe, *History of the House of Austria* (London: Henry G. Bohn, 1847), vol. 1: 214; *Allgemeine Deutsche Biographie* (Leipzig: Duncker und Humblot, 1875–1912), vol. 1: 286.

20   CARINTHIA

64. CARINTHIA, which also is a mountainous region, lies next to Carniola and adjoins Styria to the east and north; to the west and south it borders on the Italian Alps and Friuli. It contains many valleys and hills that are fertile in wheat, many lakes, and many rivers, of which the foremost is the Drava, which is no smaller than the Sava and runs through Styria and Pannonia into the Danube. The Austrians hold sovereignty over the country and call its ruler the Archduke.

Whenever a new ruler assumes office, they observe a ceremony that I have heard of nowhere else. In a spacious valley not far from the town of St. Veit an der Glan, the remains of an ancient city can be seen, whose name has been effaced by the long passage of time.[256] Nearby, in the open meadows, stands an upright marble stone. This is mounted by a peasant, to whom the duty falls by familial descent and the right of inheritance. On the right stands a scrawny black ox, on the left an equally emaciated mare. The common people and all the peasantry crowd around. Surrounded by nobles dressed in purple, the ruler then advances from the opposite side of the meadows, preceded by a banner and the insignia of sovereignty. The count of Gorizia, who supervises palace affairs, leads the way amidst twelve smaller banners, and he is followed by the other officers of state. No one in the procession seems unworthy of honor except for the ruler himself, who presents the appearance of a peasant. His clothes are rustic, his cap and his shoes are rustic, and the staff he holds in his hand identifies him as a shepherd. When the peasant on top of the stone observes him coming, he shouts in the Slavic language (for the Carinthians, too, are Slavs), "Who is this I see advancing with such pride?" The people standing around him answer that the ruler of the land is approaching. Then he asks, "Is he a righteous judge, who seeks his country's welfare? Is he a free man and worthy of of-

---

256. Probably Virunum, capital of the Roman province of Noricum.

fice? Is he a follower and defender of the Christian faith?" They all reply, "He is and he will be!" The peasant rejoins, "I therefore ask what right he has to move me from this place." The count of Gorizia answers, "We purchase this place from you for sixty denarii, and these animals will be yours," pointing to the ox and the mare. "You will also receive the ruler's robes, which he removed just now, and your house will be unencumbered and free of tax." When these words have been spoken, the peasant gives the ruler a light slap on the face and commands him to be a good judge; then he gets up and leaves the place, taking the animals with him. The ruler climbs the stone and, brandishing a naked sword in his hand, he turns in every direction and promises the people impartial justice. They say that he also drinks cold water which is brought to him in a peasant's cap, as if he were condemning the use of wine. He then makes his way to the Church of Saal, named St. Mary, which stands on a nearby hill; it is said to have once been a pontifical see.[257] Following the celebration of a mass, the ruler takes off his rustic garments, puts on a general's cloak, and, after dining sumptuously with the nobles, returns to the meadows, where, sitting in judgment, he dispenses justice to petitioners and confers fiefdoms.[258]

65. There is a story that in the year of Christ our Savior 790, during the reign of Charlemagne, the duke of this nation, called Ingo,[259] prepared a great feast for the inhabitants and ordered it

[257]. Aeneas uses the term "pontifical" (*pontificalis*) several times in this work. The German translation renders it as episcopal (*bischöfliche*, or some variation), which may, indeed be correct. In para. 105, however, Aeneas designates Cammin a "pontifical city," stating that its bishop "is subject only to the pope." To make the distinction clearer, in the same paragraph, he uses the term "episcopal see" (*episcopalis sedes*) to describe Brandenburg. For Aeneas, then, pontifical does not seem to have been a synonym for episcopal. Hence, although it is an unusual usage, we have maintained the original wording in this translation.

[258]. This fascinating custom was first documented in 1286 but is likely much older. It was continually practiced until 1579. For a discussion of the ceremony and its possible origins and meanings, see A. W. A. Leeper, *A History of Medieval Austria* (Oxford: Oxford University Press, 1941), 98–100.

[259]. Ingo may have been a clergyman rather than a duke. This story originated in a

to be served on gold and silver dishes for the peasants, who were ushered inside into his presence, but on earthenware for the nobles and grandees, who were seated far from his sight. When asked why he did this, he replied that those who lived in cities and high palaces were not as pure as those who inhabited the countryside and lowly huts. The peasants, who had accepted the Gospel of Christ and been cleansed by the water of baptism, possessed white and shining souls, whereas those of the nobles and the powerful, who practiced the foul worship of idols, were soiled and of the blackest hue. He had arranged the feast, he said, to conform with the quality of souls. Chastened by this, the nobles sought the water of holy baptism in droves and within a short time all accepted the Christian faith under the direction of Virgil and Arno, the bishops of Salzburg.[260] This is the reason why the honor of investing the ruler was granted to the peasantry.

The duke of Carinthia was also the imperial huntsman, to whom were referred all the lawsuits of hunters; when summoned to a trial in the emperor's presence, he was obliged to respond to the plaintiffs only in the Slavic tongue. They say that this country enjoyed many honors, many privileges. This is easy to believe, since there is no doubt that Emperor Louis bestowed the dukedom of the land on his firstborn son, Arnulph.[261]

66. There is another custom of this country in the town called Klagenfurt—a very harsh one to combat thieves. If anyone falls under suspicion of theft, he is quickly arrested and put to death by hanging. After inflicting punishment, they pronounce judgment on the suspect three days later. If they find that the executed man

---

late ninth-century pamphlet called *The Conversion of the Bavarians and Carantanians*; see Richard Fletcher, *The Barbarian Conversion: From Paganism to Christianity* (New York: H. Holt, 1998), 344–47. Thanks to Patrick Geary for help with this question.

260. Virgil became bishop of Salzburg in 767; Arno in 785.

261. Arnulph (r. 887–99) was the illegitimate son of Louis the German. He was appointed duke of Carinthia in 880 and became emperor after the deposition of Charles the Fat.

was guilty, they allow his corpse to hang in shame until it rots and drops of its own accord. But if not, they take it down and bury it in the cemetery, providing a proper funeral at public expense and obsequies to satisfy his soul.

67. In this country, Count Henry of Gorizia, a man more debased than a woman,[262] compelled his youthful sons to get up and drink with him at midnight, scolding them for sleeping without a thirst.[263] He was seen more often with shepherds and ploughmen than with nobles. As an old man, he played on the ice with boys.[264] He frequently bathed among common prostitutes and rarely took meals in the palace hall but visited the cook alone and gobbled down morsels of food right there in the kitchen. He dressed in cheap greasy garments, leaving his bare chest exposed. His eyes were always running. When Emperor Frederick once spotted him from the window as he was coming to see him, he called out to me and said, "Aeneas, look at the ruler hurrying toward us and tell me if you have ever seen a more elegant or handsome man!" After observing the count and his companions for some time, I was disgusted by the uncouthness with which, having attained dominance, he reduced the high nobility to servitude. His Hungarian wife, a woman of outstanding beauty and more than a man's audacity, had him imprisoned. He was soon freed through the help of Count Ulrich of Cilli and drove his wife from home. He died not long afterward, leaving his sons as heirs—young men of good character who resembled their mother more than him. [265]

262. A phrase from Justin (*Epitome* 1.3.1), citing Pompeius Trogus on Sardanapalus's excesses; cf. Orosius, *Histories against the Pagans*, 1.19.1.

263. Henry VI, count of Gorizia (r. 1415–54). His sons' names were John, Louis, and Leonard; John was betrothed to Ulrich Cilli's daughter, Elizabeth. Henry's exploits may be exaggerations on Aeneas's part (fed, perhaps, by Henry's wife, Katerina—see note 265), but Henry does appear to have indulged in undignified behavior at times. See Wakounig, "Una duplice dipendenza," 352–56.

264. This may be an eyewitness observation as Aeneas visited Henry at S. Veit an der Glan during the winter of 1443/44; see Wolkan, *Briefwechsel*, vol. 61: 248–90.

265. Katerina of Garai, Ulrich Cilli's cousin, married Henry c. 1438. She actually

21 STYRIA

68. STYRIA, which I find was once called Valeria, is neighbor to Pannonia in the east; its northern side faces Austria, and to the west and south it borders on the Carnians and Carinthians. This, too, is a mountainous country, though its eastern tract contains large plains. The famous Drava and Mur rivers irrigate its land; the Mur discharges its waters into the Drava, the Drava into the Danube. The people of the cities are mostly Germans. The Slavs, who cultivate the countryside this side of the Drava, recognize the sovereignty of the House of Austria. Styria contains an old town called Cilli, which some think was once named Sullaceum and built by Lucius Sulla; I am not able to vouch for this. Many remains of antiquity can be seen there, and marble tombstones record the names of Roman rulers. Count Frederick presided there in our time. A man excessively prone to lust, he was once infatuated with a mistress called Veronica and with his own hand murdered[266] his lawful wife, a descendant of the counts of Croatia.[267] However, his father, Herman—such is the justice of the powerful!—drowned his mistress in a stream.[268] Frederick stole wives from their husbands at random, abducted bevies of girls to the palace, treated his subjects like slaves, robbed churches of their property, and procured forgers, poisoners, soothsayers, and necromancers from all parts. In the year of Jubilee [1450], when he was ninety, he went to Rome to

---

imprisoned Henry twice: in 1443 and in 1453. According to Wakounig, he died while still imprisoned by his wife in 1454; see "Una duplice dipendenza," 351, 355.

266. Correcting van Heck's *intermisset* to *interemisset*.

267. Frederick of Cilli (d. 1454), ban of Slavonia and parts of Croatia was the father of Ulrich Cilli. His wife, Elizabeth (d. 1422), came from the powerful Frankopan family.

268. Frederick's father was Herman II of Cilli (d. 1435), the ban of Slavonia and father-in-law of Emperor Sigismund. The unfortunate Veronica survived her rival by seven years only to be accused of witchcraft by Herman and drowned in 1429. Herman's action against Veronica was intended to stave off a full-scale feud between the Cilli and Frankopan families. See Fine, *LMB*, 495–96.

obtain indulgences but showed no improvement upon his return. When he was asked what good Rome had done him, since he had relapsed into his old habits, he said, "My shoemaker, too, after seeing Rome returned to sewing gaiters."

69. Upon his death, he was succeeded by his son Ulrich, who was like him in other respects and superior only in intellect and eloquence. When he was killed (as I reported previously),[269] there were twenty-four pretenders to the inheritance. Thus the man who had provoked widespread wars while alive continued in death to foment discord. However, the nobles decreed that control of the land should be entrusted to Emperor Frederick on condition that he adjudicated the claims of the pretenders in accordance with the country's custom. The widow of Ulrich decided to defend her possessions by force of arms. Frederick, after capturing several forts with a powerful force, was finally received in Cilli[270] when John Vitovec, a Bohemian native, surrendered the citadels of the region.[271] Although he had been the count's military commander, he accepted money from the emperor and defected from his widow. But soon, overcome with regret, he dared to commit a serious and unforgivable crime, as if to redeem one wicked deed with another, and attempted to ambush the emperor at bedtime, while he was staying peacefully in Cilli with a few of his men. Having bribed a large number of the inhabitants to surrender part of the town when he arrived, he was let inside at the appointed hour with eight hundred horsemen and began to wreak havoc. Frederick was protected by divine mercy, which on that night had prompted him to sleep—contrary to his custom—in the upper citadel, a place well fortified by its natural position and human industry. The dignitaries who

---

269. Ulrich was killed on Nov. 9, 1456. See para. 10.
270. Punctuating with a comma after *obtinuisset* (Vat. Lat. 3888) instead of *Cilia*, as in van Heck.
271. Military commander Vitovec was employed by Ulrich's widow, Catherine, in an effort to maintain control over the region. He became governor of the region of Cilli; see Fine, *LMB*, 553–54.

had remained in the town were all captured. Among them was John Ungnad, the wealthiest of all the Styrians, who was abducted with his brother George. No mercy was shown to Ulrich, chancellor of Austria, although he was a bishop and had taken refuge in a church.[272] To such an extent have the laws of God and man lost their hold upon the people of our generation. Enriched by a mass of spoils, the Bohemian traitor never lacked for accomplices from that time forth.

70. There is a story, one that is very well-known among the Styrians, that there was a nobleman who often felt the impulse to hang himself. In his distress he sought a remedy against this temptation from a certain learned man. The advice he gave him was to hire a personal chaplain to celebrate daily masses for him while he stayed in a lonely castle. The nobleman complied and went for almost a year without thought of hanging himself. Eventually the chaplain asked him if he could assist a neighboring priest, who was about to dedicate a church on a nearby mountain. He gave his permission, with the intention of following a little later and joining in the mass. But he stayed for a long time, after being detained for one reason or another. He finally set out around noon and met a peasant in the woods, who said that the service on the mountain was over and that all the people had left. When the nobleman was saddened by this news and bemoaned his misfortune in not having seen that day the Blessed Sacrament, the peasant began to console him. If the noble-man wished to buy it, he said he would sell him the reward he had earned for participating in the service and asked for the nobleman's cloak as payment. After completing the sale, the nobleman never-theless climbed the mountain and prayed in the shrine. When he returned, however, he found the peasant hanged in a nearby tree, but after that he was never troubled again by terrible thoughts.

272. Ungnad was Frederick III's chamberlain, and Ulrich Hinnenberger was bishop of Gurk (r. 1453–69). These events took place between the death of Ulrich Cilli (Nov. 9, 1456) and that of Ladislas Postumus (Nov. 23, 1457).

Austria   127

71. In this country, decocted salt is imported to neighboring regions. It also contains rich iron mines and silver workings of no mean quality, though not much silver is extracted owing to the indifference of its rulers.[273]

22 AUSTRIA

72. I THINK it unnecessary to describe Austria here, since I have published a history devoted to it.[274] After the death of Emperor Albert, the people of this country entrusted themselves to Frederick with the stipulation that, if the pregnant queen gave birth to a male child, he would be its guardian; if a female, he would become ruler of the land. When Ladislas [Postumus] was born, as I described previously, Frederick took on his guardianship.[275] The soldiers who had served under Albert claimed they had been cheated of their wages and laid waste to the country with acts of brigandage and arson. Frederick bought off their harassment for seventy thousand gold pieces at the time when the Bohemians and Hungarians were raiding Austria.

73. The eldest of Ladislas's sisters married Duke Wilhelm of Saxony.[276]

74. John Hunyadi, after vainly petitioning Frederick for the crown of the Hungarian kingdom, entered Austria with twelve thousand horsemen and plundered and burned all the territory between Vi-

273. Reading *incuria* (Urb. Lat. 885) for van Heck's *in curia*.
274. The most recent edition is *Historia Austrialis* (*Monumenta Germaniae Historica*, nov. ser. 24), ed. Julia Knödler and Martin Wagendorfer (Hannover: Verlag Hahnsche Buchhandlung, 2009). A previous version of this work became known as the *Historia Friderici III imperatoris*, an unfinished history on which Aeneas worked from 1452–58. See Rolando Montecalvo, "The New Landesgeschichte: Aeneas Silvius on Austria and Bohemia," in *Pius II, 'El Più Expeditivo Pontifice': Selected Studies on Aeneas Silvius Piccolomini*, ed. Zweder von Martels and Arjo Vanderjagt (Leiden: Brill, 2003), 74–75.
275. Ladislas was born Feb. 22, 1440. See para. 6.
276. Anna (1432–62) and Wilhelm III of Saxony (1425–82), landgrave of Thuringia; the two were married in 1446.

enna and the mountains of Styria.²⁷⁷ When the emperor set out for Italy, the Austrians asked him to release Ladislas into their custody so that he might succeed his father, having now almost reached maturity. When their request was rejected, they began an armed rebellion on the initiative of two Ulrichs—one, Ulrich, the count of Cilli, the other Ulrich Eytzing²⁷⁸—and laid siege to Frederick in Wiener Neustadt as he was returning from Italy. They were joined by Henry Rožmberk,²⁷⁹ a Bohemian, with two hundred horsemen and one thousand infantry, and although they had been directed by Pope Nicholas not to interfere with the emperor's guardianship, they stuck to their criminal plan in defiance of the orders of the Apostolic See and with contempt for its supreme authority.²⁸⁰

75. It was then that the learned university of Vienna issued an ignorant opinion, when it ruled that the orders of the pope could be suspended by appealing to a future council.²⁸¹

From that time forth, the city of Vienna and all of Austria were embroiled in constant fighting and paid the penalty for this insult to religion. Frederick yielded to the fury of the populace and surrendered his ward, who was still a boy of tender age, into the hands of the count of Cilli, on condition that he summon the relatives and friends of both sides to the city of Vienna and arbitrate a defini-

---

277. Hunyadi actually invaded these regions twice in 1446. First, in March, to punish Ulrich Cilli for his raids in Slavonia and Croatia, and again in November, in the hopes of pushing Frederick III to negotiate the release of Ladislas Postumus; see Held, *Hunyadi*, 118–23.

278. Eytzing or Eytzinger (c. 1398–1460), a magnate in lower Austria, a favorite of Emperor Albert II (d. 1439), and a leader of the uprising of the Austrian Estates against Frederick III in 1452; see *Lexikon des Mittelalters* vol. 4, no. 1: 195.

279. Henry Rožmberk (or Rosenberg) (d. 1457) was a member of a powerful Bohemian baronial family; see John M. Klassen, *The Nobility and the Making of the Hussite Revolution* (New York: Columbia University Press, 1978), 40 and passim.

280. Aeneas is partial to Frederick, whose refusal to allow his ward to take power in both Hungary and Bohemia was a source of widespread discontent.

281. For more on this event and the university's long-standing support of council over papacy, see Joachim W. Stieber, *Pope Eugenius IV: The Council of Basel and the Secular and Ecclesiastical Authorities in the Empire* (Leiden: Brill, 1978), 83–84; 321–22.

tive settlement concerning the guardianship, the fortresses, and the other matters of dispute among the leaders invited to the conference.²⁸² Ladislas was received with great enthusiasm by the people of Vienna and followed the will of the count in managing all his affairs. On the appointed day of the council, Duke Ludwig of Bavaria and Duke Wilhelm of Saxony, along with Albert and Charles, the margraves of Brandenburg and Baden respectively, convened with many barons from Bohemia and more from Hungary. The emperor sent ambassadors, myself included. There was a long argument about the parties' legal rights, but, since everything was handled in accordance with the victor's will, and the laws failed to defend anyone who lacked the protection of arms, the meeting was dissolved without accomplishing anything. Everything that the Austrians had promised to the emperor was denied. Every word was taken back, and the authority of letters and seals was ignored. It was an act of barbarous faith.

76. At that conference, Ladislas raised John Hunyadi to the rank of rulership for rescuing his kingdom from the invasion of the Turks. On a raised platform in the Great Square adjoining the Church of the Carmelites, seated on a golden throne and decked in his royal mantle and crown, he conferred upon Hunyadi the countship of Beszterce. This action was wholly impermissible in that location, for it is illegal for the king of Hungary to exercise sovereignty in the Roman Empire.²⁸³ But respect for the laws is only as great as what is conceded to them, or left untouched, by armed force.

77. Count Ulrich of Cilli manipulated the king just as he pleased and, seizing total control, showed disdain for Eytzing and the Vien-

---

282. Frederick capitulated on September 4, 1452; Hungarian and Bohemian nobles, including Hunyadi, arrived thereafter to work out the details.

283. Hunyadi was awarded this title in late 1452 to compensate for his loss of the governorship. He continued, however, to wield much power as "Captain-General of Hungary," which hurt relations with Frederick and may have been the source of Aeneas's consternation. Aeneas may also simply have rejected the validity of a Hungarian ceremony on Austrian soil. See Held, *Hunyadi*, 146–47; Thuróczy, *Chronicle*, 167–68, n. 434.

nese people, bestowing almost queenly rank upon a mistress whom he had taken after killing her husband. Finally, he fell from royal favor and was driven from the court through the efforts of Eytzing. When he set out for exile he was accompanied by only four horsemen, while Albert, margrave of Brandenburg, provided security as far as the city's gate, to prevent the people stoning him in contempt. However, the shame and misery of his exodus was equaled by the pride and popularity of his return. For after a year, when the king had returned from Bohemia, he was recalled through the influence of the leading barons of Austria and made his way back to Vienna with one thousand horsemen gleaming in silver and gold.[284] Even the king came almost a mile outside the city gates to meet him, and the whole nobility congratulated him upon his return. The common people, too, who not long ago had tried to pelt him with mud and stones as he fled, did not hesitate to scatter the road on which he returned with flowers, showing their usual lack of restraint in both directions, whether of love or hate.

78. It was an amazing turnabout—a whimsical joke of fortune. Eytzing lost his influence with the king, retired to his castles, and was reconciled with the emperor, whom he had gravely offended. Not long afterward, the followers of King Ladislas had the arrogance and presumption to enter the outskirts of Wiener Neustadt, where the empress lay in childbirth during the emperor's absence, and tried to storm the city.[285] When they failed, they burned the places which they had occupied and went away. There was much discussion of making peace between the emperor and the king, but to no avail. For while he lived, the count of Cilli considered it contrary to his interests for the rulers of Austria to exist in harmony.

---

284. Ulrich of Cilli left Ladislas's court in 1453; he returned in 1455.
285. Empress Eleonora gave birth on November 16, 1455, to a boy named Christoph (d. March 1456); Katherine Walsh, "Deutschsprachige Korrispondenz der Kaiserin Leonora," in *Kaiser Friedrich III (1440–1493) in seiner Zeit*, ed. Paul-Joachim Heinig (Cologne: Böhlau Verlag, 1993), 411, n. 41.

Austria   131

But when he died, Eytzing was sent to the emperor from Bohemia and proposed peace conditions acceptable to both sides. Austria seemed on the verge of tranquility, but the sudden announcement of King Ladislas's death not only disrupted the agreement but abruptly quashed the rising hope for great initiatives which would benefit the Christian world.[286]

79. When both the emperor and his brother Albert questioned the Austrians about the transfer of power, the Austrians held a conference of their countrymen. At this, the emperor's representatives asserted that the country belonged to the senior ruler of Austria (namely the emperor). In his own name and that of his uncle Sigismund, Albert demanded a share of the royal inheritance and tried to elicit sympathy by recalling his misfortunes and his poverty, which were unbefitting a man of such noble birth. The convention replied that the people would do what law and equity prescribed, after the brothers had reached an agreement.[287] Meanwhile, some brigands crossed the Danube into Austria and occupied a fortified position on the bank of the Morava River, where they began to plague the whole area with acts of robbery and arson. Albert marched against the brigands and captured them by force of arms. A great many were killed in the fighting, but he took away 550 prisoners and hanged eighty of them on the gallows—a feat which won him great repute and popularity among the Austrians.

But Ulrich Eytzing, after going to Wiener Neustadt to visit Emperor Frederick (whose cause he supported) and returning to Vienna, received a summons from Albert and approached him confidently, suspecting nothing amiss. Albert promptly had him

---

286. Ladislas died on November 23, 1457; see para. 10.
287. Reading a comma after *dictaret* and a period after *conuenissent* (as in the 1571 edition). The previous discussions appear to have taken place in January 1458. The source of concern was Frederick III's claim to all of Austria on the death of Ladislas Postumus and Duke Albert of Austria's refusal to accept that claim. The eventual outcome of these negotiations was that upper Austria would go to Albert and lower Austria to Frederick. See Coxe, *Austria*, vol. 1: 233; *Allgemeine Deutsche Biographie*, vol. 1: 288.

arrested, chained, and confined in a private prison.[288] The townspeople found this shameful. Everyone grumbled and condemned the deed, yet no one lent assistance to the poor man.

80. Though he was often invited, the emperor put off going to Vienna for some time, fearing the chance of treachery. Meanwhile, Sigismund of Tyrol came down from the Etsch to Vienna and then traveled to Wiener Neustadt, where he received the insignia of rulership from the emperor and swore allegiance to him in the old-established manner.[289] Albert, too, was present at this ceremony and soon thereafter returned to Vienna with Sigismund. Both of them conspired against the emperor in an attempt to bring Austria beneath their own domination. When he perceived their aims, the emperor decided to visit Vienna, and, summoning Duke Ludwig of Bavaria, a ruler of great reputation, he journeyed there, followed by the empress. As he approached, the urban populace came out to meet him. Albert and Sigismund, too, greeted the emperor outside the city with an escort of noblemen. Albert had about three thousand horsemen, armed and ready for action, who revealed themselves to the emperor on a knoll not far from Vienna, striking terror into him as he drew nearer. Albert fed his suspicion by repeatedly approaching them and speaking to them privately, as if he had prepared an ambush for the emperor. They say that the captain of that force told Albert, "It is a simple matter, if it pleases you, for me to make you master of Vienna and Austria today. For who is there to prevent me from intercepting Emperor Frederick and his entourage? Just give the nod. The question of the succession will then be resolved. Laws and men favor the victor." Albert hesitated for a while and at last replied: "I could have forgiven it if you had done what you speak of without my knowledge. But I cannot command what

288. Eytzing was arrested in 1458.
289. Sigismund (1427–96), lord of the Tyrol (from 1439) and later duke of Austria. Frederick III became Sigismund's guardian on the death of his father, Frederick IV, in 1439. Sigismund finally achieved his independence in 1446 when Frederick bowed to pressure from the rebellious inhabitants of Tyrol.

is dishonorable." After they entered the city, Albert and Sigismund lived together in the so-called House of Prague. The emperor stayed in private houses belonging to citizens. The citadel was being kept under guard in the name of the Austrian people. Sigismund and Albert conspired to attack it and force their way inside by night. After arming a band of soldiers and setting forth, they bound themselves by an oath not to return home unless they had entered the citadel.

81. When the citizens noticed them, they quickly took up arms and stationed a stronger garrison in the citadel. Civil war and a bloody battle for the fortress were imminent, and it seemed certain that, if the rulers started a battle, it would be to their own great cost. For a long time, the situation hung in the balance. The citizens held firm in their resolve to defend the citadel. The lords, who had sworn to enter it, thought it shameful to return home without accomplishing their purpose but too dangerous to launch an assault. Finally, it was agreed that they should enter the citadel, stay for a little while, and leave after a drink of wine, and in this way they cheated, rather than fulfilled, their sacred vow. On the next day, the citadel was divided into three parts with the agreement of the Austrian people. Albert and Sigismund took two, the emperor the remaining one. Austrian subjects were selected to settle the brothers' disputes and vested with full power. But it is hard to pass judgment on the powerful. The nobility and church leaders are more favorably disposed toward the emperor; the common people prefer Albert.[290] "Each has a mighty judge to defend him."[291]

---

290. This meeting seems to have taken place in June 1458 and reflects the ongoing tensions between Frederick, Albert, and now Sigismund, lord of Tyrol, over Austrian territory. In addition to the division of Austria between Frederick and Albert noted in para. 79, Sigismund of Tyrol received part of Carinthia adjoining Tyrol. It was also agreed that the three rulers would share joint residence in Vienna—the previous passage suggests it was not always an amicable arrangement. Conflicts between the three rulers, especially Albert and Frederick, would continue until the former's death in 1463. After Albert's passing, Frederick successfully claimed Upper Austria. See Coxe, *Austria* vol. 1: 233; 237–38; *Allgemeine Deutsche Biographie*, vol. 1: 288–90.

291. Lucan, *Civil War*, 1.127.

82. There are many things in this statesman [Frederick] which deserve praise: a fine physique and an appearance worthy of an emperor, a calm and unruffled mind, a perceptive intelligence, an even more tenacious memory, burning religious zeal, a strong desire for peace and tranquility. He values every person's particular virtue and deems it worthy of reward. He puts up magnificent buildings, though his admiration and passion for gardens and gemstones is excessive. And in the conduct of affairs, he is rather slow and easygoing. Many have accused him of being niggardly and too careful with money.[292] This is due to his immediate predecessors, the emperors Sigismund and Albert,[293] whose prodigality makes everyone else's generosity look like greed. But Frederick neither squanders his own nor steals the possessions of others, showing equal restraint in his words and actions.

83. His brother Albert is quite different. Hasty in his undertakings, eager for war and glory, contemptuous of danger, bold, tolerant of toil and quick in action and thought, he shares his money liberally amongst his friends. A pauper in the midst of wealth and rich in his poverty, he is greedy for fame more than anything else.[294]

---

292. Aeneas could have said more about the emperor's misplaced energies and interests. He journeyed to the Holy Land (1436), supposedly on crusade, but the trip became a "shopping spree," in which he disguised himself in order to avoid being overcharged in the bazaars; see F. R. H. Du Boulay, *Germany in the Later Middle Ages* (New York: St. Martin's Press, 1983), 55. For more on Frederick, see Heinrich Koller, *Kaiser Friedrich III* (Darmstadt: Wissenschaftliche Buchgesellschaft, 2005); see also Heinig, ed., *Kaiser Friedrich III.*

293. Emperors Sigismund (r. 1411–37) and Albert II (r. 1438–39)—not to be confused with Albert VI of Austria and Sigismund of Tyrol of paras. 80–81.

294. Albert VI became known as *der Verschwender* ("the Prodigal"), but Aeneas might also have noted his interest in education, particularly the founding of the University of Freiburg in 1454.

23 MORAVIA

84. HEADING northward through Austria, one arrives among the Moravians, a fierce race, avid for plunder, who dwell on the other side of the Danube between the Hungarians and Bohemians. In our day, Emperor Sigismund made a gift of this country to his son-in-law Albert, who succeeded him as emperor.[295] When it rebelled and refused to obey his orders, Albert caused it to suffer great destruction. For he burned over five hundred farms in a single expedition, put many people to death, drove off almost all the livestock, and forced that perfidious people to bear his yoke.[296]

In this country, the cities and towns observe the ritual of the Roman Church and subscribe to the Catholic faith, whereas almost all the barons are tainted with the Hussite stain. When Giovanni da Capistrano was here, preaching the word of God, and vehemently attacked the errors of the Hussites, he achieved the conversion of an important baron called Czernahora. Renouncing his former faithlessness, he embraced the truth of the Roman See along with two thousand of his subjects. His son, a man of outstanding culture and character, obtained the see of Olomouc not long afterward.[297] This is the only city of the Moravians which has a bishop.

The Moravians once possessed an extensive and powerful kingdom, which lasted until the son of Svatopluk (whose fortunes I have described in my *History of Bohemia*). When the son of Svatopluk rejected the church of God, the kingdom was confiscated from this people and later transferred to Bohemia by the Roman emperors.[298] In this country, there are many populous and prosperous

---

295. King of Bohemia (as Albert I, r. 1438–39), Emperor Albert II (r. 1438–39).
296. Sigismund gave Moravia to Albert in 1423, but he faced opposition from Hussite nobles in the region. See para. 5.
297. Protasius of Czernahora, bishop of Olomouc (r. 1457–82).
298. See Aeneas's *Historia Bohemica*, vol. 1: 92–98. Svatopluk was king of Greater Moravia (r. 871–94). One of his sons, Mojmir II (r. 894–906), was on favorable terms with

towns, chief among them Brno and Znojmo, which is famous for the death of Sigismund. No one enjoys free passage through this land except for the armed and powerful, for all its roads of access are beset by robbers.

The people speak a mixture of German and Bohemian, but the Bohemians, who control the region, are predominant.

It is difficult to say which tribes once inhabited Moravia. But so far as I can gather from reading Ptolemy, the Marcomannians, Sudinians, and Candians seem to have settled in Moravia and the part of Austria which lies across the Danube.[299]

24 SILESIA

85. AFTER Moravia, next comes Silesia—a country of no small renown, through which flows the Oder, one of Germany's most famous rivers. Its source is in Hungary, which lies on the eastern border of Silesia, and its course ends at the Baltic Sea. This land is about two hundred miles in length and eighty miles in breadth. The people's capital is Breslau, a spacious city situated on the banks of the Oder, which is beautifully adorned with private and public buildings. Our forefathers described its bishopric as "golden," but the Hussite Wars have reduced it to mud.[300] When Wenceslas was reigning over Bohemia, a conspiracy arose in this city, and the consuls, who hold the highest power, were pitched from the windows of the town hall into the marketplace, where they were met by the

---

the pope, but his younger son, whose name is unknown, led a strong opposition to his brother and may be the son Aeneas refers to in this passage. See Jaroslav Pánek, Tůma Oldřich, et al., *A History of the Czech Lands* (Prague: Karolinum Press, 2009), 69–72.

299. Ptolemy, *Geography*, 2.11.11; Ptolemy has it as Quadians, not Candians.

300. The Hussite Wars, c. 1420–36, were led by Bohemian nobles to protest the execution of Czech reformer, Jan Hus, for heresy in 1414, and to force Emperor Sigismund to accept their demands, namely communion in both forms. For more on this conflict, see Thomas A. Fudge, ed. and trans., *The Crusade against the Heretics in Bohemia, 1418–1437* (Aldershot: Ashgate, 2002).

Silesia 137

swords and spears of the irate mob, causing a dreadful spectacle. A few years later, Emperor Sigismund beheaded the authors of this deed.[301] The dukes of Silesia are many in number, since a father's inheritance is divided individually among his sons. As a result, the country is split into many parts and endures many misfortunes, exposed as it is to constant acts of brigandage. Among these dukes, there is said to have been one called Boleslaw of Opole, who lived in Głogów.[302] A man addicted to luxury and pleasures, he was mad enough to deny the existence of heaven and hell and to believe that our souls are annihilated with our bodies. He never entered a church, or only rarely, and totally abstained from Christian sacraments except for his misuse of matrimony. For, having discarded his wife because she displeased him, he replaced her with another woman and, to prevent her being called his mistress, insisted on being united with her through the rites of matrimony.

The Silesians are subject to the Bohemians. At the present time, however, they refuse to obey their orders. Rejecting their new king, George, they follow Duke Wilhelm of Saxony, who claims the kingdom of Bohemia through his wife, the sister of Ladislas, king of Hungary and Bohemia.[303] Only the sword will settle this dispute.

The language of the race is predominantly German, though the Polish language prevails on the other side of the Oder. Therefore, some, not unreasonably, have regarded the Oder as the frontier of

---

301. A likely conflation between the First Defenestration of Prague (1419), in which German imperial officials were hurled to their death from the city hall, and a conspiracy in Breslau (1418), in which German councilmen were seized and beheaded. Sigismund retaliated for the latter crime by beheading twenty-three of the accused and burning three religious leaders at the stake. Both events reflect imperial efforts to combat Hussite power and Bohemian nationalism. See William Urban, *Tannenberg and After: Lithuania, Poland, and the Teutonic Order in Search of Immortality* (Chicago: Lithuanian Research and Studies Center, 1999), 267.

302. The Hussite Duke Boleslaw of Opole (d. 1460), who cast aside his wife Elizabeth of Pilcza in favor of his concubine and "robbed God's churches of their temporal goods"; see Dlugosz, *Annals*, 491–92, 538.

303. George Podiebrad, king of Bohemia (r. 1458–71); Wilhelm III (1425–82) was married to Anna.

Germany. As it slants northward, however, the same river flows between German peoples on both its banks.

At this point, I propose to leave the borders of Germany and to visit the peoples of Sarmatia to the east and the north.[304]

25 POLAND

86. POLAND is a vast region which lies next to Silesia in the west and borders the Hungarians, Lithuanians, and Prussians. The capital city of the kingdom is Kraków, which contains a flourishing school of the liberal arts. Zbigniew presided over this city, a bishop notable for his literary erudition and charming personality. I received many letters from him, composed with plentiful wit and Roman refinement. In recognition of his singular merits, the Roman Church sent him a cardinal's red hat.[305]

87. Apart from Kraków, the cities of Poland are less than elegant. They build most of their houses out of wood and smear the majority with mud. The region is flat and forested. The national drink is beer, which is made of wheat and hops; the use of wine is very rare, and the cultivation of the vine is unknown. The land is fertile in grain. The people own much livestock and also devote much time to hunting wild animals. They eat a woodland horse which is similar to a deer except for the horns. They also hunt wild cattle, which the ancients called aurochs. They abound in fish and fowl, but the land is lacking in silver and gold.

---

304. Sarmatia was "a roughly defined region lying between the Vistula and the Don" (*Oxford Latin Dictionary* s.v. Sarmatia).

305. Bishop of Kraków (r. 1423–55), Zbigniew Olesnicki was created cardinal by anti-pope Felix V in 1440 and confirmed by Pope Nicholas V in 1449. He and Aeneas exchanged a few letters, although Aeneas appears to have written more than he received. For more on their correspondence, see Nancy Bisaha, "'Discourses of Power and Desire': The Letters of Aeneas Silvius Piccolomini (1453)," in *Florence and Beyond: Culture, Society and Politics in Renaissance Italy*, ed. David Peterson and Daniel Bornstein (Toronto: Centre for Reformation and Renaissance Studies, 2008).

Poland 139

The king's revenues are small. Their ancestors divided the kingdom into four regions, which the king visits in rotation during the course of the year. Each region maintains the king and his court for three months. When these are over, he moves on to another region. What the people are obligated to provide is fixed by statute. If the king remains beyond the prescribed time, he must live at his own expense.

When the king of this nation died in our fathers' time, leaving a daughter, Duke Wilhelm of Austria took her hand in marriage and was placed in charge of the kingdom.[306] The Poles disapproved of a German king, so they summoned Wladyslaw from Lithuania, expelled Wilhelm, and entrusted his wife and kingdom to a new king. Wladyslaw had been a heathen and a worshipper of idols, but he agreed to accept baptism along with the kingdom.[307] After his conversion to Christ, he proved himself a pious leader, attracting many Lithuanians to the Gospel, founding several pontifical churches,[308] and treating the bishops with considerable honor. While he was out riding, he took off his cap and lowered his head whenever he saw church towers, in homage to the God who was worshipped within. He fought successfully against the Tartars who were harassing the frontiers of his kingdom. He defeated the Prussians in a great war which I will mention in my account of Prussian affairs.[309] He had no children from his first wife, with whom he was not joined in

---

306. Jadwiga (d. 1399), the younger daughter of King Louis I of Poland (r. 1370–82) and Hungary (r. 1342–82), married Wilhelm of Austria against the wishes of the Polish nobles. The marriage was, according to Waugh, "consummated but not solemnized" and thereby ruled invalid. Polish nobles drove Wilhelm out and, in an unusual move, crowned the twelve-year-old princess "king" in 1384; see W. T. Waugh, *A History of Europe From 1378–1494* (New York: Putnam and Sons, 1932), vol. 4: 405; Jerzy Lukowski and Hubert Zawadski, *A Concise History of Poland* (Cambridge: Cambridge University Press, 2001), 32–33.

307. Polish nobles forced Jadwiga to marry Wladyslaw Jogaila (later polonized to Jagiello) in 1385, and Jogaila was baptized in 1386, taking the name Wladyslaw II. He ruled as king of Poland from 1386–1434.

308. On Aeneas's use of the word pontifical, see para. 64.

309. See para. 99.

lawful matrimony. The second gave birth to two sons, Wladyslaw and Casimir, when he was nearly ninety.[310]

88. When Wladyslaw died, his son Wladyslaw received the throne of Poland while Casimir obtained the dukedom of Lithuania.[311] The former, after also being invited to become king of Hungary, fell in combat with the Turks, as I related previously.[312] When they learned of this, the nobles of Poland were worried about a successor and asked Frederick, margrave of Brandenburg, who had spent his boyhood in their kingdom and understood their national language and customs, to accept the kingship. He replied that an heir existed in the person of Duke Casimir of Lithuania, who was the dead king's brother. They should ascertain his wishes. If he desired his brother's and his father's kingdom, Frederick considered it beneath his dignity to offer any obstacle.[313] Duke Albert of Bavaria[314] showed equal restraint with regard to Ladislas [Postumus], the son of Albert [Habsburg], in refusing the kingdom of Bohemia when it was offered to him. Emperor Frederick, too, when he was invited by the Hungarians and Bohemians to succeed Ladislas, could never bring himself to listen, since it would jeopardize his cousin's rights.[315] This is a great glory of our age and a great credit to the German nation, though doubtless some attribute it less to fairmindedness than to indolence that anyone should eschew another's kingdom. For my part, I can only praise something that has all the appearance of rectitude. As for Casimir, although the Lithuanians were reluctant to

310. Wladyslaw was actually in his seventies when his sons were born—not to his second wife, but to his fourth, Sophia of Kiev; see Urban, *Tannenberg and After*, 263.
311. Wladyslaw III, king of Poland (r. 1434–44) and king of Hungary (r. 1439–44). Casimir ruled as grand duke of Lithuania from 1440 to 1492 and as king of Poland from 1447 to 1492.
312. Battle of Varna, 1444. See paras. 30–32.
313. Frederick was considered a possible candidate for the crown of Poland, but only because Casimir delayed accepting the kingship upon his election in 1446 due to pressure from the Lithuanians; Casimir IV was not crowned until mid 1447. See Długosz, *Annals*, 497–500.
314. Duke Albert III of Bavaria (r. 1438–60).
315. Frederick was the first cousin of Ladislas's mother, Elizabeth.

let him go, since they wanted to keep their own ruler with them, he entered Poland and peacefully took control of the kingdom. Not long afterward, he married the sister of King Ladislas.[316] He waged many wars against the Teutonic Brothers of St. Mary, which I will mention in my account of Prussian affairs.[317]

26 LITHUANIA

89. LITHUANIA, which is also an extensive region, adjoins Poland in the east and is almost entirely covered in bogs and forests. The leader of this land was Vytautus, the brother of Wladyslaw II, who abandoned the cult of many gods and received the sacrament of Christ along with the throne of Poland. The name of Vytautus was great in his own time. His subjects feared him so much that, if ordered to hang themselves, they would rather obey than incur their ruler's wrath. Those who resisted his rule he sewed inside a bear skin and threw to living bears, which were kept for this very purpose, to be torn to pieces; he also inflicted other cruel tortures. While riding on horseback, he always kept his bow drawn. If he saw anyone walking in a way that displeased him, he shot him down then and there. This bloodthirsty butcher also destroyed many men for amusement. In order that there should be a clear facial distinction between the people and their ruler, he ordered everyone to shave their beards. When that was unsuccessful (for a Lithuanian would more readily endure the loss of his neck than his beard), he himself appeared in public with a shaven chin and head and threatened capital punishment for any of his subjects who removed the hair from his face or head.[318] Named king of the Lithu-

---

316. Elizabeth and Casimir's fruitful marriage (they were wed in 1454) produced thirteen children.

317. See paras. 101–102.

318. Długosz, by contrast, portrays Vytautus (or Witold), grand duke of Lithuania (r. 1401–30), as generous and magnanimous, his greatest vice being that "he was more

anians by Emperor Sigismund, he died before the ambassadors who were bringing the crown arrived to meet him.

His successor, Švitrigaila, kept a bear which used to take bread from his hands and often wandered into the woods; when it returned, all the doors leading to the prince's inner chamber were left open for it. There it would rub against the door and kick it when it was hungry, whereupon the prince would open the door and offer it food. Some young nobles conspired against the prince and, after arming themselves, rubbed against the door of his bedchamber in imitation of the bear. Švitrigaila thought it was the bear and opened the door, whereupon he was stabbed on the spot by the ambushers and killed.[319] The governance of the country then passed to Casimir.

90. It is difficult to reach Lithuania in summertime, when almost the whole area is surrounded with marshy waters. Winter provides access across the frozen lakes. Merchants travel over the ice and snow carrying several days' provisions in their vehicles. There is no well-defined road, and, as at sea, one steers one's way by the course of the stars. Towns are scarce among the Lithuanians, and farms not numerous. Their wealth consists chiefly of the skins of animals known today as "sable" and "ermine." The use of money is unknown, its place being taken by skins. The commoner skins take the place of copper and silver; the more precious ones are the equivalent of coined gold.

Noble matrons openly keep paramours with their husbands' permission; they call these "matrimonial assistants." For men, it is shameful to take a mistress in addition to one's legitimate spouse.

---

ready to make love than was decent"; see *Annals*, 455. For more on bears and other farfetched barbaric stereotypes used by Aeneas, see Stephen C. Rowell, "Bears and Traitors, or Political Tensions in the Grand Duchy ca. 1440–1481," *Lithuanian Historical Studies* 2 (1997): 50–53.

319. Vytautus's brother (r. 1430–32). Aeneas conflates Švitrigaila with a later ruler, Zygimantas, or Sigismund (r. 1432–40), who was murdered in a coup—without the aid of a bear; see Rowell, "Bears and Traitors," 51–53.

However, marriages are easily dissolved by mutual consent, and they marry again and again.

The region abounds in wax and honey, produced by wild bees in the woods. The use of wine is very rare and their bread is deep black. Cattle provide their sustenance, and they consume an abundance of milk. The national language is Slavic, for this tongue is widespread and divided into many branches. Some of the Slavs follow the Roman Church, like the Dalmatians, Croatians, Carnians, and Poles. Others follow the false beliefs of the Greeks, like the Bulgarians, Ruthenians, and many of the Lithuanians. Others have invented their own heresies—like the Bohemians, Moravians, and Bosnians—a large number of whom emulate the madness of the Manichees. Others remain trapped in heathen blindness, like many of the Lithuanians who worship idols. A large number of these were converted to Christ in our time, after Wladyslaw, a member of that race, received the throne of Poland.[320]

91. I am personally acquainted with Jerome of Prague, a leading expert in sacred literature and a man famed for his purity of life and exceptional eloquence, who for over twenty years performed penance at the Camaldolese monastery in the Etruscan Apennines. When the Hussite heresy sprang up in Bohemia, he fled this noxious venom and crossed into Poland. Here he received a letter of recommendation from King Wladyslaw and made his way into Lithuania to the court of Prince Vytautus, in order to preach the Gospel of Christ. With the support of Vytautus, he converted many communities to the life-saving faith in our Lord. He came, finally, to the Council of Basel, at the summons of Cardinal Giuliano Cesarini, when the affairs of Bohemia were on the agenda.[321]

Here he told many tales about the Lithuanians which seemed scarcely credible. I used to hear his stories from others and could

320. Wladyslaw became king of Poland in 1386; see para. 87.
321. Jerome (better known as John Jerome) of Prague (c. 1370–1440), a Praemonstratensian canon who entered the monastery of Camaldoli in 1413 and performed missionary work in Lithuania sometime after 1392.

not be persuaded to believe them. I decided to visit the man myself and hear them from his own mouth.[322] My companions were Niccolò Castellano, who at that time ran the household of Cardinal Giuliano Cesarini, Bartholomaus Lutinianus, the scribe of the archbishop of Milan,[323] and Pietro da Noceto, the secretary of the cardinal of Fermo—men both serious and learned.[324] We met with him in his cell at the Carthusian monastery across the Rhine, where he told us the following story.[325]

92. The first Lithuanians whom he encountered worshipped snakes. Each head of the household kept his own snake, lying on hay in a corner of the house, to which he gave food and offered sacrifice. Jerome ordered all these to be killed, brought to the marketplace, and burned in public. Among them was found one larger than the others, which the fire wholly failed to consume despite many attempts.

Next, he discovered a tribe which worshipped a sacred fire they called "eternal." The priests of the temple kept it supplied with wood so it would not go out. These men were consulted about the lives of sick people by their friends. At night they drew near to the fire, but in the morning they provided answers to those who consulted them. They said they had seen the ghost of the sick person near the sacred fire, which, while warming itself, had exhibited tokens of death or life. If it turned its face to the fire, it portended that the sick person would live; if it showed its back, then the person would die. They urged them, therefore, to make wills and put their

---

322. John Jerome and Aeneas met at Basel in 1432.
323. Francesco Pizzolpasso.
324. Niccolò was a humanist from Città di Castello, also known as Niccolò Tifernate after the city's ancient Roman name. Lutinianus (possibly Lusimano or Lucimano) has not been identified. Pietro da Noceto was a close friend of Aeneas going back to their secretarial service to Cardinal Capranica in Siena and Basel (beginning in 1431) and a recipient of many of Aeneas's letters.
325. For more on John Jerome in Lithuania and *Europe* as a source, see William Hyland, "John-Jerome of Prague (1368–1440): A Norbertine Missionary in Lithuania," *Analecta Praemonstratensia* 78 (2002): 228–54.

affairs in order. Jerome exposed this as a fraud, and, after convincing the populace, he destroyed the temple, scattered the fire, and introduced Christian ways.

Going further inland, he found another tribe which worshipped the sun and venerated, with remarkable devotion, an iron hammer of extraordinary size. When the priests were asked about the meaning of this cult, they replied that once upon a time the sun disappeared for several months because a mighty king had captured it and confined it in the dungeon of a strongly fortified tower. A giant had then come to the help of the sun and smashed the tower with a huge hammer, releasing the sun and restoring it to humanity. The tool with which mortals had recovered light was therefore worthy of veneration. Jerome laughed at their simplicity and showed it to be an empty fable. He explained that the sun and moon and stars are actually creations of almighty God, with which he adorned the heavens, bidding them shine with everlasting light for the benefit of mankind.

Finally, he visited other people who worshipped a sacred wood; the taller a tree, the worthier of reverence they regarded it. He preached to this tribe for several days, revealing the sacraments of our faith, and finally ordered them to cut down the wood. When the populace gathered together with axes, no one was bold enough to touch the sacred wood with iron. Jerome therefore led the way by taking up a double axe and chopping down a lofty tree. He was followed by the crowd, who competed with each other to fell the wood through the various use of swords, picks, and axes. They reached the middle of the grove, where there was a very ancient oak, which in their religion was more sacred than all other trees and most particularly believed to be the home of a god. For some time, no one dared to lay a blow upon it. In the end, there always being someone bolder than the rest, a certain man jeered at his companions for fearing to strike an insentient thing like wood. Raising his axe, he aimed a great blow at the tree but struck his own shin and fell to the ground in a faint. Stunned by this, the surrounding throng began to weep and lament and to denounce Jerome for persuading them to violate the sacred dwelling of a god. Not a soul now dared to wield his blade. In response, Jerome asserted that illusions are conjured up by devils to bewitch the eyes of ordinary people and deceive them. He then ordered the man who had fallen wounded, in the way I described, to arise and showed that no part of his body had been injured. Whereupon he drove his blade into the tree and, with the help of the crowd, brought down its massive bulk with a great crash and leveled the whole grove.

93. There were several woods in that region which were held to be equally sacred. While Jerome was on his way to cut them down, a large throng of women approached Vytautus, weeping and wailing. They complained that a sacred grove had been felled and a god deprived of his habitation, where it had been their custom to seek divine assistance: from here they had obtained showers, from here sunshine. Now that the god had been robbed of his home, they didn't know where to look for him. There were some smaller groves where the gods were accustomed to respond to petitions, but Jerome wanted to destroy them, too, and was eradicating their traditions through the introduction of some new rites or other. They begged and beseeched him, therefore, not to allow the elimination of their ancestral religion. The women were followed by the men also, who insisted that they could not endure a new cult. They said they would rather abandon their land and ancestral homes than the religion which they had received from their forefathers. Vytautus was disturbed by this and, fearing a popular uprising, preferred that the people should desert Christ rather than him. He therefore revoked the letters he had given to the local governors, instructing them to obey Jerome, and ordered him to leave the country.

Jerome told us these things on oath, with a straight face and no hesitation. The seriousness of his speech and the erudition and piety of the man are an indication of his credibility. I have reported what I heard without alteration. I do not take responsibility for its truth, but my companions and I were convinced of it when we left his presence.

27 RUTHENIA

94. THE RUTHENIANS,[326] whom Strabo appears to call Roxanians,[327] border on the Lithuanians. They are a rough and barbarous race, among whom Cardinal Isidore of Santa Sabina, whom I mentioned previously, secured a wealthy diocese.[328] In this nation, there is said to be a huge city called Novgorod, which German merchants succeed in reaching only with much hardship. Rumor holds that it contains great wealth, an abundance of silver, and valuable pelts. Buyers and sellers use weighed, not coined, silver. There is a square stone in the middle of the marketplace. Whoever is able to climb this without being pulled down attains the rulership of the city. They fight over this with weapons, and they say that often several men have climbed it in a single day owing to the frequent outbreak of political strife within the population.

28 LIVONIA

95. NEXT IS Livonia, the most distant of the Christian countries, which borders on the Ruthenians to the north. It is often invaded by the Tartars, who have suffered bloody defeats there in our time. The Teutonic Brothers of St. Mary conquered this country and forced

---

326. A term which roughly corresponds to Ukrainians.
327. Strabo, *Geography*, 7.3.17 (actually Roxolanians).
328. Orthodox metropolitan of Kiev from 1436/37–42, Isidore became a Unionist and was raised to the rank of cardinal in 1439 and named Latin patriarch of Constantinople in 1452. See also paras. 19 and 43 on Isidore.

it to adopt the sacraments of Christ, for it was previously heathen and worshipped idols.[329] Its western shore is washed by the Baltic Sea, which most of the ancients thought to be the Ocean; the north was less familiar to the Greeks and Italians than it is today. The Christian religion opened up this part of the world to our generation, cleansed it of its barbarism, and revealed a gentler way of life to its ferocious tribes. The gulf of the Baltic Sea is so broad that its size seems unknown to some authors. Its starting point is the British Sea [North Sea]—which could also be called German, for it washes a large part of Germany, too. Its mouth is in the west, not far from the Cimbrian Peninsula, which today is called Denmark. As it runs east, it expands toward the north, encircling large islands. The Norwegians occupy its western shore. To the north, there are reports of a semi-savage people whom sailors are unable to converse with in any tongue; they are said to trade merchandise using only signs and nods.[330] The southern shore belongs to the Saxons and Prussians, and the eastern, as I have said, is occupied by the Livonians.

Between Livonia and Prussia, they say there is a small land, about one day's journey wide, inhabited by the Samogitians,[331] a people neither pagan nor truly Christian who are subservient to the Poles. And so the kingdom of Poland extends to the sea and the Baltic gulf, of which I have spoken.

29 PRUSSIA: THE TEUTONIC BROTHERS

96. RETURNING from Livonia to Germany along the shore of the Baltic Sea, the next people one encounters after the Samogitians are the Prussians. They inhabit both banks of the Vistula River, which forms the boundary between Sarmatia and Germany.

---

329. On the Brothers of St. Mary, more commonly known today as the Teutonic Knights, see paras. 97–104.

330. Possibly the Sami or Lapps.   331. Lit. "Massagetans."

Prussia: The Teutonic Brothers 149

It rises in the mountains which separate Poland and Hungary and irrigates part of Poland. But it runs through the whole length of Prussia from the town of Torún to Gdańsk, where it flows into the Baltic. Some, as I have done, have called this river the Vistula, which agrees with modern parlance, others the Iustula and some the Istula. The other side of the river was under Sarmatian jurisdiction, this side, German. To the east and south, the Masovians and Poles inhabit the countryside; the west is occupied by the Saxons, and the north is bounded by the shore of the Baltic Sea.

The region is fertile in grain, well-watered, and densely populated. Many impressive towns and many winding inlets of the sea contribute to its beauty. There is a great quantity of livestock, much hunting, and rich fishing. Jordanes reports that this land was once inhabited by the Ulmerigans, at the time when the Goths descended upon the mainland from the island of Scandinavia and invaded the lands of the Ulmerigans by way of the Iustula (as he calls it).[332] However, Ptolemy asserts that the Amaxobians, Alans, Venedians, and Sitonians lived by the Istula River.[333]

97. This race was uncivilized and a worshipper of idols until the time of Emperor Frederick II.[334] But during his reign, when the Christians lost the city of Acre in Syria,[335] the Teutonic Brothers of St. Mary were driven out of there and returned to Germany. Refusing to languish in inactivity, these noble and experienced warriors approached Frederick and told him that Germany's next-door neighbor, Prussia, rejected the worship of Christ. Men of that race often raided the Saxons and other neighbors, driving off great numbers of livestock and people. It was their intention, they said, to tame this uncivilized race. They asked only that the emperor grant his assent and entrust the country to the Brothers for their perpetual possession if they conquered it. For by now, the dukes of Masovia, who

---

332. Jordanes, sixth-century author of *The Origins and Deeds of the Goths*.
333. Ptolemy, *Geography*, 3.5.7–8 (Gythonians, not Sitonians).
334. Frederick II, Holy Roman Emperor (r. 1220–50).
335. Acre fell from Christian rule in 1291.

formerly claimed control of that land, had ceded their rights to the Brothers. The offer pleased Frederick, who praised their plan and granted the Brothers the bull they wanted, sealed with gold. The Brothers quickly went onto the offensive and occupied the region under Prussian jurisdiction on this side of the Vistula. They then crossed the river and, close to its bank, built ramparts around an ancient, wide-spreading oak and fortified it like a castle.[336] There they stationed a garrison and began to harass the Prussians on the other side. Many a battle was fought for the oak, and great pagan forces were put to flight and destroyed. The war dragged on for several years. Finally, fortune smiled upon the Brothers' rule and brought all Prussia beneath their sway. The defeated tribes of barbarians submitted to their yoke.[337]

98. From that time on, the German language was introduced and the worship of Christ imposed upon the tribes. Pontifical churches were also built across the Vistula in Pomesania, Chelmno, Sambia, and Warmia. When Bishop Francis died, the canons requested the appointment of my humble self to the Church of Warmia, and Pope Calixtus entrusted it to me with the assent of the consistory of cardinals.[338] This is the only church in those parts that exercises its own jurisdiction and is not subject to the Brothers. The other bish-

---

336. The castle of Thorn or Toruń.

337. The Brothers of St. Mary, or the Teutonic Knights, began as a military order in the Holy Land during the Crusades. While still based in the Holy Land, they were invited in the later 1220s by Polish Duke Conrad of Masovia to help him fight the pagan Prussians. A group of knights accepted this invitation, bolstered by the Golden Bull of Rimini issued by Frederick II in 1226, which granted the master of the Teutonic Knights the status of a prince of the Empire, lord of the province of Chelmno, and entitled the order to keep all future conquests in the region. See Jonathan Riley-Smith, *The Crusades: A Short History*, 2nd ed. (New Haven, Conn.: Yale Nota Bene Press, 2005), 196–97; Eric Christiansen, *The Northern Crusades* (London: Penguin Books, 1997. 1st edition published by Macmillan, 1980), 73–83.

338. Francis Kuhschmalz, bishop of Warmia (r. 1424–57). Aeneas was appointed his successor in August 1457 by Calixtus III, but he never claimed the position owing to a dispute over the title. For more on Aeneas's claim to Warmia and his political interests in Prussia, see William Urban, "Renaissance Humanism in Prussia," *Journal of Baltic History* 22 (1991): 29–73; see also para. 64 on Aeneas's use of the word pontifical.

Prussia: The Teutonic Brothers 151

ops are obliged to wear the habit of the order. In the place where I said the oak fortress stood, the noble city of Marienburg, with its immense and famous castle, was built.[339] This is the seat of the grand master who presides over all the Brothers living in Prussia. This order also has two other masters. One rules Livonia, the other governs the convents of Germany. The Germans were the founders of this order, and for that reason no one is accepted into it unless he is a German of noble parentage and has committed himself to fight in arms against the enemies of the saving Cross to protect the Christian Gospel. For that reason, they wear white robes into which is sewn a black cross. They all grow beards except for those who serve the holy altars. For the canonical hours, they recite the Lord's Prayer and they eschew education.

99. These men possess great wealth and power no less than that of kings. They often fought with the Poles over the boundaries of their kingdom, both suffering defeats and inflicting them in turn, and willingly accepted the risk of a full-scale battle with Wladyslaw,[340] the father of Casimir, who is still king.[341] Both sides had assembled powerful and vast forces. The Lithuanians and Tartars, led by Vytautus, were allied with the Poles. The Teutonic Brothers had recruited their strength from all of Germany. When both armies had camped about twenty stades apart, full of hope and impatient of delay, the master of the Prussians[342] sent a herald to declare war on the king. With him, he sent two swords on which victory would depend, giving his enemy the power to choose which one he want-

339. Aeneas is mistaken. The fortress of Thorn stood opposite the famous oak tree, Vogelsang; Marienburg, which was built later, became the official residence of the order in 1309. See Stephen Turnbull, *Crusader Castles of the Teutonic Knights, AD 1230–1466* (Oxford: Osprey, 2003), 8. Thanks to William Urban for help on this question.

340. Placing a period after *patre* (as in the 1699 edition) instead of *recusarunt*; van Heck's punctuation necessitates a strained interpretation of the preposition *cum*.

341. The Teutonic Order grew powerful and wealthy, reducing the Prussians to serfdom and abusing the Livonians. The order increasingly clashed with the Poles over territory, and the papacy, which had once supported it, ordered an investigation into its practices in 1310; Riley-Smith, *Crusades*, 250.

342. Ulrich von Jungingen, grand master of the Teutonic Knights (1408–10).

ed; the other one he ordered to be sent back to him. Wladyslaw received the message with alacrity and, after rewarding the herald and keeping one sword for himself, returned the other one. Without delay, the soldiers were commanded to arm themselves, and the signal for battle was given.[343]

I find it recorded that the two camps contained sixty thousand horsemen. Wladyslaw ordered the Tartars and Lithuanians to begin the battle while from the Poles he selected his reserves. On the other side, the Prussian kept his auxiliaries in the rearguard and placed the flower of his order's soldiers in the vanguard of the army. When battle was joined, the Tartars and Lithuanians were cut to pieces, almost as if they were unarmed. However, they kept pressing forward in a mass and did not dare to turn their backs from fear of the Poles. A ghastly struggle ensued on top of the corpses of the slain, with the Prussians seeming less eager to inflict wounds than the Tartars were to receive them. The battle continued for a long time, resulting in great carnage. The Lithuanians and Tartars were being butchered like cattle, but, faced with a constant succession of new foes, the Germans grew weary from so much killing and, scarcely having the strength to wield their swords, began to fight more feebly. When Wladyslaw noticed this, he finally sent in his powerful brigade of Poles, bristling with arms. They made immediate inroads, and the battle was renewed. The Germans could not withstand the onslaught of the new host; it was an unequal fight between fresh and exhausted soldiers. Soon the Brothers began to flee, with their backs exposed to the blows of the Poles. When the master of the order saw his men give way and realized he could now place no hope in his auxiliaries, he threw himself against the enemy with a select band of soldiers and was killed. The rout grew even more ignominious, and the Germans did not halt their

---

343. What follows is a description of the Battle of Tannenberg (July 15, 1410), which marks the beginning of the decline of the Teutonic Order's power in the region and international prestige. See Urban, *Tannenberg and After*, for a full discussion of the battle and its ramifications.

Prussia: The Teutonic Brothers 153

flight till the Poles stopped pursuing them. On the Brothers' side, many thousands of men perished in that battle, among them about six hundred prominent and distinguished men of knightly rank, whom they call "comturs," together with the master himself. And the Poles' victory was far from bloodless, for the majority of the Tartars and Lithuanians were killed. This battle was fought in the year of Christ our Savior 1410.

100. Prussia threw in its lot with the victorious king and defected to him in its entirety, except for Marienburg.[344] However, peace was negotiated between the Brothers and the Poles through the intervention of Emperor Sigismund, and a treaty was concluded, whereby an indemnity was paid to the king of Poland, and Prussia was restored to the Brothers. From then until the time of Frederick, the present emperor, the order has been undisturbed in the possession of its land.[345] Under his reign, however, the people found the Brothers' yoke too heavy for them and formed a league on approximately the following terms: that sixteen men should meet every year in designated locations to hear the people's complaints against the Brothers and protect any individual from undeserved harassment. Four of these men were to be drawn from the order, four from the prelates of the churches, and an equal number from the nobles and the cities; and they required everyone to obey these men.[346]

---

344. The order actually won back a number of towns on its own in the fall of 1410. Emperor Sigismund assisted the order by attacking Poland after Prussia agreed to become a vassal state to Bohemia; see William Urban, *Teutonic Knights: A Military History* (London: Greenhill, 2003), 227–28.

345. Aeneas alludes to several moments of negotiation here. The First Peace of Thorn (Feb. 1, 1411) left the order with most of its pre-1409 territories (except for Samogitia) in exchange for a heavy indemnity paid to Poland. Sigismund became involved as an arbiter in 1412; he ruled that the terms of the Peace of Thorn should stand and that the Poles must resign their claims to ancient Polish lands in Prussian territory. The Poles soon went to war with the order but were unsuccessful; they would gain more Prussian territory by treaty and conquest in the 1420s. See Christiansen, *Northern Crusades*, 228–42; Urban, *Tannenberg*, 190 ff.

346. Most likely this is the Prussian League, formed by secular nobles and towns in 1440 to check the power of the order.

101. During the same period, the order was internally divided. Some followed the grand master, others certain comturs who disapproved of the master's administration.[347] In order to win over the people, the master endorsed the league without consulting the council of Brothers. Emperor Frederick also lent strong support to the pact, though he inserted a proviso that the rights of the order should not be infringed by his letter. After the death of the master who had accepted the league, and following the appointment of his successor, Pope Nicholas sent a legate to inspect the country of Prussia. Having learned the state of affairs as reported by his legate, he condemned the people's pact and ordered them to disavow it with the threat of excommunication. When they stubbornly stuck to their purpose, the dispute was brought before Emperor Frederick by common consent of the interested parties. After hearing the case again, he condemned the pact and ordered the Prussians to return to their allegiance to the Brothers, who by their arms had rescued the country from the hands of non-believers and purchased it with copious blood.[348] When this was announced to the cities, the people immediately took up arms against the Brothers, of whom many were captured and killed. Their castles were sacked and their citadels toppled from their foundations. Fifty-five towns conspired together in that rebellion. But thinking it too dangerous to oppose the order without external help, they adopted King Casimir of Poland as their lord—a man whose family was anathema to the Brothers, who had tried their luck against his father. Casimir entered the country with an army and took control of those cities which surrendered themselves to him; the Brothers fought with him for a long time, with varying success.[349]

347. There was a schism within the order in 1438–39.
348. The pope's lawyers declared the league to be illegal in 1450. Frederick concurred in 1454.
349. Responding readily to the Prussian cities' offer to switch their allegiance from the order to Poland, the Polish crown issued an act of incorporation of Prussia in 1454. This was the start of the Thirteen Years' War.

102. There were several clashes, the most memorable of which took place at the town of Chojnice.[350] Eighteen thousand Poles, including King Casimir himself, were conducting a siege there. They had brought up siege-engines and were attacking the town by day and night. Rudolph, the ruler of Żagań, who was one of the dukes of Silesia, commanded the order's army at that time.[351] In order to aid the besieged, he boldly attacked the king with seven thousand soldiers. The battle was fought in view of the townspeople. Both sides fought with great intensity and passion and incurred many casualties. When Rudolph noticed that his men were giving ground, he held the line firm by castigating the cowardice of those who were fleeing and threatening them with execution. He then advanced into the middle with a fresh band of soldiers and renewed the fierce struggle, striking some to the ground and stabbing others. The situation changed suddenly. As Rudolph pressed forward, the Poles yielded, and it was Casimir's turn to hold his men steady and insert himself in the battle. As if starting anew, they fought with tenacious energy. Rudolph was killed in the battle, the king was unhorsed, and the better men on both sides were laid low. Finally, in the belief that their king had been killed, the Poles despaired of victory and took to flight. The king was barely snatched from disaster by the help of his friends. Rudolph, through his own death, won victory for the order. Over six thousand of the Poles are said to have fallen; of the Germans, too, there perished not a few. After that reverse, the Polish cause in Prussia began to falter, as the people leaned in the same direction as the fortunes of war. However, the outcome remains uncertain and awaits the judgment of another battle.[352]

---

350. In 1454.

351. Both Duke Rudolph of Żagań (or Sagan) and Bernard Szumborski commanded the army; Rudolph was killed in this battle.

352. The war continued for several years, but by 1457 forces at Marienburg surrendered to the Poles. In 1466 the order would lose its rich western territories to Poland in the Second Peace of Thorn.

103. There is a story amongst the Brothers that once upon a time, when a master died and they were discussing his successor, there was a man who, when asked to choose the one he thought would best serve the interests of the order, chose himself; he was unwilling, he said, to swear a false oath. He knew what he thought himself but did not know the hearts of others. If the position of master were placed in his hands, he had no doubt that he would try to serve the community well. Moved by his words, the others entrusted him with the governance, which proved to be highly effective.

30 THE SAXON NATION, POMERANIA

104. NEXT after Prussia comes the nation of the Saxons, a powerful and widely distributed people, whose western boundary is the Weser River. Most have been of the opinion that the Saxons extend as far as the Rhine.[353] The zone to their north is occupied by the Danes and the Baltic Sea, and the Franconians, Bavarians, and Bohemians are situated to the south; the region to their east is inhabited by both Silesians and Prussians. Included within these frontiers are the Thuringians, Brandenburgers, Meisseners, Lusatians, and Pomeranians, all of whom accept Saxon jurisdiction. However, people say that the Thuringians settled in this land before the Saxons and claim that the Saxons were a Greek race who arrived in fleets from Macedonia and expelled the Thuringians from their ancestral lands after exhausting them in many wars. But this seems unlikely to me. For the Saxon name is the oldest in Germany and mentioned by all the old writers. None of the ancients who enumerate the tribes of Germany name the Thuringians. It is not until the

---

353. As Aeneas admits here and in para. 111, he—like many scholars—had difficulty determining the exact borders of Saxony given his mix of classical and contemporary sources and the disparities between them.

first arrival of the Franks, who entered Germany in the time of Emperor Valentinian, that I find the Thuringians named.[354] For this reason, the story claiming that the Thuringians were in Germany earlier than the Saxons fails to square with the truth. I will admit, however, that the boundaries of Saxony contracted and expanded at different times. For, as with empires, the boundaries of countries also shift in the course of time. Emperor Charlemagne waged many wars with the Saxons before they accepted the worship of Christ and dealt them serious defeats.[355] But when the line of Charlemagne ran out among the Franks, the Roman Empire returned to the eastern Germans, and the status of the Saxons was enhanced. They produced several emperors renowned for their remarkable wisdom and great feats, especially the three Ottos who reigned in succession.[356] These men thoroughly earned the gratitude of the Roman Church, and I have no doubt that it was through their valor that the frontiers of Saxony were extended.

105. Among the Pomeranians, who inhabit eastern Saxony, the following towns deserve to be mentioned: Wismar, Stralsund, Greifswald, Stettin, and Rostock, which has a school of liberal arts that is far from contemptible; and since they lie close to the sea, they are inhabited by many rich merchants. In the inland region, there is also Cammin,[357] a pontifical city, whose diocese is very large and thought to be no smaller than that of Mainz. The bishop of that place is subject only to the pope.

354. Valentinian, r. 364–375 CE.
355. Charlemagne campaigned against the Saxons from 772 to 804, forcing them to accept baptism each time he defeated them. In turn, they repeatedly threw off both Christianity and his lordship in his absence. At one point, in 782, Charlemagne ordered the execution of 4,500 rebels in one day; Roger Collins, *Early Medieval Europe 300–1000* (New York: St. Martin's Press, 1991), 261–66.
356. Otto I of Saxony (r. 962–73) revived the lapsed office and title of Roman Emperor; Otto II reigned 973–83; Otto III, who was only three at his father's death, r. 983–1002.
357. Lat. *Caminum*. Van Heck translates this as Chemnitz, but Cammin, as Frank et al. have it, makes more sense. It was once a sizable bishopric which lies in the same region as the aforementioned cities.

The Brandenburgers are divided into two marks, one called "the Old," the other "the New." The Elbe River flows through the Old Mark, and on its banks stand the town of Stendal as well as Gardelegen, Salzwedel, and Osterburg. The Oder River, which is not much smaller than the Elbe, intersects the New Mark, and on its banks are situated Frankfurt [an der Oder], a wealthy market, and the city of Lebus. The Spree River, which is comparable to the Tiber, also waters this country, and on its banks lies the town of Berlin. There is another river, too, called the Havel, which divides the city of Brandenburg—from which the mark takes its name—into two parts, the Old and New Towns. There is an episcopal see there and a tribunal of margraves. Also situated on the banks of the same river is Havelberg, a pontifical city, and round about it a famous region called Prignitz, which is crowded with many towns and filled with a warlike population. The capital of the Meisseners is the city of Meissen, which gives its name to the district; it, too, is washed by the Elbe River. Here there is a strong castle which contains a cathedral. In this region, too, there are many towns full of warlike inhabitants, including Martinopolis, which was founded by the ancients in honor of Mars;[358] today they call it Merseburg.

31 THURINGIA, HALBERSTADT

106. IN THURINGIA is the famous town of Erfurt, which is the capital of this region; it lies under the jurisdiction of the bishop of Mainz and is famous for its schools of the liberal arts. There is also the small city of Naumburg, which is subject to the duke of Saxony. All these towns use the law and language of the Saxons and follow the same customs. But the true Saxons, as no one doubts, are thought to be the people of Magdeburg, together with those of Bremen, Halberstadt, Hildesheim, Verden, Brunswick, Lüneburg, and Lübeck.

358. Probably St. Martin, rather than Mars (van Heck).

Thuringia, Halberstadt

In Magdeburg, there is an archbishop's see and a wealthy church of square-cut stone dedicated to St. Maurice—a grand construction of the Ottos, which holds the body of St. Florentinus. It is also believed to contain one of the six jars in which the Gospels relate that our Lord and Savior turned water into wine. This they exhibit to the common people. Its material is marble-like and transparent, and it holds as much wine as a horse could carry; they claim that another smaller one exists in Hildesheim. The banner of St. Maurice is also displayed here every year.[359] The magistrate of the city reverently guards an abbreviated version of Roman civil law written in the Saxon language, which they say was approved by Charlemagne.[360] The surrounding communities turn to this in settling their lawsuits, and its laws command great prestige and veneration. The inhabitants of Bremen consider that their own most glorious achievement was to convert the Danish race to Christianity.[361]

107. I should not omit what is recorded about Halberstadt. The Holtemme River flows through this city. Roughly in its center rises a hill, on top of which is a plateau about two stades in length. In its opposite corners stand two churches, one pontifical, the other named after the Blessed Virgin. In the middle is a broad square ringed by the grand houses of the canons. This is called the "city," and the part that lies below the hill is called the "lower city";[362] no laymen live on the hill. Charlemagne is said to have founded this church, and an annual festival is celebrated in his honor.[363] It is said

---

359. The cathedral church of St. Maurice was first built in the mid tenth century but destroyed by fire in 1207 and rebuilt starting in 1209.

360. This may refer to a later translation of the *Leges Saxonum*, a brief list of compensations for injury and murder issued under Charlemagne; see Collins, *Early Medieval Europe*, 274.

361. See Adam of Bremen's eleventh-century account of medieval conversion efforts in Scandinavia, *Deeds of the Archbishops of Hamburg-Bremen*.

362. *Urbs* and *suburbium*, respectively.

363. Charlemagne was canonized by anti-pope Paschal III in 1165 at the behest of Emperor Frederick Barbarossa. His sainthood was never accepted by the larger church, but the day of his death, January 28, continued to be celebrated in parts of Germany;

to support twelve dignitaries, twenty-four canons, and over twenty archdeacons. Every year, in this church, they select a member of the population whom they deem to be stained with the worst sins. They dress him in clothes of mourning, cover his head, and lead him to church on the first day of Lent; then, after celebrating divine offices, they throw him out. On each of the forty days of Lent, he walks around the city on bare feet and visits the churches, without entering or speaking to anyone. The canons take turns in offering him hospitality, and he eats what they serve him. After midnight, he is allowed to sleep on a bed of straw. On Holy Thursday, after the consecration of the oil, he is brought back into the church. When a prayer has been said, he is absolved of his sins, and the people offer him gifts of money; these, however, are released to the church. They call him Adam and consider him free of all guilt.[364]

Around Halberstadt lies excellent farmland, fertile in wheat; when the crops ripen, they say that the stalks rise higher than a man on horseback.

32 BRUNSWICK, SAXONY

108. BRUNSWICK is a large and populous town renowned throughout Germany. It is fortified with walls and ditches, together with high towers and ramparts. Its houses are grand, its streets elegant, and its churches large and richly decorated. It possesses five markets,[365] five halls of justice, and an equal number of municipal councils which dispense justice to the citizens. The dukes of Brunswick take their name from it. They are the noblest men in all of

---

see Phyllis Jestice, *Holy People of the World: A Cross-Cultural Encyclopedia* (Santa Barbara, Calif: ABC Clio, 2004), 172–73.

364. Andreas Kotte discusses this penitential rite, which evolved into a play, in "The Transformation of a Ceremony of Penance into a Play," in *Theatrical Events: Borders, Dynamics, Frames*, ed. Vicki Ann Cremona et al. (New York: IFTR/FIRT, 2004), 53–68.

365. Lat. *fora*, which may also mean judicial authorities or tribunals.

Germany, descendants as they are of the Ottonian line, though the passage of time has diminished their fame and power. The city of Lübeck is very powerful, and without its help the kings of Denmark have hardly ever managed to control their subjects. Twelve men called consuls preside over its administration; they hold office in perpetuity and possess the rank of a knight. The inhabitants have no means of participation in the city's government unless they are convened, but the people do not appear downtrodden: each man's property is protected, and they are free to live as they wish within the laws. The councillors impart equal justice, and, if they cause offense, an appeal is made to the emperor.[366]

109. In our time, the brothers Frederick and Wilhelm are recognized as dukes of Saxony.[367] One of them bears the title of imperial elector, the other claims the right to the kingdom of Bohemia, as I mentioned earlier.[368] There was a quarrel over the electorship with the people of Brunswick. Emperor Sigismund settled the dispute, and, as often happens, his verdict favored the more powerful party.[369] The elder brother was an energetic hunter, while the younger one was ambitious for war and well trained in arms. For a long time, bitter wars flared up between them over their father's inheritance.[370] There was often talk of peace, but, owing to the opposition of Apel Viztum[371] and of many other powerful men who stood to benefit from their dissension, every discussion ended in vain. But after the fields had been devastated and the whole country was go-

366. Lübeck, one of the leading towns of the German Hanseatic League which dominated Baltic and North Sea trade in the thirteenth and fourteenth centuries, became an imperial city in 1226. This may be a reference to upheavals in the council from 1408–16 and Emperor Sigismund's intervention; see Du Boulay, *Germany in the Later Middle Ages*, 148, 152; also Philippe Dollinger, *The German Hansa* (London: Routledge, 1999), 113.

367. Frederick II (1411–64) "the Gentle," elector of Saxony (r. 1428–64); Wilhelm III (1425–82), landgrave of Thuringia (from 1445) and duke of Luxembourg (from 1457).

368. See para. 85. Wilhelm claimed Bohemia as Ladislas Postumus's brother-in-law.

369. The brothers reached an initial agreement to divide their lands in 1445, but the conflict reemerged and lasted from 1446–51.

370. Known as "the Saxon Brother War" (1446–51).

371. Saxon knight, Apel Viztum the elder (c. 1400–74).

ing to rack and ruin, and when Apel, the instigator of the brothers' quarrels, had gone to Rome in the year of Jubilee [1450], Frederick asked his brother to visit him in Leibnitz in order to discuss peace. Wilhelm agreed. Having started out, he was informed by his counselors that an ambush had been set for him and his companions, and they cautioned him not to destroy himself or drag his followers to their death. "But I will gladly die," he replied "if I see you killed first—you provokers of brotherly strife!" With these words, he ordered all who loved him to follow him and, spurring his horse, he galloped off to meet his brother. Dispensing with mediators, the two made peace in an instant and sealed a pact. He was a great man to put himself in his enemy's hands so generously. The other one showed greatness, too, in welcoming back his alienated sibling as a brother and a friend.

Apel, who had returned from Rome in the meantime, and all those who sided with him were banished from Thuringia, where they possessed numerous towns. Apel held out for a while in Coburg, a town in Franconia, but despairing of his safety there and unable to count on anybody's help, he secretly fled to Bohemia with his treasures. From that time on, the Saxons enjoyed peace, though the Bohemians demanded the return of certain castles and often threatened them with war. A truce between the two sides has held off hostilities to the present day, but now a more serious quarrel seems ready to erupt. For rumor has it that Wilhelm, as the king's brother-in-law, hankers after the throne of Bohemia, though the nobles of the land have picked for themselves another king.[372]

110. I would like to insert here the audacious deed of a private individual named Conrad von Kaufungen. Born of a noble family in Saxony, he was skilled in warfare, bold in action, and fearless in spirit.[373] Thinking that he had been unjustly expelled from his home-

372. George Podiebrad (r. 1458–71).
373. Here follows an account of what became popularly known as the *Prinzenraub* in 1455.

land and deprived of his father's inheritance by Duke Frederick, he perpetrated an incredible crime during this era. In Meissen there is a castle situated on a high mountain with sheer cliffs on all sides; the provincials call it Altenburg. At the foot of the mountain lies a well fortified and populous town. In this castle, the two young sons of Frederick, Ernst and Albert,[374] were being raised. With a few companions, Conrad hastened to this destination by forced marches in the dead of night. Raising ladders, he entered the castle through the treacherous assistance of the boys' tutor and seized the young men while they slept in bed. After threatening them with death if they uttered a sound, he bound them with ropes and dragged them out, convinced that, after taking them to Bohemia, he would ransom them for a large sum and thereby be seen to have gloriously avenged his wrongs. He had just entered the Hercynian Forest,[375] which separates Bohemia from Saxony, and now supposed that he had escaped every danger, when the younger of the captives, who was fainting from exhaustion and hunger, asked for a rest and some food. Moved by his pleas, the brigand turned aside to the house of a certain charcoal-burner and ordered him to bring bread and beer. Meanwhile, a hue and cry was raised at Altenburg when the shocking deed was discovered. The stunned townsmen immediately seized their weapons and followed the kidnapper's tracks at breakneck speed in order to recover their precious booty. Fortune smiled upon them when they entered the forest, for, among the many paths, they happened to take the one which led straight to the charcoal-burner. Conrad was taken by surprise while he was serving the boy with food and, having been delivered to the duke, paid with his head for his thoroughly audacious crime. At almost the same time as he received the news of his sons' capture and abduction, Frederick learned of their recovery and safe return home.

374. Albert III of Saxony (1443–1500) became elector in 1464.
375. In classical usage, the Hercynian Forest refers to "a vaguely defined region of forest-covered mountains extending between the Rhine and the Carpathians" (*Oxford*

111. Only a small part of Saxony proper is subject to the dukes of Saxony; for there are many other rulers in that country, many cities which are called imperial, and many bishops who control their own territory. But Meissen and the majority of Thuringia as well as most towns of Lusatia and Franconia pay homage to these dukes. However, they allege that the right of electing the Roman emperor belongs to the dukes of Saxony on account of a small principality that lies between Meissen and Silesia. Its capital is the town of Wittenberg,[376] which means White Mountain.

112. Near Goslar in Saxony, Emperor Otto I discovered silver mines, which yielded large revenues. An impressive palace was built there, too.[377] Saxony also has bitter springs from which white salt is decocted and exported to neighboring communities. There are very rich and productive salt-works at Lüneburg, from which many abbots and prelates have been accustomed to support their monasteries and churches; for the salt yielded abundant income.[378] The people of Lüneburg took forcible possession of these salt-works and were condemned for it by both Pope Nicholas V and Emperor Frederick. The municipal council which was held responsible for this action was ousted by papal authority, but through the influence of Duke Bernard of Brunswick[379] it regained its former status soon afterward, and those who had formed the new council were thrown into prison. For its rebelliousness and seizure of church belongings, the city was placed under interdict.[380] However, there are

---

Latin Dictionary s.v. 'Hercynius'); see also *The Oxford Classical Dictionary*. It may refer here to the Elbe Sandstone Mountains. Thanks to Tom Brady for help on this reference.

376. Frank et al. translate this as Weissenberg, but Wittenberg seems more likely given the latter's regional importance.

377. Goslar was probably founded in the early tenth century not by Otto, but by his father, Henry the Fowler. Systematic mining of Rammelsberg Mountain began under the Ottonians, and Henry II moved the imperial court to Goslar; an extensive palace complex was built under Henry III.

378. Lüneburg was a major supplier of salt to northwest Europe in this period.

379. Bernard of Brunswick (r. 1400–34).

380. Named the Prelates' War (1445–62), the conflict was still unresolved when Aeneas wrote.

plenty who are willing to perform the sacraments for them. Such is the contempt nowadays for the authority of the church, among both laymen and the clergy.

113. In the Mark of Brandenburg, there is a city of little importance called Havelberg, which is surrounded by water. At a rough and deserted spot in its diocese is a small town called Wilsnack, where three hosts are preserved from which a spontaneous flow of blood is said to have poured. For this reason, many people visit it on pilgrimage, and sailors fulfill their vows here. The popular name of the place is "By the Holy Blood."[381]

114. I have gone beyond my usual practice in mentioning the cities of Saxony one by one. I have done so because ancient writers were very sparing in their accounts of Germany and, as if that nation lay beyond the borders of the world, seemed to be dreaming when they touched upon German affairs. For that reason, I will be forgiven, and perhaps thanked, if in describing the regions of Germany I have been somewhat more prolix than usual and exceeded the limits of my plan, in order to bring things vividly before the eye.

33 DENMARK, NORWAY, SWEDEN

115. AT THIS point, since Denmark lies next to Saxony, I have decided to record some noteworthy facts about the kingdom of Denmark and its neighboring regions to the north before I attend to the remaining parts of Germany.[382] Extending northward, there

---

381. The controversial "miracle hosts" of Wilsnack (modern Bad Wilsnack) attracted profitable pilgrimage traffic between the 1380s and mid sixteenth century; even Margery Kempe visited the site. They drew many critics, however, including Jan Hus and Aeneas's learned colleague, Cardinal Nicholas of Cusa. See Caroline W. Bynum, *Wonderful Blood: Theology and Practice in Late Medieval Northern Germany and Beyond* (Philadelphia: University of Pennsylvania Press, 2007), 25–29.

382. Determining the most commonly accepted names of sovereigns and dates of reigns in this section was a challenge. Swedish kings did not start using numbers until the sixteenth century; they were, however, given them in retrospect by historians, and

are three kingdoms which lie next to one another: those of the Danes, which today they call Dacia,[383] the Swedes, and the Norwegians.

Denmark (or Dacia, if we defer to custom) is a part of Germany and is shaped like a peninsula. The Cimbrians once inhabited it, and from here came the flood of barbarians which was massacred by Marius of Arpinum when they marched on Italy and threatened to overthrow the Roman state.[384] Posidonius (according to Strabo)[385] infers that the army of Cimbrians, in its rootless wandering and pillaging, got as far as the Sea of Azov.[386] For he thinks it was they who named the Bosphorus "Cimmerian," that is "Cimbrian," since Cimbrians are called Cimmerians in the Greek language.

Sweden is girt by the sea on all sides and contains many islands, among which the ancients make much mention of Scandinavia. From Sweden, too, there came a vast host of people who once engulfed the whole of Europe in a whirling tempest of war. For the Goths, who defeated the Huns in battle, invaded Pannonia, Mysia, Macedonia, and all of Illyria, laid waste to Germany, Italy, and Gaul, and finally settled in Spain, originated there.[387]

---

are used here for convenience. In addition, variants of personal names were used when a king or queen ruled different countries, but only one form will appear here. Finally, the reigns of several rulers overlapped. Thanks to Erika Harlitz for her help with this section. Studies used here include Knut Helle, ed., *The Cambridge History of Scandinavia*, vol. 1. (Cambridge: Cambridge University Press, 2003); Thomas Riis, "The States of Scandinavia, c. 1390–c. 1536," in *The New Cambridge Medieval History*, vol. 7, ed. Christopher Allmand (Cambridge: Cambridge University Press, 1998). Hereafter, *CMH*.

383. "Dacia" was used by some medieval and Renaissance writers as a designation for Denmark. But as it is also the term for the former Roman province on the lower Danube, it was less preferred than "Dania."

384. The Cimbri, who had migrated from northern Germany and devastated Spain and southern Gaul, were finally defeated by Marius and Catulus near Vercellae in 101 BCE.

385. Strabo, *Geography*, 7.2.2.

386. Lat. *Meothim*, or Maeotic Marsh in classical usage.

387. Reading *nam Gothis ... hinc fuit origo. Norvegia ... contermina est* (Urb. Lat. 885) for van Heck's *nam Gothi ... consedere. Hinc fuit origo Norvegie, ... nomen*. Aeneas follows Jordanes who claimed the Goths originated in Scandinavia/Scandia.

Denmark, Norway, Sweden

Norway, which took its name from the word north itself, is joined to the continent via the Ruthenians;[388] it stretches toward the North Pole and is bounded by an unknown land or, according to popular legend, an ocean made of ice. In the east and south, it is washed by the Baltic Sea; in the west, it ends at the North Sea.

116. The Germans today call Dacia the Mark of the Danes [Denmark], and its language is unknown to the Germans. They think that the people who occupied the territory of the Cimbrians came from Norway. Within our fathers' memory, Valdemar reigned in this land, Magnus in Sweden, and Haakon in Norway, who is said to have been a godlike man, worshipped by the people of his country with extraordinary love and reverence.[389] His wife was Margaret, the daughter of Valdemar, who gave birth to Olaf. Olaf succeeded his father but soon died and left the kingdom to his mother. She acquired her father's kingdom, too, when Valdemar passed away.[390]

But when Magnus departed this life in Sweden,[391] Duke Albert of Mecklenburg received the crown at the invitation of the people.[392] Albert felt contempt for the government of his female neighbor and began to provoke war with Denmark and Norway.

---

388. Here the sense is probably Russians, where otherwise it refers to Ukrainians.

389. Valdemar IV Atterdag, king of Denmark (r. 1340–75). Magnus Eriksson was king of Sweden (r. 1319–63) and ruler of Norway (as Magnus VII) (r. 1319–55); he was co-ruler of Norway with his son, Haakon VI from 1355–74. Haakon was king of Norway (r. 1355–80) and co-ruler of Sweden (r. 1362–63). Some historians date the start of Haakon's rule in Norway to 1343/44, but as he was underage, others date it as 1355.

390. Margaret I (1353–1412) married Haakon (Magnusson) of Sweden in 1363. Her son, Olaf, was king of Denmark (as Olaf V) (r. 1375–87) and king of Norway (r. 1380–87). Margaret ruled as Olaf's regent and wielded a great deal of power even during her husband's life. After Olaf's death, Margaret was elected queen of Denmark in 1387 and Norway in 1388.

391. Reading *hominem exiente*, the text of the (superior) class A manuscripts cited by van Heck; *hominem exire/exuere* (to depart from or shed human existence) is a medieval euphemism for death (cf. para. 233, *hominem exuit*). The meaning would be inaccurate as Magnus was deposed before Albert took the crown, but Aeneas does not go on to discuss him, so he may have been under the assumption that he had died. Van Heck, following the class B manuscripts, has *hominem exigente*, which is obscure.

392. Albert of Mecklenburg was ruler of Sweden from 1363–89.

Margaret mustered her troops and came to meet him, and on a wide open plain they fought a battle which made it seem as if she had donned the spirit of a man and her enemy that of a woman. Defeated, taken prisoner, and led in a triumphal procession, Albert lost his kingdom. When he was finally released, he lived out his old age in disgrace in his father's home.[393] A woman of great fame, Margaret ruled three kingdoms and governed her subjects with majesty and devotion until her old age. Ultimately, when she was enfeebled by age and unable to manage so great an empire by herself, she adopted as her son the fourteen-year-old Duke Erik of Pomerania,[394] entrusted her kingdoms to him, and married him to Philippa, daughter of the king of England.[395] After his wife died without producing an heir, he refused to marry again and ruled for fifty-five years until he was finally deposed by a popular uprising in the reign of Emperor Frederick. Duke Christopher of Bavaria, his nephew on his sister's side, was appointed in his place and allowed his uncle to rule the isle of Gotland during the ten years of his own reign.[396] When Christopher passed away, Christian received the crown of Denmark and Norway.[397]

117. The Swedes, however, disagreed over the choice of king, some wishing to entrust the kingdom to Karl, a distinguished knight, others to Knut, his younger brother.[398] While the matter of

---

393. With the support of Swedish nobles who proclaimed Margaret rightful ruler in 1388, Albert was defeated and imprisoned in 1389. He was released six years later.

394. Erik of Pomerania (c. 1382–1459) was proclaimed hereditary king of Norway in 1389 and elected king of Denmark and Sweden in 1396. He was crowned in Kalmar in 1397, where the Kalmar Union of the three countries was proclaimed. Despite Erik's title, Margaret continued to rule until her death in 1412.

395. Philippa (1394–1430), daughter of Henry IV; she married Erik in 1406.

396. Erik was deposed in Denmark (1438) and Sweden (1439) and Norway (1442). Christopher III of Bavaria was elected king of Denmark (r. 1440–48), Sweden (r. 1441–48), and Norway (r. 1442–48).

397. Christian I Oldenburg, elected king of Denmark (r. 1448–81) and Norway (r. 1450–81). He also briefly reigned in Sweden (1457–64).

398. Karl Knutsson Bonde (d. 1470), who had served as captain of the realm and regent, became King Karl (VIII) of Sweden in 1448, but not without opposition. He had

the election was still pending, Karl sent soldiers in and secretly occupied the town of Stockholm, where the king's residence is maintained. Knut assaulted the fortress with the help of his supporters, and thus began a war between the brothers over the kingship. For a long time, the struggle was indecisive. At last, after many had been killed on both sides, an armistice was arranged on the condition that the power of choosing a king should fall to the common people and that the nobility be excluded. Since Karl enjoyed greater popularity, sovereignty was placed in his hands. Knut pursued the life of a private individual. Karl, on the other hand, was puffed up and arrogant over his new power and sent an armed fleet to expel the aging Erik from Gotland, where he was harming nobody and keeping to himself.[399] He is still alive today and is said to be living in his homeland of Pomerania, content with little. By his example, he teaches how precarious and vain are the affairs of mortals, for, having been stripped of three powerful kingdoms, he was not even able, despite his advanced years, to retain until his death the small island on which he had lived in seclusion for ten years. But neither did the crimes of Karl go unpunished. In the midst of persecuting Christian churches, flouting religion, robbing priests, prohibiting the observance of feast days, and generally disrupting the laws of God and man, he was defeated in a great battle by Jöns Bengtsson, the bishop of Uppsala, a shrewd and energetic man who had roused the nobles of the realm to action.[400] Driven from his kingdom, he is spending his exile on a small island not far from the mouth of the

---

a tumultuous and fragmented reign in Sweden (r. 1448–57; 1464–65; 1467–70). His half brother, Knut Stensson, was a knight of minor importance who is rarely mentioned in studies dealing with Karl. Aeneas's intriguing description of an armed conflict between the brothers over the throne of Sweden does not appear in other sources. Thanks to Thomas Lindkvist and Erika Harlitz for help on this question.

399. Not so peaceful on Gotland, Erik tried to regain the throne until 1449 and engaged in piracy.

400. Jöns Bengtsson Oxenstierna, archbishop of Uppsala (r. 1448–67), led the revolt in 1457 and placed Christian I Oldenburg on the throne. Karl Knutsson Bonde returned to power in 1464.

Vistula. Christian, a man superior to him in piety and justice, was chosen in his place and in our time has once again combined the three kingdoms into one. Gotland, too, which was once the abode and homeland of the Goths, is subject to his rule.

34 BOHEMIA

118. THE GEOGRAPHICAL order of places would now require me to take up the deeds of the Bohemians and describe their location, for they border the Saxons in the south. Many things of note have happened among them in the present age; many battles have been fought there and much blood spilled; cities have been razed to the ground, religion spurned and trampled upon. The heresy of the Hussites emerged; the madness of the Adamites sprang up; the armies of the Taborites and Orphans ran riot;[401] the two thunderbolts of war, Žižka and Prokop, looted the country at their pleasure.[402] Jan Hus and Jerome of Prague deceived the people and were finally burned at the stake at the great synod of Constance.[403] Jacobellus, Koranda, Rokycana, and Peter the Englishman, all of them corruptors of the Gospel, were regarded as teachers of the

---

401. "Adamites" was a name attributed to a radical offshoot of the Hussites led by Martin Huska, who supposedly imitated Adam's innocence by going naked and having sexual relations at will; their beliefs may have been fabricated by their enemies. The Taborites and Orphans were military wings of the Hussites; see Malcolm Lambert, *Medieval Heresy: Popular Movements from Bogomil to Hus* (London: E. Arnold, 1977).

402. Jan Žižka and Prokop Holý (i.e., the Bald) were military leaders of the Hussites. Žižka (d. 1424), from the lesser nobility of southern Bohemia, rose to become a brilliant military leader of the Taborites (a peasant military wing of the Hussites) and continued to press for acceptance of Hus's reforms after his death. He is known for the military innovation of mobile artillery; see Fudge, *Crusade in Bohemia*, and John Martin Klassen, "Hus, the Hussites, and Bohemia," in *CMH*, vol. 7. For more on Aeneas's impressions of the Hussites, see Howard Kaminsky, "Pius Aeneas among the Taborites," *Church History* 28, no. 3 (1959): 281–309.

403. Reformers Jan Hus (1369–1415) and Jerome of Prague (c. 1365–1416)—not to be confused with John Jerome of Prague—were condemned and burned as heretics at the Council of Constance, despite assurances of protection from Emperor Sigismund. See para. 85. Centuries later, Pope John Paul II apologized for Hus's death.

truth.⁴⁰⁴ Four kings were unable to eradicate the deadly venom: Wenceslas, Sigismund, Albert, and Ladislas (who is believed to have been poisoned to death there).⁴⁰⁵ Finally, George Podiebrad was made king, who is thought to be tainted with the Hussite stain, though in other respects he is a great man and famous for his deeds in war. But all these matters have been written up in the *History of Bohemia*, which I published recently.⁴⁰⁶ I have also described there, to the best of my ability, the topography of the region and its national customs. Therefore, whatever appears to be missing from the present work on the subject of Bohemia will have to be acquired from there. Continuing on the path I began, I will run through the countries of lower Germany and then return to its upper regions.⁴⁰⁷

35 FRISIA

119. THE FRISIANS, who live next to the ocean, border on Saxony to the east and Westphalia to the south; in the west they adjoin the territory of Utrecht (though the people of Utrecht, too, are alleged to be Frisians by many authors, including Otto, bishop of Freising, who wrote a history of Germany that is not without merit).⁴⁰⁸ Albert, bishop of Mainz, who built the monastery of Fulda, was killed by the Frisians and crowned with martyrdom while striving to convert them to Christianity.⁴⁰⁹

---

404. Jacobellus of Mies took up and expanded Hus's agenda at the University of Prague following Hus's death. Václav Koranda of Plzen was a radical Hussite preacher. Hussite priest Jan Rokycana (or Rokyzana) was named archbishop of Prague, but the pope never confirmed him. Oxford Wycliffite Peter Payne joined the faculty at Prague in 1418.
405. The Utraquists, a Hussite group who demanded communion in both forms, would continue to fight for recognition until they were granted full rights by the crown in 1485. On Ladislas's death, see para. 10.
406. See *Historia Bohemica*, eds. Hejnic and Rothe.
407. Classical terminology referred to northern Germanic regions as "lower Germany" and the southern regions as "upper."
408. See Otto of Freising's chronicle, *The Two Cities* (1146).
409. The name Albert (or Adalbert in Urb. Lat. 885) is puzzling as the description

This race is fierce and proficient in arms, powerful and tall in physique, confident and fearless in spirit—and it prides itself on its independence. Although Philip, the ruler of Burgundy, calls himself master of the land, in reality Frisia is free and follows its own customs, neither enduring subjection to foreigners nor aspiring to dominate them; in defense of freedom the Frisian willingly embraces death.[410] These people dislike men of military rank and do not tolerate the ambitious man who exalts himself above others. They select annual magistrates to administer the state with impartial justice. They punish the lasciviousness of women very severely and are reluctant to accept unmarried priests, for fear they might pollute the beds of others; for they think it scarcely possible and contrary to nature for a man to restrain his desires. Their assets lie entirely in cattle. The land is flat and marshy, and very rich in grass. It lacks wood, so they feed their fires with bituminous sod and dry cow-dung.

Cornelius Tacitus records that two ambassadors from this race, Veritus and Malorix, came to Rome during Nero's reign. Upon entering the theater of Pompey, they saw some men in foreign dress sitting among the senators and when they realized that this honor was granted to the ambassadors of nations who excelled in courage and friendship toward Rome, they exclaimed that no men surpassed the Germans in arms or loyalty and went down to sit among the senators. Because of this, Nero rewarded them both with citizenship.[411]

---

matches that of St. Boniface (born Winfrid), who was archbishop of Mainz (745), founder of the monastery of Fulda (744), and martyred by the Frisians in 754. Perhaps Aeneas conflates Boniface with St. Adalbert, archbishop of Prague, who was martyred by the Prussians in 997.

410. Duke Philip III of Burgundy (r. 1419–67) was attempting to extend control or influence over areas of Holland like Utrecht and Frisia to the north; see David Nicholas, *The Northern Lands: Germanic Europe, c. 1270–1500* (Malden, Mass.: Wiley Blackwell, 2009), 31–40.

411. However, Nero refused their primary request: permission for the Frisians to settle or keep lands on the right bank of the Rhine near Roman territory; see Tacitus, *Annals*, 13.54.

36 HOLLAND, UTRECHT, DORDRECHT, WESTPHALIA

120. HOLLAND, which is also a German country, is washed by the ocean on its northern edge; the rest of it is cut off by branches of the Rhine River, which form an island. It is marshy, rich in pasture, and interspersed with numerous lakes and inlets of the sea.[412] Some say that the famous city of Utrecht is located in Holland. To me, it does not seem strange that Utrecht has at one time been attributed to Frisia, at another to Holland, since frontiers are often altered by the decrees of rulers. Indeed, in our time it is assigned to neither Frisia nor Holland. The bishopric of Utrecht is subordinate to the emperor alone and owns extensive land, which is hemmed in by various channels of the Rhine. The Frisians adjoin it in the east and the Westphalians in the south; Holland borders it in the north, and in the west, the duchy of Guelderland, of which I will speak in due course, is separated from it by the Rhine River. With downright ignorance, not to say mendacity, some have recently maintained that Utrecht is a city of the French nation, when the election of its bishop was under discussion.[413] For how can we assign Utrecht to France when it is situated on the other side of two branches of the Rhine, and when it is agreed that even people who live this side of the Rhine, such as the inhabitants of Cologne and Cleves, are Germans? Indeed, the location, the way of life, and the language of the people of Utrecht are clearly German.[414]

Utrecht is a rich and populous city, whose bishop leads forty

---

412. Reading *sinibus* (Urb. Lat. 885) for van Heck's *finibus*.

413. Perhaps a reference to Philip of Burgundy forcing the city to accept his illegitimate son, David, as bishop of Utrecht in 1456, a year after he had persuaded Pope Nicholas V to appoint him.

414. Aeneas likely reflects the position of the imperial court, which questioned Burgundy's claim to several areas, including Alsace and Lotharingia (Lorraine); see Nichol, *Northern Lands*, 34–40.

thousand soldiers to war whenever there is a pressing need. The men and women are extremely good-looking. They are protected from foreign invasion both by floodwaters and their own courage. Their national drink is beer, though wine is imported by merchants.

121. Many feuds occurred in this city within our memory, when one faction rejected the bishop that had been accepted by another.[415] Desiderius once maintained peace within the diocese but was then expelled by the citizens and appealed to the Roman pontiff and neighboring rulers for assistance against his rebellious subjects.[416] The citizens adopted a certain Diepholt[417] as their prelate, contrary to civil and divine law. Pope Martin V pronounced anathema against them. But, since the stubborn people scorned the sword of excommunication, it was necessary to resort to warfare. Large forces belonging to the duke of Burgundy and neighboring rulers were directed against the people of Utrecht, but they fought without success. The victorious and defiant populace disregarded the commands of the church for seven years. When Desiderius died in exile, the canons, who on his account had been expelled from their country, chose Walram von Moers, the brother of the archbishop of Cologne, to succeed him as bishop.[418] The case was discussed in the Council of Basel, and his election was confirmed. For a second time, the synod condemned the rebellion of the Utrechtians; for a second time a war was fought in vain. In the end, Jean, bishop of Conserans, who was later called to the honor of the cardinalate with the title of Thérouanne, was sent as a legate by Eugenius.[419]

---

415. Dating the reigns of bishops of Utrecht is complicated given the lack of clarity between an election, a claim, and residence as bishop; the following dates that are provided, therefore, may differ from those of other scholars.

416. Desiderius, or Zweder, von Cullenborch (d. 1439), bishop of Utrecht (r. 1425–33).

417. Rudolph of Diepholt, bishop of Utrecht (r. 1432–55).

418. Reading *archiepiscopi* (Urb. Lat. 885, Vat. Lat. 3888) for van Heck's *archiepiscopum*. Walram von Moers, bishop of Münster (r. 1450–56), was the brother of the powerful Dietrich von Moers, elector and archbishop of Cologne (r. 1414–63). Walram fought unsuccessfully for this position from 1433–48.

419. Jean le Jeune (1411–51) was appointed bishop of Conserans in 1433 but appears

Holland, Utrecht, Dordrecht, Westphalia

When he reported that the only way of pacifying the country was to forgive Diepholt and to grant him the bishopric of this nation, to the exclusion of Walram, the rebellious population was appeased.[420] A fine thing, indeed! The laws never support the losers and power triumphs over holy statutes. The people of Utrecht intended to evade the authority of Calixtus, too, when they refused to accept the bishop that he gave them on the death of Diepholt. But they were intimidated by the armaments and power of Duke Philip of Burgundy and, after failing in their initial efforts, they desisted from their madness and complied.[421]

122. The most distant Germans toward the north and west are the Hollanders—island-dwelling people located opposite the mouths of the Rhine, among whom the inhabitants of Dordrecht are considered paramount. This city is strongly fortified, rich in resources, and suitably positioned for trade. No small part of it is said to have been destroyed by fire last year.[422] It is agreed that this happened through the negligence of the citizens, though many miracles are also alleged; these I pass over, since they are not confirmed by evidence of sufficient reliability. The town of Brielle, too, is not without repute; it is surrounded by waters, and there, as well, many merchants dock their ships.

123. I will not yet cross the Rhine in order to describe the German peoples who live there. I will have the opportunity to discuss them in due course.

Meanwhile, I will continue with the peoples of ancient Germany, as it is strictly defined, and give an account of those who adjoin the Utrechtians and Frisians in the south. Westphalia is bounded by the Rhine River in the west and the Visurgis—which today they call the Weser—in the east; to the north it abuts Frisia and the ter-

---

not to have formally occupied the see; he was transferred to the see of Thérouanne in 1436. In 1439 he was created cardinal.
    420. In 1448 the two parties were reconciled, and Walram resigned his claim.
    421. David, the illegitimate son of Philip, was appointed bishop of Utrecht in 1455.
    422. Dordrecht suffered a great fire in 1457.

ritory of Utrecht; in the south it ends at the mountains of Hesse, which Ptolemy seems to call the Anobian Mountains.[423] These are the source of the Ems River, which, splitting the country roughly into two halves, flows past the well-known cities of Paderborn and Münster and then runs through Frisia down to the sea. The Lippe River also waters Westphalia. When Drusus Germanicus was campaigning between this river and the Rhine, he overcame the enemy but met his death in the hour of victory.[424]

124. It is difficult to say how antiquity described the inhabitants of this land owing to the disagreement among authors. Strabo seems to call those who lived near the Rhine in this area the Sygambrians.[425] These men waged wars with the Romans under their leader Melo and, after being defeated, provided hostages and obtained peace; however, they trampled on their word and betrayed their hostages by starting a revolt.[426] Ptolemy also relates that along the Rhine River, starting from the northern part of Germany, lived the Bussatorians, known as "the Small," the Sicambrians, the Oquenians, and the Langobards.[427] I find in Strabo that around the Ems River lived the Bructerians, whom Drusus overcame in a naval battle;[428] however, after being defeated in war, the Bructerians dispersed from the south toward the north as far as the ocean. On this basis, I am able to conjecture that these are the people who are now called Prutenians [Prussians]—the northern people of whom I spoke before; for the tongue easily converts "Bructerians" into "Prutenians."

125. Charlemagne waged many wars against the Westphalians, inflicted on them many defeats, and compelled them to abandon the

---

423. Ptolemy, *Geography*, 2.11.5 (Abnobian, not Anobian).
424. Nero Claudius Drusus, brother to Tiberius Caesar, died in 9 BCE returning from the front.
425. Strabo, *Geography*, 7.1.4.
426. In 17 or 16 BCE Melo defeated a Roman army under Marcus Lollius in Gaul.
427. Ptolemy, *Geography*, 2.11.6 (listing the lesser Bructerians, Sygambrians, and Suevian Langobards; Aeneas's *Oqueni* is an error, presumably based on a faulty text of Ptolemy).
428. Strabo, *Geography*, 7.1.3.

worship of idols and embrace Christianity.[429] But because they frequently renounced it and failed to keep their oath, he appointed secret judges, in order to repress rebellion through the fear of punishment. Whenever they had established that someone had committed perjury, broken his word, or perpetrated any other crime, he gave them the power of punishing that man immediately, as soon as he could be arrested, without issuing a summons in advance or allowing him to defend himself. He chose sober and righteous men, who were unlikely to penalize the innocent. This terrified the Westphalians and at last kept them faithful, now that they often came across the hanged bodies of nobles and commoners in the woods, without having heard of a prior accusation. However, to anyone who investigated the reason it became clear that the men found killed had broken their word or committed some serious crime. This court has survived to our own times and is called "the forbidden." Those who preside over it are named *scabini*, whose effrontery is such that they wish to extend their jurisdiction throughout Germany. They have secret rituals and mysterious proceedings for denouncing malefactors; thus far, no one has been induced to disclose these either by bribery or intimidation. The majority of the *scabini* themselves operate under cover. As they range through different districts, they identify those guilty of an offense and refer them to the court, where they accuse them and prove their guilt in accordance with their procedures. The condemned are written down in a book, and their execution is entrusted to junior *scabini*. The defendant is ignorant of his conviction and suffers the penalty wherever they find him.

This court has degenerated, however; for some worthless individuals are being admitted and are daring to take up civil cases when they were granted authority over criminal ones alone.[430]

---

429. Charlemagne first defeated the Westphalians in 775.
430. A branch of the fehmic or vehmic courts, which met in secret and date back to Charlemagne's reign or earlier Saxon practice. Scott questions their sinister reputation, arguing they functioned more as a private court of appeals. He also notes the prolifera-

126. In Westphalia, the people of Soest defected from the Church of Cologne within our time. Though exhausted by a lengthy war, defeated on many occasions, and oppressed by a determined siege, they would not restore their allegiance. Dietrich von Moers, the archbishop of Cologne (who is considered the ruler of the Westphalians), and Jean, the duke of Cleves, fought over this with no little hatred, since the people of Soest had turned for protection to the people of Cleves, and the archbishop of Cologne had summoned to his assistance the dukes of Saxony and a considerable force of Bohemians.[431] There was also a fierce struggle at Münster, a city of the same country, on account of a church which Walram, the brother of Dietrich, considered his due. Many of the enemy were killed in this battle, and one of the leading men of Brunswick, who commanded their forces, was taken prisoner and placed in the hands of the archbishop of Cologne.[432]

127. Westphalia is a frigid region, poor in crops. They eat black bread, and their drink is beer. Wine is imported via the Rhine and commands a high price; only the wealthy partake of it, and that seldom. The populace is warlike and shrewd. There is said to be a proverb about them which goes: "Westphalia breeds rogues and liars more easily than fools."

128. Since I happened to mention Dietrich, it would be appropriate here to report a few facts about him—a man to whom no one would deny a place among the leading lights of our generation.[433]

---

tion of the courts, which led to variations and conflicts in judgments. See Tom Scott, "Germany and the Empire," in *CMH*, vol. 7: 354.

431. Soest threw off Dietrich's jurisdiction in 1443. The struggle continued until 1449 when the town came under the duchy of Cleves. For more on the battle over Soest, see *Commentaries*, Bk III (Meserve and Simonetta, vol. 2: 42–45; Gragg and Gabel, vol. 2: 208–10).

432. Dietrich attempted to gain control of Münster for Walram in 1450 upon the death of their brother Henry, who was bishop of the city.

433. Born in 1385, Dietrich was archbishop of Cologne (r. 1414–63) and a major political figure who labored intently to further his family's interests, often by military force. Aeneas speaks of him at greater length in the *Commentaries*, Bk XI (Gragg and Gabel, vol. 5: 748). For more on his governing methods, see Georg Droege, *Verfassung und Wirtschaft in Kurköln unter Dietrich von Moers* (Bonn: Ludwig Röhrscheid Verlag, 1957).

He was born into a family of Moers which was highly respected among the rulers of Germany. He had three brothers, who all lived beyond sixty: Henry, the eldest, governed his father's dominion; Johann administered the Church of Münster for many years until the end of his life—and to the highest acclaim;[434] and Walram aspired in vain to the Church of Utrecht and, when his brother passed away, the Church of Münster, even though, in the case of Utrecht, he benefited from the support of the Council of Basel and, in that of Münster, from a directive of Pope Nicholas. Dietrich, while studying canon law in Bologna, received the Church of Cologne from Pope John XXIII, over which he has presided now for forty-six years[435] with the full support of the commons and nobility. Although, with varying results, he has waged numerous wars in defense of the church, fulfilling the roles of both an energetic soldier and a valiant general, he has never neglected his priestly duties or the civil administration at home. His physique is handsome, his stature taller than average, his spirit large and generous—his palace always stood open to distinguished guests.

37 HESSE

129. BETWEEN Westphalia and Franconia lies Hesse, a mountainous region which stretches north from the Rhine and joins Thuringia. The ruler of the nation, Landgrave Ludwig, was invited to become emperor in our time, but he said that he was unequal to so heavy a burden and preferred to rule efficiently the small realm bequeathed to him by his parents than to accept a large one and squander it.[436] It also stood in the way of his governing the Chris-

---

434. Aeneas confuses Henry and Johann; on Walram and Henry, see paras. 121, 126.
435. He was appointed to the bishopric in 1414, so it would have been forty-four years in 1458.
436. Ludwig I, landgrave of Hesse (r. 1413–58), was offered the imperial crown in 1439 before it was offered to Frederick III. For more on Ludwig, see *Allgemeine Deutsche Biographie*, vol. 52: 115–18.

tian world, he said, that he was not a scholar. However, he was a guardian of the laws, which he ordered to be translated for him into his native tongue. In all the cases tried before him, he was never found to have passed an unjust sentence. When he entered a certain monastery under his jurisdiction in order to institute reform, he was invited to eat with the monks and is believed to have swallowed poisoned food during the meal. For both he and the abbot, who had requested the reform, are said to have died shortly afterward.

38 THE FRANKS

130. AFTER this comes Franconia, a decidedly well-known and very powerful region, which was named after the Franks who settled there. In fact, the Franks were originally Trojans, who, after the destruction of Troy, followed the leadership of Priam, the nephew of Priam the Great on his sister's side, and made their way into Scythia through the Black Sea and the Sea of Azov. There they built a city called Sicambria, from which they took the name of Sicambrians. For it is known that, after the conquest and burning of Troy, those who survived its destruction divided into three bands and fled into exile. Some, under the leadership of Aeneas, headed for Italy; from them the Albans were descended and later the Romans, who gained control of the whole world. Others under Antenor slipped through the midst of the Achaeans, and, after making their way through the gulfs of Illyria and reaching the kingdom of the Liburnians in the innermost recess of the Adriatic Sea,[437] they founded the city of Padua; tradition holds that Antenor was buried there. Antenor took refugees of the Enetians with him, and from them the Venetians were later named, who today wield immense power by land and sea. The third group, as I said, entered Scythia,

---

437. Virgil, *Aeneid*, 1.242–44.

where they evolved into a great race.[438] When many of the Scythians became subjects of the Roman Empire, the Sicambrians also paid tribute and remained liable to taxation until the time of Emperor Valentinian, during whose reign the Alans began to harass the empire.[439] However, the emperor issued an edict promising freedom for a period of ten years to any who could curb the ferocity of the Alans. Enticed by this prize, the Sicambrians took up arms, defeated, and destroyed the Alans. The emperor rewarded them for this with freedom for the duration of ten years and changed their name to "Franks," which in the Attic language [i.e., Greek] sounds like "fierce" or "noble;"[440] in Italian "Franks" means "free" (*franci*).

131. When the ten years had passed and the Romans demanded the usual taxes, the Franks, made headstrong by their freedom, refused to obey. The rulers of the Franks at that time were Priam and Antenor, who matched their ancient namesakes in valor. Under the command of these captains, the Franks fought a battle with the Romans, in which Priam and the bravest of his people fell. Those who survived the disaster left Scythia, traveled to Germany, and settled in parts of Thuringia together with their leaders, Marcomer and Suno, the sons of Priam and Antenor. Suno died childless; Marcomer had a son called Faramundus, who was elected king by the Franks and became the first to reign over them.[441] His son was Clodius the Long-Haired, from whom the kings of the Franks were named "the Long-Haired." During the same time, the Goths, who had already forced their way into the city of Rome, invaded

---

438. Aeneas may be drawing on several sources for myths and history of the Franks, including Otto of Freising and Ekkehard of Aura (van Heck). For more on Trojan migratory myths and the Franks, see Heath, "Renaissance Scholars"; also R. E. Asher, *National Myths in Renaissance France: Francus, Samothes, and the Druids* (Edinburgh: Edinburgh University Press, 1993).

439. Cf. para. 21.

440. From Otto of Freising, *Chronicle*, Bk I: 25. The Greek allusion is obscure.

441. Marcomer and Suno battled Roman troops under Arbogast on the Rhine frontier and formed a treaty state in 384 CE.

the settlements in Gaul beyond the Loire River. The Burgundians, also, lived near the Rhone, and they, too, began to be ruled by kings a little later. As for the Franks, they crossed the Rhine and routed the Romans who occupied those places. Gradually gaining strength, they attacked Mainz, Trier, Cologne, Tournai, Cambrai, Reims, Soissons, and Orléans, thereby extending their empire from Aquitania to Bavaria. When Clodius died, he was succeeded by his son Meroveus,[442] after whom the Franks were called Merovingian. After Meroveus, Childeric[443] became king, but owing to his dissipated way of life he was driven out by his own people and replaced by Egidius Romanus.[444] Deprived of his kingdom, Childeric took refuge with King Bisinus of Thuringia, whose wife he defiled with adultery. When he was recalled after eight years, however, he attacked Cologne, expelled the Romans, and recovered a large part of his kingdom. On the death of Egidius, his son Syagrius reigned in the city of Soissons. As for Queen Bisina, when she learned that Childeric had recovered his kingdom, she deserted her husband and fled to him. Childeric welcomed her and treated her like his wife. She bore him Clovis, who later assumed the kingship and became the first of the Frankish kings to accept Christianity when he was baptized by the sainted Bishop Remigius.[445]

132. However, there is no basis to the popular tradition that Cologne was so named from being colonized by the Franks. For before the Franks entered Germany, it was called the Colony of the

---

442. Merovech, king of the Salian Franks, fl. 450 CE; Aeneas's text has *Glodoveus* (or Clodoveus) instead of Clodius, which seems a textual error as it does not correspond to Ekkehard and there is no antecedent mentioning Clodoveus; see Ekkehard of Aura in *Patrologia Latina*, vol. 154: 715.

443. Childeric, Merovech's son and successor, d. 481/82.

444. Egidius, or Aegidius (d. 465), a Roman general in Gaul who broke away from the Empire when Ricimer took control in 461.

445. Clovis (c. 466–511) was the first king of the Merovingian dynasty. The date of his baptism is a matter of debate. See William Daly, "Clovis: How Barbaric, How Pagan?" *Speculum* 69, no. 3 (1994): 619–64. Remigius (437–533), later canonized a saint, played a central role in Clovis's relations with the church.

The Franks

Romans, having been founded by the emperor Claudius and named after his wife, Agrippina.[446] Between Clovis and Syagrius a number of wars took place. In the end, Syagrius was defeated and fled for refuge to Alaric, king of the Goths,[447] the ninth in succession from Alaric the Great.[448] Clovis demanded the return of Syagrius and, after obtaining him, had him killed; the remaining Romans who lived in Gaul were also annihilated.[449] Clovis brought the Alemannians beneath his sway, declared war on the Goths and Aquitanians, and defeated them, killing King Alaric in the process.[450] They say that when he went to war, he vowed that, should he emerge victorious, he would dedicate a horse to St. Martin, who had passed away 112 years ago. After winning the victory, he delivered the horse but wanted to buy it back for a hundred gold pieces. The horse stood stock-still until the sum was doubled, which prompted the king to remark that Martin was "a good ally, but an expensive dealer." This same Clovis took as his wife Clothild, the daughter of the king of the Burgundians. Although she was a Christian, she was married to him when he was still a pagan and insistently pleaded with her husband to accept baptism; she also secretly baptized the sons that were born to them. However, they say that the reason why Clovis became a Christian is that, when he was fighting the Swabians and found himself on the verge of defeat, he vowed that he would become a Christian if he escaped from the battle. Because of this his fortune changed, and, plucking victory from defeat, he overcame the Swabians and committed himself to the Christian religion. His descendants reigned in France until Pepin the Short, the father

---

446. Aeneas refers to Cologne in this passage by the ancient name Agrippina. Agrippina was born at Oppidum Ubiorum, later named Colonia Agrippinensis by Emperor Claudius.
447. Alaric II, king of the Visigoths (r. 484–507).
448. Alaric I (r. 395–410), who was responsible for the sack of Rome in 410.
449. Syagrius was killed in 486; the Romans of Gaul were not annihilated but in fact played an important role in the Merovingian kingdom, particularly as clergy, as Gregory of Tours' chronicle demonstrates.
450. In the year 507.

of Charlemagne. At that time, Childeric [III] was dispossessed of the kingdom because of his cowardice, and, when he had been shaved and thrust out of sight in a monastery, Pepin assumed the throne.[451]

133. In Francia at that time, the kingdom was governed by Mayors of the Palace. In the year of our Lord 710, when Dagobert the Younger, king of the Franks, died, his little son, whom others say was the son of Ansegisil, came under the guardianship of Pepin the Fat and perished through treachery.[452] Then Grimoald, the legitimate son of Pepin the Fat, tried to usurp the throne, was taken prisoner by the kinsmen of Dagobert, the dead king, and died in captivity.[453] During the same period, the Gauls who lived between the Seine and Loire rivers fomented wars against the Franks and ventured abroad as far as the city of Mainz, to which they laid siege.[454] The Franks, who lacked a king, wished to elevate Charles Martel to the throne; he refused the crown but accepted leadership and forcibly checked the advance of the Gauls.[455] He ordered the country between the Loire and the Seine, which was then known as Gaudina, to be called Carlinga after himself, and this name was long preserved among the Germans. This same Charles was the son of Alpheida, an aristocratic mistress of Pepin the Fat. He was an illustrious man and a strong warrior, who put to the sword many thousands of Saracens.[456] He was also the father of Pepin the

---

451. With the blessing of Pope Zacharias, Childeric III (the text incorrectly states Childeric II) was deposed in 751 and Pepin the Short was crowned king, thus inaugurating the Carolingian dynasty.

452. Aeneas's chronology is slightly off. The reigning king of Austrasian Francia in 710 was Childebert III (r. 695–711). He was succeeded by his son Dagobert III (r. 711–15). Pepin II of Heristal, from the powerful Arnulfing family, was Mayor of the Palace (r. 679–714).

453. Grimoald was murdered in 714.

454. This probably refers to the combined attacks of the Neustrians, based in northwest Francia south of the Seine, and the Aquitanians, based in south-central Francia south of the Loire, in 718–19; see Collins, *Early Medieval Europe*, 248.

455. Charles was sole Mayor of the Palace from 719–41.

456. A reference to Charles's victory over Muslim forces at Poitiers/Tours in 732.

Short,[457] who sired the world-famous emperor Charlemagne upon his wife, Berta, whom he brought from Greece.[458]

134. And so it was that this race of Franks, after coming from Scythia to Germany and settling there for a long time, became German and named the land which they had first occupied "Francia," after themselves. But as their power increased, Francia, too, grew so large that almost all of Gaul and a great part of Germany from the Pyrenees to the borders of Pannonia was designated Francia; for they called Francia whatever was subject to the Franks. It was divided into two parts: the part consisting of Gaul was called "West Francia," the part consisting of Germany, "East Francia." (And indeed they expanded Germany to the present-day limit of the German language; for the German-speaking regions on this side of the Rhine belonged to East Francia.) Under Charlemagne, this race earned title to the Roman Empire, when he brought relief to the Apostolic See, hard-pressed as it was by war with the Lombards.[459] Although he won control of Gaul, Charlemagne was in fact a German who had been born and raised in Germany, and he usually resided in Aachen, which is a German city. That is where his palace and his head may be seen. His descendants reigned in both Gaul and Germany during their imperial tenure. But when his male line came to an end, the empire reverted to the Germans—that is, to the eastern Franks—of whom Otto was the first to be elected.[460] In fact, the empire does not belong to the Germans in the sense that

---

457. Pepin "the Short" (Aeneas calls him "the dwarf") (714–68); Mayor of the Palace (r. 741–51) and king of Francia (r. 751–68).

458. Charlemagne was born in 742. His mother Bertrada was Frankish, not Greek. Her supposed Greek birth may point to legends supporting Charlemagne's claim to the Roman Empire.

459. Charlemagne was crowned Roman Emperor by Pope Leo III in 800, largely as a reward for defending Leo, who had been assaulted by Roman enemies. Charlemagne's father, Pepin, first defended papal territory in central Italy against the Lombards in 754, and Charlemagne attacked the Lombards again in 773–74—long before he was crowned emperor.

460. Otto I (r. 962–73).

no one except a German can be emperor; but since the authority to choose the emperor was handed to the Germans, a German is usually elected. That is why, when the position of emperor became vacant on the death of Louis, the son of Boso, the Germans, having that power, selected a man who was a German and a Frank from eastern Francia.[461]

I wanted to include this preface, since the subject of Franconia had arisen. For there are many who claim that only those who live around Paris are Franks and that the empire was assigned to them. It would be more accurate to call these people descendants of the Franks.[462]

39 FRANCONIA

135. FRANCONIA, as it is understood in our time, borders on the Swabians and Bavarians in the south, the Rhine in the west, and the Bohemians and Thuringians in the east; the Thuringians also adjoin it to the north, along with the Hessians. A river of no little renown called the Main flows through the land. Ptolemy seems to call this river the Obrinca, which according to him separates the Upper from the Lower Germans. For there is no other river which could mark that separation more suitably than the Main; even today, in fact, the Lower Germans extend as far as Mainz, and from there on they are called Upper Germans. The Main rises in the mountains of Bohemia and empties into the Rhine right opposite Mainz. For that reason, many people have believed that "Maguntia" [Mainz] is really "Moguntia" and was named after the river Moganus [i.e., Main]. The same river flows through several cities, of which the most cel-

---

461. Louis III "the Child" (r. 899–911); the next king of Germany was Henry the Fowler of Saxony (r. 919–36), but the imperial throne remained vacant until Henry's son Otto was elected in 962.

462. *Francigenae.*

ebrated are Würzburg and Frankfurt. In Würzburg is the famous see of a bishop who is also known as the duke of Franconia; when he celebrates mass, he keeps a naked sword in front of him on the altar. In Frankfurt, there is a well-known market, where the Upper and Lower Germans meet twice a year. There, too, the emperor is chosen in accordance with a long-established custom.[463] This makes it clear that the empire was given to the Germans, since it is among them that the emperor is elected and crowned—even if the culmination of his glory comes when he is crowned again in Rome. In Franconia, there is also the famous Church of Bamberg, which stands by the Pegnitz River. It was founded by Emperor Henry II, whom the locals venerate devoutly and hold to be a saint.[464] This is where Berengar is buried, who usurped the throne of Italy.[465] After being captured by Otto I, he was brought to Germany and died there in exile.

136. On a high mountain above the city is a castle well fortified by nature and human ingenuity, where I once lunched with the local bishop.[466] Albert, the most noble count of the Franconians and grandson of Duke Otto of Saxony, through his daughter, took refuge in this castle after killing Count Conrad, who was said to have been the son of King Louis, and for a considerable time withstood the king's siege.[467] Storming the place seemed difficult, so the king resorted to trickery and enlisted Otto, bishop of Mainz, as

463. The Golden Bull of 1356 decreed that all future imperial elections would be held at Frankfurt.
464. The cathedral was built in 1004 by Henry II (r. 1002–24); he was canonized in the twelfth century.
465. Lombard magnate Berengar (c. 900–66) seized the throne of Italy in 951 and married the widow of Lothar, his predecessor.
466. Bishop Anthony von Rotenham (r. 1431–59).
467. Albert of Bamberg killed Conrad "the Old," who was the head of a rival Franconian aristocratic family (but not related to King Louis IV) in 906. This story can be found in Otto of Freising's *Chronicle*, 6:15. See *The Two Cities: A Chronicle of Universal History*, trans. and ed. Charles Mierow, Austin Evans, and Charles Knapp (New York: Octagon Books, 1966), 374–75, for translation and notes. Thanks to Patrick Geary for help identifying this event.

his accomplice in the crime. Otto went to see Albert, and, claiming to be a mediator in the dispute, he asked Albert to come down to the emperor's camp, promising that he would either offer him a peace settlement or escort him back to the castle safe and sound. Albert believed him and, after accepting Otto's solemn oath, he followed him. Scarcely had they left the castle when Otto said, "I'm afraid our meeting with the emperor may last a long time; perhaps it would be best to eat first." Albert approved of the prelate's suggestion, returned to the castle, and served Otto with lunch. After the meal, he accompanied him to the emperor, where he was quickly arrested and sentenced to death. When he invoked the archbishop's promise of safe conduct, the unscrupulous priest replied that he had kept his word, since he had already taken Albert back unharmed when he went in with him for lunch; he had not promised to do it twice. The unfortunate Albert was put to death by the sword. The Romans behaved better than this, when one of the captives whom Hannibal had sent to Rome tried a similar deception and they tied him up and sent him back. "For," in the words of the greatest orator, "deceit does not dissolve but solidifies a false oath."[468] The estates which Albert owned later passed to the Church of Bamberg.

137. Franconia is partly flat, partly mountainous, though the mountains are not inaccessible. The farmland is not very fertile, for it is sandy to a large extent. In many places, the hills are planted with vines and produce a pleasant wine, especially at Würzburg. There are many forests and much hunting. The land is distributed among many owners. Although, as I mentioned before, they call the bishop of Würzburg the duke of Franconia, the Churches of Mainz and Bamberg possess many territories, and the count Palatine, too, owns a considerable portion. The margraves of Brandenburg are also powerful here, and likewise the burgraves of Nuremberg. Furthermore, there are many flourishing imperial cities in Franconia.

---

468. Cicero, *On Duties*, 3.113.

Franconia 189

As for Nuremberg, it is uncertain whether to assign it to Franconia or Bavaria. The name itself suggests that the city belongs to the Bavarians, for Nuremberg means "mountain of Noricum," and so it was clearly a city of the Noricans. However, the Noricans were succeeded by the Bavarians, and that portion of Bavarian land which lies between the Danube and Nuremberg is now called Noricum. Nevertheless, the city is in the diocese of Bamberg, which belongs to the Franconians. The Nurembergers themselves wish to be seen as neither Bavarians nor Franconians, but a third and distinct people. Their famous city is adorned with splendid public and private buildings, and through it flows the Pegnitz River. Because it stands on infertile and sandy land, its population is devoted to business; for all are either artisans or traders—hence their abundant wealth and great reputation in Germany.[469] It is a most fitting residence for the emperors, being an autonomous city and situated roughly in the center of Germany. Between Bamberg and Nuremberg lies Forchheim, a town that is famous for its white bread; its inhabitants mistakenly believe that it was the birthplace of Pilate.

138. Frederick, the margrave of Brandenburg, whom Emperor Sigismund counted among his intimate friends, held great power in this country.[470] He had four sons: Johann, Frederick, Albert, and another Frederick. Johann, as the firstborn, was entitled to the imperial electorship, but his father's judgment gave precedence to Frederick, his second son, since he seemed more suited to the performance of imperial duties. Therefore, before he died, he divided his inheritance between his sons.[471] He appointed Frederick elector

---

469. Nuremberg began to abolish restrictions against foreign traders at the end of the fourteenth century and to stimulate support for industry, particularly the metal industry, initiating a period of growth and prosperity for the town; see Fritz Rörig, *The Medieval Town* (Berkeley: University of California Press, 1967), 103–4.

470. Frederick I (1362–1440) was granted the margravate of Brandenburg and invested with electoral status in 1417.

471. In 1437 Frederick I named Frederick II (r. 1440–70) his heir as elector of Brandenburg and divided family possessions in Franconia among his other sons. Albert III

and showed good judgment in this; for Frederick was renowned for his wisdom among the rulers of Germany. Through his diplomacy, many regions were restored to peace—and on more than one occasion. He is also hailed as a champion of justice and honor, for, when he could have ascended to the throne of Poland by virtue of the barons' choice, he turned down their offer, as I related previously, in order not to wrong the true heir.[472] His brother Albert, on the other hand, attracted the support of almost all the rulers of Germany when he waged war on the people of Nuremberg; the cities, however, sent aid to the Nurembergers.[473] It was a harsh and terrible war, involving as it did so many powers, which collided and fought with the bitterest hatred for two full years. They say that there were nine battles, eight of which were won by Albert, who succumbed to defeat in only one. There was no peace agreement until the combatants ran out of money and supplies, after the fields had been burned, the settlements ruined, the cattle stolen, and the peasants killed. Even then, peace was made more on Albert's terms.

This Albert was trained in arms from childhood—"from his tender nails," as the saying goes—and participated in more battles than other captains of his time either witnessed or read about. He campaigned in Poland, fought in Silesia, encamped in Prussia, routed the enemy in Bohemia, served in Austria, and plundered Hungary. There was no corner of German territory on which he had not trodden in arms. He commanded countless armies, thrashed the fiercest foes, and sacked the best defended cities. In battles, he was the first to enter the fight and the last to leave it, as the vic-

---

"Achilles" received Anspach as his duchy and became elector of Brandenburg (r. 1470–86) on his brother's death.

472. Frederick II brought stability to the area of Brandenburg by curbing the violence of the nobility; Scott, "Germany and the Empire," 360. He was offered the throne of Poland in 1444; see para. 88.

473. Albert came into conflict with Nuremberg when the city claimed the right to extend burghers' privileges to the feudal subjects of local lords and complained about unsafe roads and excessive tolls. This culminated in the Second Cities' War (1448–53); see Scott, "Germany and the Empire," 359–60.

tor; in assaulting towns he was often the first to climb the wall; he was frequently challenged to single combat, never declined, and never failed to strike down his enemy. In military games, where men contend with lances, he was the only one never to be thrown from his horse and to overthrow all those who rode against him. At tournaments, he always emerged victorious. On seventeen occasions, protected only by a shield and helmet and with the rest of his body uncovered (as in a type of duel practiced by the Germans), he charged with pointed lance in hand against challengers armed in the same way, without ever suffering an injury or failing to unhorse his opponents. For these deeds he was named, not without justification, the German Achilles. The skills of a soldier and the qualities of an emperor—his noble lineage, too—shown forth in him with extraordinary grace. His stature and handsome looks, his physical strength, and the eloquence of his tongue made him an almost divine figure of awe.[474]

40 BAVARIA, THE PALATINATE, SWABIA

139. BAVARIA abuts the northeast of Franconia and a part of its southern border.[475] It, too, is an extensive and wealthy land. In the south, it is bordered by the Italian Alps; the Swabians lie to its west, the Austrians and Bohemians, to its east.[476] The Danube flows roughly through its center. Some have set the Enns River as the frontier between Austria and Bavaria, others the Inn River; the Lech River marks the boundary between the Swabians and Bavarians. The Noricans once inhabited this region, and a portion of it

---

474. Albert was also extremely brutal toward his enemies and made no exceptions for civilians or the clergy; see Brady, *German Histories*, 95.
475. Lit. "toward the summer sunrise and a portion of its midday region."
476. Lit. "The Swabians receive its setting sun, the Austrians and Bohemians, its rising sun."

situated across the Danube is still called Noricum, as I mentioned before.

140. I cannot easily tell from where the Bavarians got their name or took their origin. But when I find that the oldest manuscripts use the name Boioaria for what our contemporaries call Bavaria, it is not hard for me to believe that the people of Boioaria were named after the Boians and that once it was a Gallic race. Strabo adds support to this opinion in his fifth book when he says (with reference to the Po River): "Therefore, in olden times, as I have said, a great many Gallic tribes lived by the river. The most numerous of these were the Boians, the Insubrians, and the Senonians, who with the Gesatans once attacked and captured the city of Rome. In later years the Romans utterly destroyed the latter and expelled the Boians from their territory. Migrating from there, they settled with the Tauriscans in the vicinity of the Danube, where they engaged in constant warfare with the Dacians."[477] It is apparent, then, that the Boians settled in Pannonia and in the course of time were able to migrate from there without difficulty into the bordering region of Noricum. In identifying the lake which is now called Constance, Strabo also says that the Rhaetians lived a short distance from it, the Helvetians and Vindelicans further away.[478] Beyond the Vindelicans, he states that the unpopulated territory of the Boians reached as far as the Pannonians.[479] By this he makes it clear enough that the land of the Bavarians was inhabited by the Boians. Strabo, once again, in describing Germany, asserts that the Boians previously inhabited the Hercynian Forest and that the Cimbrians assembled an army and invaded the region but were repelled by the Boians.[480] We are therefore justified in concluding that the name of the Bavarians descended from the Boians; for their land on the other side

---

477. Strabo, *Geography*, 5.1.6.   478. Strabo, *Geography*, 4.3.3.
479. Strabo, *Geography*, 7.1.5.
480. Strabo, *Geography*, 7.2.2. In this passage, the modern Black Forest corresponds to a small (western) portion of what the ancients called Hercynian.

Bavaria, The Palatinate, Swabia 193

of the Danube includes a large part of the Hercynian Forest. The race is now German and speaks the German language. It is not an "unpopulated territory," as Strabo reports, though perhaps it was in his time. Today it is highly cultivated and contains large and ostentatious cities and towns of great renown; I know of none in all of Europe which could surpass their splendor. It has five pontifical cities, one of which is metropolitan. They call it Salzburg after the river by which it lies; the ancients called it Iuvavia.

141. In Bavaria Ludwig, son of Ludwig, a man disfigured by a hump and a goiter, embarked on impious wars against his father—a venerable and august old man, who had once governed the kingdom of France—and besieged him in a strongly fortified castle. But the powers of heaven demanded vengeance for so heinous a crime, and he was struck down with a fever and died before he could bend his father's mind to his own will. His father later fell into the clutches of Henry, a duke of the same family, and died shortly thereafter.[481] Nor did Henry long survive him. After forbidding his subjects to go to Rome in the year of Jubilee from fear that the country would be drained of money, he joined his forefathers in the same way. He was succeeded by his son Ludwig, whom he had fathered with the sister of Emperor Albert. Ludwig was a young man of high spirit, eager for glory and contemptuous of money. He posted edicts in public places banishing all Jews from his dominions.[482] He married a wife from Saxony, the niece of Emperor Frederick.[483] Through his authority, he settled many disputes in Germany, though despite many earnest attempts, he was unable to reconcile King Ladislas [Postumus] with the emperor.

481. Ludwig VIII (r. 1443–45) "the Hunchback" of Bavaria-Ingolstadt, son of Ludwig VII (r. 1413–43) "the Bearded." Ludwig VII's sister was Isabella, the wife of Charles VI and held great sway with the mentally incapacitated French monarch. Ludwig VIII was imprisoned by Henry XVI of Bavaria-Landshut in 1445 or 1446 until his death in 1447.

482. Ludwig IX "the Rich" of Bavaria-Landshut (r. 1450–79), son of Henry and Margaret of Austria. He issued this decree against the Jews in 1450, reversing his father's policies toward them.

483. Amalia; the couple were married in 1452.

142. Albert is a ruler of the same land and family. When his father Ernst ordered a female bath-attendant, whom Albert desperately loved and proposed to marry, to be drowned in the waters of the Danube at Straubing, he lived in mourning for a long time.[484] At length, when his grief had run its course, he took a wife from the House of Brunswick, who bore him a handsome set of children. In the reign of Frederick, while suffering from the gout, he put aside all other cares and devoted himself to music, delighting his soul with a stream of songs and melodies; sometimes he also occupied himself with hunting.[485]

In Salzburg, which, as I mentioned, holds the metropolitan see in Bavaria, there were three archbishops. The last of these, named Sigismund, when still a provost, nobly supported the Roman Church during the raging storm of schism.[486] But when he was appointed archbishop by Pope Nicholas V, he forbade the publication in his church of the apostolic letter that flung the thunderbolt of censure against the Austrians who had rebelled against the emperor, either through fear of their power or because he thought there was a better chance of working out a peaceful settlement if the excommunication was suspended.[487] He himself went down into Austria and devoted no small effort to arranging one.

143. In the region around the Rhine, which in our time displays Germany at its finest, there were frequent quarrels between Dietrich, the archbishop of the Church of Mainz, and Ludwig, count

484. Duke Albert III of Upper Bavaria-Munich (r. 1438–60) and Duke Ernst of Bavaria-Munich (r. 1397–1438). Agnes Bernauer was the ill-fated object of Albert's affections. For more on Agnes, contemporary interpretations, and the popularity of her story, see Lyndal Roper, "Gorgon of Augsburg," in *Women, Identities and Communities in Early Modern Europe*, ed. Susan Broomhall and Stephanie Turbin (Burlington, VT: Ashgate, 2008), 113–36.

485. Albert married Anna, the daughter of Eric I of Brunswick. His love of music dates back to his education in Prague, where he lived with his aunt. See *Allgemeine Deutsche Biographie*, vol. 1: 231.

486. Archbishop Sigismund of Volkertsdorf (r. 1452–61) was preceded by Johann of Reisberg (r. 1429–41) and Frederick of Emmerberg (r. 1441–52).

487. Nicholas V issued the bull on April 4, 1452; see Stieber, *Pope Eugenius IV*, 322.

Bavaria, The Palatinate, Swabia 195

palatine of the Rhine.[488] It very often came to blows, and the whole surrounding area was ravaged with pillage and arson. The bishop of Mainz received assistance from the margraves of Baden and Brandenburg, while the count palatine was supported by Jakob, bishop of Trier, and a number of cities.[489]

Count Ludwig had married the widow of King Louis of Sicily. When Ludwig died, his brother Frederick, with the agreement of the nobles of the land, adopted the infant son to whom she had given birth and took over the government of the state as if he were its ruler. He claimed he was an imperial elector and promised to remain unmarried forever, in order not to compromise the rights of his adopted son by taking a wife. When Pope Nicholas V was consulted, he confirmed this form of adoption, but Emperor Frederick rejected it, despite frequent and assertive petitions.[490]

144. In Swabia, Albert, the brother of Emperor Frederick, waged war against several cities with varying success. Through a judicial decision, he acquired the countship of Rothenburg from the people of Ulm.[491]

---

488. Dietrich von Erbach, elector and archbishop of Mainz (r. 1436–59); Ludwig IV, count palatine of the Rhine (d. 1449).

489. Margraves Jakob I of Baden (r. 1431–53) and Frederick II of Brandenburg (r. 1440–70); Jakob I of Sierk, elector and archbishop of Trier (r. 1434–56). The source of these quarrels was most likely territorial disputes and division among the electors (c. 1446) as to whether to support the Council of Basel, as did Jakob, or the papacy, as Dietrich eventually did. See Izbicki et al., *Reject Aeneas*, 367–70.

490. Margaret of Savoy married Ludwig, count palatine of the Rhine, in 1445. Frederick I (1425–76) became elector in 1451 and guardian of Ludwig's son Philip. Frederick eventually married in 1472, but while one of his two sons (Ludwig, Count of Lowenstein) survived him, he kept his word and Philip succeeded as elector and count palatine of the Rhine in 1476.

491. In 1450.

41 THE MARGRAVATE OF BADEN, THE TYROL, SWITZERLAND

145. IN THE margravate of Baden, the ruler was Jakob, a man whose reputation for justice and wisdom made him celebrated among the Germans. Because it pained him that the only thing he lacked for human happiness was a knowledge of letters, he compelled the children whom he had fathered with his lawful wife to study literature. When he had divided his inheritance among them and arranged for his firstborn son, Carl, a remarkably industrious youth, to marry the emperor's sister, he passed away, without reluctance, in the fullness of his years.[492]

146. The Tyroleans, who inhabit the valleys of the Inn and Etsch, petitioned in vain for the return of their ruler Sigismund, who lived under the guardianship of Emperor Frederick and by now was quite grown-up. Resorting to arms, they threw out the local governors whom the emperor had installed. When the people of Trent remained loyal to the emperor at the bidding of the bishop to whose authority they were subject, the Tyroleans went there with an army, captured the terror-stricken city through treachery, and forced the surrender of the citadel after wearing it down by assault. Having come to terms with the emperor, they subsequently obtained their own ruler, though with a less fortunate outcome than they had imagined.[493]

147. The Swiss are a fierce mountain people. When the people

---

492. Jakob Margrave of Baden (r. 1432–53), nicknamed "Solomon." He devoted himself to scholarly studies in his mature years and provided a secular education for his sons Carl and Bernard, and religious educations for the others. His son Carl married Katherina Habsburg; see *Allgemeine Deutsche Biographie*, vol. 13: 532–34.

493. The Tyroleans rebelled in 1446, prompting Frederick to release his ward as their ruler. Aeneas had tried to shape the young man's character through his letters, but Sigismund did not develop into an impressive ruler. See Piccolomini, *Selected Letters*, trans. Albert Baca (Northridge, Calif.: San Fernando Valley State College, 1969), 1–22.

of Zürich reneged on a pact that they had formed with them, they mustered an army and marched into their territory, destroying everything in their path.[494] When the people of Zürich ventured to meet them in battle, they were massacred. Such was the brutality and savagery of the Swiss toward their defeated foes that they held a feast on the very spot where they had won the victory. They piled up the bodies of the slain to make tables and chairs, and, slitting open the corpses of the enemy, they drank their blood and tore out their hearts with their teeth.[495]

42 ALSACE, THE VOGTLAND, SAVOY, ARLES

148. IN ALSACE, which was once called Helvetia, a country formerly under French but now German rule, Louis, the dauphin of Vienne,[496] led almost the whole French army into the territory of Basel and struck great fear into the people of that city. The Swiss, in accordance with a treaty of alliance, sent four thousand soldiers drawn from the pick of their young men to reinforce the city. When the dauphin observed them approaching, he positioned himself with his whole army midway between Basel and the Swiss. The Swiss did not shrink from battle, though they had to fight on foot and could see that a line of thirty thousand horsemen stood facing them. Both sides fought with all their strength. Finally, the Swiss, less vanquished than exhausted by victory, paid the penalty for taking on too audacious a task. Except for a handful who escaped by

494. A reference to the Old Zürich War (1436–50), which arose over claims to the Toggenburg territory between Zürich, an imperial free city, and members of the Swiss Confederation; see Scott, "Germany and Empire," *CMH*, vol. 7.
495. The battle of St. Jakob an der Sihl, July 22, 1443. The burghers of Zürich were quickly routed by the Swiss confederates, who then proceeded to loot and burn the suburbs and countryside around the city. See E. Bonjour, et al., *A Short History of Switzerland* (Oxford: Clarendon Press, 1952), 115–16.
496. Louis (1423–83), later King Louis XI of France (r. 1461–83).

flight, they all lay slaughtered on the field of battle.⁴⁹⁷ Nevertheless, few of the Swiss died unavenged. Many who had been pierced with lances slipped through the rain of spears to kill an enemy and exact retribution for their wounds.

149. In Vogtland, there is a well-known city called Freiburg, which for many generations was under the control of the House of Austria. But in our time, since it owed so much money to Duke Louis of Savoy that the citizens were unable to repay it either from private or public funds, it was finally placed under the jurisdiction of the Savoyards during the reign of Frederick.⁴⁹⁸

In keeping with the fact that Vogtland marks the furthest reach of the German language, I here bring to a conclusion my discussion of German affairs. Let me next relate the deeds of France and, in particular, those of Savoy.

150. Amedeo of Savoy, the first duke of that people,⁴⁹⁹ held the rudder of state for almost forty years after his father's death. To the neighboring peoples and their rulers, he seemed admirable for having increased his father's dominions, formidable for having established peace on all sides, and filled with wisdom for having accumulated wealth.⁵⁰⁰ In the end, however, he resigned the insignia of princely glory and retreated to a hermitage, where together with six elderly men of knightly rank he donned a monk's habit,

---

497. Summoned by Frederick III to defend Zürich in 1444, Louis gathered up the unoccupied, troublesome free companies and led them to Lorraine against the bishoprics of Metz, Toul, and Verdun. Swiss troops, whose numbers may have been as small as 1,600, came out to meet his army of 30,000 near Basel on August 26 and inflicted great losses before they were annihilated. The tenacity of the Swiss was enough to move Louis to seek terms with Basel and turn aside toward Alsace; see Paul M. Kendall, *Louis XI, The Universal Spider* (New York: W.W. Norton, 1970), 57–58; Bonjour, *Switzerland*, 117.

498. Duke Louis I of Savoy (r. 1440–65); Freiburg came under the suzerainty of Savoy in 1452.

499. Reading a comma after *Sabaudia* rather than *dux*, as in van Heck. The title of duke was awarded to Amedeo in 1416.

500. An unwieldy sentence whose precise articulation is ambiguous. Other interpretations are possible.

took up a twisted staff, and renounced the world and its vanities.[501] Finally, the Council of Basel offered him the honor of the papacy during the church's schism, and he accepted it, with little approval from the powers of heaven. He shaved his beard, which he had allowed to grow long, surrendered his dukedom to his firstborn son, and quickly learned the ceremonies of the church and its forms of prayer. Then, surrounded by a large company of nobles and accompanied by a brilliant escort, he traveled to Basel, where, amidst a huge throng who had poured in from everywhere to witness this great event, and flanked by his two sons—fine-looking young men, one of whom was the duke of Savoy, the other the count of Geneva[502]—the traditional ceremony was performed, and he was crowned pontiff of the Roman Church by those who thought they made up a general council.[503] He celebrated many holy masses, blessed the people, organized the duties of the Curia, and appointed cardinals of outstanding erudition and prestige.[504]

151. Amedeo negotiated with King Charles of France, King Alfonso of Aragon (who was then an enemy of Pope Eugenius), Duke Filippo of Milan, and many others about recognizing his authority, but all to no avail.[505] Emperor Frederick also met him in Basel, but secretly and in the dead of night, so he might not seem to have worshipped an idol.[506] The only people who revered him as the vicar of Jesus Christ were his own subjects, the Swiss, the inhabitants of

---

501. Duke Amedeo VIII of Savoy (r. 1391–1440) retired to the monastery of Ripaille in 1434.

502. Louis (d. 1465) was duke of Savoy; Philip (d. 1444) was count of Geneva.

503. Understanding *se*, which Aeneas tends to omit in indirect statements; see van Heck, *De Europa*, 7.

504. The Council of Basel deposed Pope Eugenius IV and elected Amedeo as Pope Felix V in 1439; Aeneas was a witness of these events, including the coronation on July 24, 1440; initially, he was a supporter of Felix. For more on Aeneas's shifting views of conciliarism, see Emily O'Brien, *The Anatomy of an Apology: The War against Conciliarism and the Politicization of Papal Authority in the Commentarii of Pope Pius II (1458–64)*, Ph.D. diss., Brown University, 2005.

505. Charles VII, Alfonso V, Eugenius IV, Filippo Maria Visconti.

506. Felix and Frederick met privately at Basel on November 15, 1442.

Basel and Strasbourg, and those who held allegiance to Duke Albert of Bavaria. There was much hope of winning over Germany, since six prince-electors had made a pact that, unless Eugenius acceded to their demands (demands which certainly had to be denied), they would transfer their allegiance to Amedeo, whom they called Felix V. But when Frederick upset their plans and ordered the departure of those who were living in Basel under the pretext of the synod, Amedeo lost hope of a more successful outcome and, through the mediation of the envoys of King Charles of France, he restored peace to the church and was reconciled with Pope Nicholas. He relinquished the name of pope and kept the rank of cardinal, which he held until he passed away soon afterward, not without the reputation of a good man.[507] He was a fortunate[508] ruler—fortunate beyond measure, had he not besmirched his old age with ecclesiastical titles.

152. Bolomier, who had once been his principal and dearest counselor and who had amassed great wealth in his service, incurred the hatred of the nobility and was put on trial for treason. He was sentenced to death and drowned in Lake Geneva, into which he was thrown with a large rock tied to his neck.[509] In consequence, the nobility attracted the anger of the new duke and fled to the king of France, who used his influence to help them return home.

153. Juan de Segovia, a Spaniard of outstanding character and knowledge, equaled the most eminent teachers of theology in his learning and had received the distinction of the cardinalate from Amedeo, while he called himself pope. Later, he consented to the reunion, gave up the title of cardinal, and was appointed by Pope

---

507. Frederick began to withdraw his support for the council in August of 1447. Amedeo relinquished his claim to the papacy on April 7, 1449, and was named cardinal on June 18 that same year. He died in 1451.

508. Lat. *felix*, a probable pun on Amedeo's papal name, as suggested by Frank et al. in the German translation.

509. During his interrogation, Guillaume Bolomier accused another individual of treason and was executed for calumny in 1446; see *DBI*, vol. 11: 358–60.

Nicholas as head of the Church of Caesarea, where he lived in seclusion high in the mountains, content with a small monastery. Summoning teachers of Arab law from Spain, he made a new translation into our language of the book which they call the Qur'an, which contains the mysteries, or rather the ravings, of the false prophet Muhammad, and he exploded its follies with convincing and vivid arguments and proofs.[510]

154. In Arles, the tomb of Louis, cardinal of St. Cecilia and bishop of that city, whom I saw presiding over the assembly of fathers in Basel, gained a great reputation for miracles, and sick people flocked there from all quarters in the hope of a cure.[511]

43 FRANCE

155. WHEN Count Jean of Armagnac was stricken with an incestuous passion for his sister and tried to marry her, King Charles of France judged him worthy to be expelled by force from his father's inheritance.[512]

---

510. Juan de Segovia (c. 1390–1458), an ardent conciliarist, served on the committee that elected Felix V at Basel and was created cardinal in 1440 by Felix. He resigned the cardinalate in 1449 and was appointed titular bishop of Caesarea, but he retired to Aiton, France, where he collaborated with Muslim jurist Yça Gidelli on a translation of the Qur'an, which was never finished. See Ann Marie Wolf, "Precedents and Paradigms: Juan de Segovia on the Bible, the Church and the Ottoman Threat," in *Scripture and Pluralism: Reading the Bible in the Religiously Plural Worlds of the Middle Ages*, ed. Thomas Hefernan and Thomas Burman (Leiden: Brill, 2005).

511. Louis d'Aleman (c. 1390–1450), archbishop of Arles (1423) and cardinal (1426), was a reformer who supported Felix V at Basel and helped elect him, but was later reconciled with Nicholas V. He was buried at St. Trophime in Arles and was beatified in 1527; see *New Catholic Encyclopedia* (Detroit: Thomson Gale, 2003), vol. 8: 805; Alban Butler, *Butler's Lives of the Saints*, ed. Paul Burns (Collegeville, Minn: Liturgical Press, 2003), 154.

512. Count Jean V of Armagnac (r. 1450–73) fathered children with his sister Isabelle and unsuccessfully sought papal dispensations to marry her. Charles VII expelled him from France, more for political reasons than his incestuous relationship, but Louis XI allowed him to return. For more on this bizarre story and the count's later absolution by Pius himself, with heavy penance, including a promise to partake in crusade against

156. In the kingdom of France itself, it happened in our time that a young girl from Lorraine named Jeanne, following instructions from God (as they believe), dressed and armed herself like a man and took command of the French army. Fighting herself in the front ranks—miraculous to relate!—she rescued much of the kingdom from the hands of the English.[513]

157. After Duke Philip of Burgundy had put behind him the injustice of his father's death, abandoned the English, and defected to the French, major disputes and rivalries arose between King Charles and his son Louis, the dauphin of Vienne.[514] At that time, Charles of Anjou, the dauphin's uncle, held a great deal of influence with the king. Since Duke Jean of Alençon could not abide his power, and the ruler of Bourbon and his bastard brother also regarded the government of Anjou with animosity, they persuaded the dauphin to desert his father.[515] For this, they said, might prompt the king to reject Charles out of love for his son and to use better counsel in ruling the kingdom, which seemed to be going to ruin in that man's hands. The dauphin was swayed by them and left for Nevers without paying his respects to his father. When he learned of this, the king hurriedly assembled an army and led it into Alençon, where he seized numerous fortifications without much difficulty and accepted the duke's surrender. Next, he moved against his son. Since the cities of Nevers did not dare to protect the dauphin against his father's power, they asked him to leave. He then took himself to Bourbon, where shortly afterward the duke of Bourbon, in fear of

---

the Turks, see *Commentaries*, Bk IV (Gragg and Gabel, vol. 3: 315–20). See also *Nouvelle Biographie Générale* (Paris: Firmin Didot Frères, 1853–66), vol. 3: 257–59.

513. Jeanne d'Arc (c. 1412–31). For a fuller treatment by Aeneas, see *Commentaries*, Bk VI (Gragg and Gabel, vol. 4: 436–43).

514. Philip's father, John II "the Fearless" (r. 1404–19), was assassinated by a follower of the dauphin Charles, later Charles VII, king of France (r. 1422–61); Louis, dauphin of Vienne, would later become King Louis XI (r. 1461–83).

515. Charles of Anjou was Queen Marie's brother; Duke Jean II of Alençon (r. 1415–76); Duke Charles I of Bourbon (r. 1434–56); his brother Alexander was called "the bastard."

the king's wrath, reconciled the son with his father.[516] This, however, did not turn out well for his bastard brother, who was captured a little later and drowned in a river as punishment for interfering with a father's authority over his son.

158. Not much time had elapsed after this when René d'Anjou, who had been evicted from the kingdom of Sicily, married his daughter to King Henry VI of England with the approval of the king of France.[517] Through this marriage, Charles obtained a truce of several years with the English, which benefited both him and his kingdom. When this was settled, the king felt secure at home and decided to give France a respite from the plundering and arson of soldiers that had troubled it for so long by sending the dauphin with a large part of his army against the Swiss, as I related previously.[518] With the rest of the army, he himself set off for Lorraine, where he harried the territory of Metz and Toul and seized from the Church of Metz a town of some significance called Épinal, when it was surrendered by the inhabitants.

159. After this, François l'Aragonnais stealthily captured the town of Fougères in Normandy, which belonged to the duke of Brittany, and by this act appeared to have broken the peace between the two mighty kings of France and England.[519] While the matter was under discussion, and deputations were being sent back and forth, Floquet, whom the king of France had placed in command of a large troop of horsemen, concealed a body of armed men in hay wagons and ordered peasants, as instructed, to drive

---

516. This 1440 revolt against Charles (known as "La Praguerie," in reference to the Hussite uprising) was a reaction to Charles's poor conduct of the war and general misgovernment, but the conspirators also had personal goals for greater power, as Aeneas suggests. Louis was only sixteen at the time. See Kendall, *Louis XI*, 47–48.

517. René I, duke of Anjou (r. 1430–80) and king of Naples (r. 1435–42); Margaret of Anjou (1430–82) and Henry VI were married in 1445.

518. See para. 148.

519. François de Surienne of Aragon attacked the town on March 24, 1449; see John Wagner, *Encyclopedia of the Hundred Years War* (Westport, Conn.: Greenwood Press, 2006), 128–29.

them through Pont-de-l'Arche next to the Seine River (which is the boundary between France and Normandy) and halt in the middle of the bridge before the gate to the fortress. He himself remained in hiding with his troops and waited for the signal. When this had been received, and the soldiers had slipped out of the hay, they attacked the gate, butchered the guards, and held the position until Floquet rushed to the scene and took control of both the bridge and the fortress.[520] When news of this got around, King Charles personally transported forces into Normandy across the same bridge, and François, the ruler of Brittany, led an army from another direction.[521] Duke Edmund of Somerset governed this land in the name of the king of England. When he learned he was the target of such a mighty campaign, he ordered Talbot, an illustrious commander noted for his exploits, to stay with him in Rouen, hoping through his counsel and armed strength to maintain the loyalty of the city, whose mood he saw was wavering.[522] However, his plan came to nothing. For when they learned that the king was approaching, the people of Rouen sent ambassadors to him and, after bargaining for the safety of themselves and their property, promised to receive his army into the city and carry out his orders. The king commended the ambassadors and sent them home with an armed escort, whereupon the city was surrendered to him. Talbot took refuge in the citadel with the duke and all his men. When an assault on it was initiated, an agreement was reached through the intervention of King René,[523] whereby the English would vacate all the towns in Normandy that they occupied, and the duke and Talbot go free

520. Floquet was bailli and captain of Evreux; the battle at Pont-de-l'Arche took place on May 16, 1449.

521. Duke François I (r. 1442–50).

522. Edmund Beaufort (c. 1406–55) became earl of Somerset in 1444 and duke of Somerset in 1448. John Talbot (c. 1384–1453)—a much-admired soldier and general who served Henry IV, Henry V, and Henry VI—became the first earl of Shrewsbury in 1442; see Wagner, *Hundred Years' War*, 46–47; 293–94. For more on Talbot, see A. J. Pollard, *John Talbot and the War in France: 1427–1453* (London: Royal Historical Society, 1983).

523. René d'Anjou, king of Naples (r. 1435–42).

with their men. But when the governors of the towns failed to obey, the duke of Somerset abandoned Talbot and his two stepsons in the citadel and secretly returned to England. The citadel was surrendered after that, and the duke's stepsons together with Talbot fell into the hands of the king.[524] But Talbot, thanks to his excellent reputation in all quarters, which he had won not though dishonest means but in open battle through his strength and ingenuity, was allowed to go free, after giving his word that he would never again bear arms against the French.

160. This man came to Rome in the year of Jubilee [1450] to obtain the remission of his sins, though some believe it was to seek a release from the promise he had made to the king of France. I have been unable to verify this. What is certain is that, upon his return to England, when the king of France had conquered all of Normandy and also subdued Bordeaux, Talbot was sent by his king to Gascony in command of a large army and recovered Bordeaux.[525] He also stormed many other castles which had defected from English rule or retrieved them through voluntary surrender. When the king of France became aware of this, he at once equipped two armies, one of which was commanded by Count Jean of Clermont, his son-in-law and the son of the duke of Bourbon.[526] He ordered this army to march straight to the city of Bordeaux with fifteen thousand soldiers, who comprised the élite of his entire armed forces; the other one, which he led himself, was conscripted from his courtiers—among them the count of Étampes[527]—and accompanied by eight hundred hand-picked young horsemen from Brittany. Keeping the count in his own company, the king ordered this army, too, to go on before him. When they had halted seven leagues (so called) away from Bordeaux, they began to attack a small castle, after oc-

---

524. October 1449.
525. Bordeaux was recaptured by the English in October 1452; Talbot was about sixty-six years old.
526. Jean de Clermont (1426–88); duke of Bourbon, as Jean II (r. 1456–88).
527. Jean, count of Nevers and Étampes (1415–91).

cupying a certain tower located between Bordeaux and this castle and manning it with a garrison of archers. When Talbot perceived he had to fight two armies, he decided to attack first the one which he was confident of overcoming with less difficulty.[528] Therefore, when evening had fallen, he emerged with the flower of his army and approached the tower whose occupation I have described. This he stormed in the first assault and killed all the archers captured there—about fifty in number. When he left there in the morning and heard that the king's army was preparing to flee, he was afraid that his prey would slip through his fingers, as it were. Without delay, he ordered the others to follow him and, accompanied by five hundred helmeted soldiers and eight hundred archers, dashed on ahead toward the enemy and entered into a makeshift battle. For some time, the enemy had discussed among themselves whether they should take to flight, but they felt ashamed in the king's presence and had decided to try their luck in battle. They had about three hundred bronze cannon, which they had brought with them on carriages, and these they pointed toward the road by which Talbot was expected to arrive; they also positioned many artillery pieces on both sides of the road, to decimate the enemy before they knew what was happening.

Knowing nothing of the artillery, Talbot's soldiers made a wild charge down the only road that gave access to the enemy's camp, and, when the cannon were fired, almost three hundred of the English perished from the bombardment in the initial encounter. When he observed this, Talbot urged his son, who had accompanied him, to leave and preserve himself for better times.[529] But when his son replied that he could not flee from a battle in which his father was about to risk his life, Talbot replied: "My son, thanks to my many illustrious feats, I can neither die without glory nor flee without

---

528. The following account refers to the Battle of Castillon, July 17, 1453.

529. Talbot's son, John, viscount of Lisle. The following description can also be seen in Shakespeare's *Henry VI, Part I*; see Pollard, *Talbot*, 3.

disgrace. You, however, are beginning your military career, and neither will flight discredit you nor death bring you fame." When the son's sense of filial duty prevailed over his father's advice, Talbot exhorted his comrades to take courage and renew the battle. Forming a *testudo*,[530] he bravely attacked the enemy, who had never ventured outside the fortifications of their camp, and wreaked great slaughter upon them. However, the enemy held the upper hand, owing partly to their position, partly to their artillery and numbers. After Talbot's leg had been smashed with a cannon-ball and most of his men had been killed, he too finally collapsed and fell with his two sons—one legitimate [John], the other born out of wedlock—and one of his sons-in-law.[531] Such was the end of this celebrated man, who had won so many victories over the enemy; it was principally the determination and daring of the Bretons which brought him down. Bordeaux again reverted to the king's control.

161. They say that the duke of Brittany, the brother of the man who now holds power, was unable to produce offspring for a long time and made a vow that, if heaven should grant him sons, he would consecrate the first two to religious orders, one to the Friars Minor [Franciscans], the other to the Preachers [Dominicans]. When his prayers were answered, he named his first-born son François, the second Dominique.[532] A third son was also born to him, whom he sent to England to be raised. When his father died, he returned to Brittany during the rule of François and was arrested by him and put to death in prison.[533] The story goes that when he was handed over to be killed, he condemned the sacrilege of his brother,

---

530. See note in para. 38.

531. The other, illegitimate, son who fought at Castillon may have been Henry Talbot or Sir John Ripley; see Pollard, *Talbot*, 61, 115.

532. Duke Jean V of Brittany (r. 1399–1442). His first two sons were François I (r. 1442–50) and Pierre II (not Dominique) (r. 1450–57).

533. This son, Gilles (d. 1450), was a personal friend of Henry VI of England and forcefully advocated for the English cause. He was arrested and executed for allegedly spying for the English. See *Nouvelle Biographie Générale*, vol. 18: 500–503.

who, not content with usurping his kingdom, was wicked enough to deprive him of his life as well; he summoned François to appear before the tribunal of God within a year to answer for the murder of his kin. And so, when François fell ill from dropsy and died within the specified time, he was commonly believed—the French being a God-fearing nation—to have been punished by divine judgment. Dominique [i.e., Pierre] took his place, and when he died this very year without children, he was succeeded by his uncle Arthur, commander of the French army, a man respected for his wisdom no less than his military prowess.[534]

162. Duke Charles of Orléans, who had once been captured by the English in a great battle, was sent home in his old age and, on the death of Filippo Maria, adorned himself with the titles belonging to the dukedom of Milan, as if it was owed to him by virtue of succession.[535]

44 GHENT

163. IN FLANDERS, the people of Ghent revolted against Duke Philip of Burgundy and were defeated in several battles. In the end, after losing over twenty thousand of their citizens in one battle, they admitted their error, surrendered to Philip, and accepted the victor's terms.[536] The same Philip, not without provoking the ire of King Ladislas [Postumus], also seized the very large and well-fortified town of Luxembourg, which had come under Saxon rule by way of a dowry.[537]

---

534. Duke Arthur III (r. 1457–58) was constable of France when he succeeded his nephew in Brittany.

535. Duke Charles (r. 1407–65) was the son of Filippo Maria Visconti's sister, Valentina. He was captured at Agincourt (1415) and claimed Milan in 1447 but never gained possession of it.

536. The Ghent War of 1449–53; the last and greatest battle, mentioned here, was at Gavere, July 23, 1453.

537. Philip conquered Luxembourg in 1443. Prior to that, it was ruled by the house

164. When the dauphin of Vienne tried to murder a strikingly beautiful woman called Agnes who was loved by his father, he once again incurred the king's wrath, and since he thought he would be safe nowhere else, he fled for refuge to the court of the rich and powerful Philip.[538] As soon as he met Philip, the dauphin said, "Have mercy on me, kinsman. Although I am the son of a king, I am without a country." Philip replied, "As long as I have a country, do not say you lack for one. For the lands that are subject to me are yours too, and I desire them to obey you no less than me." After this, he showed him the prosperous towns of Brabant and the proud cities of Flanders, and ordered him to be addressed as lord and prince in his presence.[539]

45 ENGLAND

165. I HAVE reached a place from which the crossing to England is very short, for the sea which flows between Flanders and England is no more than thirty miles wide. Now that I have completed my account of France, it would be fitting to cross the sea and record as briefly as possible the changes that took place in England, once named Britain, during the reign of Frederick.

In England, which the ancients sometimes called Albion, sometimes Britain, Henry, desiring solitude and leisure, governed the kingdom more through the judgment of others than his own.[540]

---

of Luxembourg, including Ladislas's father, Albert II, and brother-in-law, Wilhelm of Saxony.

538. Agnes Sorel (c. 1422–50), the acknowledged mistress of Charles VII from 1444. She died of dysentery shortly after giving birth to her fourth child; some contemporaries claimed that Louis had her poisoned. Charles himself may have suspected Louis and a member of the royal council, Jacques Coeur, who assisted Louis in various ways. A more likely source of tension between father and son was Louis's marriage to Charlotte of Savoy against Charles's wishes in 1451. See Kendall, *Louis XI*, 74–75.

539. See Kendall, *Louis XI*, chap. 8, on the dour and socially maladroit Louis's stay at the glittering Burgundian court in 1456–57.

540. King Henry VI (r. 1422–61 and 1470–71).

Duke William of Suffolk held influence with him and was the one to whom he listened above all others. This man imposed laws arbitrarily on the people and the nobility, suppressing those whom he hated and, in turn, elevating those he loved.⁵⁴¹ But when the fortunes of England had begun to wane in France, and French power was rising to its former glory, Duke Richard of York conscripted a substantial force and, accompanied by many barons, came to London to change the king's policy and, so he said, to protect the interests of the king and the kingdom. The duke of Suffolk did not wait for his arrival but swiftly commandeered a ship and attempted to save himself by fleeing down the Thames River. But who can escape one's destined end? Those who were sent to arrest him headed off his escape by taking shortcuts, and, after intercepting him, slaughtered him then and there on the prow of the ship that was carrying him.⁵⁴² The duke of Somerset, too, who had come back to England after the loss of Normandy and was thought to hold influence with the king, was thrown into prison.⁵⁴³ A good many noblemen were murdered, and no mercy was shown to those in holy orders, including my friend Adam de Moleyns, keeper of the king's secret seal and a literary scholar, who was beheaded and lay mutilated on the ground.⁵⁴⁴ Not long afterward, when the duke of York had returned home, the duke of Somerset was released from

541. William de la Pole (1396–1450) became earl of Suffolk in 1415 and the first duke of Suffolk in 1448. In 1429 he was taken prisoner by Jeanne d'Arc's forces. He was a royal councillor in the 1430s and 1440s; see Wagner, *Hundred Years War*, 259–60.

542. Richard, the third duke of York (r. 1415–60), the father of kings Edward IV and Richard III. De la Pole fell into disgrace when he was blamed for the loss of Normandy. Parliament impeached him and he was accused of corruption and treason in 1450; the king dismissed the charge of treason, but ordered him into exile, whereupon his ship was attacked, likely on Duke Richard's orders; see Wagner, *Hundred Years War*, 260.

543. Edmund Beaufort, duke of Somerset (r. 1448–55), was King Henry's cousin. As one of the commanding officers of Normandy, he surrendered Rouen in 1449 and Caen in 1450. Labeled a traitor by Duke Richard of York, he was imprisoned in the Tower from 1453–54 while Richard was Lord Protector.

544. Adam de Moleyns (or Molins), bishop of Chichester, was killed in 1450 by rioting soldiers whom he had come to pay. He was a friend and correspondent of Aeneas; see Izbicki at al., *Reject Aeneas*, 151–52.

prison and began to govern the kingdom with the king's permission. This was the cause of his final downfall. For the duke of York was provoked by this and hastened to London with more troops than before. When the king came out to meet him with the duke of Somerset, expecting to placate him with seductive words or deter him by the weight of royal majesty, he got nowhere. For, being far more powerful, the duke of York, after ordering the king to withdraw to the side, rushed upon the duke of Somerset and his cavalry, took him prisoner, and beheaded him on the spot.[545]

46 SCOTLAND, IRELAND

166. SCOTLAND is the farthest tip of the island that contains England; it faces north and is separated from England by rivers of no great size and a mountain range. I was there in the winter, when the sun lit the earth for little more than three hours a day.[546] At that time the king was James, a stocky man weighed down by a fat paunch. He had once been captured in England and spent eleven years in custody. When he was finally released, he took an English wife and returned home, where he executed a good number of chieftains and was finally assassinated himself by members of his own household. After taking revenge on them, his son succeeded to the throne.[547]

167. I had heard that in Scotland there was once a tree grow-

---

545. This battle at St. Albans (May 22, 1455) marked the beginning of the Wars of the Roses.

546. In late 1435 Aeneas traveled from Basel to the court of King James I in Scotland on a mission to persuade the king to assist the French in the Hundred Years' War by raiding in northern England. He spent several months in Scotland and England.

547. King James I (r. 1406–37) was captured by English sailors in 1406 at age 12. He was educated in England where he met and married Joan Beaufort, Henry VI's cousin, in 1423. In 1427 he returned to Scotland but was killed in a coup led by Walter Stewart, earl of Atholl, in 1437. The conspirators were defeated and the king's son, James II (r. 1437–60), was put on the throne. For more on James and Scotland, see Jenny Wormald, "Scotland: 1406–1513," *CMH*, vol. 7: 514–31.

ing on the bank of a river which produced fruits shaped like ducks. When these were nearly ripe, they dropped down of their own accord, some onto the earth, and some into the water. Those that landed on the earth rotted away, but those that sank into the water instantly came to life, swam out from below the water, and immediately flew off into the air, equipped with feathers and wings. When I eagerly investigated this matter, I learned that miracles always recede further into the distance and that the famous tree was to be found not in Scotland but in the Orkney islands.

Nevertheless, I did witness the following wonder in Scotland. I noticed that semi-naked paupers who were begging outside churches went away happily after receiving stones as alms. This kind of stone, which is loaded with sulfur or some other rich substance, is burned for fuel instead of wood, which the region lacks altogether.

168. I ought now to deal with Ireland, which is divided from Britain by a narrow strait. Part of it is independent and enjoys friendship and alliance with the Scots, whereas part is subject to English rule. However, since I have heard of nothing memorable that was done during the era with which this treatise is concerned, I hasten on to the affairs of Spain.

47 SPAIN, CASTILE, NAVARRE, PORTUGAL

169. THE HUGE expanse of Spain, a land powerful in men and arms which bears comparison with the very best, is distributed among five kings at the present time. They call the king of Castile the first and greatest of these; next to him, the king of Aragon; in third place, the king of Portugal; in fourth, the king of Navarre; the king of Granada, because it rejects[548] the Gospel of Christ, is placed last.

---

548. Or "which rejects" (understanding *quod* [*regnum*]). Either interpretation involves a grammatical difficulty.

Spain, Castile, Navarre, Portugal 213

170. In Castile, a renowned kingdom with far-flung dominions, whose kings spring from the blood of the Goths and have never varied their stock,[549] Álvaro de Luna, an Aragonese by race and a man of noble birth, though born out of wedlock, once wormed his way so deeply into the favor of King Juan that he alone seemed to wield power over the kingdom and the king.[550] When King Juan of Navarre and Enrique, master of the Military Order of Santiago,[551] tried to impose their own power and govern the kingdom, Álvaro forcibly drove them off. Later, however, when the queen[552] turned against him, they returned and gained control over the king. Álvaro was expelled from the court and lived for some time as a private individual on his estates—a fortunate man, if only he had known how to enjoy the leisure afforded him! But there is no peace for those deposed from power. And so, in an attempt to win back his lofty position, from which he would be hurled again with even greater ruin, he secretly persuaded the king to come out to the woodlands near his home on the pretext of hunting. He said that he would come to meet him with a powerful force and that beyond doubt the nobles of the kingdom would assert the king's freedom. It was not hard to persuade him. The king went out with a few men, inadequately guarded because the name of Álvaro had been almost forgotten, and came to the place of ambush, where Álvaro, raising

549. Aeneas makes this same assertion about Alfonso of Aragon in para. 275. It is noteworthy given Aeneas's harsh comments about the Goths as pillagers of Rome in other writings. Perhaps his recent familiarity with Jordanes's *History of the Goths* had improved his opinion of them; see R. J. Mitchell, *The Laurels and the Tiara: Pope Pius II 1458–64* (London: Harvill Press, 1962), 264.
550. King Juan II of Castile-León (r. 1406–54). Luna (c. 1390–1453) was a court favorite who proved an able administrator and exercised great influence over Juan from a young age.
551. Juan and Enrique were sons of Ferdinand I of Aragon (and brothers of Alfonso V). Juan married Blanca of Navarre and became king–consort in 1425; he became king of Aragon on Alfonso's death, ruling as Juan II (1458–79). Enrique (d. 1445) was master of the Order of Santiago (de Compostela). Juan was a strong guiding presence behind young King Juan of Castile; Enrique vied for control over the king as well. See Thomas Bisson, *The Medieval Crown of Aragon: A Short History* (Oxford: Clarendon Press, 1986).
552. Isabella of Portugal.

a shout and exulting in the midst of his picked soldiers, hailed the king as a free man and took him away with him. As soon as news of this spread abroad, an amazing turnabout of power took place, and for a second time the government of the kingdom devolved upon Álvaro. Not long after this, a terrible battle was fought with the same Juan and Enrique, in which many perished on both sides, and victory fell to Álvaro. Enrique died a few days later as a result of a wound in the hand which he had received in the battle. Álvaro took over his mastership [of Santiago] and for some time afterward was looked upon as the father of the king and the governor of the kingdom.[553] In the end, however, he fell victim to strong resentment. For when he ordered a certain nobleman to be thrown from the window of his house for bringing him a displeasing message under orders of the king, he was arrested and condemned to death in the center of the marketplace. However, he did not die like a coward. After enumerating his meritorious services to the king and the realm, he offered his neck to the sword neither weeping nor wailing, but with an eager expression, as if he had been invited to a banquet—a man of proud spirit, famous in peace no less than in war, whose mind was always fixed upon great designs.

171. For some years, Juan then governed the kingdom by himself.[554] When he passed away, his son Enrique ascended the throne—a zealous young man with a hunger for rectitude. After leaving his first wife because she was infertile, he took another from Portugal, the sister of the empress [Eleonora], and marching with an army into the kingdom of Granada, he plundered and destroyed a large part of the enemy's territory.[555]

553. Luna rescued Juan from rebel nobles, including Enrique, in 1420. He was appointed constable in 1423. Ousted from power in 1427 and 1438, Luna regained his position both times.

554. Actually only for a year after Luna's death—Juan II of Castile-León died in 1454.

555. Enrique IV, "the Impotent" (r. 1454–74), took Juana of Portugal as his second wife. After doubts arose about the paternity of Juana's children, he was forced by the nobles to name Isabella I his heir; she took the throne in 1474 with her husband

Spain, Castile, Navarre, Portugal 215

In this kingdom [Castile], where he was born, Cardinal Juan of Ostia, a man of the highest integrity and an eminent authority on the law, whom I myself as a young man assisted in the drafting of letters, gave up his soul to God, enfeebled by old age.[556]

In the kingdom of Navarre, a son took up arms against his father and father against son. At length, the son was driven from the kingdom and, after traveling through France, took refuge with his uncle Alfonso V, king of Aragon and Sicily. Alfonso dispatched two exceptional men, Luis (master of Montesa) and Juan Ferrandez, who are now striving to reconcile the son with his father.[557] Joanna [i.e., "Maria"], the sister and wife[558] of King Alfonso, for many years during her husband's absence held jurisdiction in the kingdoms of Aragon and Valencia, over so many powerful cities, and so many rulers of the highest nobility—a pure and saintly woman, who deserved to bear children to Alfonso.

172. In Portugal, Pedro, titled the Infante (for that is what the king's sons are called before they reign), a ruler of great repute, who had traveled through almost all of Europe giving proofs of his virtue, governed the realm for some time in the capacity of guardian—to the highest acclaim. Just as faithfully, he restored it to Afonso, his nephew on his brother's side, who was also his son-in-law. Finally, however, quarrels arose on both sides, and, as their

---

Ferdinand II of Aragon. Enrique's raid near the city of Granada (1455) has been characterized as weak and half-hearted. Pope Calixtus III and Pius II himself would later suspect him of misusing crusade funds. See John Edwards, "Reconquista and Crusade in Fifteenth-Century Spain," in Housley, *Crusading in the Fifteenth Century*, 163–81.

556. Juan Cervantes, bishop of Ostia and cardinal of San Pietro in Vincoli (d. 1453), whom Aeneas met at the Council of Basel. Cervantes was born and died in Seville.

557. Carlos of Viana, Juan of Navarre's oldest son, attempted to seize control of Navarre, while his father ruled Aragon for Alfonso. Carlos visited both Charles VII of France and his uncle Alfonso in 1456–57 seeking their aid. Alfonso allowed him to live comfortably in exile in Naples while he sent Luis Despuig and Juan Ferrandez de Hijar, his majordomo, to negotiate a truce; see Ryder, *Alfonso*, 422–23.

558. *Soror et coniunx*—a Virgilian reference to Juno (*Aeneid*, 1.47). Alfonso's wife, Maria (not Joanna), was his first cousin (d. 1458). She governed Aragon in Alfonso's frequent and long absences and produced no children.

hatred grew, it ended in warfare.⁵⁵⁹ Pedro was pierced by a random arrow and perished—a man of great achievements, who had once served under Emperor Sigismund and won for himself no small glory fighting the Turks.⁵⁶⁰

173. Afonso, a most civilized leader, high-minded, and blessed with remarkable wisdom (for the royal blood of Portugal has never been passed on to fools), ruled peacefully after this. When his dearly beloved wife, who was also his cousin, passed away, he could not be persuaded to take another to replace her. His whole attention was directed instead toward doing something that would win praise for himself and benefit the Christian religion. He therefore summoned the nobles of his kingdom and, after publicly receiving the sign of the cross, pledged a fleet and expeditionary force against the Turks.⁵⁶¹

48 ITALY: GENOA

174. NOW THAT I have traversed the furthest bounds of Europe and covered as much of the north as I had planned, I finally return to my homeland. Since I am faced with the task of recording new developments in Italy, I think I should certainly begin with the city whose constant revolutions are an object of amazement to both East and West.

559. Pedro the Infante, regent of Portugal (r. 1438–48) for Afonso V, was an able ruler who strove to balance competing noble and municipal interests in the kingdom while taking steps to centralize royal power. See Armindo De Sousa, "Portugal," *CMH*, vol. 7: 639–41.

560. Pedro served Sigismund from 1426–28; see Francis Rogers, *The Quest for Eastern Christians: Travels and Rumor in the Age of Discovery* (Minneapolis: University of Minnesota Press, 1962), 55.

561. Despite the promise Aeneas saw in Afonso V (r. 1438–81), he ultimately demonstrated little of his uncle's prudence and devoted most of his time and resources both to crusading in North Africa (which complicated trade relations) and to pursuing a claim to the throne of Castile, which ultimately proved futile; see De Sousa, "Portugal," 641–42.

175. This is Genoa, the mistress and queen of the Ligurians, which within our memory was racked by civil strife and lost command of the sea. In Genoa, after the expulsion of Duke Filippo of Milan and the murder of his governor, Opicino Alciati, eight Captains of Liberty were appointed on the initiative of Francesco Spinola.[562] When the loss of liberty led to their ejection a short while later, Isnardo Guarco,[563] a man of over seventy years, accepted the dogeship at the suggestion of Tommaso Fregoso, who had himself once held the office of doge before the domination of Filippo. Since a man of such advanced age seemed unfit to govern, Guarco was allowed to rule for barely seven days, when Tommaso robbed him of his office.[564] When Tommaso had governed for four years, his brother Battista deposed him—for about sixteen hours. For Tommaso, recovering his strength, quickly expelled his brother from the palace and subsequently ruled the city for three years and a few months until the city again claimed its liberty at the prompting of Gianantonio Fieschi.[565] In the former manner, eight captains were selected to govern the state, who threw Tommaso Fregoso into prison, having now served three times as doge of his native city. Their leaders were the aforementioned Gianantonio, a soldier of knightly rank,[566] and Raffaele Adorno, a jurist.[567]

176. But this freedom, too, lasted only a few months, since the

562. The Genoese were under Milanese domination from 1421–35. They revolted and murdered the Milanese governor on December 27, 1435, partly in reaction to Filippo Maria Visconti's sudden generosity toward Alfonso and the Aragonese cause after Genoa's role in capturing him at the battle of Ponza. See para. 178.

563. Guarco was elected doge March 28, 1436; he was deposed in one week. See Stephen Epstein, *Genoa and the Genoese 958–1528* (Chapel Hill: University of North Carolina Press, 1996) for dates and details on the doges and various conspiracies in this section.

564. Tommaso Fregoso was first elected doge in 1415. He became doge again on April 3, 1436, after deposing Guarco with the support of other nobles. He presided over a lavish court and patronized humanists but was known to be harsh.

565. Fregoso was deposed in December 1442 but was soon allowed to retire to his family's estates in Sarzana.

566. Gianantonio Fieschi (c. 1400–47) was later executed on suspicion of treason.

567. Elected doge January 28, 1443. Adorno abdicated January 4, 1447.

title of captain appealed less to Raffaele than that of doge. After securing the support of his own kindred and the leading men of the Spinolas, he deposed his colleagues from the magistracy and assumed the insignia of doge. He enjoyed these for a little over two years, when he was ousted from the government by his kinsman and cousin, Barnabò.[568] But Barnabò completed not even a month as ruler before Giano Fregoso, with the support of Gianantonio Fieschi and the Doria family, drove him from power.[569] Soon after that, in payment for the service he had received from Gianantonio, Giano arranged his death, employing his kinsman Giovanni Filippo to strike him down and rewarding him with the dead man's castles. Giano himself died in office, after ruling for a little more than two years, and was succeeded by his brother Ludovico, who was thrown from his exalted position by his cousin Piero.[570] This is the Piero Fregoso who has ruled with such mental and physical vigor in recent times, though despised by the magnates of the city and by almost the whole nobility. Because he suspected that his kinsman and cousin Niccolò Fregoso, an honorable man noted for his philosophical studies, aspired to become ruler, he invited him to the palace for a visit and had him assassinated in a prepared ambush.[571] When he had ruled for four years at the head of both his own and other noble families, he was driven from the city, and his cousin Ludovico, whom he himself had previously deposed, was appointed in his place. When Ludovico realized he was unacceptable to the magnates, he sent for the same Piero, whom he had ousted from power, to assist him. On the third day after returning from exile, Piero removed his cousin from his position as doge

---

568. Barnabò Adorno, elected doge in January 1447.

569. Giano Fregoso was elected doge on Jan. 30, 1447.

570. Giano Fregoso d. December 1448; Ludovico Fregoso, elected doge December 1448; Piero Fregoso, elected Dec. 8, 1450.

571. Niccolò Fregoso (c. 1410–52) was trained in the humanities by Giovanni Toscanella and elevated to captain general of Genoa in 1450. He attended Frederick III's coronation in Rome in 1452, where he likely met Aeneas.

and expelled all his enemies from the city. Their leaders turned to the flourishing court of Alfonso, king of Aragon and Sicily, and obtained from him a large and formidable fleet, with which they have now pressured Genoa by land and sea for almost two years. They often reached the city walls, and some fighting occurred within the suburbs. This year, however, when the signal for attack was given, the fighting erupted everywhere, both in the harbor and in front of the city walls.[572] The Aragonese gained entry and routed the doge's soldiers throughout a large part of the city, defiling it far and wide with slaughter and pillage. But Piero came to the rescue with a select force of young men. He compelled his fleeing soldiers to make a stand and, by slipping in among the Aragonese, inflicted great destruction and retrieved the city from the brink of capture. However, it would have been all over for him if the enemy had fully secured the gate which they had captured, so it could not be closed again from above, and thus kept the entrance open for the naval allies coming behind them. Now both sides are making virtually a new start in their preparations for war, though there is a rumor that Piero is discouraged and begging the French for assistance, with the intention of selling the dogeship to their king, since he is unable to retain it for himself.[573]

49   ITALY: MILAN

177. AMONG the northern Italians and in the world-famous city of Milan, Duke Filippo Maria, who had once brought Genoa beneath his sway, married the daughter of Duke Amedeo of Savoy.[574]

---

572. Probably a reference to the assault on Genoa by Genoese exiles and Aragonese forces on Christmas Day, 1457; see Ryder, *Alfonso*, 403. See also para. 271 for further discussion of these battles.

573. Genoa submitted to King Charles VII of France in May 1458.

574. Duke Filippo Maria Visconti of Milan (r. 1412–47) married Maria of Savoy (d. 1469) in 1428.

178. Filippo defeated the mighty King Alfonso in a naval battle, together with his two brothers—one the king of Navarre, the other master of the Military Order of Compostela—and many other lesser rulers. When Alfonso was taken prisoner and brought before him, Filippo, with extraordinary generosity, presented him with splendid gifts and gave him his freedom.[575]

179. Filippo did not deign to visit Emperor Sigismund when he was staying in Milan on his way to Rome.[576] He delivered Bologna, Forlì, and Imola from the hands of tyrants and restored them to the holy Church of Rome.[577] He subdued in war the savage nation of the Swiss.[578] He frequently triumphed over the Florentines and Venetians through the agency of his captains and once caused all Italy to tremble. Then, as his fortunes waned, he lost Genoa, his highly trusted general Niccolò Piccinino died, and his army was routed and stripped of its camp by enemy forces led by Micheletto da Cotignola at Casalmaggiore near the Po River, where a large number of horsemen and foot soldiers were captured.[579] All of which made him a figure of contempt not only to the Venetians but to all the communities and rulers surrounding him. Indeed, after crossing

575. In an attempt to seize the port of Gaeta, and ultimately full control of the kingdom of Naples, King Alfonso V of Aragon (r. 1416–58) and his brothers, Juan and Enrique (see para. 170), were captured at the Battle of Ponza (Aug. 4, 1435). After the battle, Alfonso was delivered to Visconti, who soon agreed to become his ally.

576. Sigismund stayed in Milan in 1432 and received the ceremonial iron crown of Lombardy. Filippo, at this point, avoided public appearances; Cecilia Ady, *A History of Milan under the Sforza* (London: Methuen and Co., 1907), 15.

577. Probably a reference to two moments: the first, Filippo's (temporary) restitution of Imola and Forlì to the papacy in 1427; the second was Filippo's act of selling the liberties of Bologna to the papacy in late 1441, a move made possible by the presence of his condottiere Niccolò Piccinino in the city as a protector against the anti-Bentivoglio faction. See Cecilia Ady, *The Bentivoglio of Bologna: A Study in Despotism* (London: Oxford University Press, 1937), 17–22; *DBI*, vol. 68: 707. Thanks to Jane Black for help on this question.

578. Reference to the Battle of Delebrio in the Valtellina (1432).

579. Niccolò Piccinino, one of the leading condottieri of Renaissance Italy, died on Oct. 15, 1444; Micheletto Attendolo da Cotignola (c. 1390–1451), a soldier of fortune and Francesco Sforza's uncle, was fighting on behalf of Venice at the time. The battle of Casalmaggiore took place on September 28, 1446.

the Adda River and encamping in the territory of Milan, the Venetians struck such terror into him that he thought of relinquishing power. He sought reinforcements from kings on both sides of the Alps, but the same man whom all thought worthy of honor and applause when he enjoyed good fortune and was trampling on his foes was abandoned by everyone in his hour of crisis, as if he deserved to be hated. Alfonso alone, remembering the kindness he had received from him, prepared to bring assistance.

180. His expedition was too late, however, for in the meantime Filippo first lost his eyesight through poor health and then, after suffering the severe shock of hearing the crash of the enemy's artillery from his own citadel, he passed away, weary of life and exhausted, having named Alfonso his heir.[580]

181. A man of large physique, Filippo was lean in his youth, extremely fat in old age; he had an ugly and frightening face, eyes which were shifting and enormous, and an acute and clever mind. He was lavish in spending, lax in saving money; difficult to approach but, once he had entered into conversation, mild-mannered and agreeable; neglectful of grooming, elegance, and all personal embellishment; and passionate for hunting and devoted to horses. Impatient of repose and avid for the exercise of power, he looked for war in peacetime and for peace in war. He was a first-rate master of both simulation and dissimulation and more indulgent toward soldiers than civilians. He rarely appeared in public and was quick to believe informers. So prone was he to suspicion that he often renounced his truest friends for the most trivial reasons. He was reluctant to allow people dressed in mourning to approach him, unwilling to hear talk about death, and astonishingly fearful of thunder and lightning. He ordered those who were stricken with

---

580. As Aeneas states in the next paragraph, Filippo's will was destroyed immediately after his death. Whatever claims circulated as part of his last will and testament were forgeries. See Jane Black, *Absolutism in Renaissance Milan* (Oxford: Oxford University Press, 2009), 78.

the wasting disease to move out of the cities into the countryside and their homes to be burned; through these precautions he kept the innumerable population of Milan largely untouched by that plague for many years.[581]

When he departed from this life, he received a funeral unworthy of so great a leader and his ancestors, and he was not honored with a tomb.[582] When they learned of the duke's death, the people proclaimed themselves free and elected twelve men to govern the state.[583] The castle of Porta Giovia, which resembled a magnificent palace, was seized and demolished, and Filippo's will was ripped to shreds.

182. Many yearned to rule Milan but only four had plausible claims. Emperor Frederick contended that rule had fallen to him because Filippo had died without legitimate children;[584] Alfonso claimed the inheritance on the strength of the will; Duke Charles of Orléans, who came from the blood of the Visconti,[585] said that the dukedom rightly belonged to him in the absence of a will; and Francesco Sforza-Visconti asserted that his wife, Filippo's daughter, should be recognized as her father's heir.[586] The deputations

---

581. Piero Candido Decembrio relates similar stories in his biography of Visconti (1447) and may have been a source for Aeneas; see *Vita di Filippo Maria Visconti*, translated into Italian by Elio Bartolini (Milan: Adelphi Edizioni, 1983).

582. Visconti died on August 13, 1447. Described by Lauro Martines as "bungling and terribly secretive," he was not mourned by the Milanese, who had not seen the recluse for fifteen years but felt the heavy burden of his wars and taxes; see *Power and Imagination: City-States in Renaissance Italy* (1979. Reprint. Baltimore: Johns Hopkins University Press, 1988), 140–41.

583. The Ambrosian Republic was formed on August 14, 1447—one day after Visconti died. Its chief governing body was the Consiglio delle Provvisioni, comprised of a vicar and twelve councillors.

584. Milan was, at least in theory, a vassal state of the Holy Roman Empire.

585. Charles of Orléans claimed Milan as Visconti's nephew; see para. 162.

586. Better known as Francesco Sforza (1401–66), duke of Milan as of 1450. He married Bianca Maria Visconti, the illegitimate daughter of Filippo Maria, in 1441. For more on Aeneas's relationship with Sforza before and after his election as pope, see Marcello Simonetta, "Pius II and Francesco Sforza. The History of Two Allies," in *Pius II, 'El Più Expeditivo Pontifice,'* ed. Zweder von Martels and Arjo Vanderjagt (Leiden: Brill, 2003), 147–70.

of all were heard in the senate of Milan. Some sought dominion in unambiguous terms, whereas others, under the pretence of offering help against the Venetians, strove to worm their way into the people's favor and claim dominion bit by bit. But the city, which was now rejoicing in its liberty and whose desire to exercise power had prompted it to hire the army of the dead duke, assented to no conditions which seemed in any way to place a yoke over the citizens' heads. However, it offered the emperor the annual tribute of a golden goblet, provided it was allowed to remain free under its own laws. Meanwhile, the legacy of Filippo was systematically torn to pieces. The Venetians occupied Piacenza, Crema, Lodi, and many other smaller towns. Duke Louis of Savoy seized Valence and Conflans;[587] the people of Asti defected to Duke Charles of Orléans and, after receiving large reinforcements from the king of France, began to harass the territory of Alessandria; the people of Pavia, who were racked by internal divisions, were for a long time undecided about which side to join; the peoples of Novara, Como, Alessandria, and Tortona accepted the rule of Milan; the people of Parma were admitted into an alliance of some sort.

183. During this time, Francesco Sforza was operating in the Marches,[588] although by now he had lost most of that region. Not long before he died, Filippo was reconciled with him through mutual friends and invited him back to fight against the Venetians, having asked King Alfonso to pay him in his own name the sum of seventy thousand gold pieces. When this had been done, and the troops assembled and equipped, Francesco had just gotten ready for the journey when the news of Filippo's death drove him to double his pace, for he had long coveted the wealth of Milan. As soon as he entered Lombardy, the people of Milan, uncertain of his intentions, sent spokesmen and hired his services through the offer of a large

---

587. Louis of Savoy claimed Milan through his sister, who was Filippo Maria Visconti's widow.

588. Aeneas uses the classical term *Picenum* for this region.

stipend to prevent him from opposing their own initiatives, either on his own or in league with the Venetians. And as soon as they had appointed him commander of their army, they ordered him to besiege Piacenza with all his forces.[589] He obeyed their word, and while laying siege to Piacenza, he received the surrender of the people of Pavia, who had now rejected the rule of Milan, finding it haughty and overbearing.[590] This greatly perturbed the minds of the Milanese, who said that Francesco was prohibited by their agreements from occupying any of the cities which Filippo had held. Francesco, however, said that he had not occupied the city but only received its voluntary surrender. Since they feared his power, the Milanese decided it was best to turn a blind eye. Francesco continued the siege of Piacenza and finally launched an all-out assault on the city. Although it was defended by a large and courageous troop of soldiers, he took it by storm and sacked it.[591]

184. At this time, the government of Milan was in the hands of the nobles and Filippo's former counselors. As a result, the state was faring prosperously under the direction of wise men, and a considerable force of Frenchmen which had crossed the Alps—about three thousand select horsemen—had been routed and destroyed at Alessandria.[592] The Venetians, too, had been overcome in a great battle at Caravaggio and lost almost all their troops, and Lodi, which had

---

589. The new government of Milan hired Filippo's condottiere, Sforza, to deal with the cities that revolted after Visconti's death. Information and dates in the notes to the following section were largely drawn from Ady, *Milan under the Sforza* and *Storia di Milano* (Milan: Fondazione Treccani degli Alfieri per la storia di Milano, 1953–66), vols. 6–7.

590. Pavia offered itself to Sforza on Aug. 17, 1447.

591. The sack of Piacenza, which began in Nov. 1447 and stretched into December by some accounts, was thorough and violent. Although Sforza has been credited for his attempts to protect women and children by guarding hospitals and monasteries, Francesco Filelfo, for one, decried the atrocities in the *Sforziad*; see Diana Robin, *Filelfo in Milan* (Princeton, N.J.: Princeton University Press, 1991), 67 ff; Ady, *Milan under the Sforza*, 42.

592. Milanese forces commanded by condottiere Bartolomeo Colleoni won a victory at Alessandria in October 1447.

Italy: Milan 225

been snatched from their control, had fallen again beneath the sway of the Milanese.[593] At this juncture, Francesco Sforza, who had been sent to harass the people of Brescia, entered preemptively into a treaty with the Venetians,[594] either because he anticipated that this was the only way to achieve the leadership of Milan, which he had dreamed of for so long, or because he thought it necessary to forestall the Milanese, who were seeking friendship and alliance with the Venetians behind his back, so as not to be left in isolation for both peoples to prey upon. In addition to many other promises on both sides, it was agreed that the senate of Venice would help Francesco with money and arms when he set out with his forces to win control over the city of Milan. When the pact was confirmed, he marched at once into Milanese territory.[595] The Bracceschi were serving on the side of the Milanese at the time, but, after routing Luigi dal Verme and some other troops of Francesco at Monza, they eventually deserted the Milanese and defected to Francesco.[596] Francesco betrothed his daughter to Jacopo Piccinino.[597]

185. But Carlo Gonzaga, a well-known commander who somewhat earlier had defected from Milan and come over to Francesco, observing that the Milanese had been forsaken and left without a leader, abandoned Francesco and once more switched his allegiance to the Milanese.[598] This man had a massive build, a giant-

---

593. Milanese troops under Sforza defeated Venetian forces at Caravaggio on Sept. 15, 1448. Venice relinquished Lodi by treaty on October 18, 1448.

594. Reading a comma after *censuit* instead of a period as in van Heck.

595. Sforza entered into an alliance with Venice in October 1448.

596. "Bracceschi" refers to Braccio (Fortebraccio) da Montone's army, which was led by his successor Niccolò Piccinino and his sons Jacopo and Francesco after Braccio's death. The company defected to Sforza on December 19, 1448. Luigi (or Ludovico) dal Verme was a captain serving under Sforza.

597. Drusiana (1437–74), Sforza's illegitimate daughter, eventually married Jacopo in 1464.

598. Carlo Gonzaga (c. 1417–56) and Sforza initially worked together to further their own territorial interests while serving as condottieri of the Ambrosian Republic of Milan. When Sforza allied with Venice in October 1448, Gonzaga turned against him. He became captain of the people in Milan on November 14, 1448; Ady, *Milan under the Sforza*, 50–53. For more on Gonzaga, see *DBI*, vol. 57: 693–96.

like appearance, and physical strength proportional to his size. He was a distinguished orator and well educated in Greek and Latin, but fickle in mind and naturally disposed to action of every kind, whether honorable or wicked.[599] He had high hopes of suppressing freedom in Milan and usurping control of the city. But now that the fortune of the Milanese was turning sour,[600] the people of Piacenza, Tortona, and Novara defected and accepted garrisons from Francesco. When the Alessandrians saw that no hope could be placed in the Milanese, they entrusted themselves to the rule of Guglielmo, the brother of the ruler of Monferrato.

186. In the meantime, the government had fallen from the hands of the nobility into those of the common people, and twelve lowborn and obscure men, who had been chosen from the dregs of the populace to preside over the city in the traditional way, were holding office.[601] Suspecting the nobility—whom they had offended in many ways—of siding with Francesco, and egged on by Gonzaga—who thought this offered him the most convenient path toward usurping leadership of the city—these men suddenly seized seven nobly born and affluent citizens of the highest rank during the night and murdered them, exposing them in the marketplace as a spectacle for the common people. Among them lay the supine and mutilated body of Giacomino Bossi, who was completely innocent—a fine young man of gentle character and scholarly training, who was linked to me in friendship. And not long afterward, they cruelly tortured and killed Giovanni Caimi, a venerable old man, and his son Francesco, a handsome youth, who were entrapped by no other charge than that of being related by blood to Bianca Maria, the wife of Francesco Sforza.[602] After that, the jurist Giorgio Lampugnano

---

599. The younger son of Marquis Gianfrancesco of Mantua, Carlo, like his brother Ludovico, was educated by the celebrated humanist Vittorino da Feltre at the court of Mantua.
600. Lit. "was becoming a stepmother."
601. The elite Ghibelline faction began losing power to middle-class Guelphs in 1448.
602. Aeneas had been part of the embassy sent by Frederick III to persuade Milan to

Italy: Milan 227

was taken prisoner and killed in Monza on the pretext of his having been sent on an embassy to the emperor; he was a great defender of liberty and the man who had previously torn up Filippo's will to show his support of popular rule. Nor did they spare Teodoro Bossi, who was very highly regarded in the city; after imprisoning him for a long time, they finally executed him. Galeotto Toscano, too, another nobly born and wealthy citizen, was put to death.[603]

187. No form of liberty now remained. With tyrannical arrogance, the twelve men defiled the city with their slaughter and rapacity, and, by prohibiting the election of successors, prolonged their own power against the wishes of the people. The city was at last aroused and provoked into taking up arms, electing a new administration from the nobility, deposing the tyrants, and throwing them into prison.[604] Not even this allowed the populace to catch its breath, for, after it had lost everything except the cities of Como and Parma (which remained loyal to the end), Francesco now laid the city under a harsh siege. This inflamed the common people again, who drove the nobles from the palace, freed the tyrants from prison, and restored them to their former position, as if they were lovers of liberty and had earned the deepest gratitude of the state. Reverting to their former ways, these men acquired a large number of armed retainers and at the urging of Carlo Gonzaga committed many acts of plunder and thoroughly persecuted the nobility, though they did not afford him an avenue for seizing leadership.

---

accept imperial suzerainty in late October 1447; see *Storia di Milano*, vol. 6: 413. He may have come to know several of these individuals during that time.

603. The events described previously began to unfold around January 1449. Teodoro Bossi (c. 1400–49) and Giorgio Lampugnano (c. 1385–1449) were among the jurists who formed the Ambrosian Republic in 1447. Toscano (d. 1449) was one of the Ambrosian captains. Fearing a deterioration of republican principles under Gonzaga's sway, Lampugnano, Bossi, and Toscano were secretly negotiating surrendering the city to Sforza. See *DBI*, vol. 13: 338–39.

604. The captains and defenders who were elected in February 1449 for a two-month term refused to hold elections until June. The newly elected government punished previous officials with imprisonment and other harsh reprisals, prompting a riot in July; see Ady, *Milan under the Sforza*, 52–53.

When he observed this and realized it was now dangerous for him to stay in Milan, he was reconciled with Francesco through intermediaries. Enticed by large rewards, he betrayed Lodi to Francesco and, breaking his word for the third time, to the great detriment of Milan and the consternation of the common people, crossed over to Francesco's side.[605]

However, the tyrants showed spirit enough to request reinforcements from all quarters in an attempt to shake off the yoke of Francesco now hanging over their necks. After asking others in vain, they at last convinced the Venetians not to abandon them. For it seemed to the Venetians contrary to their own interests that Francesco, a man in the prime of life and highly skilled in warfare, whose military abilities had already caused them heavy loss, should obtain a power that ultimately might appear to rival their own.[606] The Venetians therefore struck a treaty with the Milanese and enacted laws which were to be binding on all of northern Italy,[607] instructing Sforza to be content with specified forces and frontiers and to leave the Milanese in peace.[608] Knowing that he would soon perish if he obeyed the Venetians, Sforza ignored their bidding. Although he seemed abandoned by everyone (for only the Florentines—and they grudgingly—were supplying him with aid), he decided to persevere with the siege.

188. By this time, Francesco Piccinino had died and his brother, Jacopo, had crossed over to the Venetians with the Bracceschi. Leonardo Venier, who had been sent as an envoy by the Venetian

---

605. Sforza's siege of Milan began in September 1449. Gonzaga left Milan on September 11, 1449, to negotiate with Sforza, offering him Crema and Lodi in exchange for the concession of Tortona and Casalmaggiore as well as a payment of 18,000 ducats; *Storia di Milano*, vol. 6: 438.

606. Reading *quod* for mss. *quo*, which yields a smoother sense.

607. Lit. "Cisalpine Gaul."

608. The Venetians, who had made an alliance with Sforza in October 1448, feared his growing power and reversed its position in a treaty published September 24, 1449. The treaty divided large tracts of northern Italy between Venice and Milan and left only a few towns for Sforza.

senate, had entered Milan and was promising that reinforcements and a large supply of provisions, which the city sorely needed, would arrive very soon. Both in Francesco's army and in the city, the extreme dearth of all things made it seem debatable whether he should be called the besieger or the besieged. He had scarcely two thousand horses left which were capable of carrying a rider, and the soldiers, cheated of their wages, had stripped themselves of their arms for food; for Francesco had no money with which to pay the soldiers. Alternating between hope and fear,[609] and with only words to offer instead of deeds, he drew out the siege day after day. As for the city, all its grain had been consumed and no other form of sustenance remained, so that dogs, horses, and other animals of that sort were now being eaten. When the people could endure the famine no longer, they congregated at the Porta Vercellina and burst into the marketplace brandishing weapons. Here they came across Leonardo, the Venetian ambassador, whom they pierced with their swords and tore to pieces. After routing the tyrants' bodyguards, they next attacked the palace. This they took without resistance and clapped in irons the tyrants whom they found there.[610]

189. After that, they sent deputies to Francesco to offer him rulership of the city. He soon entered the city and accepted control, and after a few days returned with his wife and children, and, decked out in a duke's regalia, processed into the city like a triumphing general.[611] After receiving the surrender of Como and Parma and taking Alessandria from Guglielmo of Monferrato, he then waged a protracted and major war against the Venetians and King Alfonso in alliance with the Florentines. When the pressure became too severe (for he had proved unable to match their mighty power), he induced King René with generous wages and assurances to come to

---

609. Horace, *Epodes*, 5.85

610. Venier was killed in this uprising at the palace of Milan on February 24, 1450. Sforza entered the city on the 26th and began to arrange terms.

611. Sforza and his family most likely made their ceremonial entry on March 22, 1450; some sources say March 25; see Ady, *Milan under the Sforza*, 65.

his aid from France with his powerful cavalry.⁶¹² When René had crossed the mountains and descended into Italy, he compelled Guglielmo of Monferrato to lay down his arms through their friendship and family ties. Then, having joined his camp with Francesco's, he swooped down upon the enemy's territory, swiftly capturing a number of castles and butchering everyone he caught inside them in the French fashion.⁶¹³ Soon, such terror seized the Venetians that they no longer dared to pitch their camp opposite the enemy's, nor even trusted their ability to retain Brescia or Bergamo now that they had lost the open country. And since war with the Turks was endangering their maritime empire,⁶¹⁴ the Venetians suddenly, and contrary to everyone's expectation, made peace with Francesco at Lodi.⁶¹⁵ Peace had been long and fruitlessly discussed in the consistory of cardinals but was finally achieved through the intervention of an obscure but respected monk of upright character,⁶¹⁶ and without the knowledge of the king. This outcome was as vexing to the king⁶¹⁷ as it was beneficial to Francesco and necessary for the Venetians. Francesco soon restored the castle which had been wrecked by the enraged and frenzied populace, and through the extraordinary providence of fortune or almighty God⁶¹⁸ that famous

612. Sforza allied with Florence in July or August 1451, but it was not until February 1452 that an alliance was concluded with Charles VII of France, René's brother-in-law; the war began two months later.

613. René's troops were so uncontrollable that Sforza's troops were forced to turn against them at the sack of Pontevico "to prevent the wholesale massacre of the inhabitants"; see Ady, *Milan under the Sforza*, 69.

614. A reference to the fall of Constantinople on May 29, 1453.

615. Milan and Venice signed the Peace of Lodi on April 9, 1454. In the following months, this became a general peace between all major powers in Italy that would last, more or less, for the next forty years; see Vincent Ilardi, "Peace of Lodi," in *Encyclopedia of the Renaissance*, ed. Paul Grendler (New York: Charles Scribner's Sons, 1999), vol. 3: 442–43, hereafter, *ER*. See also paras. 218 and 238.

616. Fra Simonetto da Camerino; see para. 238 for more on his role in negotiating the Peace of Lodi.

617. It is unclear if this refers to René or Alfonso, as the peace was vexing to both; it is most likely René here, judging by the context.

618. Punctuating after *restauravit* (Vat. Lat. 3888) instead of *providentia*, as in van Heck.

and magnificent building was speedily rebuilt by the same hands that shortly before had torn it down.[619]

190. Francesco Filelfo, a famous author of satires, turned to epic poetry during this time and began to write about the deeds of Sforza.[620] Leodrisio Crivelli began to achieve fame in both prose and poetry.[621]

50 ITALY: VENICE

191. AMONG the Venetians, who wield enormous power by land and sea and have made the name of Italy famous among foreign[622] nations far and wide, the son of the doge Francesco Foscari[623] was driven into exile on the grounds of plotting against the state. Subsequently recalled, he was charged again with suspicion of crime and most cruelly tortured. Though he admitted no wrongdoing, he was banished to the Peloponnese and there came to the end of his wretched life.[624] The son-in-law of the same doge, Andrea Donato,

---

619. Known today as the Castello Sforzesco.

620. Francesco Filelfo (1398–1481), a famous and controversial humanist who studied in Greece and briefly taught in Florence before falling out with Cosimo de' Medici. He spent most of the last decades of his life in Milan under Visconti and Sforza's patronage and wrote a sixteen-book epic Latin poem, the *Sforziad*, in Francesco Sforza's honor; for more on Filelfo, see Diana Robin's article in Grendler, *ER*, vol. 2: 362–64.

621. Crivelli (1420–76) was Filelfo's student; he later wrote an account of Pius II's crusade.

622. Lit. "barbarian."

623. Doge Francesco Foscari (1373–1457); (r. 1423–57).

624. The situation was more complex. Jacopo Foscari was first accused of accepting bribes in exchange for public offices in 1445 and banished for life to Modon in Venetian Greece. When he fell ill two years later, the republic recalled him and cancelled his sentence at his father's request. In 1450 he was accused, on weak evidence, of murder and exiled to Crete; he did not confess to this crime, even under torture. In Crete, however, he began a secret exchange with Mehmed II in order to escape the island in 1456. He was charged in Venice, readily confessed his crime, and again was banished to Crete, this time with a year's sentence in prison. He died six months later. See John Julius Norwich, *A History of Venice* (New York: Vintage Books, 1989), 334–38; Dennis Romano, *The Likeness of Venice: A Life of Doge Francesco Foscari 1373–1457* (New Haven, Conn.: Yale University Press, 2007). Lord Byron adapted the story in *The Two Foscari* (1820).

had been named duke of Crete while governing the island on behalf of the Venetian empire, but he was summoned home, deprived of the honor, fined a large sum of money, and sent into exile.[625]

Ermolao, a man who held high rank and influence among the Venetians, was struck and killed by a spear as he returned home late at night from the council.[626] The person who perpetrated such a wicked crime was not discovered, though an accusation was laid against the son of the doge.

Francesco Barbaro, who excelled in the liberal arts and published many small works that were highly praised, departed from life at a ripe old age, having earned a distinguished reputation.[627]

Emperor Frederick visited Venice on his return from Rome together with his wife, King Ladislas [Postumus] of Hungary, and his whole retinue.[628] He was welcomed with gladness and goodwill and heaped with unbelievable honors.

192. Francesco, the doge of this people, had ruled the city for thirty-five years to the highest acclaim. He had stolen Brescia and Bergamo from Duke Filippo of Milan and routed his troops in several places.[629] He had beheaded Francesco Carmagnola, a famous commander, on suspicion of treason.[630] He had also seized and killed Marsilio of Carrara, whose ancestors had long ruled as tyrants over Padua, when he attempted to claim his paternal in-

---

625. Husband of Camilla Foscari and duke of Crete, Donato was sentenced in 1447 for accepting bribes from Francesco Sforza; see Romano, *Likeness of Venice*, 201–3.

626. Senator Ermolao Donato (d. 1450) was serving on the Council of the Ten when he was murdered.

627. Francesco Barbaro (1390–1454), one of Venice's most prominent humanists and author of *On Wifely Duties* (c. 1416) among other works.

628. Frederick visited Venice in May 1452 with his bride, Eleonora of Portugal, and his ward, Ladislas.

629. During its 1425–28 war with Milan, under the generalship of Carmagnola, the Venetians acquired Brescia in 1426 and Bergamo in 1428.

630. Francesco Bussone, called Carmagnola (1390–1432), first served Filippo Maria Visconti as condottiere with stunning results. He fell out of grace by 1425, however, and sought employment with Venice. When hostilities resumed with Milan in 1431, Carmagnola came under increasing suspicion for double dealing through a series of inexplicable delays, inaction, and half-hearted battles. He was executed for treason on May 5, 1432. For more on Carmagnola, see Mallett, *Mercenaries*, passim.

heritance.[631] He had concluded a peace with the Turks that was less honorable than necessary, and he had vastly expanded the power of the Venetians on land and sea.[632] In the end, he was forced to step down from government, since his old age made him seem unfit to serve the state. Outraged and unable to stand the sight of his ungrateful homeland or live a life without power, he retired from the public palace into a private house where, having resigned the rulership to his citizens, he forthwith returned his grieving soul to nature.[633] Battista Piasio,[634] the astronomer from Cremona, had predicted his fall several months previously, as if he had seen it coming. When he died, Francesco was not far from his ninetieth year of life, a venerable old man graced with outstanding physical majesty. He remembered everything that he had seen or heard since infancy, possessed a rich eloquence and a keen, exceptionally agile mind, and handled the reins of the senate with the greatest skill. When his father was doing business in Egypt, he consulted a prophet of that region about the future and received the reply that he had a son who would one day achieve leadership over his city.[635]

193. Francesco was replaced by Pasquale Malipiero, a man of remarkable good sense and civilized character. People think he will undertake no wars as doge unless they are necessary or offer the prospect of great glory.[636]

---

631. Marsilio da Carrara (c. 1390–1435), son of Francesco Novello, lord of Padua. The family lost control of the city to Venice after the death of Marsilio's brother, Ubertino, in 1407. Marsilio tried for many years to regain control of Padua from Venice but never succeeded.

632. Venice reached a trade agreement with Mehmed II in 1454, albeit with less generous terms than it had enjoyed under Byzantine rule; Norwich, *Venice*, 332.

633. Foscari was forced to resign in October 1457. He died November 1 of the same year.

634. Battista Piasio (1412–92), reading *Piasius* (Vat. Lat. 3888) for van Heck's *Prasius*. Thanks to Michael Shank for help with this identification.

635. Aeneas appears to be the only written source for this apocryphal story, which is mentioned again in para. 232 regarding Pope Eugenius IV's birth. See Romano, *Likeness of Venice*, 7–8.

636. Doge Malipiero (r. 1457–62) followed a cautious policy of avoiding war, as Aeneas predicted in 1458.

51   ITALY: MANTUA

194. LUDOVICO, marquis of Mantua, a man of considerable fame among the rulers of our generation, who is both cultured and experienced in military matters, sided with Francesco Sforza in the war with the Venetians after he had seized sovereignty over Milan, giving a great boost to Sforza's cause.[637] His brother Carlo, who had broken faith with Francesco and been thrown into prison, was released on Ludovico's guarantee, but, when he failed to honor his word even on these terms, he was deprived of all the towns which he controlled in Mantuan territory. While serving with the Venetians, he led a large force of them into the territory of Mantua, where he devastated and burned the fields over a wide area.[638] Since fortune had granted Carlo a successful start to this war, and the Mantuans were now stricken with fear and seemed to despair of their situation, Ludovico, having sent for reinforcements from Milan, brought up his soldiers into line and offered battle to his brother. Carlo accepted the contest, and a fierce battle ensued in which the two brothers—both of them in the prime of life, both experts in warfare, both excelling in strength of body and mind—strove with all their might for glory, power, and life itself. In the end, Ludovico was victorious. Having routed Carlo and put him to flight, he inflicted great casualties and captured all the commanders of his troops and his cavalry captains. Exiled from his homeland and destitute, Carlo later succumbed to disease and died.[639]

---

637. Ludovico Gonzaga, marquis of Mantua (r. 1444–78), was under contract as a condottiere for Venice in 1448; he switched to Sforza's side in 1450 and won considerable gains against Venice. For more on the Gonzaga family, see Kate Simon, *Renaissance Tapestry: The Gonzaga of Mantua* (New York: Harper and Row, 1988).

638. Carlo Gonzaga (1417–56) (see para. 185) was imprisoned by Sforza in early 1451 and released on March 17, 1451. He began commanding Venetian forces in 1451 but used them to threaten Mantuan territory in 1452–53.

639. The battle between the brothers took place on June 14, 1453; Carlo died in 1456.

52 ITALY: FERRARA

195. IN FERRARA, Niccolò d'Este died—the most fortunate of all the rulers of our generation had he, once upon a time, not been forced to take vengeance for his wife's adultery, not only on her but his dearly beloved son.[640] Leonello then took power, a peaceable ruler who was well versed in literature and devoted to music. When he passed away, his brother Borso, who was also the son of Niccolò by his mistress Ptolomea of Siena,[641] was invited to rule—a young man of fine appearance who had acquitted himself admirably in arms and was skilled in both word and action.[642] After lavishly entertaining Emperor Frederick during his journey to Rome and again on his return, he received the title of Duke of Modena and Reggio and was the very first in the Este family to be named a duke.[643]

196. While Pope Eugenius was holding a council with the Greeks at Ferrara, Ugo da Siena, who at that time was considered the leading doctor, invited to his home all the Greek scholars of philosophy who were thought to have assembled there. When he had served them with a rich and sumptuous banquet, and the meal had ended, and the dishes and tables had been cleared away, he gently

---

640. Niccolò d'Este (1383–1441). His illegitimate and favorite son, Ugo, was accused of adultery with Niccolò's wife, Parasina Malatesta. Both were executed in 1425.

641. Also known as Stella de Tolomei or Stella dell'Assassino. See Werner Gundersheimer, *Ferrara: The Style of a Renaissance Despotism* (Princeton, N.J.: Princeton University Press, 1973), 77.

642. Leonello d'Este (r. 1441–50) was taught by renowned humanist Guarino da Verona and trained in arms by the condottiere Braccio da Montone. He brought several artists to Ferrara, including Andrea Mantegna and Pisanello, as well as the scholars Leon Battista Alberti and Theodore Gaza. Borso d'Este (r. 1450–71) was also a soldier, scholar, and patron; he expanded the Palazzo Schifanoia. For more on the Este family, see Gundersheimer, *Ferrara*.

643. These events took place in 1452. For more on Borso's reasons for seeking the title and his efforts to convince Frederick to bestow it, see Gundersheimer, *Ferrara*, 152–54.

lured them step by step into a debate. When Marquis Niccolò appeared and many excellent philosophers attending the synod had arrived, he brought up for discussion all the topics of philosophy about which Plato and Aristotle seem to argue in their works and hold widely differing opinions. He himself, he said, would defend whichever side the Greeks opposed, whether they supported Plato or Aristotle. The Greeks agreed to the competition, and the debate went on for many hours. Finally, when Ugo, the host of the banquet, had defeated one after another of the Greek philosophers with his eloquent arguments and forced them into silence, it became clear that the Latins, who had long ago surpassed Greece in the arts of war and military glory, were in our time also outstripping them in literature and every[644] branch of learning.[645]

197. However, the House of Este was always a friend to learned men. In our time, it not only attracted the aforementioned Ugo with its generous inducements but honored many men in the sphere of civil law and more in the other disciplines. In the field of oratory, it numbered among its household Giovanni Aurispa of Sicily, an expert in Greek and Latin studies, well-known for his poetry and prose, and made him rich and prosperous.[646]

198. Guarino da Verona, too, the father and instructor of virtually all who in our time have acquired a knowledge of Greek literature—an admirable old man deserving of every honor, who had devoted his whole life to reading, teaching, and writing—found there the sole refuge of his old age and one indeed that was honorable and worthy of his activities and virtues.[647]

644. Reading *omni* for mss. *omnium*.
645. Ugo da Siena, or Ugo Benzi (c. 1370–1448), physician of Niccolò III d'Este, was also a philosopher and a professor in Siena and Ferrara. For more on the Council of Ferrara-Florence (1438–39), see paras. 19 and 205. Aeneas likely heard this story directly from his friend Ugo, who may have embellished. On Benzi, see *DBI*, vol. 8: 720–23.
646. Sicilian humanist Giovanni Aurispa (c. 1369–1459) studied Greek in Constantinople and acquired over two hundred Greek manuscripts, which were highly sought after in Italy. He served as a papal secretary for a time and taught in several cities including Florence and Ferrara.
647. Humanist Guarino Guarini da Verona (1374–1460) learned Greek in Constan-

53 ITALY: BOLOGNA

199. BOLOGNA may be called not so much the mother of learning as the nurse of sedition—the twin sister of Genoa, consistent only in its inconsistency. When it had violently evicted the faction of the Zambeccari and many of the citizens, it began to be governed by a general council of the Canetoli and Bentivogli.[648] The leaders of the factions were Battista Canetoli and Annibale Bentivoglio: both bloodthirsty men, both notorious for the commission of murders. Although they were linked by the sacred bond of godparentage, they behaved no better in their dealings with one another. Annibale had just raised Battista's son from the holy font and, while following his fellow-parent [Battista] to visit the new mother, had taken Battista's hand to congratulate him on the birth of his son, when Battista's bodyguards suddenly rushed in and killed him; this made it clear that Battista had sought the sacrament of baptism not for the sake of strengthening a bond but of committing murder. But the death of Annibale did not go unavenged, for soon afterward the adherents of his party armed themselves, routed their adversaries, and took control of the street. On information given by a boy, Battista was finally discovered skulking in an underground cellar with most of his accomplices and, after being forced out by smoke, was pierced on the spot with many wounds. His corpse was dragged into the marketplace and long subjected to mockery. Many tore at his heart with their teeth like wild beasts and felt no qualms about drinking his blood before his body was finally burned.

---

tinople and briefly taught in Florence, Venice, Padua, and other towns before settling permanently at the Este court. His teaching methods were widely admired and emulated, and his translations of Greek works and passion for the Greek language helped significantly increase its study in Italy; see William McCuaig's article in Grendler, *ER*, vol. 3: 97–99.

648. Part of the Papal States, Bologna revolted against the papacy in 1438, led by the pro-Bentivoglio faction, and invited Annibale Bentivoglio (1413–45) to become leader of the city.

200. During this time, Sante, an illegitimate son of Ercole Bentivoglio whom Pope Eugenius had once ordered, or at least allowed, to be killed, was living in obscurity in Florence, eking out a life of poverty through wool working and barely aware of his father's identity. All of a sudden, the people of Bologna called for him and, when he demurred, brought him back to his homeland seemingly against his will.[649] From a wool worker they turned him into a knight and appointed him the guardian of Annibale's son[650] and ruler of the republic. Such was the courage that he showed in adversity and such his moderation in success that all recognized him as the son of Ercole. When some exiles entered the city one night through an act of betrayal and with puffed up arrogance[651] began to throw their weight around like victors, he did not lose his presence of mind but roused his supporters, took up arms, and attacked them. After killing and capturing many, he drove them headlong from the city in defeat.[652]

201. At this time, Cardinal Bessarion of Nicaea, a Greek of remarkable sagacity and an expert in our language as well as his own, was governing in Bologna on behalf of Pope Nicholas V.[653] He performed the role of legate up until the pope's death and was equally dear to the nobility and the common people, though it has come to the point in the city where the legates of the pope can only make

649. Sante Bentivoglio (c. 1424–63), son of Ercole (d. 1424), was sponsored by Cosimo de' Medici and led the government of Bologna from 1445 until his death in 1463. Shortly after Sante took power, Bologna negotiated the capitulations of 1447, which granted the pope limited authority over the city as its suzerain; see Cecilia Ady, *The Bentivoglio of Bologna: A Study in Despotism* (London: Oxford University Press, 1937), 37–39; *DBI*, vol. 8: 641–44.

650. Giovanni II (1443–1508).

651. Reading *tumore* for mss. *rumore*, which makes poor sense; this is possibly the reading of Urb. Lat. 885, which is barely legible on microfilm here.

652. There were multiple plots against Sante. This seems to refer to an attempt in 1451 in which 3,000 men led by heads of the Canetoli, Zambeccari and other families entered the city, but were defeated by Sante's forces; see *DBI*, vol. 8: 643.

653. Bessarion (1403–72), a celebrated Greek humanist and clergyman who helped promote the union of the Greek and Latin churches, was named cardinal in 1439. He served as papal governor of Bologna from 1450 to 1455. For more on Bessarion, see John Monfasani, *Byzantine Scholars in Renaissance Italy: Cardinal Bessarion and Other Emigrés* (Aldershot: Variorum, 1995).

requests rather than issue commands. This is clearly what Luis, cardinal of Santi Quattro Coronati, is now experiencing as legate.[654] Although he abounds in talent and enjoys the prestige that is due to a nephew of the supreme pontiff, he can achieve no more in the city than what is acceptable to the senate and Sante.

202. In the territory of Bologna, a number of small ants climbed a dry pear tree to find food. A large number of bigger ants then arrived, which killed some of them and dislodged others. After about two hours, such a multitude of small ants had been aroused that the whole field seemed covered with a black column. They approached in a pack and, after surrounding the tree-trunk on all sides, gradually began to ascend it. When the bigger ants noticed the presence of the enemy, they massed together above and awaited battle. When their front lines came together and battle was joined, the bigger ants used their fierce bite to kill one group of small ants after another and quickly dispatched so many that a large pile of fallen and dying ants accumulated on the ground at the foot of the pear tree. But the smaller ants pressed on obstinately, with one formation following hard upon the heels of another; twenty or more would surround single enemies, attacking them from the front and rear and also piercing their unprotected flanks. At length, the bigger ants were defeated and completely wiped out, thus paying the penalty for rashly initiating the battle.[655]

This took place in sight of the army of the Roman Church, when Eugenius IV occupied the throne of Peter.[656] It was reported to me by someone who said he witnessed it, a man worthy of trust and respect—Niccolò of Pistoia, an expert in both fields of law [i.e., civil and canon], who was then representing Nerio, bishop of Siena, in the papal army.[657]

---

654. Luis Juan del Milà (c. 1430–1510), nephew of Pope Calixtus III, served as governor of Bologna from 1455–58. He was created cardinal in 1456.
655. There happens to be a Monte delle Formiche ("Mount of Ants") near Bologna.
656. Pope Eugenius IV (r. 1431–47).
657. Niccolò Fortiguerri (1418–73), bishop of Pistoia, was Aeneas's cousin and would

203. This is similar to something that occurred in Belgium not far from the city of Liège, according to an old legend. A falcon had built itself a nest, either in a tree or a cliff, and was warming the eggs in eager expectation of the chicks hatching. Some ravens that happened upon the scene drove off the falcon, broke open its eggs, and ate them. This was witnessed from nearby by some ploughmen, who noticed the agitated falcon fleeing away. On the following day—marvelous to relate!—falcons and ravens formed up in ranks, as if they had been summoned to battle from all over the world, with one side taking up position to the north, the other to the south, and, as if they were capable of reason, placing some to guard the wings and others to lead the central columns. After this, they fought a bitter and ferocious battle in the air. Now the ravens, now the falcons gave way, and then, recovering their strength, resumed the struggle until the whole field underneath was covered with feathers and corpses. In the end, victory fell to the falcons, who, fighting fiercely with their claws as well as their beaks, wiped out the ravens.

A short time later, two rivals for the Church of Liège, one chosen as bishop by Gregory XII, the other by Benedict XIII (who were involved in a dispute over the papacy), converged upon the same place with their armies in order to join battle. Duke John of Burgundy assisted one of them with his forces, while the people of Liège supported the other.[658] When they came to blows, both sides fought with the utmost intensity, and a terrible and bloody battle took place, in which John was finally victorious, killing thirty thousand of the enemy. A shrine was built to commemorate this event,

---

later be elevated by him (in 1460) to the rank of cardinal and trusted adviser. Nerio de Monte Garulo, bishop of Siena (r. 1444–49), was Aeneas's predecessor in that office.

658. The Battle of Othée, Sept. 23, 1408. John of Bavaria was backed by the duke of Burgundy (and Gregory XII, pope of the Roman obedience) as bishop; Theodore de Perwez was backed by the town of Liège; see Wim Blockmans and Walter Prevenier, *The Promised Lands: The Low Countries under Burgundian Rule, 1369–1530*, trans. Elizabeth Fackleman; trans. revised and ed., Edward Peters (Philadelphia: University of Pennsylvania Press, 1999), 59.

which I saw filled with the bones of the slain while later passing along that way.

But as for the battle of the falcons and ravens, I leave it to each person to form his own opinion and refer its veracity to the verdict of tradition.

54 ITALY: FLORENCE, LUCCA, SAN CASCIANO

204. FLORENCE, a city built on the banks of the Arno from the ruins of Fiesole, was called Fluentia by the ancients. Founded under lucky auspices, it began to outstrip the neighboring cities all around it and to extend its power with extraordinary success, whereupon the name of Florentia became much more appropriate than Fluentia.

205. In this city, Pope Eugenius IV brought to a splendid conclusion the council that he had begun with the Greeks at Ferrara. There were several controversies between the Greeks and Latins over the mysteries of orthodox faith. The greatest and most intractable concerned the procession of the Holy Spirit, for the Greeks claimed that the Paraclete proceeds only from the Father, whereas we say it proceeds from the Father and the Son. After many long, drawn-out debates in which Niccolò Sagundino,[659] a skilled speaker in both languages, equally quick in thought and expression, acquired a distinguished reputation as interpreter, they finally agreed with the Latin Church on one creed.[660]

206. The Greek emperor, the patriarch of Constantinople, and their whole retinue were liberally and sumptuously entertained by

---

659. Or Nikolaos Sekoundinos; see para. 22.

660. The Council of Florence, or Ferrara-Florence (1438–39), ended with compromises on key issues like the procession of the Holy Spirit, the use of leavened vs. unleavened bread in communion, and purgatory. Especially helpful to Pope Eugenius IV, it affirmed his authority in both East and West at a time when he was challenged by the Council of Basel; see Joseph Gill, *The Council of Florence* (Cambridge: Cambridge University Press, 1959). See also para. 19.

the city. The patriarch died there of old age and was buried inside the church of the Order of Preachers.[661] Maffeo Vegio, a poet from Lodi of no small fame, composed his epitaph in uneven couplets.[662]

207. The exiles of Florence issued an invitation to the illustrious general Niccolò Piccinino, who entered the territory of Mugello, ten miles from Florence, and plundered everything in hostile fashion. Not long afterward, when he had made war on Pope Eugenius and Florence simultaneously, he was defeated and crushed in a great battle in the territory of Arezzo at Anghiari.[663] Ludovico, the archbishop of Florence, was then commander of the papal forces. He was made famous by this victory and a little later promoted to cardinal.[664] For after Eugenius had achieved union with the Greeks and put aside his fear of Piccinino, he felt more confident and created seventeen cardinals—men who were either distinguished by birth, outstanding in merit, or conspicuous for their holy way of life. Among them two Greeks were also chosen: Isidore, archbishop of the Ruthenians, and Bessarion, bishop of Nicaea, whom I mentioned previously.[665]

208. King Alfonso of Aragon was asked by Filippo Maria [Visconti] to assist him against the power of the Venetians, as I related earlier.[666] When Alfonso had gathered a large army, he set out on

---

661. Some seven hundred Greek delegates were hosted by the city of Florence. Patriarch Joseph II (d. June 10, 1439) is buried in the Dominican church of Santa Maria Novella.

662. Priest, poet, and humanist, Vegio (1406–58) taught jurisprudence at Pavia and was later attached to the papal court. The epitaph, composed in the elegiac meter, is extant.

663. Niccolò Piccinino (1386–1444) was serving Filippo Maria Visconti of Milan as condottiere at this time. In concert with Rinaldo degli Albizzi and other Florentine exiles, he attacked territories in the papal state near the Florentine border. Florentine and papal forces defeated Piccinino at the Battle of Anghiari (June 29, 1440); see D. S. Chambers, *Popes, Cardinals and War* (London: I. B. Tauris & Co, 2006), 45; John Najemy, *A History of Florence, 1200–1575* (Malden, Mass.: Blackwell Publishing, 2006), 289.

664. Ludovico Trevisan, also called Scarampo (1401–65), led papal forces in concert with those of Francesco Sforza; he was apostolic chamberlain, patriarch of Aquileia, and archbishop of Florence (r. 1435–39). Shortly after the Battle of Anghiari, he was awarded the cardinal's hat; see Chambers, *Popes, Cardinals and War*, 45.

665. See paras. 19 on Isidore and 201 on Bessarion.

666. In the following paragraphs, Aeneas draws heavily from Bartolomeo Facio,

Italy: Florence, Lucca, San Casciano 243

his journey to northern Italy. But Filippo died before Alfonso departed from Tivoli, to which he had now proceeded.[667] Hearing of his friend's death, and because he had been named by him as heir, he set out for the Sabine country [central Italy] and held a magnificent funeral service for Filippo. He then crossed the Tiber and marched straight into Florentine territory with the intention, so he said, of forcing the Florentines to recall their troops from Lombardy. In this way, he could proceed through a pacified and friendly Tuscany to bring help to the people of Milan, who were hard pressed in war by the Venetians.[668] When Alfonso asked the Florentines, they refused to abandon their alliance with Venice, so he marched into the territory of Volterra and, on the same day that he arrived, threw his troops around Pomarance, a town of some importance which had dared to close its gates to him, took it by force, and plundered it.[669] He then advanced to Castelnuovo in the same territory, whose inhabitants, after hearing of the fate of Pomarance, immediately surrendered without a struggle. A number of nearby fortresses did the same. Next, he laid siege to Montecastello, which was well protected by nature and human skill. At this juncture, there arose rainstorms and gales of such scale and intensity that the soldiers could find no rest either outside or inside their tents,[670] many of which were torn to shreds or snatched into the air. Suffering from a lack of rations,

---

Rerum gestarum Alfonsi regis libri, books 9–10; the text has recently been edited and translated into Italian by Daniela Pietragalla (Alessandria: Edizione dell'Orso, 2004). For more on Aeneas's use of Facio, see the introduction. Much of the information on Alfonso in the following notes derives from Alan Ryder's excellent and thorough study, *Alfonso the Magnanimous*.

667. The verb *appello* usually means "put into, reach by sea." Filippo Maria Visconti died on August 13, 1447. Alfonso had been encamped at Tivoli for eight months, against the will of the papacy; see Ryder, *Alfonso*, 258.

668. Milan would remain at war with Venice until 1449.

669. Alfonso began his campaign in the region in November 1447, taking several small towns and fortresses, while others successfully resisted.

670. Reading *neque extra tentoria <neque in tentoriis>* for mss. *neque extra tentoria*. The passage is a verbatim borrowing from Facio, *Rerum gestarum*, 9.63; the missing phrase must have dropped out through scribal error.

Alfonso therefore marched his troops from there to Campiglia.[671] But since the Florentines had reinforced that town with a garrison and provisions, his efforts there were in vain. However, he captured a few neighboring fortresses in Gherardesca (as that region is called) and restored them to the people from whom they had been previously confiscated by the Florentines. The king's retinue included Simonetto, leading a thousand horsemen, who had crossed over to his side after the Florentines ceased to employ his services.[672]

Meanwhile, the king waited day by day for Sigismondo Malatesta, whom he had hired along with eighteen hundred horsemen and six hundred infantry before he entered Tuscany. Sigismondo, however, went over to the Florentines.[673] Federico, lord of Urbino, a well-known and distinguished soldier, was also in the pay of Florence.[674] Since the Florentines were in no way inferior to the king in cavalry or infantry and thwarted his every opportunity of capturing towns by force, the king decided not to persevere in the siege of Campiglia, especially since, in the mountains, he was hard pressed by a shortage of provisions.

209. Therefore, he turned aside to the coastal region and camped at the once-famous but now ruined city of Populonia, where grain and machines of war could be easily shipped to him from the kingdom of Naples. About three miles from here is the well-known town of Piombino. While the king labored over the siege of Piombino,[675] of which I will speak later, Castiglione della Pescaia, itself

---

671. Alfonso began attacking Campiglia in December 1447.

672. Simonetto da Castel San Pietro, or di Castelpiero (d. 1460), whom Aeneas later praises in the *Commentaries* (Book IV) for his conduct in battle on behalf of papal forces aiding Ferrante of Naples; see *Commentaries*, Book IV (Meserve and Simonetta, vol. 2: 246–47, 258–60, 290–95; Gabel and Gragg, vol. 3: 310, 313, 323–24); see also www.condottieridiventura.it.

673. Malatesta, lord of Rimini, was hired by Florence in 1448. For more on him, see para. 256.

674. Federico da Montefeltro, condottiere, lord of Urbino (r. 1444–74), and later, duke of Urbino (r. 1474–82); he signed a *condotta* with Florence in 1447.

675. Begun on June 25, 1448, the siege of Piombino was abandoned in September 1448.

Italy: Florence, Lucca, San Casciano 245

a town of no small importance, was betrayed by its garrison of Florentines and handed over to him, except for its citadel;[676] Simonetto laid siege to the citadel and accepted its surrender a few days later. Just before this, while the king was living in his winter quarters at Acquaviva, he was approached by ambassadors from Milan, who begged his assistance and prevailed upon him to declare war then and there on the Venetian senate.[677] For at this time, Francesco Sforza, resentful toward the people of Milan and relying on the help of the Venetians, was trying his utmost to subject the same people whose territory and armed forces he had recently expanded. When the king returned to Naples after raising the siege of Piombino and withdrawing into the country of the Pelignians,[678] the Florentines sent him ambassadors to sue for peace. After receiving safe conduct, the ambassadors entered his camp, where they laid out their instructions and made excuses for the war. A few days later, through the efforts of Cardinal Antonio of Lérida, a theologian of the first rank who had undertaken this duty in accordance with the wishes of the pope, peace was granted to the people of Florence on the condition that Castiglione della Pescaia and the island of Giglio, which had been wrested from Florence during that war, should remain in the power of the king.[679] But when Sforza had gained possession of Milan[680] and was demanding that Venice return all bridges and

676. Castiglione della Pescaia had gone over to Alfonso in December 1447, much earlier than Aeneas suggests here. The acquisition of this coastal town and the island of Giglio helped keep Alfonso's campaign alive and allowed it to receive supplies from Naples, Sicily, and Sardinia; see Ryder, *Alfonso*, 278.

677. The chronology is compressed and out of order. Campiglia fell in December 1447; the siege of Piombino took place in the summer of 1448; Alfonso, moreover, did not sign the treaty with the Ambrosian Republic of Milan until March 1449; see Ryder, *Alfonso*, 278–81.

678. The classical name for central Italian people of Sabine origin, who dwelled in the northern central Apennines. The name survives in towns in the Abruzzi today, such as Pratola Peligna and Taranto Peligna. Pietragalla renders it as *Sannio* in her translation of Facio's *Rerum gestarum Alfonsi regis libri*.

679. The treaty was signed on June 21, 1450. Cardinal Antonio de la Cerda, called Lérida, was the dedicatee of this work. See dedication letter.

680. February 1450.

castles along the Adda River on the grounds that they belonged to the territory of Milan, Alfonso, who was hostile toward Francesco, considered it in his best interests to prevent his power from taking root so deeply. He therefore settled his differences with the Venetians through the mediation of Leonello, marquis of Este. After forming a pact of friendship with them, he declared war again on the Florentines, who had thrown in their lot with Francesco and were aiding him with arms and money.[681] He decided to send his son Ferrante on an expedition against them.[682] Ferrante was then quite a young man, with an exceptional intelligence, amenable to instruction in all the best pursuits. Educated in the liberal arts and well trained in the science of handling arms, he was eager for glory and tolerant of hunger and hard work. His father entrusted him with six thousand horsemen and two thousand infantry, and his army included Count Everso and Napoleone Orsini—by no means contemptible commanders.[683] Federico of Urbino, who had fought on the side of Florence in the previous war, also served in his army.

210. When they perceived the storm of war bearing down upon them, the Florentines hired Astorre of Faenza, Simonetto (whom I mentioned previously), Sigismondo Malatesta, and finally Alessandro Sforza, who, after combining their forces, had over ten thousand horsemen and a large number of foot soldiers in their camp.[684] However, Ferrante led his forces through the territory of Cortona to Arezzo. Here he took by force and plundered some insignificant strongholds and commenced an assault on Foiano, a town of no

681. Alfonso concluded an alliance with Venice on Oct. 24, 1450, but he did not formally declare war on Florence until June 2, 1452; see Ryder, *Alfonso*, 283–85.

682. Alfonso's illegitimate son Ferrante (1423–94), duke of Calabria and later king of Naples (r. 1458–94).

683. Everso of Anguillara (c. 1400–64) and Napoleone Orsini (c. 1400–80); Aeneas discusses both condottieri at several points in the *Commentaries*, taking special care to note Everso's many crimes in Book II (Meserve and Simonetta, vol. 1: 250–55; Gragg and Gabel, vol. 2: 133–35).

684. Astorre Manfredi, lord of Faenza (1412–68); Alessandro Sforza (1409–73), Francesco's brother, was lord of Pesaro. On Malatesta, see para. 256.

Italy: Florence, Lucca, San Casciano 247

small importance, whose surrender he received after eight days when the enemy failed to bring assistance.[685] At Montepulciano, he routed and put to flight the cavalry of Astorre, capturing many and killing not a few. In the territory of Florence, he stormed Rencine, but after he had laid siege to Castellina, he yielded to the deepening chill of winter and retreated to the coast at Acquaviva as his father had done.[686] At the same time, Antonio Olzina captured the coastal town of Vada with his fleet and fortified it on the land side with a deeper ditch; from this base he threatened the region of Pisa and Volterra.[687] Meanwhile, the Florentine commanders had moved camp to Foiano, and Ferrante had set out to relieve the besieged, when a severe epidemic erupted. Owing to the number of the sick, he was barely able to move camp, let alone conduct a campaign. In the meantime, therefore, Foiano was attacked in full force and, though defended with no less courage, was at length surrendered by the townsmen without the knowledge of its garrison. Nevertheless, the townsmen themselves fell prey to the victors shortly afterward, when the town was set afire and razed to the ground.[688]

211. During the same time, Gherardo Gambacorta, who wanted to cede to Ferrante four castles in the Apennines which his father had received from the Florentines, was betrayed by one of his people, lost the castles, and for a long time followed the king around like a beggar.[689] Later, when peace was achieved at Lodi [1454], as I have mentioned, Ferrante was recalled by his father and withdrew

685. Foiano surrendered on September 2, 1452.
686. Ferrante's troops began to withdraw on November 5, 1452.
687. Vada, some twenty miles south of Livorno, was captured by the Aragonese fleet on Dec. 15, 1452. Olzina served Alfonso as a secretary and *escriva del racio*, whose duties included provisioning naval expeditions and building fortifications; see Ryder, *Kingdom of Naples*, 88, 229.
688. Florentine forces recovered the town in 1453, but the troops could not be controlled, and they sacked it. Machiavelli notes this and other points which follow in *Florentine Histories*, Bk VI.
689. Gambacorta, the lord of Val di Bagno and a longtime ally and beneficiary of Florence, secretly negotiated with Alfonso in 1453, but local magnates aided by Florentine forces prevented the exchange.

to the kingdom of Naples, whereupon the Florentines recovered everything that they had lost. Baldaccio, an infantry commander of no small repute, decisive and bold, who had long been employed by Florence, was finally summoned to the palace. When he answered the magistrate defiantly, he was seized and thrown from the highest window into the square. Although he had already died from the great fall, his neck was severed with an axe.[690]

212. Among all the Florentines who flourished in my time, Cosimo de' Medici was pre-eminent in wisdom and prestige. Regarded as the city's leader, he steered the senate in whatever direction he pleased, legislated for the city at his own discretion, enriched a great many impoverished citizens, arranged many marriages with dowries supplied from his own money, built sumptuous villas, made valuable donations to churches, and erected the large and gleaming monastery of San Marco from its foundations upward.[691] Displeased by the church of his own parish, he demolished it and raised in its place a building of superb workmanship made from the stone of Fiesole. Although he had erected for himself a most elegant mansion, he planned a more impressive structure and, at a prominent location in the city, built a tall and massive palace of dressed stone, so beautiful and spacious that it beggars comparison with any other in all of Florence.[692]

213. The wisdom of the Florentines is to be commended in many

---

690. This description matches that of Baldaccio d'Anghiari (d. 1441), whose death Machiavelli attributes to his friendship with the anti-Medicean Capponi family. This event seems out of place among developments from the 1450s, but in a few other passages Aeneas similarly mentions noncontemporaneous events from the same region without the benefit of a transition; see, for instance, para. 259.

691. Cosimo il Vecchio (the Elder) (1389–1464) was the unofficial leader of the Florentine Republic from 1434–64. He and his brother, Lorenzo, funded work on the monastery and library of San Marco under the direction of the architect Michelozzo from 1437–44. See B. L. Ullman, *The Public Library of Renaissance Florence: Niccolò Niccoli, Cosimo de' Medici, and the Library of San Marco* (Padua: Editrice Antenore, 1972).

692. The Medici built the parish church of San Lorenzo, whose façade remains unfinished. Palazzo Medici (1445–60), designed by Michelozzo, is now known as Palazzo Medici Riccardi.

respects, above all because in selecting their chancellors they focus not on legal skill, like most cities, but on oratory and what they call the humanities. For they understand that Cicero and Quintilian, not Bartolo or Innocent,[693] teach the art of writing and speaking correctly. I have known three men in that city, renowned for their expertise in Greek and Latin and the fame of their publications, who held the chancellorship one after another: Leonardo and Carlo, both from Arezzo, and Poggio, a citizen of the same republic, who as apostolic secretary once composed letters for three popes.[694] Preceding them was Coluccio Salutati, whose powers of speech were such that Giangaleazzo, lord of Milan, who in our fathers' memory waged a most grievous war against the Florentines, was frequently heard to say that one thousand Florentine horsemen were less harmful to him than the writings of Coluccio.[695]

693. Bartolo da Sassoferato, Roman law commentator (c. 1313–57) and Innocent IV, commentator on canon law before his elevation to the papacy. On the rhetorical shift Aeneas refers to, heralded by Valla's attack on Bartolo, see Paul F. Grendler, *Universities of the Italian Renaissance* (Baltimore: Johns Hopkins University Press, 2002), 211; also Jerrold Seigel, *Rhetoric and Philosophy in Renaissance Humanism* (Princeton, N.J.: Princeton University Press, 1968), chap. 7.

694. Leonardo Bruni (c. 1370–1444), one of the greatest humanists of the quattrocento, was a secretary at the papal chancery before he attained the coveted position of chancellor of Florence (1427–44). Among his works were *The History of the Florentine People* (1415–44), *Panegyric on the City of Florence* (1404?), *Lives of Dante and Petrarch* (1436), and an edited volume of his familiar letters. He also translated Aristotle's *Ethics* (1416) and *Politics* (1438). Carlo Marsuppini (1399–1453), humanist and chancellor of Florence from 1444–53. Poggio Bracciolini (1380–1459), humanist and chancellor of Florence from 1453–59. Like Bruni, he served as a secretary for the papal court prior to this appointment. Best known for his dialogues, he composed such works as *On Avarice* (1428), *On the Vicissitudes of Fortune* (c. 1448), and *Against the Hypocrites* (1449). His humorous *Facetiae* (1438–52) were also well-known. See James Hankins's article in Grendler, *ER*, vol. 1: 301–6; Albert Rabil, ed., *Renaissance Humanism: Foundations, Forms and Legacy*, 3 vols. (Philadelphia: University of Pennsylvania Press, 1988), passim.

695. Coluccio Salutati (1331–1406), humanist chancellor of Florence from 1375–1406 and author of such works as *On the Labors of Hercules* (c. 1391), *On Destiny and Fortune* (c. 1396), and *On Tyranny* (1400), was a powerful advocate for the Florentine republic during its wars with Milan; see Ronald Witt's article in Grendler, *ER*, vol. 5: 389–92. Giangaleazzo Visconti, ruler of Milan (r. 1385–1402; duke as of 1395), waged three expansionist wars (1390–92; 1397–98; 1400–02) in northern and central Italy, threatening Florence in the process.

214. There was a long controversy among the Florentines over monetary taxation, which was squeezing the citizens of lesser means more than the rich. As things stand now, with Cosimo's consent, they have begun to compile a new *catasto* (that is, a census of each citizen's wealth), which is said to have rarely been achieved without popular uproar and commotion. But at present, it is proceeding in peace and tranquility.[696]

215. The people of Lucca have in recent memory twice endured a siege by the Florentines and twice defended their liberty with the help of Duke Filippo of Milan.[697] But ultimately, since they were unable to match the strength of their neighbors or easily find someone to help them whenever they came under attack, they struck a treaty with Florence for fifty years, submitting to conditions dictated by the more powerful party.[698]

216. Between Florence and Siena in the town which they call San Casciano, in the sixth year after the Jubilee, some clouds at a height of twenty cubits (so called) above the ground appeared to do battle with each other, propelled by extraordinary blasts of wind. One group buffeted another, and, in constant succession, those which had struck a blow were struck in turn. Meanwhile, the roofs of houses were tossed through the air, walls overthrown, and massive rocks dislodged by the intense and unbelievable violence of the wind. The oldest olive trees and the trunks of ancient oaks were torn from their roots and shattered; people and animals were picked up and swept through the sky for long distances. Men who said they witnessed it reported this to me. But I was more influenced to believe it by the letters which some highly respected

---

696. The catasto, last conducted in 1427, was unpopular with the elite of Florence who stood to lose the most by its implementation. The Medici quietly allowed the catasto to be sidelined, but the Signoria conceded to popular pressure and reinstated it in 1458; see Najemy, *History of Florence*, 291–94.

697. The sieges took place in 1430 and 1437.

698. Reference to the fifty-year league with Florence (1441); see M. E. Bratchel, *Lucca 1430–1494* (Oxford: Clarendon Press, 1995).

persons wrote to King Alfonso about these events and which were read in my presence while I was visiting him.[699]

55 ITALY: SIENA

217. THE CITY of Siena, which is my own place of origin, today holds the second place in Tuscany. It is located in a delightful spot and, if I can be trusted, has a population which is neither coarse nor unsophisticated. Its rulers, after pushing aside the nobility (which in that city was renowned throughout Italy) and crushing the party of the people which they call "the Twelve," carried on peacefully for many years, but at length began to divide into two factions. These allied themselves either with the people or the rulers of Italy, according to what they thought best served their interests.[700]

218. But when King Alfonso marched against the Florentines, as I described previously, these factions were revealed more clearly. One of them considered that the king should be helped in his war against the Florentines; the other, not daring to advocate that Florence should be assisted, recommended that the war be ignored. At first, the friends of the king carried the day and sent provisions into his camp. But when the king encamped close to the city at the sixth milestone, the supporters of the Florentines spread a rumor among the people that Alfonso was trying to take over Siena rather than

---

699. Aeneas heard about this destructive tornado while at Alfonso's court in Naples. He arrived there in April 1456 to seek the king's help in negotiating peace between Siena and Jacopo Piccinino, the details of which he describes in paras. 219–20; see Cecilia Ady, *Pius II* (London: Methuen and Co., 1907), 143–45 on Aeneas's visit to Naples.

700. A popular revolt in 1355 supported by Emperor Charles IV deposed the governing body of the nine and installed a new governing body, comprised of twelve lords of the guilds. Several coup attempts followed, including one in 1384, in which the Piccolomini and other noble families tried to take over the government, but were exiled in 1385. Among the many vicissitudes in Sienese politics in this period, the city surrendered itself to Giangaleazzo Visconti from 1399 to 1404 to seek protection from Florentine aggression; see Martines, *Power and Imagination*, 134–35; Samuel Cohn, *Popular Protest in Late Medieval Europe* (Manchester: Manchester University Press, 2004), 112–18.

Florence. This caused trepidation throughout the city, and armed men were posted at the gates, who kept an eye on Alfonso's soldiers as if they were plotting against their liberty. Francesc Martorell, a man of outstanding intelligence whom the king was happy to have in his employ, was sent to them as an ambassador and for a while allayed the people's suspicion.[701] But since the policies of the republic were being disrupted less by love or hate of the king than by private quarrels of the citizens,[702] they allowed so meager a supply of food to be brought into the king's camp that they seemed to be making fools of both the Florentines and the king at the same time.[703] The same happened on another, later occasion when Ferrante, the king's son, also led an army against the Florentines;[704] for they failed to provide him with sufficient support when he first arrived. However, the Venetians, who were joined in alliance to the Sienese and to the king, pestered the Sienese so much with delegations that they, too, finally allied themselves with the king and publicly declared war on Florence. This war soon subsided when the Venetians accepted peace at Lodi without consulting the king.[705]

219. Immediately after this, another war broke out between the Sienese and Count Aldobrandino of Pitigliano in which they employed Sigismondo Malatesta and Giberto da Correggio as commanders, whose power the enemy had less reason to fear than the Sienese themselves.[706] When dissension arose between Sigismondo and the Sienese, and he observed that he was under suspicion, he

701. Martorell was chief secretary in the chancery of Alfonso.

702. Reading *civium* (as in the 1571 edition) for mss. *civibus*.

703. The Sienese eventually refused to allow Alfonso's troops to camp in their territory in the fall of 1447 when he began his campaign against Florence; see Ryder, *Alfonso*, 277–78.

704. Beginning in July 1452.

705. On the Peace of Lodi, see para. 189.

706. The conflict began in late 1454. Aldobrandino Orsini (d. 1472) was a condottiere and the lord of Pitigliano, a minor town south of Siena. Giberto (or Roberto) (d. 1455) was lord of Parma and captain general of Siena at the time; see Serena Ferente, *La Sfortuna di Piccinino: storia dei bracceschi in Italia 1423–1465* (Florence: Olschki Editore, 2005), 48–49; www.condottieridiventura.it.

pulled out—to his own detriment and that of the Sienese. Giberto persevered with the Sienese. Meanwhile, Count Jacopo Piccinino, who had long served the Venetians and won praise for his success as their commander, lacked employment now that a general peace had been achieved. He therefore hastened to Tuscany and, in the name of the friendship the Sienese enjoyed with his father, sent ambassadors and asked them to lend him twenty thousand ducats.[707] When he failed in this attempt, he turned his forces against them and, after entering Sienese territory, plundered several towns, some of which he had captured by force, some by betrayal. Calixtus III, who had just begun his papacy, sent his troops to the aid of Siena, as did Francesco Sforza and the Florentines.[708] The Venetians also provided help, albeit niggardly, when requested to do so in accordance with the treaty. An impromptu battle was fought, from which the participants emerged without great loss. Jacopo was forced to retreat with his army to Castiglione della Pescaia, a town which I said belonged to the king, who had taken it from Florence in the previous war; but despite a fierce assault, he did not succeed in capturing it. In the meantime, Giberto came under suspicion of colluding with Piccinino, a charge for which there existed ample proof. Having been summoned to the city, he was put to death in the Sienese senate and flung through a window into the marketplace.[709]

220. Shortly afterward, Piccinino obtained the town of Orbetello, a place strongly defended by its natural position, through an act of betrayal. For there is access to it only by a single road—one, too, that is very narrow and protected by the citadel facing it. Its other sides are hemmed in by a swamp which is navigable only by small sail-

---

707. The Peace of Lodi had left Piccinino without employment or a means to pay his troops; see Ludwig Pastor, *The History of the Popes from the Close of the Middle Ages* (London: Kegan Paul, Trench, Trübner & Co, 1899), vol. 2: 360–64.

708. Piccinino's forces entered Sienese territory in early 1455. Papal forces, including some which had been readied to fight the Turks, were diverted to aid Siena in the summer of 1455.

709. Giberto was executed on Sept. 6, 1455.

boats or skiffs. Finding a plentiful store of grain and wine, Piccinino stayed here until a peace settlement was concluded by the king of Aragon, when he [Piccinino] returned to the kingdom [of Naples].[710]

221. But although this peace released Siena from external war, it entangled it more and more in an internal one. For, as if they had caused the wars and fostered the ambitions of Piccinino, some of the king's friends were beheaded, some banished. Many, when they saw the danger threatening them in their homeland, fled into exile of their own accord, and suspects were treated with such severity that it seemed cruel even to the Florentines. There is no end yet to these evils, for in this city, which is so far from achieving tranquility, new conspiracies are formed or discovered daily, and the marketplace is sprinkled with the blood of citizens.

Perhaps this trouble was foretold in the year of Jubilee by that pregnant pony, which expired while giving birth in front of the gate that leads to Rome as a large crowd looked on. For, although it showed no trace of the female sex, it was a hermaphrodite.

222. Among other banished men whom the citizenry considered innocent, there were two who had been friends from childhood and united by their shared intellectual pursuits, though one practiced the science of civil law, the other poetry: Gregorio Lolli[711] and Francesco Patrizi.[712] Many of Francesco's poems survive, which are praised by men of the highest erudition and considered to have saved his life. During the same time, Mariano Sozzini[713] was es-

---

710. Jacopo Piccinino took Orbetello, the port of Siena, in October 1455. Alfonso aided negotiations with members of the League of Lodi to buy off the condottiere's aggression in Tuscany, and he allowed Piccinino to withdraw with his troops to Naples. Aeneas talks more openly about Alfonso's role in secretly supporting Piccinino's plan to disrupt Sienese territory from the beginning in the *Commentaries*, Bk I, passim. See also Ferente, *La Sfortuna di Piccinino*, 52 ff.; Pastor, *History of the Popes*, vol. 2: 362–64.

711. Gregorio (Goro) Lolli, Aeneas's cousin and lifelong friend. He would later become a trusted secretary to Aeneas when he was pope.

712. Francesco Patrizi, humanist, political writer, and bishop of Gaeta (r. 1461–94).

713. Professor of law and humanist, Sozzini was Aeneas's favorite teacher at the Studio of Siena. He encouraged Aeneas to write his famous *Tale of Two Lovers* (1444).

teemed far and wide for his knowledge of the law, not only in Siena but throughout Italy.

56 ITALY: PIOMBINO

223. THE FAMOUS town of Piombino is thought to have been built from the ruins of Populonia; some think it should be called Populino. It is situated on the shore of the Tuscan Sea opposite the island of Elba, whose inexhaustible deposits of iron provide the lord of Piombino with a large annual revenue. The ruler of this town was Jacopo d'Appiano, son of Paola, a most noble woman who was the sister of Pope Martin V.[714] He was a peaceful ruler and loved by his neighbors. When he failed to obtain male offspring from his wife, he looked for an heir outside of marriage and began a love affair with a certain concubine. When her belly had swollen and the time for giving birth was imminent, Jacopo was overcome with incredible joy and pleadingly invited the Florentines and Sienese to send representatives to raise the newborn baby from the holy font and become godfathers; they consented, and the representatives arrived on the appointed day. The woman, after completing a long labor under the care of midwives, finally gave birth to a dark-skinned baby.[715] As well as provoking the people's merriment and guffaws, this put an end to the matter of godfathers and to the ruler's happiness. There happened at this time to be a Moorish flute-player in his household, who was believed to be the father. As soon as he learned that his misconduct had been found out, he ran away to save himself.

224. When Jacopo died, he was replaced by Rinaldo Orsini—a sharp-witted man, experienced in the art of war—not through his own entitlement but that of his wife, who had been Jacopo's daugh-

---

714. Jacopo II d'Appiano (r. 1405–41), son of Paola Colonna, who acted as regent from 1441–45 after Jacopo's death.
715. Lit. "Ethiopian."

ter.⁷¹⁶ When Alfonso was detained in Tuscany by the war against the Florentines, he discovered that Rinaldo was supporting the enemy. He therefore moved his camp to Piombino, blockaded him inside the walls, and launched an all-out assault by land and sea. However, Rinaldo defended his citizens from within no less courageously than the king's soldiers attacked the walls from without. The fighting continued for a long time with fierce intensity, so that many were slain on both sides, and a considerable number of the wounded fell into the hands of the enemy.⁷¹⁷

Many men showed conspicuous courage in this battle, including the two Antonios, Fuxanus and Caldora,⁷¹⁸ who approached the walls together and were observed fighting bravely among the rest. But most admired of all was Galeotto Baldassino, a Sicilian by birth, who on three occasions attempted to break into the town by climbing to the top of the wall where it had been shattered by artillery.⁷¹⁹ However, he was kept at bay by boiling water and quicklime, which was poured down on him amidst a volley of missiles and burned his limbs when it penetrated to the skin. He was finally dislodged by the blow of a heavy rock which broke off part of the rampart.

Galeotto was of above-average height, with powerful, shapely limbs, and his strength was proportional to his size. He was second to none in wrestling, throwing, and running, and his spirit

716. Rinaldo Orsini, lord of Piombino (r. 1445–50); his wife, Caterina, was actually Jacopo II's sister.

717. On the siege of Piombino (December 1447–September 1448) by Alfonso's forces, see para. 209.

718. Fuxanus is perhaps Antonio de Foxa, an Aragonese castellan of Trani (1459–61); see Francesco Senatore, "Pontano e la Guerra di Napoli," in *Condottieri e uomini d'arme nell'Italia del Rinascimento*, ed. Mario Del Treppo (Naples: Liguori, 2002), 282, n. 11. Pietragalla identifies him as Giannantonio Fossano; see Facio, *Rerum gestarum*, 439. Antonio Caldora (c. 1400–77) served as condottiere for René d'Anjou; he was named duke of Bari and viceroy of Abruzzi and taken prisoner in 1442. While supporting Alfonso at this time, he continued to pursue his own interests and change sides until Ferrante defeated him in 1465; *DBI*, vol. 16: 633–37.

719. Galeotto Baldassino (also spelled Bardassino or Bardaxi) (d. 1477), lord of Martini; see Ryder, *Kingdom of Naples*, 275. This passage draws almost verbatim from Facio, *Rerum gestarum*, 9.100ff.

was equal to his brawn. Both on horseback and on foot, he was a fearsome warrior. Helmeted and clad in heavy armor, he would stand on the ground, holding the saddle with his left hand and a lance in his right, and mount a tall horse with an energetic leap. He fought in single combat on four occasions—twice in Italy, twice in France—and emerged as victor every time. When he was attacked by three enemy horsemen in the same war against Florence, one he knocked half dead from his horse with the hilt of his sword, another he pulled from his saddle and threw to the ground after clasping him around the waist at full gallop, and the third he put to flight after seriously wounding him in the elbow. On top of this, he was so modest that he never talked about himself, even at the request of his friends, and he was popular and loved by all for his mode of life and refined manners.

225. Alfonso persisted at Piombino for several days, but since it seemed difficult to capture the town—his camp lacked provisions and his horses had eaten all the leaves from the trees and were dying of hunger—he lifted the siege and withdrew. Not long after this, Rinaldo became sick and died. His wife, Caterina, in fear that the king would punish her for her husband's offense, sent envoys and promised to pay him the annual tribute of a golden cup worth five hundred ducats for as long as she lived.[720]

226. When she died, the townspeople fretted over whom it would be best to select as their lord. While neighboring potentates used various wiles to try to win them over, it was reported that Emanuele d'Appiano,[721] a member of their ruling family, was still alive, and they could entrust themselves to him. This man had served as a soldier for many years but had neither amassed a fortune nor

---

720. Almost two years actually intervened between Alfonso's withdrawal from Piombino (September 1448) and Rinaldo Orsini's death (July 5, 1450); in the interim, he served Florence as a military commander. The agreement between his wife and Alfonso was reached as part of a treaty with Florence on June 21, 1450; see Ryder, *Alfonso*, 282; www.condottieridiventura.it. Thanks to Bill Caferro for help on this question.

721. Emanuele d'Appiano, son of Jacopo I (r. 1451–57).

acquired a reputation through any remarkable feat. Therefore he had now given up soldiering and taken a wife in Troia in Apulia. There he was living a modest life, with the thought of ruling furthest from his mind, when he was officially invited by the people of Piombino. When he first heard the news, it seemed to him like a dream. Willingly embracing this jest of fortune, he then became a different man, as if he had slept through his life up till now. Despite his advanced age, he took up the rulership and governed for many years thereafter with the approval of his subjects and the friendship of his neighbors. He served, moreover, in the army of Alfonso, who had been his patron, and also paid him tribute. He died having named as his heir the younger of the two sons born to him outside of matrimony,[722] because the city preferred him to the older one.

57 ITALY: VITERBO

227. IN VITERBO, there were great upheavals. For, during the papacy of Nicholas V, Princivalle Gatti, the ruler of that city, was set upon and murdered by his enemies at Lago di Vico while returning from Rome.[723] Then, during the papacy of Calixtus III, his nephew Guglielmo was killed at home during the night.[724] This gave rise to a restless quest for vengeance, and the city endured great sufferings while the malefactors were tracked down, some taking to flight, others receiving punishment.

---

722. Jacopo III d'Appiano (r. 1458–74).
723. Princivalle was murdered in 1454 by the rival Mondaleschi faction.
724. Guglielmo Gatti was murdered in 1456.

58 ITALY: ROME

228. AT LONG LAST, I am faced with the affairs of the city of Rome, which call for their own narrative. I will try to do them justice while adhering to my principle of brevity.

In Rome, Giovanni Vitelleschi—patriarch of Alexandria, cardinal, legate, governor of the Patrimony of St. Peter, and commander of the papal army, who had defeated and killed in battle the tyrants of Foligno and Camerino, the prefect of Rome, Count Antonio da Pisa,[725] and many others who insulted the church—was suddenly attacked by the guards of Castel Sant'Angelo while trying to cross the Sant'Angelo bridge over the Tiber in order to move troops into Tuscany. He was wounded, taken prisoner, and hustled into the castle, where he met his death a few days later, either from drinking poison or as a result of his wound.[726]

229. Ludovico Scarampo, a cardinal himself and the patriarch of Aquileia, who was already widely known for his achievements and friendship with the pope, then took over his responsibilities.[727] After calming the situation in the city, he prepared for the return of Pope Eugenius. The Romans had arrested Eugenius, proclaimed their freedom, and kept him under guard at Santa Maria in Trastevere; when he tricked his guards and fled by boat down the Tiber, they had pursued him with spears and arrows, for the people were

---

725. Corrado Trinci of Foligno, defeated in 1439; Piergentile of the Varano family, lord of Camerino, executed in 1433. Count Antonio da Pisa is Antonio da Pontedera, whom Vitelleschi captured and hanged in 1436. See John Law, "Giovanni Vitelleschi: prelato guerriero," *Renaissance Studies* 12 (1998): 40–66.

726. Giovanni Vitelleschi (1396–1440) commanded papal troops from the late 1430s to 1440, winning numerous, often brutal, victories. He became titular patriarch of Alexandria and archbishop of Florence in 1435 and cardinal in 1437. It was rumored that he wished to seize the papacy for himself. On the day Vitelleschi was set to depart for Umbria (March 19, 1440), Antonio Rido, the castellan of Castel Sant'Angelo, waited until the cardinal's troops had passed over the bridge and seized him. Vitelleschi died on April 2, 1440; see Chambers, *Popes, Cardinals and War*, 42–45.

727. Ludovico Scarampo (1401–65); created cardinal July 1, 1440; see para. 207.

furious at the invasion of a hostile army which was ravaging the Roman countryside and making off with men and livestock. But after Eugenius had been absent for several years, the rich and poor citizens alike had come to see that without the Papal Curia, Rome was less like a city than a vast and empty cave. They therefore sent envoys to Eugenius and ardently begged him to return to his city. He returned in the ninth year after he had fled, and the ignominy of his expulsion was eclipsed by the glory of his welcome home.[728]

230. There was a dangerous war with Francesco Sforza in the Marches, and in other places, which I will speak of later. Supported by King Alfonso, Eugenius brought this war to a conclusion through the mediation of Cardinal Ludovico and Niccolò Piccinino, who had now been reconciled with him. Francesco Sforza had planned to lead his army to the city of Todi, which was friendly to him (for he had once controlled it and ruled the people mildly), and then to Rome. For among the cardinals, there were some who resented the power of Ludovico and issued invitations to Francesco, in opposition not so much to Eugenius himself as to his policy. They say that among these was Niccolò of Capua,[729] who held influence and power in the City [Rome]; for during this time, Eugenius saw to his removal from Rome on suspicion of this very thing. But when the church's reinforcements hastily arrived on the scene, Francesco withdrew without achieving his aim. As for Eugenius, he had once been an enthusiastic supporter of the Venetians and Florentines, but because they were now providing military and monetary aid to his enemy Francesco in opposition to the church, he, too, switched sides to that of their enemies, King Alfonso and the lord of Milan.[730] Indeed, through his persuasion the king had come as far as Tivoli to

---

728. Eugenius IV (r. 1431–47) fled Rome during an uprising on May 29, 1434. He resided in Florence until his return to Rome on September 28, 1443.

729. Niccolò Acciapacci, called the cardinal of Capua (r. 1439–47); see Peter Blastenbrei, "The Soldier and His Cardinal: Francesco Sforza and Nicolò Acciapacci (1438–1444)," *Renaissance Studies* 3 no. 3 (1989): 290–302.

730. Discussed in paras. 248 and 270.

help Filippo, whose power seemed to have almost collapsed, with the intention of marching either into Tuscany against the Florentines or into northern Italy against the Venetians.

231. But after creating four cardinals, from whom he prescribed that his successor should be chosen, Eugenius, while lying in his sickbed, joined his forefathers a few days later and was buried in St. Peter's Basilica next to Eugenius III.[731] Before he passed away, however, the Germans, who, after observing the rivalry of the two popes, had maintained a kind of neutrality and refused to obey either of them, dispatched envoys to Rome—including me, as an emissary of Emperor Frederick—and restored their allegiance to Eugenius when he was close to death.[732] For his part, Eugenius altered his ruling and reinstated Dietrich and Jakob, archbishops of Cologne and Trier, whom he had deprived of their episcopal rank, in their former positions.[733]

232. Eugenius was without doubt a great and distinguished pope. He scorned money and loved virtue above all. He was neither puffed up by success nor broken by adversity. Hope did not increase his joy, nor fear his sadness. His calm spirit displayed itself in his unchanging countenance. His speech was concise[734] and all the weightier for being so. Though strict and severe in dealing with his enemies, he was kind to those whose loyalty he had regained. Added to this were a tall build, comely looks, and an august nobility in old age. On those who enjoyed his confidence he relied somewhat more, and conferred greater power, than was fitting. When his father was doing business in Egypt in company with the father of

---

731. The last four cardinals created by Eugenius in 1446 were Enrico Rampini, Tommaso Parentucelli (later Pope Nicholas V), Juan Carvajal, and Giovanni de Primis. Eugenius IV died on February 23, 1447; Eugenius III reigned 1145–53.

732. The two rival popes were Eugenius IV (r. 1431–47) and anti-pope Felix V (r. 1440–49). Papal-imperial negotiations began during the summer of 1446, and a formal settlement was reached on February 7, 1447; see Mitchell, *Laurels and the Tiara*, 89–91.

733. Dietrich von Moers and Jakob of Sierk were deposed by Eugenius on January 25, 1446. Eugenius softened his stance on the two shortly before his death, but they were not reinstated until September 1447 by Nicholas V; see Stieber, *Pope Eugenius IV*, 310.

734. Reading *sermone* (Urb. Lat. 885, Vat. Lat. 3888) for van Heck's *sermonem*.

Francesco Foscari,⁷³⁵ whom I have already mentioned, he received a prophecy no less auspicious than the one received by Foscari from the hermit whom they visited together. For one learned that his son would become ruler of his country, the other that his son would rise to the supreme priesthood.

233. Eugenius was baptized with the name of Gabriele. When he had grown up and his parents had been laid to rest, he heeded the message of the Gospel and dispersed the considerable fortune which he had inherited from them among the poor of Christ. Then, accompanied by Antonio Correr, a young man of equal fervor, he entered a religious order, where his conduct earned the highest praise.⁷³⁶ He lived there with Antonio until Angelo Correr, under the name of Gregory XII, obtained the see of Peter.⁷³⁷ Since the two men were inseparable, he sent for them both and appointed Gabriele bishop of Siena and Antonio bishop of Bologna. And, after a short interval, he honored them both with the cardinalate, in which they both shone.⁷³⁸ But Eugenius, after attaining the papacy, distinguished himself more. Although a schism emerged at the beginning of his papacy, and he struggled with the Council of Basel until his death, he nevertheless crowned Sigismund as emperor, achieved union with the Greeks and Armenians, recovered the cities of the church which had been lost, eliminated tyrants in the surrounding area, curbed the obstinacy of the Roman people, and departed from life in victory and renown.⁷³⁹ Although I had once

---

735. Francesco Foscari, doge of Venice (r. 1423–57). See paras. 191–92.
736. Eugenius was born Gabriele Condulmer in Venice, c. 1383. Antonio Correr was his cousin. The two young men entered the order of Augustinian Canons in 1400.
737. Correr, Gabriele and Antonio's uncle, was elected Pope Gregory XII by Roman cardinals during the Schism (r. 1406–15).
738. Gabriele became bishop of Siena in 1407; Antonio, bishop of Bologna in 1407. Both became cardinals in 1408.
739. The Council of Basel repeatedly challenged Eugenius's authority and eventually claimed the right to depose him and elect anti-pope Felix V. Eugenius crowned Sigismund (elected emperor in 1411) in Rome in 1433. Union with the Greeks and Armenians was declared at the Council of Ferrara-Florence, 1438–39. See para. 229 on Eugenius's exile from Rome.

Italy: Rome 263

sided with the Council of Basel against him in the belief that I was serving God (for at that time the whole church was wavering in allegiance), he received me kindly when I came to see him, appointed me one of his secretaries, and bestowed upon me the honor of an apostolic sub-deaconship.[740] A few days before he died, moreover, after hearing a false rumor that the see of Trieste was vacant, he marked it out for me alone of all the many candidates; his successor later fulfilled his wishes.[741]

234. Nicholas V, a Tuscan from the town of Sarzana and the son of a doctor, a man famed for his theological erudition and distinguished in almost every branch of learning, was chosen to succeed Eugenius on the throne of Peter. A few months earlier, he had received a cardinalate from Eugenius after completing a successful mission as legate in Germany, and shortly before that the bishopric of Bologna.[742] Nicholas adorned Rome with many buildings on a grand scale. If his projects could have been completed, they would have rivaled in magnificence any erected by the ancient emperors. But the buildings and their mighty looming walls[743] still lie unfinished. He eradicated the schism in the church which was still flourishing among the people of Savoy, restored Amedeo to favor when he renounced the papacy, and left him the rank of cardinal and the office of legate in his ancestral domain. He stripped of their rank several cardinals created by Amedeo. He blessed the Romans with a long peace. The year of Jubilee [1450] which he held was a success, except that around two hundred people are agreed to have perished when a crowd of people suddenly converged on the Sant'Angelo Bridge and they were either trampled or thrown into the river.[744]

---

740. On Aeneas's previous support of the Council of Basel and anti-pope Felix V, see Izbicki et al., *Reject Aeneas*, passim; see also O'Brien, *The Anatomy of an Apology*.

741. Nicholas V named Aeneas bishop of Trieste on April 17, 1447.

742. Nicholas, born Tommaso Parentucelli (1397–1455), was appointed bishop of Bologna in 1444 and created cardinal on December 16, 1446. He was elected pope on March 6, 1447.

743. Virgil, *Aeneid*, 4.88.

744. The accident occurred on Dec. 19, 1450; Nicholas later erected two chapels at

He raised Bernardino of Siena to sainthood, a brother in the Order of Friars Minor who had died shortly before.[745] He joined Emperor Frederick III and Eleonora Augusta in marriage and anointed and crowned them in the traditional manner, entertaining their households with a sumptuous and elegant feast.[746] He twice created cardinals. Indeed, on the first occasion he chose only you, Antonio, a native of Majorca, whom he named Cardinal of San Crisogono; he picked you from among all others as his equal in philosophical studies and knowledge of the mysteries of sacred theology.[747] On the second occasion, he created six cardinals who were renowned for their erudition or noted for their family's distinction. Among them was his brother, Filippo, a man of gentle character and incorruptible integrity, whom he named Cardinal of Santa Susanna.[748]

235. He ordered books to be tracked down throughout Greece and brought to him, and he saw to it that they were rendered into Latin, offering large rewards to their translators. His favorite translators were George of Trebizond, Lorenzo Valla, Pier Candido Decembrio, and Gregorio of Castello, together with the Greek Demetrius.[749] Their prose so marvelously beguiled the ears of the pope

---

the site to offer daily prayers for the victims' souls; see *International Dictionary of Historic Places*, ed. Trudy Ring (Chicago: Fitzroy-Dearborn Publishers, 1995–96), vol. 3: 588.

745. The popular Franciscan preacher (1380–1444) was canonized on May 24, 1450.

746. Nicholas entertained the imperial couple in March 1452.

747. Antonio de la Cerda (1390–1459), the dedicatee of *Europe*, was created cardinal of San Crisogno on Feb. 16, 1448; he was appointed cardinal of Lérida on March 28, 1449.

748. Filippo Calandrini (1403–76), Nicholas V's half brother, became cardinal in December 1448.

749. Nicholas provided generous support to the scholars he brought to Rome. George of Trebizond (c. 1396–1473), a Cretan humanist who worked for many years at the papal curia in Rome, translated works by such authors as Aristotle, Ptolemy, Eusebius, John Chrysostom, and other Greek church fathers. Valla (1407–57), a Roman humanist and gifted philologist, translated such authors as Thucydides and Herodotus; he worked as a scriptor and secretary under Pope Nicholas. Milanese humanist Decembrio (1399–1477) translated such works as Plato's *Republic*. Umbrian humanist Gregorio di Città di Castello (better known as Gregorio Tifernate; c. 1415–66) translated works by Aristotle and Strabo, among others, under Nicholas's patronage. "The Greek Demetrius" has yet to be identified but is possibly Demetrius Chalcondyles (1423/24–1511), who spent time in Rome during Nicholas's reign and was a member of Cardinal Bessarion's circle. Thanks

that they never failed to obtain from him whatever they requested. He keenly desired the poetry of Homer to be made into a Latin epic poem, and a great many tried to oblige him, but only one man succeeded in meeting his exacting standards. This was Orazio Romano who, having been appointed as a papal secretary for this purpose and enticed by large promises, took on the *Iliad* and translated several of its books into Latin; these deserve the admiration of our own age and would have escaped criticism even in antiquity.[750] Niccolò Perotti, too, with his agreeable and elegant translation of Polybius, Giovanni Tortelli of Arezzo, with his skillfully written book *On Orthography*, Alberti of Florence, with his excellent volumes *On Architecture*, and other authors almost beyond count earned the favor of this pope with their new compositions.[751] For Nicholas so keenly stimulated and fostered gifted writers that it would be hard to find an age in which the study of the humanities, eloquence, and all the other noble arts flourished more than in his. Certainly no one would deny that more volumes were inscribed to him by leading scholars than we find dedicated to his predecessors or any of the emperors. However, I am surprised that he neglected one scholar: Flavio Biondo of Forlì, who with astonishing organization, laid out the history of the world in two *Decades*, from the decline of the

---

to Neils Gaul for help with this figure. For more on these and other scholars in this section, see Charles Stinger, *The Renaissance in Rome* (Bloomington: Indiana University Press, 1985); Grendler, *ER*; Rabil, *Renaissance Humanism*; and Mario Cosenza, *Biographical and Bibliographical Dictionary of the Italian Humanists and of the World of Classical Scholarship in Italy 1300–1800* (Boston: G. K. Hall, 1962–1967).

750. A little-studied humanist from Viterbo, Romano served Nicholas V, Calixtus III, and Pius II. He died sometime before 1467; see Anna Maria Oliva, "Orazio Romano" in *Roma nel Rinascimento* (1994): 23–29.

751. Perotti (1429–80), who later became a papal secretary and archbishop of Siponto, translated Polybius; his other notable works were a Latin grammar and an expansive commentary on Martial. Tortelli (1400–66) was Nicholas's trusted librarian, responsible for procuring and curating the many volumes in the papal collection. Florentine humanist and polymath Leon Battista Alberti (1404–72) served as a papal secretary under Eugenius IV and Nicholas V. He wrote *De re aedificatoria* in Rome, and is known for his treatises on painting and a dialogue on the family. He also designed several churches or elements of them, such as the famous façade of Santa Maria Novella in Florence.

Roman Empire to our own era. He restored Rome in describing it; he illuminated Italy; and, when he undertook to write of the triumphant City, he revealed to us the whole of antiquity.[752] But this is the way of the world: rarely does a pope praise anyone who was loved by his predecessor. However that may be, Nicholas built up a library richly stocked with ancient and modern manuscripts, in which he deposited around three thousand volumes.[753]

236. He wonderfully adorned the papal sacristy with vessels of gold and silver and priestly vestments. For the altar, he purchased ornaments and tapestries of amazing workmanship woven with gold. Throughout the palace, he provided the necessary furnishings on a most magnificent scale, doubling and tripling it in quantity.

His responses to the embassies which he heard in public were of such quality that one hardly knew what to admire more: his wisdom or his eloquence. If he learned that any foreigners worthy of esteem were visiting the city, he immediately honored them by sending gifts of welcome. When nobles who had been banished from their own homes came to him, he took generous care of them. To the poor of Christ, he gave liberal alms and saw to it that mendicant friars lacked nothing essential. He contributed numerous gifts to the churches of the city. In the Patrimony of St. Peter, he built a large number of well-fortified castles in strategic locations.[754]

237. Even so, there was no lack of conspirators against the life of this pope, a life so much to be admired and desired. Stefano of Rome, a knight of reduced means from the Porcari family, often fomented sedition in the City.[755] For that he was banished to Bologna,

---

752. Flavio Biondo (1392–1463), one of the greatest Renaissance historians of ancient Rome, served as papal secretary to Eugenius IV, Nicholas V, Calixtus III, and Pius II. Biondo is credited with early archaeological studies of ancient Rome as well as systematic historical study of Rome and medieval Europe. Here Aeneas refers to his *Decades* and three other works, *Roma Instaurata*, *Italia Illustrata*, and *Roma Triumphans*.

753. Nicholas's patronage and passion for book collecting became the foundation of the Vatican Library.

754. These include Spoleto, Nepi, and Città Castellana; see Chambers, *Popes and Cardinals*, 47.

755. Stefano Porcari (c. 1400–53). Influenced by his humanistic studies and service

but he left Bologna in secret and returned to Rome in rapid stages. He promptly convened his friends and explained his purpose, insisting that it was disgraceful for the city which had brought the whole world beneath its sway now to be subservient to the power of priests; one would more rightly call them women than men. He had come prepared to strike the yoke from his fatherland, which would be easy to accomplish if only they were men. Pope Nicholas could be apprehended without much trouble on the festival of the Epiphany as he was about to celebrate mass in the Church of St. Peter. The people loved liberty and would quickly assist them in their venture when they heard of its proclamation. To bind the pope, he brought with him a golden chain which he had acquired some time ago and showed it to the gathering. For, he said, it was not in their interest to kill the pope immediately, but to guard him until they had recovered Castel Sant'Angelo through his help. Since he was an eloquent speaker, Stefano easily got the group to support his idea, and all the more easily because he had invited men who were impecunious, loaded with debt, and fearful of being tried for the crimes they had committed—men whom peace offered nothing to hope for. But Nicholas got wind of the plot and sent soldiers with orders to arrest the man. They found him in his sister's house, broken-spirited and hiding in a chest. His accomplices were attacked and captured in the house where they had met. One of them, Battista Sciarra, with boldness and a fearless spirit, cleared a path with his sword through the midst of the papal guards and escaped.[756] Stefano met his end by hanging in Castel Sant'Angelo,

---

in Florence as captain of the people (1427–28), Porcari began to envision a return to republican rule in Rome and delivered public speeches to that effect. Despite these leanings, he was employed by the papacy and entrusted with various missions. Exiled to Bologna in 1452 for suspicion of treachery, he later returned to Rome in secret and was apprehended while plotting an insurrection. He was tried and executed on January 29, 1453. For more on Porcari, see Anthony D'Elia, "Stefano Porcari's Conspiracy Against Pope Nicholas V in 1453 and Republican Culture in Papal Rome," *Journal of the History of Ideas* 68, no. 2 (2007): 207–31.

756. Sciarra, Porcari's nephew and co-conspirator, was later apprehended in Venice and executed at Città di Castello.

the others on the Campidoglio. And so it was that the supreme pontiff was rescued from great danger and preserved the prestige and power of the Roman see.

238. The pope was blessed with the greatest good fortune in everybody's judgment, except that, as I related previously, the sack of Constantinople by the Turks occurred during his reign—an everlasting memorial to the sloth and faint-heartedness of Christians.[757] There was something else, too, which diminished his glory to no small extent. After being chosen unanimously by the various parties to initiate and arbitrate a peace settlement in Italy, which was then being ravaged by sword and flame, he dragged out the deliberations day after day and came to be suspected by Francesco Sforza, now lord of the Milanese, and by the Venetians of being unwilling to pronounce a decision that seemed to bring peace to others but war to the church.[758] Thanks to the intervention of the monk Simonetto,[759] a member of the Order of the Hermits of St. Augustine, who was insignificant and completely unknown before this but a man of unimpeachable integrity, the Venetians met with Duke Francesco and negotiated the terms of an agreement, setting a deadline by which their allies in the war would ratify the peace.[760] It seemed miraculous to everyone that a humble and unknown monk had brought peace to Italy.[761] But when Alfonso rejected the peace, which had been declared without his knowledge, Nicholas revealed the emptiness of the suspicion he had incurred

757. Constantinople fell on May 29, 1453.
758. Nicholas held peace talks in Rome from November 1453–March 1454. His ill health, pressure from Alfonso V, and possibly concerns about papal territories, as Aeneas notes, combined to hinder negotiations; see para. 189.
759. Fra Simonetto da Camerino was sent by Venice to negotiate with Sforza in secret.
760. Sforza and Venice signed their treaty at Lodi on April 9, 1454.
761. Florence, Venice, and Milan entered into a twenty-five year treaty/defensive league of mutual protection on August 30, 1454. They invited Alfonso and the pope to join the league, provided they accept the territorial concessions made at Lodi. Alfonso refused.

by sending Cardinal Domenico Capranica of Santa Croce, a man of singular wisdom and conspicuous probity, as a legate to Alfonso.[762] When he reached Gaeta and then Naples, he was joined by emissaries sent by the Venetians and other parties. After they had made a fresh start and discussed all their differences, he not only persuaded King Alfonso to make peace but concluded a pact of twenty-five years among all the powers of Italy, which the pope was appointed to preserve and adjudicate.[763]

239. But, having suffered greatly from arthritic pains through almost his whole papacy, Nicholas grew more and more exhausted every day, and, when his pure soul could no longer endure its unclean mortal companion, departed from this life.[764] He not only confirmed the duties with which Pope Eugenius had entrusted me but added the rank of bishop and assigned to me first the Church of Trieste, then that of Siena.[765]

240. After him, Calixtus III obtained the throne of St. Peter.[766] He was Spanish in origin, born of a noble family in the kingdom of Valencia. He was the most eminent of all jurists in his time and had presided for many years over the council of King Alfonso, whose skills and circumspection he displayed in his own person.[767] No sooner had he risen to the summit of the papacy than he turned

762. Capranica (1400–58; cardinal as of 1430), Aeneas's first employer and a correspondent of his; it was he who brought the young humanist to the Council of Basel.

763. Alfonso signed the pact on January 26, 1455, but only after the other powers agreed to exclude Genoa, against which Alfonso still harbored animosity; the Genoese, for their part, wanted to retain the option of attacking Alfonso if the need arose; see Epstein, *Genoa*, 285.

764. Nicholas died on March 25, 1455.

765. Aeneas became bishop of Trieste on April 17, 1447, and Siena on Sept. 23, 1450.

766. Calixtus, born Alfonso de Borja (or Borgia) (1378–1458), was trained as a canon lawyer and was secretary and chief councillor of King Alfonso V of Aragon from 1417 to 1444. He was created cardinal in 1444 and elected pope on April 8, 1455; see Michael Mallett, *The Borgias: The Rise and Fall of a Renaissance Dynasty* (New York: Barnes and Noble, 1969), 61–62.

767. The interpretation of the second half of this sentence is uncertain (*et qui consilium regis Alfonsi, in quo multis annis presederat, illiusque artes ac cautiones pre se ferret*). Perhaps a word or more has dropped out.

his mind toward destroying the religion and race of the Turks, and he made a solemn vow to that effect. He sent the leading cardinals of the Holy Roman Church as legates to France, Germany, Hungary, and the East, of whom none has yet returned; however, people think that Alain, cardinal of Santa Prassede, a very talented man with a confident and powerful mind, will return from France any day now.[768] He built shipyards in Rome, a thing previously unheard of, and on the bank of the Tiber in the Leonine City he constructed and armed a great many galleys which he launched against the Turks.[769] When Count Jacopo Piccinino attacked the Sienese in force (as I have described), the pope restrained him by sending his own troops.[770] When King Alfonso asked how they were going to get along with one another, he replied, "Let Alfonso rule his own kingdoms and leave to me the control of the supreme apostolate." A large part of Italy believed that their genuine disagreements on many matters were feigned and fabricated; among those who thought their rivalry was real, some blamed Calixtus, some Alfonso, some both, inasmuch as one of them could not endure the king whose subject he had been by birth, the other the supreme pontiff to whom he owed obedience as the vicar of God.

241. Calixtus twice created cardinals. On the first occasion he named three, of whom two were his nephews. Although they were somewhat younger than seemed appropriate for such rank, their learning, discretion, and attractive characters are held to have justified this honor.[771] The third was Jaime of Portugal, a scion of royal blood, conspicuous for such modesty, such seriousness, such shrewd intelligence, such scholarly zeal, and such love of virtue that, although he was still a young man, everyone thought that he

768. Alain de Coëtivy (1407–74), created cardinal in 1448.
769. For Calixtus's devotion to crusading, see Setton, *Papacy and Levant*, vol. 2: chap. 6.
770. See paras. 219–21.
771. Luis Juan del Mila, Rodrigo de Borja (both nephews of Calixtus), and Jaime of Portugal were all between the ages of twenty-three and twenty-six when they were created cardinals in September 1456.

rose too slowly to that rank.⁷⁷² On the second occasion, six cardinals were chosen, who were by no means unworthy of such high office—with the sole exception of me. However, in my opinion no one deserved this honor more than Juan, bishop of Zamora, an eminent authority on civil law, who throughout thirty-nine years of attending the Roman Curia had remained pure and blameless in the performance of almost all its duties.⁷⁷³ Calixtus assigned the chancery, which had been vacant since the time of Nicholas, to his nephew Rodrigo, the cardinal of San Nicola in Carcere and legate of the Marches.⁷⁷⁴ He also placed that man's brother, Pedro de Borja, a young man of splendid promise and disposition, in command of the church's army; subsequently he entrusted to him the prefecture of the city.⁷⁷⁵ To Luis, cardinal of the Santi Quattro Coronati, who was another of his nephews, he assigned the legation of Bologna.⁷⁷⁶

242. Among the company of the saints, he enrolled Vincent of Spain and Osmund of England, who were celebrated for their miracles.⁷⁷⁷ He sent legates to Scythia, Persia, and Ethiopia to keep Christians of the East within the faith and arm them against the enemies of religion. He paid subsidies to Skanderbeg in Albania⁷⁷⁸ and many others in Greece who were suffering from the war with the Turks. He instituted the festival of the Transfiguration of Our Lord and ordered it to be celebrated in public.⁷⁷⁹ He predicted his

772. Jaime of Portugal (1433–59) was the nephew of King Afonso V of Portugal.
773. Juan de Mella (1397–1467), professor of canon law and bishop of Léon and Zamora. He and Aeneas were created cardinals in December 1456.
774. Rodrigo de Borja (more commonly Borgia) (1431–1503), later the infamous Pope Alexander VI, was appointed legate *a latere* in the March of Ancona in December 1456 and vice chancellor of the papal court in 1457; the latter position had been vacant since 1453; Pastor, *History of the Popes*, vol. 2: 459.
775. Pedro was appointed captain-general of the church in 1456 and prefect of the city of Rome in 1457.
776. Luis was appointed governor of Bologna in 1455. After becoming cardinal, he was appointed legate *a latere* to the city in 1457.
777. St. Vincent Ferrer (1350–1419), canonized June 3, 1455; St. Osmund (d. 1099), canonized January 1, 1457.
778. George Castriot; see para. 57.
779. August 6, 1456. This feast had been long observed in Eastern rite churches.

elevation several years before he was chosen pope and also prophesied the defeat which the Turks sustained at Belgrade in Hungary.[780] Even now he promises many great things for the future, which I hope that the goodness of God will not deny.

243. On the death of Count Giovanni of Tagliacozzo, who came from the stock of the Orsini, the Orsini claimed his inheritance by right of kinship, since he lacked male offspring. This vexed Count Everso [Anguillara], whose son was married to Giovanni's only daughter, and a violent struggle ensued. The Colonnas lent their assistance to Count Everso.[781] Then, at the urging of the pope, Cardinal Prospero,[782] the nephew of Martin V—a most sagacious and successful pope in his time, who was the most respected man of that family and widely renowned for his scholarship—withdrew his kinsfolk from the war. To this day, the unfriendly feelings between the Orsini and Everso remain unassuaged. Cardinal Latino of Santi Giovanni e Paolo, the distinguished head of the Orsini family, a man of nimble intelligence, noted for his knowledge of the law and a mind that attended to profound matters and disdained the petty, departed from the City and retired to his own towns, as if he thought Rome too unsafe for him, either fearing the count's treachery or disturbed by the pope's anger; despite being recalled, he has refused to return to this very day.[783]

Among all the cardinals, two in particular have been heard and received by Calixtus up to now: Guillaume of Rouen, a man of pleasant nature and distinguished lineage, and Pietro of San Marco,

---

Calixtus declared it a universal feast day to commemorate the Christian victory at Belgrade; see *Dictionary of the Middle Ages*, ed. Joseph R. Strayer (New York: Scribner, 1982–), vol. 12: 126.

780. July 22, 1456.

781. This conflict between the Orsini and Colonna erupted over the disputed lordship of Tagliacozzo on the day of Calixtus's coronation (April 20, 1455); see Pastor, *History of the Popes*, vol. 2: 338–39.

782. Prospero Colonna (c. 1410–63), cardinal as of 1426.

783. Latino Orsini (c. 1410–77), created cardinal in 1448. Orsini also played a role in keeping the peace after Calixtus's election; see Pastor, *History of the Popes*, vol. 2: 339.

the nephew of Eugenius IV, a scion of a noble Venetian family and a man of exceptional diligence.[784] Either he believed there was much of value in their counsels or he thought that the former could guide the kingdom of France, the latter the republic of Venice.

He held such esteem for Simone of Rome, who excelled in philosophical studies and the art of medicine, that he presented a cardinal's hat to his brother Giacomo, bishop of Montefeltro—chiefly out of respect for Simone, though his brother was a man of outstanding virtue.[785]

244. In hearing embassies and the cases of private individuals, he far surpassed the ability of his predecessors. He dictated letters to kings and friends on his own and willingly and cheerfully devoted time to signing petitions. When consulted about the law, he replied with alacrity; the laws and canons he had at his fingertips, as if he had left law-school just yesterday or the day before; for nothing slipped from his memory that he thought worthy of retention. Moreover, no faculty seemed to him more important than knowledge of the law, in which he so excelled that scarcely one or two of his predecessors could be found to compare with him.

245. After enrolling me in the order of cardinals, he also entrusted me, at the request of the canons, with the Church of Warmia, which is situated by the Baltic Sea among the Sarmatians. As yet, I have been unable to take possession of it owing to the cruel and bloody wars which are raging in that region.[786]

---

784. Guillaume d'Estouteville (1403–83), French noble related to the royal family. Aeneas portrays a very different side of the cardinal in his famous account of his own election as pope in book I of the *Commentaries* (Meserve and Simonetta, vol. 1: 178–99; Gragg and Gabel, vol. 1: 93–105). Pietro Barbo (1417–71), Venetian patrician, cardinal in 1440, and later Pope Paul II (r. 1464–71). Pietro was also instrumental in establishing peace between the great Roman families at this time.

785. Simone Tebaldi was Calixtus's physician. Giacomo (d. 1465) was created cardinal in 1456.

786. Appointed to the bishopric of Warmia in 1457, Aeneas was never able to claim it as the inhabitants of the diocese opposed his appointment. See para. 98.

59 ITALY: UMBRIA, THE MARCHES

246. IN UMBRIA, which is now contained[787] within the duchy of Spoleto, few cities were free from internal discord. Norcia, once the homeland of Quintus Sertorius,[788] has only recently enjoyed a respite from repeated disruption by the intrigues of the Guelph party. Narni, which is ringed by a white river with sulfurous waters and hard to approach on its double ridge,[789] was once oppressed by the faction of the Ghibellines but now enjoys tranquility under the political guidance of the Guelphs. The people of Amelia, Rieti, Foligno, Ortona, and finally Spoleto all experienced their own calamities.[790] But the city of Assisi turned out to exceed them all in misery. By admitting at one time the faction of Braccio, at another that of Sforza, and expelling now the stronger party, now the one reputed to be weaker, it has been brought so low that its population could be described not just as reduced but rather nonexistent, the city having been almost deserted.[791]

247. The region of Picenum, known in our time as the Marches, was appropriated by Francesco Sforza in virtually a single expedition, when Pope Eugenius IV was occupied with affairs in Basel and embroiled in disputes not only with Filippo Maria but also King Alfonso. Francesco retained continuous possession of it for some years afterward.[792]

787. Reading *continetur* for mss. *continentur*.
788. Roman soldier (d. 73 BCE), who served Marius and set up an independent state in Spain, successfully fighting back several attempts by Roman troops to defeat him until he was assassinated by jealous officers under his command.
789. Martial, *Epigrams*, 7.93.1–2.
790. A reference to the Ghibelline uprisings against the Avignonese papacy in the early to mid fourteenth century in Umbria, which were harshly put down by Cardinal Gil Albornoz in the 1350s and 1360s; see Chambers, *Popes, Cardinals and War*, 25–32.
791. Condottiere Braccio da Montone (1386–1424) took control of Assisi, along with several other central Italian cities, in 1416; the pope recognized his rule of Assisi in 1419. The city changed hands several times in the next few decades between the Bracceschi faction and the Sforzescha faction. Niccolò Piccinino's troops brutally sacked the city in 1442.
792. Dissatisfied with the rule of papal legate Giovanni Vitelleschi, several towns in

Italy: Umbria, the Marches 275

Meanwhile, Sforza fell in love with a girl who was one of his wife's handmaids and who caused much trouble for Francesco as well as her own death. She was called Perpetua, the daughter of high-ranking parents in Novara.[793] She possessed beauty and an honorable character, except for being deceived by the flatteries of her powerful master into exchanging virginity for adultery. When her belly gradually began to swell, she was betrothed to a man who had been found to marry her in order to conceal the transgression. On the appointed day of their nuptials, after inviting his friends and preparing a grand banquet, the bridegroom joyfully awaited the arrival of his new bride in the town where he lived not far from the court of Francesco. The woman was brought with an escort of many nobles, but after she entered the town, and people thought that she would dismount at the house of her fiancé, she was ordered to keep going and hustled into the citadel, leaving no further opportunity for her unlucky husband to see his bride. When Francesco's wife, Bianca, who was a very shrewd woman, learned of this, she did not rest until she had sent assassins to kill the girl, although she was closely guarded. Francesco, despite being deeply upset by this, thought he should forgive his wife as her resentment was justified.[794]

248. After this, Pope Eugenius, who had now been reconciled with Filippo Maria and King Alfonso, sent Niccolò Piccinino with an army to confront Francesco and also urged the king to invade the Marches. Alfonso agreed. After levying troops, he arrived in

---

the March of Ancona offered themselves to Sforza in December 1433, prompting Pope Eugenius to declare him marquis of the Marches, vicar of Fermo, and gonfaloniere of the church in February 1434; see Ady, *Milan under the Sforza*, 16–18. Sforza lost all but Jesi in 1445 and finally signed that town over to the papacy on Aug 4, 1447.

793. Perpetua da Varese, mother of Polidoro Sforza, who was legitimized by Nicholas V in 1448.

794. Bianca's assassination of the woman cannot be verified, as Aeneas seems to be our only source; see Marcello Simonetta, *Rinascimento segreto: il mondo del segretario da Petrarca a Machiavelli* (Milan: F. Angeli, 2004), 101–2. The story seems questionable given the considerable number of Sforza's mistresses and illegitimate children that Bianca must have known about.

the Marches with the flower of his cavalry and infantry, joined camps at Visso with Piccinino, who was made commander of the whole army, and forced the terrified townsmen to surrender to the church.[795] The inhabitants of Sanseverino followed their example and sent him the keys to their gates. When Francesco learned of this, he distributed his troops among the better defended towns of the region, thinking it to his advantage to prolong the war. After Pietro Brunoro,[796] one of his military commanders, went over to the king with eight hundred horsemen, and the inhabitants of Macerata and Tolentino surrendered to the church, Francesco, with the agreement of the Venetians and Florentines and through the mediation of his friends, pretended to renew his friendship with Duke Filippo of Milan in order to escape the king's power. Filippo believed him and via letters and emissaries asked Alfonso to return his forces to the kingdom of Naples—in vain, for the king considered it dishonorable to leave the mission unaccomplished contrary to the will of Eugenius.[797] He therefore persevered and, applying pressure more intensely, received the surrender of the town of Cingoli into the hands of the church and stormed Castel del Piano, which he allowed his soldiers to plunder. Nor was he alarmed when Filippo, who was upset by this, made peace with the Venetians and Florentines. On the contrary, he made for Jesi with his army and, when Troilo, a commander in whom Francesco had the greatest confidence (for he had led the front line of his cavalry for many years and married his sister), handed over the city and surrendered

---

795. Under the pretext of defending papal territory from the usurper Sforza, Piccinino (fighting on behalf of the pope and Visconti) arrived in the Marches in the spring of 1442. In June 1443 Pope Eugenius and Alfonso were reconciled when the pope formally recognized Alfonso and his heirs as rulers of Naples. Alfonso's armies arrived in the Marches in July and August 1443; see Ryder, *Alfonso*, 255–56; also Giuseppe Galasso, *Il Regno di Napoli (Storia d'Italia XV)* (Turin: Unione Tipografico-Editrice Torinese, 1992), 587–88.

796. Mercenary captain (d. 1468).

797. Sforza pleaded with Visconti for protection, and Visconti soon backed out of the alliance against his son-in-law—at least until early 1445, when they had another falling out and the alliance against Sforza was reestablished; see Ryder, *Alfonso*, 255–57.

Italy: Umbria, the Marches 277

himself, he brought him into his own retinue.[798] Then, after attacking Roccacontrada, which was defended by Francesco's nephew Roberto, for many days without success, he marched without a break to the Metauro River above Fano, where Francesco had retreated with the rest of his cavalry.[799]

249. There a certain herald[800] came from Francesco to Alfonso's camp and, having obtained permission from the king to speak more frankly, in accordance with the custom of his rank, he heaped many vile reproaches on Niccolò (who was present) in the name of Francesco, calling him a traitor and a perjurer and advising the king not to entrust himself to a man who specialized in deceit.[801] Finally, in the words of Francesco, he challenged Niccolò to a contest, in which the leaders themselves and their forces would fight for glory and prestige; one battle, he said, would reveal the mettle both of the commanders and their knights. At the same time, he asked the king to be present at the battle as an impartial witness. Niccolò was enraged right from the beginning as he listened to this and, hurling equally harsh insults at the absent Francesco and proving his own good faith with many examples, he replied that, much to his frustration, his body had been weakened by a wound in the neck. If only fortune had not robbed him of the ability, he would demonstrate in single combat which of them should be branded with the stigma of treachery. However, with the permission of the king, he gladly accepted the proposed terms of a battle between their armies; on the following day he would present himself with his forces on an open plain beneath the city of Fano. The king, observing that Niccolò was asking this of him to protect his honor,

798. Troilo (Orsini or di Mura) da Rossano (d. 1476) was married to Sforza's stepsister, Bona Caterina; he surrendered Jesi in August or Sept. 1443; see *Storia di Milano*, vol. 6: 352.
799. Sforza took refuge in late 1443 at Fano with one of his few remaining supporters, Sigismondo Malatesta.
800. Lit. "trumpeter."
801. The story described here is taken almost verbatim from Facio, *Rerum gestarum Alfonsi regis libri* 8.101–8.

agreed to guarantee the security of each side. On the appointed day, Niccolò advanced onto the plain with his men and, taunting the walls of the city,[802] raced up to its gates, while the king halted with his army a mile away in order to leave the field free for both sides. But Francesco, either because he had little trust in the king or feared to risk his own glory, which was certainly at stake on this occasion, kept his men inside the city.

Between Francesco and Niccolò, there was not only a strong rivalry over military glory, in which each claimed supremacy, but also intense animosity stemming from old differences between Braccio and Sforza, the latter being Francesco's father, the former Niccolò's teacher and commander.[803] And so they waged war with each other not just as public but as private enemies and could not be induced to serve under one and the same leader.

250. Niccolò gained the name of Piccinino from his short stature, but to whatever extent his height fell below the mean, the greatness of his mind surpassed it. He was a man of few words—unpolished ones at that, but which grasped the essence of many important matters. He was indulgent toward his soldiers, generous toward his friends, harsh and pitiless toward the enemy, fond of fighting, impatient of inactivity, avid for glory, quick to respond, and calm in facing dangers. He resorted to battle as soon as opportunity offered, forestalled the enemy with his speed, and wore him out with sudden charges, using light-armed cavalry more than infantry. He loved brave and aggressive soldiers and could not be deterred by the number of his foes. After celebrating many triumphs over the enemy through these means, both in the north and in the rest of Italy,

---

802. A borrowing from Facio (*Rerum gestarum* 8.107), which Pietragalla translates "jumping on the walls." However, this seems unlikely in itself and inconsistent with Piccinino's approach to the gates. The translation offered here is in line with Aeneas's other uses of the verb *insultare* in *Europe*.

803. Braccio da Montone and Muzio Attendolo Sforza. The following three paragraphs also borrow from Facio (8.24–27) but not quite as heavily as the previous passage.

Italy: Umbria, the Marches 279

he succeeded beyond question in surpassing his teacher Braccio in the magnitude and glory of his achievements.[804]

251. Francesco, on the other hand, had a handsome physique, a far taller than average height, a large chest, powerful and well-proportioned limbs, an attractive face, and cheerful eyes. His baldness lent him a venerable air and he possessed a flowing eloquence, a sharp intellect, and a spirit that thirsted for great things. He was a skilled administrator, tireless in performing labors, perceptive and shrewd in noting future opportunities, ingenious and wily in deceiving enemies, and wary and prescient in foreseeing and evading trickery and in anticipating the stratagems of his foes. He rarely clashed with the enemy except by design and more often destroyed them through siege than open battle. He held the infantry in high regard, and wished his soldiers to be decked in silver and gold. In executing plans he was swift and resolute, and in performing every activity he was extraordinarily well equipped with presence of mind, endurance, experience, skill, and good sense. Through these qualities, he quickly became so great that, of all the generals, only he could challenge Niccolò for military preeminence. Because they seemed equal in knowledge of warfare and prestige, it was uncertain for a long time which of the two should be ranked above the other. However, this debate was settled once and for all by the rout of Niccolò's army a little while later,[805] together with Francesco's long run of victories and the entrusting to him of the fortunes of Milan, with its overflowing prosperity.[806]

252. In any case, when the king realized it would be very difficult to capture Fano, well-defended as it was not only by the presence of Francesco, a great and highly experienced commander, but also

---

804. For more on Piccinino and his sons, see Ferente, *La Sfortuna di Piccinino*.
805. Reference to the Battle of Monteloro; see para. 252.
806. For more on Sforza's rule and military activities, see Ady, *Milan under the Sforza*; *Storia di Milano*, vols. 6–7; and *Dispatches with Related Documents of Milanese Ambassadors*, ed. Vincent Ilardi and Paul Kendall; trans. Frank J. Fata (Athens: Ohio University Press, 1970–81).

because the city lay next to the sea and could not be blockaded to stop provisions getting in, he departed from there and marched to Fermo. When Alessandro, Francesco's brother, made a sortie from Fermo and attacked his rear-guard, he turned his standards against him and drove the enemy back inside the city. A terrible battle was fought in front of the walls, and the outer wall, which functioned as a palisade,[807] was stormed. The king then reformed his column and came to Torre di Palme, where a letter of Francesco's which had been intercepted was delivered to him. It was addressed to Troilo and Pietro Brunoro and contained, among other things, words to the effect that they should delay no longer and hasten now to carry out their plans. Suspecting them both of treachery, the king therefore deprived them of weapons, horses, and all their trappings, put them in chains, and sent them to Aragon, where he ordered them to be kept under guard in the castle of Xàtiva in the territory of Valencia.[808]

Not long after this, following the surrender of the Teramitans,[809] Alfonso departed for his kingdom after transferring two thousand horsemen to Piccinino, who had halted at Monteloro with his army. But before they arrived, Piccinino was surprised by a sudden attack of Francesco, routed, and repulsed.[810] The hill where his camp was pitched and the neighboring town preserved the scattered fugitives. Elated by this victory as well as the king's departure, Francesco began a triumphant tour of the Marches, harassing the region as he went.

Alfonso was asked by Eugenius to return to the Marches, but, after making preparations for the journey, he was detained at home

---

807. Or "took the place of a palisade."
808. Brunoro and Troilo da Rossano (d. 1476) were imprisoned by Alfonso for ten years. Sforza may have been the one who betrayed them; see Geoffrey Trease, *The Condottieri: Soldiers of Fortune* (New York: Holt, Rinehart and Winston, 1971), 261; Mallett, *Mercenaries*, 204.
809. Reading *Teramitani* for mss. *Temaritani*. See Facio, *Rerum gestarum*, 8.128.
810. The Battle of Monteloro took place on November 8, 1443.

Italy: Umbria, the Marches 281

by upheavals in his new kingdom. He then sent Lope de Urrea, Orsini, and Garcia with substantial forces to confront Sforza.[811] Meanwhile, Niccolò Piccinino had been recalled to the north of Italy by Filippo and left his son Francesco with a part of his army in the Marches. Sforza defeated and captured Francesco at Montolmo before the king's reinforcements had reached him.[812] After this, Ludovico Scarampo, the patriarch of Aquileia, having been charged with responsibility for this region by Eugenius, appointed Giovanni Ventimiglia commander of his entire army—a general of surpassing reputation who had been sent by the king with a large body of cavalry and infantry.[813] Through the efforts of Ventimiglia, the patriarch received the surrender of the town of Alfedena,[814] which had been laid under siege.

A considerable force of Filippo's, which had been sent against Francesco, was stationed at this time in the town of Cingoli. For when Filippo finally realized that Francesco's reconciliation was a pretense, he had sent Taliano Furlano, a well-known warrior, to assist the pope's cause there.[815] Since the patriarch [Scarampo] and Ventimiglia were unable to join him by a direct route (for Francesco occupied the intervening region), they reached him by means of forced marches through the mountains. Learning of this, Fran-

---

811. Lope Ximénez de Urrea, an Aragonese noble who was appointed viceroy of Sicily in 1443; Garcia de Cabanyells (d. 1452), a Catalan knight and count of Troia. See Ryder, *Alfonso*, 366 and 241; idem, *Kingdom of Naples*, 323; Facio, *Rerum gestarum*, 8.150. Orso Orsini, condottiere and lord of Bracciano and Nepi (d. 1456); see www.condottieridiventura.it.

812. While Niccolò Piccinino was in Milan consulting with Filippo Maria Visconti, Sforza defeated Francesco Piccinino at Montolmo (August 16, 1444), and routed Piccinino's army in the Marches.

813. See para. 55 on Ventimiglia.

814. Lat. *Aufida*; possibly Offida.

815. Condottiere Taliano Furlano (d. 1446), lord of Urbisaglia, Pizzighettone, Castelleone, Piadena, and Castellazzo; Filippo Maria Visconti began to suspect Francesco Sforza's loyalty when the latter signed a three-year contract with Venice and Florence. Visconti concluded a treaty with Pope Eugenius IV against Sforza on July 30, 1445; *Storia di Milano*, vol. 6: 357–58; www.condottieridiventura.it.

cesco left the Marches and retreated into the territory of Urbino. The patriarch besieged Montemilone and captured it. Next, he stormed the town of Sant'Angelo, which he allowed his soldiers to plunder. Shortly afterward, while withdrawing from there through the territory of Fermo to take up winter quarters in the kingdom [of Naples], Ventimiglia halted not far from Montesanto. Terrified by his arrival, the townspeople sent spokesmen to him and surrendered, as did the surrounding strongholds. He then proceeded to Montalto and remained there for several days.

253. In the meantime, the inhabitants of Fermo hatched a plot, and, in the expectation that help was close at hand, they defected from Francesco and forced his brother Alessandro to retreat into the citadel with a large part of his cavalry.[816] Ventimiglia and the pope's forces soon provided them with assistance. But since the citadel was built so strongly that it could only be captured through starvation, Ventimiglia fortified parts of the city in case of a descent from the citadel and withdrew to winter quarters, as he had planned. The following year, Alfonso sent Ramón Boyl with one thousand horsemen and an equal number of infantry to the patriarch in the Marches. When he reached the encampment of the church with Giacomo da Caivana,[817] Taliano Furlano was instantly arrested on the instructions of Filippo Maria and, three days later, beheaded at Roccacontrada by order of the patriarch. They then captured Montefabbri and seized several castles from Federico, lord of Urbino. But after the Florentines and Venetians had sent two thousand horsemen to augment Francesco's army, and Filippo's army had been routed and stripped of its camp by the Venetians at Casalmaggiore on the banks of the Po, Filippo recalled his forces from the Marches and demanded further reinforcements from Eugenius and the king. At the pope's bidding, two thousand five hundred horsemen were

---

816. November 1445.

817. Condottiere Giacomo da Caivana, or Gaivano, (d. 1446) began his career as a lieutenant of Niccolò Piccinino; for more on him, see *DBI*, vol. 51: 313–16.

transferred to him from the church's encampment. However, Francesco, who now held the upper hand in the war, stormed Monteloro and another neighboring stronghold that belonged to Sigismondo Malatesta, who had now abandoned him and thrown in his lot with the church;[818] he also besieged the town of Gradara, another possession of Malatesta's. Meanwhile, the king sent the patriarch other reinforcements, with which he returned to the Marches. He then executed Giacomo da Caivana at Roccacontrada, where he had also ordered the death of Taliano, on suspicion of treason. After that, he did nothing else worthy of note until Francesco became reconciled with Filippo and withdrew from the Marches to enter the service of Filippo, having been named commander of the campaign against the Venetians.[819] Subsequently, not only the citadel of Fermo but almost the whole territory was brought under Francesco's control.

60 ITALY: ASCOLI PICENO

254. IN ASCOLI, Giosia, a son of noble parents who was still a youth, entered into a conspiracy with a few others and, taking him by surprise, murdered Francesco Sforza's brother Giovanni, a young man of great spirit who had admirably defended that city throughout the duration of the war.[820] But when Giosia, too, played the tyrant in his own fatherland, he was driven into exile. The city then enjoyed tranquility under the church, though last year this

---

818. Sigismondo joined forces with Sforza's enemies in the spring of 1445 after Sforza gave Pesaro to his brother Alessandro, instead of to Sigismondo as he had once promised; see Ady, *Milan under the Sforza*, 29.

819. Filippo Maria Visconti and Sforza were reconciled in the summer of 1447. Sforza surrendered his last possession in the Marches, Jesi, to the pope on Aug. 4, 1447, and returned to Lombardy to help defend Visconti against the Venetians, whom the Milanese had provoked by attacking contested possessions.

820. In the summer of 1445, Giosia d'Acquaviva, lord of Teramo and duke of Atri, incited a revolt in Ascoli in the name of Alfonso of Aragon, which killed the governor, Sforza's half brother, whose name was Rinaldo da Fogliano, not Giovanni; see Ferente, *La Sfortuna di Piccinino*, 20, 71; *Storia di Milano*, vol. 6: 362.

same Giosia filled the people with great anxiety by joining with a large band of brigands and occupying, close to the city, a certain castle which is well defended by its natural position. This did not end well for him. For Cardinal Rodrigo Borgia, the legate of that territory, laid siege to the place and, after capturing the citadel, arrested Giosia and sent him to Rome in chains.[821]

61 ITALY: URBINO

255. IN URBINO, Oddantonio, the people's duke and son of a most noble mother from the Colonna family, was killed in a popular uprising after running wild in his lust for noble matrons and setting no limit to his wanton behavior.[822] The promoter of his wickedness and corruptor of his youth was the apostolic protonotary Manfredo Pio of Carpi, a man of noble origin but evil nature, who had assaulted numerous married women and virgins and through all manner of crimes attained the pinnacle of vice. He paid the price for his inexhaustible lust by being killed on the same night as his protégé. His corpse was carried into the marketplace, and his genitals were sliced off and stuffed between his teeth.

Before marrying a wife from the Colonnas, Oddantonio's father, Guidantonio,[823] was worried about how to perpetuate his family's power, since he lacked male offspring. He therefore pretended that he had made a concubine pregnant and ordered the son of his relation, the illustrious general Bernardo della Carda, who happened just to have been born, to be passed off as his own and raised under

---

821. Rodrigo Borgia captured Giosia in 1457.

822. Oddantonio da Montefeltro (1427–44) was the son of Caterina Colonna, the niece of Pope Martin V; he became duke of Urbino in 1433. Only sixteen years of age at accession, he was surrounded by courtiers who failed to restrain his cruelty. Oddantonio and two of his associates were murdered on July 23, 1444; see Cecil Clough, "Montefeltro Family," in Grendler, *ER*, vol. 4: 174–76.

823. Duke Guidantonio da Montefeltro (r. 1404–43).

the name of Federico.⁸²⁴ But when he entered into marriage and had a legitimate son, he transferred his attention to him and enlisted Federico, though still a boy, in the army, where he remained until manhood. Then, when Oddantonio died, Federico was summoned by the people and made lord of Urbino.⁸²⁵ He was a distinguished man, superbly trained in the military arts, who never lacked judgment in the conduct of war or courage in facing dangers, and who was as famous for his loyalty as he was for his deeds. This became most evident during the war in the Marches, when he steadfastly helped and supported Francesco Sforza, who had taken refuge with him, having been all but abandoned by the winds of fortune. He certainly did not deserve to lose his right eye in a jousting tournament.⁸²⁶

62   ITALY: RIMINI

256. IN RIMINI, a city of Emilia, Sigismondo Malatesta, a man notorious for his crimes, held power.⁸²⁷ After uniting in marriage with Francesco Sforza's daughter, he supported Francesco's side in the war in the Marches for some time, then served under the church. He campaigned in the north against the Venetians and in

---

824. Federico da Montefeltro (1422–82) was raised as the son of Bernardo, but later acknowledged by Guidantonio as his natural son.
825. Federico became lord of Urbino in 1444 and was named duke in 1474. He was one of the most successful and sought after condottieri of quattrocento Italy. For more on him, see *DBI*, vol. 45.
826. The tournament was hosted by the new duke of Milan, Francesco Sforza, in 1450.
827. Sigismondo Malatesta (1417–68), the illegitimate son of Pandolfo Malatesta of Fano, became lord of Rimini in 1432 on his uncle Carlo's death and married Polissena Sforza in 1441. He served Francesco Sforza and Pope Eugenius IV as condottiere. Pius's *Commentaries* are filled with colorful descriptions of Sigismondo's many crimes, for which Aeneas, as pope, took the unusual step of condemning his soul to hell while the man still lived (see Meserve and Simonetta, vol. 1: 326–31; Gragg and Gabel, vol. 2: 167–70; vol. 3: 374–76; 380).

Tuscany against the king of Aragon.[828] This later caused him much harm. For when negotiations were held in Naples to achieve peace throughout Italy, the king remembered this insult and wanted Sigismondo to be excluded from the general peace, since he had not remained loyal to him. He then sent a force against him under Count Jacopo Piccinino and Federico, lord of Urbino, who deprived him of several important towns and laid waste to his land with sword and fire. After vainly begging for help from all quarters, Sigismondo finally decided to settle his differences with Alfonso and sent an emissary,[829] which was his only means of salvation. His pleas have yet to be heeded, though the king's clemency has aroused no little hope of an agreement.[830]

63   ITALY: FAENZA, FABRIANO

257. IN FAENZA, on the death of Guidantonio, of whom there are reported many illustrious feats in war, his brother Astorre,[831] who was also well-known as a soldier, seized the rulership. Because he campaigned for the Florentines against the king, he was declared an enemy by Alfonso, just like Sigismondo, and excluded from the general peace.[832]

258. The people of Fabriano, who had long been oppressed by

---

828. Malatesta had been hired and paid by Alfonso to assist him in his Tuscan campaign in 1447, but he failed to appear, taking up arms on Florence's behalf instead in 1448; Ryder, *Alfonso*, 277–80.

829. Adding *nuntio* (Urb. Lat. 885) to van Heck's text, *misso ad eum*.

830. Alfonso obtained a loophole in the Peace of Lodi (1454), which allowed him to attack Sigismondo at will for his disloyalty in 1447. Federico da Montefeltro was eager to curb his neighbor Sigismondo's power and campaigned with Piccinino (who was being funded by Alfonso) in Sigismondo's territories in late 1457. Sigismondo, meanwhile, sought to appease Alfonso, but only the latter's death in June 1458 saved him; see Ryder, *Alfonso*, 405.

831. Astorre II Manfredi (r. 1448–68).

832. Astorre, like Sigismondo, had reneged on an agreement with Alfonso and was not protected by the Peace of Lodi (1454).

a tyranny, finally killed fifteen members of the family which had usurped rule; the rest fled.⁸³³ After this, they returned to the rule of the church and for many years led a quiet and peaceful existence. This year, they threw into prison some citizens who had been incited to rebel and either consented or were suspected of doing so; after extracting a confession of treason through torture and interrogation, they imposed on them the supreme penalty.

64 ITALY: AQUILA

259. IN AQUILA, a city of the Marsians,⁸³⁴ it happened within living memory that the much-feared general Braccio of Perugia died after besieging the city for a year and being defeated by the army of the blessed Pope Martin V.⁸³⁵ Saint Bernardino of Siena, having traveled throughout Italy preaching the name of Christ, completed the course of his mortal life. He was buried there in Aquila and is said to be famous for his miracles.⁸³⁶

260. Bernardino came from a high-ranking family in Siena. There is no truth to the allegation of those who assert that Massa was his native town, though he completed some of his early training there as a boy because his mother was from Massa. But his father and a long line of ancestors were counted among the nobility

---

833. The ruling Chiavelli family was murdered in the church of Fabriano in 1435.

834. The classical name for the ancient peoples who dwelled in the Apennines southeast of Avezzano. Today, the name survives in towns like San Benedetto dei Marsi and Luca dei Marsi. Pietragalla renders it as *Marsica* in her translation of Facio's *Rerum gestarum Alfonsi regis libri*.

835. Braccio da Montone (1368–1424), renowned condottiere and ruler of Perugia (r. 1420–24), was campaigning in Aquila in the service of Alfonso of Aragon in his bid for the kingdom of Naples. He was captured in battle by his nemesis, Francesco Sforza, and his former comrade in arms, Jacopo Caldora, and died of his wounds on June 5, 1424; see Mallett, *Mercenaries and their Masters*, 73–74.

836. St. Bernardino of Siena (1380–1444) died in Aquila. Miracles were attributed to his intercession and a basilica (completed in 1472) was built in his name to house his relics.

of Siena, where he himself was born, received the majority of his education, and, when he grew up, devoted himself to the study of canon law.[837] After burying his parents, he came to the realization that the seductions of this world are deceptive and its promises empty; he then distributed his belongings among Christ's poor, entered the order of St. Francis, and scrupulously observed the rule prescribed for him. Turning down larger communities, he became a leader and teacher of those called the Observant Friars. However, it was in instructing the common people that he showed the greatest zeal. Rich in eloquence and noted for his erudition, he was listened to by all with a concentration beyond belief and, as if he was a second Paul, admired and revered as the "vessel of election."[838]

Three populations—those of Urbino, Ferrara, and Siena—selected him as their bishop. But he chose not to confine to one city a tongue that could minister to all of Italy.

65   ITALY: NAPLES

261. LET ME now enter the kingdom of Naples and turn my pen to the prosperous and amazing career of Alfonso.[839]

After the unsuccessful naval war which he waged against the Genoese, Fortune seemed to have recognized her error in thwarting so great a leader and, changing her step-motherly hatred into

---

837. Aeneas is eager to claim Bernardino as a native and noble of Siena, given his own connection to the city and his admiration for Bernardino, but the saint was in fact born at Massa Marittima while his father was serving as governor; see *New Catholic Encyclopedia*, vol. 2: 320–21.

838. Acts 9:15.

839. Alfonso I, king of Naples (r. 1442–58); Alfonso V, king of Aragon (r. 1416–58). He was named heir by Joanna II of Naples (r. 1414–35) in 1420 and entered the city in 1421. After a falling out with Alfonso, she named Louis III of Anjou as her heir in 1423. Upon Louis's death in 1434, his brother, René of Anjou, became her heir. When Joanna died the following year, René's imprisonment provided Alfonso a good opportunity to make his bid for Naples. See Ryder, *Kingdom of Naples*, 25 ff.

maternal love, she became as favorable toward him as she had once been hostile. For when the king was brought in captivity to Duke Filippo of Milan, Filippo recognized that he, the victor, was far inferior to the one he had vanquished and immediately exchanged enmity for friendship. He ordered the king to be freed, formed an alliance with him on equal terms, presented him with generous gifts, and released him.[840]

262. Meanwhile, Isabella, the wife of Duke René of Lorraine, a rival of Alfonso's for the kingdom of Naples, who was then being held in captivity by Duke Philip of Burgundy,[841] had come with her two small sons to Gaeta and, after strengthening it with a garrison, continued on to Naples.[842] But Pedro of Aragon, Alfonso's brother, who had escaped from the naval battle with a few galleys and repaired his fleet in Sicily, was unexpectedly invited by another faction in Gaeta and took possession of the city after making his way there by night.[843] Having expelled the enemy's garrison, he imposed his own and sent ships to Alfonso to bring him from Portovenere. Soon after, Alfonso put in at Gaeta with the same ships.[844] He then made for Capua, which, despite being fiercely attacked in the meantime by Isabella and Jacopo Caldora,[845] had nevertheless remained loyal to him owing to the courage of its governor,

---

840. Alfonso and over one hundred nobles from Spain, Italy, and Sicily were captured in a naval battle near Ponza by the Genoese (August 4, 1435); see para. 178. Filippo, who had as recently as September 21, 1435, signed a pact with René of Anjou, supporting his claim to Naples, concluded a treaty of alliance with Alfonso on October 8, supporting Alfonso's claim and offering every assistance in return for promises of mutual aid; see Ryder, *Alfonso*, 207–8.

841. René was held captive by Alfonso's ally, Philip the Good, from 1431–32 and late 1434–37 over territorial disputes regarding Lorraine and, later, Anjou and Provence. René was released after paying a heavy ransom and conceding territorial losses in 1437.

842. Isabella arrived in Naples on October 18, 1435. The daughter of Duke Charles II of Lorraine, she married René of Anjou in 1420. René later became duke consort of Lorraine (r. 1431–53) and king of Naples (r. 1435–42).

843. Pedro of Aragon (c. 1406–38) captured Gaeta on December 25, 1435.

844. Alfonso arrived in Gaeta on February 2, 1436.

845. Jacopo Caldora (c. 1370–1439), Neapolitan captain general who served Queen Joanna II of Naples before Isabella. He became duke of Bari in 1430.

Giovanni Ventimiglia. Here in Capua, Raimondo, lord of Nola,[846] was reconciled with Alfonso, who soon received the surrender of Scafati, which is located on an island in the Sarno River, and of Castellammare.[847]

When she realized that she was unequal to the strength of Alfonso, Isabella sought help from Pope Eugenius,[848] who sent her Giovanni Vitelleschi, patriarch of Alexandria, with three thousand horsemen and the same number of foot soldiers.[849] Entering Campania, the patriarch assaulted and captured some castles and would have besieged Capua had not Giovanni Ventimiglia launched a surprise attack and routed and taken prisoner eight hundred horsemen whom the queen had sent to him. However, the patriarch attacked Giovanni Antonio, lord of Taranto,[850] at Montefóscolo, stormed his camp, and took him away in captivity, releasing him only on condition that his brother enter the service of the pope with five hundred horsemen.[851] The patriarch and Jacopo Caldora campaigned jointly and amicably on behalf of the queen, but when quarreling broke out between them, they separated their forces. Meanwhile, a truce of two months was arranged between the patriarch and Alfonso. While this was in force, the patriarch was reconciled with Jacopo and, after uniting their forces, decided to catch Alfonso unawares before news of the reconciliation reached him.

Alfonso was relaxing in his camp at Giugliano, three miles from Aversa, when he was informed that the enemy had broken the truce and was drawing close, and that it was too risky for him to await his attack. He therefore struck camp and hastily retreated to

846. Raimondo Orsini, count of Nola, defected from René and Isabella's side to that of Alfonso in the winter of 1436.
847. Castellammare was captured in December 1436.
848. As suzerain of Naples, Eugenius IV agreed to back René secretly in January 1436; the pope's preference became clear to Alfonso in February; see Ryder, *Alfonso*, 214–15.
849. Vitelleschi's army arrived in the fall of 1436.
850. Giovanni Antonio Orsini del Balzo (d. 1463).
851. July or August 1437.

Capua—though not without loss to those bringing up the rear of his column.[852]

When the patriarch asked of Isabella that Aversa be handed over to him for his billet, and Jacopo opposed this, their enmity flared up again.[853] But when the people of Trani (except for its citadel) hailed Alfonso as their ruler, and an assault on the citadel began, the patriarch marched there with his army and established a siege. He was joined by Jacopo Caldora (at Isabella's request), Giovanni Antonio Orsini, and many others. But after laying the siege, the patriarch grew afraid of being cut off, since Giovanni Antonio was thought to lack enthusiasm for the war, and the king's fleet was rumored to be on its way to aid the people of Trani. He therefore put to sea in a small ship and sailed to the Marches, on the pretext of seeking funds from Eugenius; he then proceeded to Rome.[854] Left without a leader, his soldiers joined Caldora. The citadel then surrendered to Alfonso, and Giovanni Antonio returned to Alfonso's side.

263. In the meantime, René had been released from captivity and came to Naples with ten galleys.[855] After summoning Jacopo Caldora, he made for Scafati on his advice and accepted its surrender. He then marched to Sulmona and, after besieging the city unsuccessfully, laid waste to its land with fire.[856] Alfonso was not inactive in the meantime but, after subduing the territory of Albe and Celano, had come to Castelvecchio, located in the Subequana Valley. René declared war on him by throwing down the gauntlet in the soldierly fashion. Alfonso accepted the challenge, but asked whether they should enter into single combat or fight a pitched battle with their whole army, adding that he was ready for either. When René replied that he wished to stake his chances on a full-scale general engage-

---

852. December 25, 1437. Alfonso and his men had to flee so quickly that they left rich booty, including Christmas dinner, for the approaching army; see Ryder, *Alfonso*, 225.
853. January 1438.
854. Vitelleschi left Apulia in the spring of 1438.
855. René arrived in Naples on May 19, 1438.
856. The siege of Sulmona lasted from September 1438 to April 1439.

ment, Alfonso declared his agreement; but since by ancient custom the party who was challenged had the prerogative of naming the day and place, he would march his army into the plain between Acerra and Nola, whose broad expanse would suit them both, and would expect René there on the eighth day hence.[857] From this, there arose a disagreement, when René said they should choose Alfonso's present location, and so the battle was cancelled. Alfonso went on to Nola. René led his army onto the former site of Alfonso's camp, and in this way each of them thought he had satisfied his honor.

René then marched into the territory of the Pelignians and subdued Castelvecchio. Alfonso marched to the Caudina Valley where he took the town of Arpaia by assault and captured Marino Boffa, lord of the valley.[858] From the ruler of Caserta he received an assurance of loyalty. Marching into Lucania, he occupied the town of Angri after exhausting it with a siege and took Lucera, when it was surrendered by the townspeople. There were now fifteen thousand horsemen in his camp. Placing his trust in them, he headed for Naples while René was absent and, together with his brother Pedro, laid siege to the city with two encampments, stationing ten galleys in the harbor. The city was attacked in full force, and the inhabitants fully applied themselves to their defense. But while Pedro was wandering along the shore some way from the camp to conduct a reconnaissance, he was struck in the head by an artillery shot from the Church of the Carmelites and instantly collapsed.[859] He was a man popular among all ranks and a born soldier, excelling in nobility of mind and physical strength, fearless in facing dangers, and energetic and decisive in action. The army was so dismayed by his death that

857. Alfonso elected to do battle at the field of Maddaloni on September 9, 1438, a shrewd answer given René and Jacopo's predicted refusal to fight a pitched battle so close to Naples; see Ryder, *Alfonso*, 229; Galasso, *Regno di Napoli*, 578–79. See also Facio, *Rerum gestarum*, 6.14–18 from which Aeneas draws liberally and, in places, verbatim.

858. Boffa, a Neapolitan noble who had sided with René of Anjou, surrendered to Alfonso in March of 1439. He maintained his feudal and other possessions and became a leading royal administrator under Alfonso. See Ryder, *Kingdom of Naples*, 46, 99, 101.

859. Pedro was killed by a shot fired from Santa Maria del Carmine on Oct. 17, 1438.

the attack was suspended for that day. When Alfonso viewed his brother's maimed corpse lying on the ground, he said, "Brother, I brought you on this campaign to win me the kingdom through your bloodshed and death."[860] He ordered the body to be placed in a coffin and carried to the castle by the sea, so that later, when he found a suitable time, he could hold a funeral worthy of his lineage.

264. But when the attack was renewed in the days following, there was such a deluge of rain that it was necessary to abandon the siege, and the phenomenon was interpreted as a portent. Alfonso next obtained the town of Caivano,[861] which was betrayed by a certain soldier, and killed many of its inhabitants; the citadel was starved into surrender. René, meanwhile, having returned to Naples from the Pelignians and learned of the developments, stormed the Torre di San Vincenzo, which was strategically placed in the sea to protect the royal citadel.[862] He then attacked the citadel itself for many days and took control of it when it was surrendered by the governor, who had completely run out of provisions.[863] Alfonso, after trying in vain to aid the besieged, crossed into Lucania and received the surrender of the Salernitans and almost the entire region, along with many of the Abruzzesi.

Jacopo Caldora, a man of outstanding intelligence, who was not averse to literary studies, and a soldier of exceptional expertise who had served under Braccio, was taken ill with a discharge of catarrh and died while attempting to capture a castle that belonged to Jacopo Lagonissa.[864] He was a famous captain, without question, and

860. Possibly a question: "Did I bring you ... ?" Facio, incidentally, also attributes last words to Alfonso (Book VI, 36), but Aeneas's version is completely different.
861. Reading *Cayvanum* (Urb. Lat. 885; Vat. Lat. 3888) for van Heck's *Caietanum*. As further support for this reading, Aeneas's description of the capture of this town matches Facio's description of the capture of Caivano; see *Rerum gestarum*, 6.44–50.
862. The attack on Torre San Vicenzo, in which Genoese allies of René played a major role, was begun on June 10, 1439.
863. Late August 1439.
864. Caldora died in November 1439 at the town of Colle in Abruzzi; castellan Lagonissa had fought on René of Anjou's side, but was pardoned by Alfonso in 1444; see

one worthy of great praise if only his good faith and keeping of promises had equaled his industry and knowledge of warfare.

During the same time, Giovanni Ventimiglia took control of Acerra, when it was betrayed by the townspeople, including its citadel, which was suffering from starvation.[865] The people of Aversa also defected from René and admitted Alfonso, who, being unable to storm the citadel without difficulty, since it was highly fortified and defended with a strong garrison, isolated it with large ditches and ordered it to be assaulted daily.[866] René set off to join Antonio, Caldora's son, in Apulia, and when he observed that this failed to alleviate the assault on the citadel of Aversa, he made his way down to Nola, followed by Antonio, first through the Caudina Valley and then, after being blocked by Alfonso, who had advanced to meet him, via a transverse route through the mountains. However, he did not venture to aid the besieged at Aversa, since Alfonso, in his camp there, seemed more powerful. But when René returned to Naples, he ordered Antonio Caldora to be arrested on suspicion of treachery and thrust into prison.[867] This caused him great damage. For when Antonio's soldiers, who were encamped on the edge of the city, ran riot and demanded back their leader, Antonio was freed and, resenting the insult he had been handed, immediately crossed over to Alfonso and brought about the surrender of the citadel of Aversa, which had now been besieged for seven months; he did so through a persuasive letter to Santo, a man who had campaigned with his father and who commanded the garrison in Aversa.[868] However, Antonio defected from Alfonso soon afterward, and

---

Ryder, *Kingdom of Naples*, 139. For more on the Caldora family, see Galasso, *Regno di Napoli*, 385–87.

865. December 25, 1439.

866. Aversa eventually capitulated in January 1440.

867. Antonio Caldora (c. 1400–66) succeeded his father as duke of Bari and leader of his troops. He was accused of treachery and placed under arrest in early July 1440 after failing to aid René in battle outside Benevento.

868. Antonio surrendered the castle of Aversa to Alfonso and performed homage to him in July 1440. The intermediary was Santo di Maddaloni (d. 1445).

then was reconciled with him at Benevento, after the citadel had been betrayed and the distraught townsmen too had fallen into the hands of Alfonso. At this time, Alfonso also subdued Caiazzo and the castle of Padula with the help of siege-engines and encamped in front of Orsara di Puglia.

265. At the same time, René's ally, Francesco Sforza, was taking possession of Ariano, Troia, Manfredonia, Lucera, and many other towns in Apulia, which he consigned to the safekeeping of Cesare Martinengo[869] and a large detachment of cavalry. While Francesco himself was campaigning in the Marches, Cesare, out of enmity toward Alfonso, had twice dared to fight him outside the walls of Troia and twice been routed by Alfonso and retreated into the city in ignominious flight.[870] Not long afterward, the town of Biccari was taken by force despite the resistance of its inhabitants; the soldiers were permitted to plunder it, but the honor of its women was protected in accordance with the king's custom.[871] Alessandro, however, the brother of Francesco Sforza, launched a sudden attack on Raimondo Caldora, Riccio, and Giosia,[872] who was on his way with troops to join Alfonso, and routed them in a minor battle near the city of Chieti. Riccio and Giosia saved themselves by headlong flight; Raimondo was captured and, being Antonio Caldora's uncle, caused a rift between him and Alfonso for the second time.[873] Giovanni, cardinal of Taranto, also entered the kingdom, leading the forces of Eugenius against Francesco d'Aquino.[874] But Alfonso went to meet him and drove him back. He then took Rocca-

---

869. Martinengo, count of Orzivecchi (d. 1461), was one of Sforza's lieutenants.

870. The more noteworthy of these battles took place on July 10, 1441.

871. Biccari was taken in July 1441; on Panormita and Facio's praise of Alfonso's conduct at this siege, see Ryder, *Kingdom of Naples*, 75, 284; Facio, *Rerum gestarum*, 7.36.

872. Riccio da Montechiaro (d. 1445), lord of Arpino; Giosia d'Acquaviva, duke of Atri (d. 1462). Raimondo Caldora, as Aeneas goes on to explain, was Antonio's uncle.

873. The battle took place on July 5, 1441.

874. Cardinal Giovanni Berardi (1380–1449); Francesco d'Aquino, master chamberlain to Alfonso and count of Loreto and Satriano (d. 1449); see Ryder, *Kingdom of Naples*, 169–70.

guglielma, which is situated on a high mountain, after occupying the castles in the vicinity and starving it into submission; and soon after that he gained the town of Capri, located on the island of the same name—once the favorite resort, or if you prefer, the lair of Tiberius Caesar—when it was surrendered to him by some of its inhabitants. Then, without pausing, he pitched camp at Naples and simultaneously besieged Pozzuoli, which, after resisting stoutly for some time, finally opened its gates to the king when it ran short of grain. He also received the surrender of the place called Torre del Greco.[875]

266. In the meantime, the people of Naples were suffering from a lack of provisions and could only hope that either the Genoese would bring them help by sea or Francesco Sforza and Antonio Caldora by the overland route. A certain bricklayer called Anello, who had been forced by famine to leave Naples, went to Alfonso and, for a reward, showed that the city could be captured with little risk to his soldiers. He revealed a water-conduit, through which two hundred brave men were selected to enter the city by night with Anello and his brother and occupy the walls; meanwhile the king waited in readiness with his army for their signal. They arrived at a house in which there was only an old woman[876] and a young maiden. When the mother began to shout, she was quickly suppressed and prevented from uttering a sound; her daughter kept quiet of her own accord. The sun had now risen, and no more than forty of the whole number had climbed out of the well. The one who was supposed to report their entry to the king failed to give him the signal, whether from negligence or for some other reason. Alfonso thought that the men he had sent in had either been killed or been too frightened to sally forth. Approaching closer, he attacked the

---

875. The two coastal towns Pozzuoli and Torre del Greco (or the Tower of Octavius, as Aeneas calls it) were taken in December 1441.

876. The woman is named Ciccarella in some accounts, which contain similar versions of the following story; see Benedetto Croce, *Storie e leggende napoletane* (Bari: Giuseppe Laterza e Figli, 1919), 286–91.

Italy: Naples

city in the section which was supposed to be occupied. René galloped to the walls post-haste with a company that he had prepared for sudden emergencies and pushed the enemy well back.

267. Those who had emerged from the well were gripped by great fear and confusion. They dared neither to return to the well, in case the clashing of their weapons should give them away, nor to break out on account of their small number. When Alfonso saw that his men were causing no disturbance within the city, he abandoned hope of success and returned to camp. René, thinking he had repelled the danger, left guards behind and retired to his palace.

Without delay, a messenger raced to Alfonso and reported that many men had emerged from the well and were hiding silently in the house out of fear. He therefore approached the walls again and renewed the battle, in order to embolden the concealed men to break out. Meanwhile, the son of the old woman I have mentioned came home from his post and beat on the door, demanding that it be opened for him. His mother and those inside were frightened out of their wits and did not know what to do. At length, they decided to crack the door open, grab hold of him, and, after taking him prisoner, order him to keep quiet. But when he saw the armed men, he recoiled at once in fear and shouted out that the enemy was inside the city; he then flew at once to René and reported what he had seen. But those who were inside rushed out of the house in a body, and, with their first assault, took possession of the adjacent walls and tower, where they found only a single sentinel.

268. Aroused by the messenger and the tumult, René quickly returned to the walls and attacked the enemy. Alfonso ordered ladders to be moved up, in order to encourage his men. But the inhabitants easily defended that part of the wall, throwing down heavy rocks to hinder those who were climbing the ladders into the captured tower. During the fierce fighting, Alfonso rode up to the walls and noticed that a certain spot had been neglected, so he ordered ladders to be brought there in a hurry and seized the

wall. As for those who had occupied the tower, some had given up fighting after being seriously wounded and some had thrown themselves headlong from the wall. René was on the point of recapturing the tower when, with a great shout, the enemy suddenly attacked from the rear and caused a panic. One of Alfonso's soldiers, who had entered the city across the walls, increased the alarm of the townspeople when he mounted a horse which he happened to find idle, charged the enemy, and created the impression that the nearby gate had been captured and smashed in. René, however, did not lose his presence of mind. Encouraging those who were near him, he courageously charged the enemy and held back their attack for a little while. But soon, when he observed that his men were terrified by the enemy's increasing number, he began to fall back little by little and, after many of the enemy had entered through Porta San Gennaro, retreated into the royal citadel [Castelnuovo] with a few men. The enemy then burst in through the gate of the cattle market and other parts of the wall from different directions and spread out to plunder. They held back from bloodshed, however. In fact, the entrance of the king soon put an end to the looting also.

269. The memory of this year, the year of Christ our Savior 1442,[877] is illuminated by the capture of this great city, which was taken in the same way as when Belisarius seized it from the hands of the Goths one thousand years ago.[878] This was the twenty-first year since the beginning of the war.

On the following day, two huge cargo-vessels sent by the Genoese put in with grain. When they learned of the city's capture, they withdrew to the foot of the citadel and carried René away, who had given up all hope of recovering the city. Three citadels—the Capuan, Mountain, and Royal[879]—still remained loyal to René.

---

877. The text reads 1440; Naples was actually captured on June 2, 1442.

878. Procopius describes a similar strategy of Byzantine general Belisarius using aqueducts to take the city in 536. It is possible that Alfonso knew of this through Bruni's recent translation of *The Gothic Wars*. See Ryder, *Alfonso*, 244.

879. "Mountain" is most likely Castel Sant Elmo; "Royal" refers to Castelnuovo.

Italy: Naples

The Capuan arranged a truce of a few days and gave itself up before René's departure; the Royal was surrendered shortly after that and the Mountain later still.

René took refuge with Eugenius who was staying in Florence; he then departed for France.[880] Alfonso, after fortifying Naples, led his army against Antonio Caldora and pitched camp at Carpenone. There, when Antonio offered battle, Alfonso's captains said that they would enter the fight if it were not for their leader's presence.[881] To which Alfonso responded, "So I, who have been used to inspiring my soldiers, shall now cause them fear by my presence! Far be it from one of my blood to entertain such madness!" And, after donning his helmet, he promptly gave the signal for battle. The struggle went on for some time with victory wavering in the balance. Finally, the enemy's army was routed, and Antonio himself was taken captive.[882] When he begged forgiveness for his error, Alfonso not only pardoned him but left untouched the towns which Antonio had received from his father and possessed by right of inheritance; and he treated the other captives with great humanity. Nor did he take anything from Antonio's many accoutrements except a crystal goblet.[883] After this, he subdued the Pelignians and Marsians, took control of Manfredonia and shortly afterward its citadel, and stamped out all the remnants of war in Apulia. Having pacified the whole kingdom, he returned to Naples and entered the city in the triumphal manner, amidst the jubilation of the people and with the most magnificent pomp.[884]

270. After this, Alfonso and Eugenius entered into peace nego-

---

880. René left Naples in July; he arrived in Florence in mid-August, and in Provence in October 1442.

881. In other words, because so much depended on his safety; see Facio, *Rerum gestarum*, 7.122.

882. June 28, 1442.

883. Antonio was left with the county of Trivento, inherited from his mother, but he lost the duchy of Bari to his rival, Prince Giovanni Antonio of Taranto; see Ryder, *Alfonso*, 248.

884. A lover of spectacle, Alfonso was given a triumph in the style of an ancient Roman commander on February 26, 1443.

tiations. Cardinal Ludovico of Aquileia, who wielded influence through his own merits as well as the pope's authority, was sent to the king for this purpose and achieved a settlement.[885] Its terms were defined as follows: Pope Eugenius was to issue a decree naming Alfonso king of Naples and grant the right of succession to Ferrante, the king's son, to whom the king had assigned the realm after his death; he was also to add Terracina to the kingdom. Alfonso, on the other hand, was to submit to the authority of Eugenius and assist in winning back the Marches, which Sforza had occupied. If ever the pope should mount a campaign against the Turks or Moors, the king was to help with his fleet; he was to recall the priests of his kingdoms who had gone to Basel on the pretext of attending the council;[886] he was not to permit three of his subjects who had been created cardinals under Amedeo of Savoy to be received or regarded as cardinals when they returned;[887] he was to hand over the ducal city of Amatrice and Accumoli, towns in the Marsian region, to the Church of Rome.[888]

Alfonso then crossed into the Marches and successfully accomplished the things described previously.[889] Returning home, he made peace with the Genoese under the dogeship of Raffaele Adorno, with the stipulation that no one should have the right of reclaiming what had been lost in war and that neither the people of

885. Cardinal Ludovico Scarampo and Alfonso reached the following accord at Terracina on June 14, 1443.

886. Alfonso sent delegates to the Council of Basel in 1436, but in February 1440 he publicly professed neutrality, moving him closer to an agreement with the pope.

887. One of these cardinals was probably Niccolò de Tudeschi, archbishop of Palermo and head of the Aragonese delegation sent by Alfonso to Basel; see Ryder, *Alfonso*, 215; Pastor, *History of the Popes*, vol.1: 332. He was created cardinal by Felix/Amedeo in November 1440. Jordi de Ornos, created cardinal in October 1440, also seems likely. The third may be either Juan de Segovia or Otón de Moncada de Luna, both created cardinal in October 1440.

888. Aeneas fails to mention the most important outcome of this treaty for the papacy: it was only after this point that Eugenius could safely return to Rome. He triumphantly entered the city on Sept. 28, 1443; Stieber, *Pope Eugenius IV*, 197.

889. Alfonso began campaigning jointly with papal forces led by Scarampo and Milanese forces led by Niccolò Piccinino in August 1443. See paras. 248–53.

Genoa nor the king should receive one another's enemies or assist them with provisions.[890] As a mark of respect, the Genoese were to donate a golden bowl to the king every year for as long as he lived and send it to Naples.

271. After this, Antonio, a Centelles on his father's side, a Ventimiglia by way of his mother, who had performed many fine services for Alfonso in Apulia,[891] came with three hundred horsemen to Fons Populi[892] not far from Teano, where the leading men of the realm had been ordered to meet. When he was accused before the king of planning to kill one of the more influential courtiers, he fled under cover and brought the town of Catanzaro back beneath his control. In an attempt to revive the extinct controversy of the kingdom, he sent letters and messengers not only to the neighboring lords but also the Venetians and other Italian powers, urging them to take up arms against the king. But all his efforts came to naught; for the king marched against him with an army and deprived him of the city of Crotone and all the land remaining to him.[893] Antonio himself he confined in Catanzaro and forced him to surrender unconditionally. Moreover, Giovanni della Noce, who had encouraged Antonio's insubordination, was stripped by him of all his towns and ordered to leave the kingdom.[894] Soon after that came the king's expedition to Tuscany, which has been described in its own place.[895]

Upon his return, and before much time had elapsed, he was vis-

---

890. Negotiations with Genoa began in June 1443 and were concluded on April 7, 1444.

891. Ryder calls Centelles "the noble of Catalan-Sicilian origin who had done most to win the toe of Italy for Alfonso and had since governed it as a viceroy"; see *Alfonso*, 375. He was also the marchese of Crotone.

892. Possibly Fontanelle, which is a few miles from Teano, or *la fonte del Pioppo* ("fountain of the poplar") as Pietragalla translates it; see Facio, *Rerum gestarum*, 7. 118.

893. These events occurred in the autumn of 1444.

894. Della Noce, who fought under Centelles, was the count of Rende in Calabria.

895. See paras. 208–11. Alfonso's attacks on Florentine possessions and allies began in the autumn of 1447; he concluded peace with Florence on June 21, 1450.

ited by Emperor Frederick and the Empress Eleonora, his niece on his sister's side, whom he entertained with such great honor that even the finest orator would hardly have the eloquence to describe it; he sent them both home with splendid gifts.[896] Although, as I related previously, he had granted peace to the Florentines at their request, nevertheless, following the capture of the city of Milan by Francesco Sforza, he set aside his enmity with the Venetians and entered into a treaty with them through the mediation of Leonello, marquis of Este. He then waged another war in Tuscany; on this campaign he sent his son Ferrante, of whom I have spoken enough in connection with the affairs of Tuscany.[897] Peace with the Genoese also broke down after the capture of a ship which was heading for Genoa from the island of Chios, as I will relate subsequently.[898] When the people of Genoa became agitated over this, Giovanni Filippo, a scion of the Fieschi family, sailed with fourteen high-decked ships to the port of Naples, in order to set fire to the king's galleys and cargo-vessels. However, he was repulsed by cannon and withdrew ingloriously. Not many days later, the king's fleet pursued six of the Genoese ships to Monte Circeo and, after the crews had slipped away, seized their valuable cargos and sank them.[899] Because of this, though almost all of Italy had reached a peace agreement, there could be no friendship between the Genoese and the king. When exiles from Genoa took refuge with the king, he put a fleet at their disposal, which, as I have told, harassed the coast of

---

896. The couple arrived in Naples in March 1452.

897. Alfonso declared war on Florence, again, on June 2, 1452; see paras. 210–11.

898. Alfonso was looking to unseat Doge Piero Fregoso, who was unfriendly to him. A ship owned by the Genoese Uberto Squarciafico, returning from the East with a valuable cargo, was seized by the Neapolitans in June 1453; Ryder, *Alfonso*, 265. Aeneas does not go on to discuss this in detail, at least not in *Europe*.

899. Probably a reference to the Genoese ships that blockaded Naples for several days in June 1454 after sacking Trapani; in October 1454 another Genoese fleet met Neapolitan ships in battle near Ponza and were routed, losing half their ships; see Ryder, *Alfonso*, 266; Galasso points to slightly different events in the summer of 1454; see *Regno di Napoli*, 607–8.

Liguria and was bold enough to attack the city itself. The same war is now being resumed with greater forces.[900]

272. When Emperor Frederick visited him, Alfonso was about fifty-eight years old. He had a slender build, a face that was pale but cheerful in expression, a hooked nose, shining eyes, and black but now graying hair which reached to his ears. He was average in height, ate and drank moderately, and only used wine if it was highly diluted with water. He applied himself to literary studies throughout his life and was especially skilled in grammar, though he very rarely spoke Latin. He was devoted to all historical works but did not ignore poets and orators. He solved logical problems with ease and demonstrated familiarity with all areas of philosophy. He had thoroughly studied all the mysteries of theology, and to anyone who questioned him about the foreknowledge of God, the free will of man, the incarnation of the Word, the sacrament of the altar, the Trinity, and other perplexing questions, he gave a prompt and sagacious answer.[901]

273. In making replies, though pithy and concise, he was never shallow. His way of speaking was pleasant and polished. His chief concern was that no one should depart from him unhappy. He preferred to postpone rather than reject unwelcome petitions. He supported religion and scrupulously attended to divine affairs. The priestly vestments and altar ornaments which he provided are

---

900. In early 1456 Genoese exiles from the Adorno and Spinola families made a pact with Alfonso's admiral Vilamari. They began naval operations in September 1456 and did some damage to Genoese shipping. Vilamari and the exiles again attacked Genoese towns and shipping beginning in September 1457 and attempted an assault on Genoa itself on December 25. Neapolitan hopes to overcome Genoa, however, ebbed in the spring of 1458 when the republic signed a pact with France, recognizing Charles VII as its suzerain, and the French sent a fleet to protect Genoa. See Ryder, *Alfonso*, 401–4; Epstein, *Genoa*, 284–86.

901. Alfonso supported numerous humanists at his court in Gaeta and Naples including Lorenzo Valla, Giannozzo Manetti, Bartolomeo Facio, Antonio Beccadelli (Panormita), and George of Trebizond. He also generously patronized poets, musicians, and architects; see Jerry Bentley, *Politics and Culture in Renaissance Naples* (Princeton, N.J.: Princeton University Press, 1987).

beyond compare. He collected sacred and domestic furnishings of gold and silver that inspired wonder and amazement. He purchased pearls of different sorts and sizes, diamonds, and other precious stones from all over the world. He decorated the walls of the chapel where he attended mass and those of the halls in which he lived with rich golden cloths. He dressed himself elegantly rather than expensively, and rarely used silk or a purple cloak. A great part of his life he devoted to hunting. In war he was stern and ruthless, in peace merciful and mild. He readily spared those who had taken up arms against him and was reluctant to shed human blood. However, he abhorred crime and did not permit his subjects to commit offenses with impunity. The kingdom, which for many previous generations had been a lair of brigands, he has made so peaceful and secure that wherever one travels there is no fear of robbers. He lavishly entertained all ambassadors who visited him and went outside the city to meet cardinals sent as papal legates, whom he honored like fathers. He constructed ships of extraordinary size, such that someone seeing them from afar might think that they were tall castles moving through the sea. He erected buildings in many places but in Naples with a splendor and magnificence beyond description.[902] He demolished from its foundations the royal citadel called Castelnuovo and rebuilt it. It is not only awe-inspiring and impregnable in construction but resplendent in opulence, with its circular towers of dressed stone, crafted with amazing skill, its walls of unprecedented thickness, and its huge triumphal arch of the whitest marble.[903] He also repaired the castle of San Salvator in the sea, named Castel dell'Ovo, whose impregnable site was con-

---

902. Reading *quam* for van Heck's *quem*. See Ryder, *Alfonso*, 347–57, for more on Alfonso's love of pomp and gems and the visit of Frederick III and Eleonora, which included a hunting expedition and a tour of the arsenal and mole of the harbor of Naples. Aeneas did not accompany his sovereign to Naples as he had to stay behind in Rome to care for (and guard) Frederick's ward, Ladislas Postumus, who was ill, but he visited the court in 1456; on Aeneas's visit to Naples, see para. 216.

903. Begun in 1455, Castelnuovo was not completed until Ferrante's reign.

verted to the function of a luxurious palace. He also enlarged the city's harbor by raising a tall jetty in the depths of the sea, complete with a massive wall and defensive towers. By draining the marshes, he brought health to the city.

274. He is unquestionably a great ruler and one who has been tested by both extremes of fortune. Among other adversities, he endured an earthquake two years ago which affected almost the whole kingdom and is said to have exceeded anything seen or heard of in our own or our fathers' memory.[904] Many towns of the realm collapsed to the ground, among them Ariano, which was swallowed up as if it had vanished into a chasm. Rare was the city that survived without notable destruction, and around thirty thousand people are said to have perished amidst the falling buildings. The finer houses of Naples were torn apart and shattered, and there was not a church in the city that did not suffer damage. But today the city has almost been restored through the diligence of its citizens and the generosity of the king.

275. Though many of them exceed the time limit I have set, it would not be unfitting in conclusion—as a kind of peroration—to summarize very briefly the glorious deeds of this illustrious king, who illuminated our era like a brilliant star. The most celebrated are as follows. When as a youth, following the death of his father Ferdinand,[905] he had wisely governed Aragon for some time, along with the kingdoms in Spain that he had inherited, he was adopted by Queen Joanna of Naples as her son and, against the advice of his friends, undertook an expedition to Italy to bring assistance to the queen.[906] In several battles, he crushed Duke Louis of Anjou, who claimed that the kingdom was owed to him by hereditary right, and expelled him. When the queen listened to bad advice and de-

---

904. A strong earthquake hit the region on December 5, 1456; a second followed on December 30.
905. Ferdinand I of Aragon (d. 1416).
906. Joanna II of Naples (d. 1435).

serted him, he did not so much punish as restrain her.⁹⁰⁷ René, a second rival for the kingdom, he defeated in battle and forced to step aside. When Giovanni Vitelleschi, the patriarch of Alexandria, invaded with large forces, he drove him in flight from the kingdom. He twice captured Gaeta: once by defeating it in a fierce battle; a second time when a faction within the city invited him in after it had defected.⁹⁰⁸ He captured Naples by assault, despite the presence of René and a large population. When his brother King Juan of Navarre experienced difficulties in Spain, he lent him military assistance. He occupied and plundered Marseilles, the famous city of Provence, in a nocturnal attack.⁹⁰⁹ He blockaded the island of Djerba (called the Land of the Lotus-eaters by the ancients), which lies four miles from the continent of Africa. When Abd al-Aziz, the king of that region, approached with his forces, Alfonso defeated him on the neighboring coast and compelled him to flee from his smaller to his larger camp; not long afterward he received tribute from the same barbarians.⁹¹⁰ From Pope Eugenius, who opposed him on the matter of the kingdom, he finally obtained the peace terms which he wanted. He forcibly expelled Francesco Sforza from the Marches, and both in Albania and in the East he harassed the Turks through his captains and caused them major losses. Twice he crushed the Florentines in battle on account of matters involving France; twice he acquiesced when they sued for peace. But the greatest thing of all and most worthy of admiration and awe is that, when he had been defeated by the Genoese in a naval battle (as I described previously), taken prisoner by Duke Filippo of Milan,

907. See n. 839 on the vicissitudes of Joanna's choices for heir to the kingdom.
908. Gaeta was captured only once. See para. 262. It is unclear if Aeneas believed the city to have fallen twice to Alfonso or if "Gaeta" is a scribal error in this passage.
909. Alfonso attacked Marseilles in November 1423.
910. The blockade of Djerba took place between August 15 and September 9, 1432. Abd al-Aziz II, Abu Faris, the ruler of Tunisia (r. 1394–1434), narrowly escaped capture, but Alfonso's victory was far from decisive, nor is it clear he received tribute apart from a trade agreement and a present of lions from Tunis; see Ryder, *Alfonso*, 186–88; 237; *DBI*, vol. 2: 324–25. Aeneas draws from Facio, *Rerum gestarum*, 4.10–39.

and subsequently released, he shortly gained possession of a mighty kingdom, took tribute as the victor from his former vanquishers, and found such favor with Filippo that he was named his heir in his last will and testament.[911]

Alfonso is a true scion of the Goths, from whom the royal family of Spain into which he was born is undoubtedly descended. It was the way of the Goths to triumph in battle and subdue kingdoms.[912] Following in their footsteps, Ferdinand fathered a son not unlike himself. As he himself had done to Aragon, Catalonia, Valencia, and Sicily, so Alfonso, by fighting, pressing forward, and defeating his foes, subdued the part of Italy that was once called Greater Greece. He has become the keeper of peace in Italy and also seems to be the guide and arbitrator of affairs in Spain.

911. See para. 180.
912. A reference to the Visigothic rulers of medieval Spain, who began to rule the Iberian peninsula in the fifth century CE, and established kingdoms in the north of the peninsula after the Muslim invasion of the early eighth century.

APPENDIX
BIBLIOGRAPHY
INDEX

APPENDIX
REIGNS OF SELECTED RULERS

POPES

Martin V	1417–31
Eugenius IV	1431–47
[Felix V	1440–49]
Nicholas V	1447–55
Calixtus III	1455–58
Pius II	1458–64

HOLY ROMAN EMPERORS

Charles IV	1346–78
Wenceslas	1378–1400
Rupert	1400–10
Jobst	1410–11
Sigismund	1411–37
Albert II	1438–39
Frederick III	1440–93

BYZANTINE EMPERORS

Manuel II	1391–1425
John VIII Paleologus	1425–48
Constantine XI Paleologus	1448–53

OTTOMAN RULERS

Osman	d. ca. 1326
Orhan	1326–62

OTTOMAN RULERS (cont.)

Murad I	1362–89
Bayezid I	1389–1402
Mehmed I	1413–21
Murad II	1421–51
Mehmed II	1451–81

RULERS OF HUNGARY

Louis I	1342–82
Maria	1382–95
Sigismund	1387–1437
Albert	1438–39
Vladislas IV (Wladyslaw III of Poland)	1439–44
Ladislas Postumus	1445–57
Matthias Corvinus	1458–90

RULERS OF SERBIA

George Branković	1427–56
Lazar Branković	1456–58

RULER OF BOSNIA

Stefan Tomas	1443–61

RULERS OF BOHEMIA

Wenceslas IV	1363–1419
Sigismund	1419–37
Albert I	1438–39
Ladislas Postumus	1453–57
George Podiebrad	1458–71

RULERS OF POLAND

Louis I	1370–82
Jadwiga	1384–99
Wladyslaw II Jagiello	1386–1434
Wladyslaw III (Vladislas IV of Hungary)	1434–44
Casimir IV	1447–92

Appendix

RULERS OF LITHUANIA

Jogaila (Wladyslaw II of Poland)	1377–1401
Vytautus	1401–30 (de facto ruler 1392)
Švitrigaila	1430–32
Sigismund	1432–40
Casimir	1440–92

RULERS OF DENMARK

Valdemar IV Atterdag	1340–75
Olaf V	1375–87
Margaret	1387–1412
Erik (co-ruler with Margaret)	1396–1438
Christopher	1440–48
Christian I (Oldenburg)	1448–81

RULERS OF NORWAY

Magnus VII Eriksson	1319–74
Haakon VI	1355–80
Olaf	1380–87
Margaret	1388–1412
Erik (co-ruler with Margaret)	1389–1442
Christopher	1442–48
Christian I (Oldenburg)	1450–81

RULERS OF SWEDEN

Magnus (II) Eriksson	1319–63
Albert	1363–89
Margaret	1389–1412
Erik (co-ruler with Margaret)	1396–1439
Christopher	1441–48
Karl (VIII)	1448–57; 1464–65; 1467–70
Christian I (Oldenburg)	1457–64

RULERS OF FRANCE

Charles VII	1422–61
Louis XI	1461–83

Appendix

RULER OF ENGLAND

Henry VI — 1422–61, 1470–71

RULERS OF SCOTLAND

James I — 1406–37
James II — 1437–60

RULERS OF CASTILE-LEÓN

Juan II — 1406–54
Enrique IV — 1454–74

RULER OF NAVARRE

Juan II — 1425–79

RULERS OF ARAGON

Alfonso — 1416–58
Juan II — 1458–79

RULERS OF PORTUGAL

Pedro the Infante (regent) — 1438–48
Afonso V — 1438–81

DUKES OF MILAN

Giangaleazzo Visconti — 1395–1402
Gian Maria Visconti — 1402–12
Filippo Maria Visconti — 1412–47
[Ambrosian Republic — 1447–50]
Francesco Sforza — 1450–66

DOGES OF VENICE

Francesco Foscari — 1423–57
Pasquale Malipiero — 1457–62

RULERS OF NAPLES

Joanna II — 1414–35
René of Anjou — 1435–42
Alfonso I — 1442–58
Ferrante — 1458–94

Appendix

DUKES OF BURGUNDY
John the Fearless	1404–19
Philip III	1419–67

DUKES OF SAVOY
Amedeo VIII	1391–1440
Louis I	1440–65

DUKES OF BRITTANY
Jean V (or VI)	1399–1442
François I	1442–50
Pierre II	1450–47
Arthur III	1457–58

ELECTORS OF SAXONY
Frederick II	1428–64
Albert III	1464–1500

ELECTORS OF BRANDENBURG
Frederick I	1417–40
Frederick II	1440–70

GRAND MASTERS OF THE TEUTONIC KNIGHTS
Ulrich of Jungingen	1407–10
Henry of Plauen	1410–13
Michael Küchmeister	1414–22
Paul of Rusdorf	1422–41
Conrad of Erlichshausen	1441–49
Ludwig of Erlichshausen	1450–67

BIBLIOGRAPHY

COMMON ABBREVIATIONS

CMH   *New Cambridge Medieval History*
DBI   *Dizionario biografico degli italiani*
ER   Grendler, *Encyclopedia of the Renaissance*
LMB   Fine, *Late Medieval Balkans*

MANUSCRIPTS OF *DE EUROPA*

Biblioteca Apostolica Vaticana, Rome
Urbinas Latinus 885
Vaticanus Latinus 3888

PRINTED EDITIONS OF *DE EUROPA*

De Europa. Edited by Adrian van Heck. Vatican City: Biblioteca Apostolica Vaticana, 2001.
De Europa. In *Cosmographia*, 87–151. Paris, 1509.
De Europa. In *Opera Geographica et Historica*, 218–374. Helmstadt, 1699.
De Europa. In *Opera quae extant omnia*, 387–471. Basel, 1571; repr., Frankfurt: Minerva, 1967.
Enea Silvio Piccolomini, Europa. Edited by Gunter Frank and Paul Metzger, translated by Albrecht Hartmann. Heidelberg: Verlag Regionalkultur, 2005.
La Europa del mio tiempo. Edited and translated by Francisco Socas. Seville: University of Seville Publications, 1998.

OTHER PRIMARY SOURCES

Adam of Bremen. *Deeds of the Archbishops of Hamburg-Bremen*. Translated and edited by Francis J. Tschan. New York: Columbia University Press, 1959.
Aethicus. *Die Kosmographie des Aethicus*. Edited by Otto Prinz. Munich: Monumenta Germaniae Historica, 1993.

Bibliography

Augustus. *Res Gestae*. Edited by John Scheid. Paris: Les Belles Lettres, 2007.

Biondo, Flavio. *Italia Illustrata: Text, Translation, and Commentary*. 2 vols. Edited and translated by Catherine J. Castner. Binghamton, NY: Global Academic Publishing, 2005; 2010.

———. *Italy Illuminated*. Edited and translated by Jeffrey A. White. Cambridge, Mass.: Harvard University Press, 2005.

Cicero. *Brutus, Orator*. With an English translation by G. L. Hendrickson and H. M. Hubbell. Cambridge, Mass.: Harvard University Press, 1962.

———. *De Officiis [On Duties]*. With an English translation by Walter Miller. Cambridge, Mass.: Harvard University Press, 1913.

Curtius, Quintus. *History of Alexander*. 2 vols. With an English translation by John C. Rolfe. Cambridge, Mass.: Harvard University Press, 1946.

Decembrio, Pier Candido. *Vita di Filippo Maria Visconti*. Translated into Italian by Elio Bartolini. Milan: Adelphi Edizioni, 1983.

Długosz, Jan. *The Annals of Jan Długosz*. Translated and abridged by Maurice Michael. West Sussex: IM Publications, 1997.

Doukas. *Decline and Fall of Byzantium to the Ottoman Turks*. Edited and translated by Harry J. Magoulias. Detroit: Wayne State University Press, 1975.

Facio, Bartolomeo. *Rerum gestarum Alfonsi regis libri*. Edited and translated by Daniela Pietragalla. Alessandria: Edizioni dell'Orso, 2004.

Fudge, Thomas A., ed. and trans. *The Crusade against the Heretics in Bohemia, 1418–1437*. Aldershot: Ashgate, 2002.

Homer. *Iliad*. 2 vols. With an English translation by A. T. Murray (revised by William F. Wyatt). Cambridge, Mass.: Harvard University Press, 1999.

Horace. *Odes and Epodes*. Edited and translated by Niall Rudd. Cambridge, Mass.: Harvard University Press, 2004.

Ilardi, Vincent, and Paul M. Kendall, eds. *Dispatches with Related Documents of Milanese Ambassadors in France and Burgundy, 1450–1483*. Translated by Frank J. Fata. Athens: Ohio University Press, 1970–1981.

Imber, Colin, ed. and trans. *The Crusade of Varna, 1443–1445*. Aldershot: Ashgate, 2006.

Infessura, Stefano. *Diario della Città di Roma*. Edited by Oreste Tommasini. Rome: Forzani E. C. Tipografi, 1890.

Isidore. *Etymologiae*. 2 vols. Edited by W. M. Lindsay. Oxford: Clarendon Press, 1911.

Jones, J. R. Melville, trans. and ed. *The Siege of Constantinople 1453: Seven Contemporary Accounts*. Amsterdam: Adolf M. Hakkert, 1972.

Justin. *Epitome Historiarum Philippicarum Pompei Trogi*. Edited by O. Seel. Stuttgart: Teubner, 1972.

Kottanner, Helene. *The Memoirs of Helene Kottaner*. Translated by Maya Bijvoet Williamson. Rochester, N.Y.: D. S. Brewer, 1998.

Kritovoulos. *The History of Mehmed the Conqueror*. Edited and translated by Charles T. Riggs. Princeton, N.J.: Princeton University Press, 1954.

Bibliography 319

Leonard of Chios. *Historia Constantinopolitanae urbis a Mahumete II captae*. Edited by J. P. Migne, *Patrologia Graeca*. Vol. 159: 923–41. 1866.

Lucan. *Civil War*. With an English translation by J. D. Duff. Cambridge, Mass.: Harvard University Press, 1928.

Machiavelli, Niccolò. *Florentine Histories*. Translated by Laura F. Banfield and Harvey C. Mansfield Jr. Princeton, N.J.: Princeton University Press, 1988.

Martial. *Epigrams*. 3 vols. Edited and translated by D. R. Shackleton Bailey. Cambridge, Mass.: Harvard University Press, 1993.

Nepos. *Vitae cum fragmentis*. Edited by Peter K. Marshall. Leipzig: Teubner, 1977.

Orosius. *Histoires (Contre les Païens)*. 3 vols. Edited by M.-P. Arnaud-Lindet. Paris: Les Belles Lettres, 1990–91.

Otto of Freising. *The Two Cities: A Chronicle of Universal History*. Translated and edited by Charles Mierow, Austin Evans, and Charles Knapp. New York: Octagon Books, 1966.

Pertusi, Agostino, ed. *La caduta di Costantinopoli*. 2 vols. Arnoldo Mondadori Editore, 1976.

———, ed. *Testi inediti e poco noti sulla caduta di Costantinopoli*. Bologna: Pàtron Editore, 1983.

Philippides, Marios, ed. and trans. *Mehmed II the Conqueror and the Fall of the Franco-Byzantine Levant to the Ottoman Turks*. Tempe: ACMRS, 2007.

Piccolomini, Aeneas Silvius (Pope Pius II). *Commentaries*. 2 vols. Translated and edited by Margaret Meserve and Marcello Simonetta. Cambridge, Mass.: Harvard University Press, 2003; 2007.

———. *Commentaries of Pius II*. 5 vols. Translated by Florence Alden Gragg and edited by Leona C. Gabel. Northampton, Mass.: Smith College, 1951.

———. *Der Briefwechsel des Eneas Silvius Piccolomini*. Edited by Rudolf Wolkan. In *Fontes rerum austriacarum*. ser. 2, vols. 61, 62, 67, 68. Vienna: Alfred Holder, 1909–18.

———. *Descripción de Asia*. Edited and translated by Domingo F. Sanz. Madrid: Consejo Superior de Investigaciones Centificas, 2010.

———. *De viris illustribus*. Edited by Adrian van Heck. Vatican City: Biblioteca Apostolica Vaticana, 1991.

———. *Epistola ad Mahomatem II (Epistle to Mohammed II)*. Edited and translated by Albert Baca. New York: Peter Lang, 1990.

———. *Historia Austrialis (Monumenta Germaniae Historica*, nov. ser. 24). 2 vols. Edited by Julia Knödler and Martin Wagendorfer. Hannover: Verlag Hahnsche Buchhandlung, 2009.

———. *Historia Bohemica*. 3 vols. Edited by Joseph Hejnic and Hans Rothe. Cologne: Bohlau Verlag, 2005.

———. *La Discrittione de l'Asia et Europa di Papa Pio II*, translated by Sebastiano Fausto. Venice, 1544.

———. *Opera quae extant omnia*. Basel, 1571; repr., Frankfurt: Minerva, 1967.

———. *Reject Aeneas, Accept Pius: Selected Letters of Aeneas Sylvius Piccolomini (Pope Pius II)*. Introduced and translated by Thomas M. Izbicki, Gerald Christianson, and Philip Krey. Washington: The Catholic University of America Press, 2006.

———. *Selected Letters*. Translated by Albert Baca. Northridge, Calif.: San Fernando Valley State College, 1969.

Pliny. *Natural History*. 10 vols. With an English translation by H. Rackham, W. H. S. Jones, A. C. Andrews, and D. E. Eichholz. Cambridge, Mass.: Harvard University Press, 1938–63.

Polybius. *Histories*. 6 vols. With an English translation by W. R. Paton (revised by F. W. Walbank and Christian Habicht). Cambridge, Mass.: Harvard University Press, 2010–12.

Pomponius Mela. *Chorographie [Description of the World]*. Edited by A. Silberman. Paris: Les Belles Lettres, 1988.

Ptolemy. *Geographia*. 2 vols. Edited by K. Müller. Paris: Firmin-Didot, 1883–1901.

Spandounes, Theodore. *On the Origin of the Ottoman Emperors*. Edited and translated by Donald M. Nicol. Cambridge: Cambridge University Press, 1997.

Strabo. *Geography*. 8 vols. With an English translation by Horace Leonard Jones. Cambridge, Mass.: Harvard University Press, 1917–32.

Tacitus. *Histories*. 2 vols. With an English translation by Clifford H. Moore. Cambridge, Mass.: Harvard University Press. 1925–31.

Thuróczy, János. *Chronicle of the Hungarians*. Translated by Frank Mantello. Foreword and commentary by Pál Engel. Bloomington: Indiana University Press, 1991.

Virgil. *Aeneid*. 2 vols. With an English translation by H. Rushton Fairclough (revised by G. P. Goold). Cambridge, Mass.: Harvard University Press, 1999–2000.

SECONDARY SOURCES

Ady, Cecilia M. *A History of Milan under the Sforza*. London: Methuen and Co., 1907.

———. *Pius II (Aeneas Silvius Piccolomini) the Humanist Pope*. London: Methuen and Co., 1913.

———. *A History of Milan under the Visconti*. London: Methuen and Co., 1924.

———. *The Bentivoglio of Bologna: A Study in Despotism*. London: Oxford University Press, 1937.

Akbari, Suzanne Conklin. "From Due East to True North: Orientalism and Orientation." In *The Postcolonial Middle Ages*. Edited by Jeffrey Jerome Cohen, 19–34. New York: St. Martin's Press, 2000.

———. *Idols in the East: European Representation of Islam and the Orient, 1100–1450*. Ithaca, N.Y.: Cornell University Press, 2009.

Bibliography

Allgemeine Deutsche Biographie. Leipzig: Duncker und Humblot, 1875–1912.

Allmand, Christopher, ed. *The New Cambridge Medieval History.* Vol. 7. Cambridge: Cambridge University Press, 1998.

Asher, R. E. *National Myths in Renaissance France: Francus, Samothes, and the Druids.* Edinburgh: Edinburgh University Press, 1993.

Avery, Catherine B., ed. *New Century Italian Renaissance Encyclopedia.* New York: Appleton-Century-Crofts, 1972.

Babinger, Franz. *Mehmed the Conqueror and His Time.* Translated by Ralph Manheim. 1953. Rev. ed. Princeton: Princeton University Press, 1978.

Bak, János. "The Late Medieval Period, 1382–1526." In *A History of Hungary*, edited by Peter F. Sugar and Peter Hanak, 54–82. Bloomington: Indiana University Press, 1990.

Baldi, Barbara. "Enea Silvio Piccolomini e il *De Europa*: umanesimo, religione, e politica." *Archivio storico italiano* 161 (2003): 619–83.

———. *Pio II e le trasformazioni dell'Europa cristiana, 1457–1464.* Milan: Unicopli, 2006.

Balsdon, J. P. V. D. *Romans and Aliens.* London: Duckworth & Co., 1979.

Barker, John W. *Manuel II Paleologus (1391–1425): A Study in Late Byzantine Statesmanship.* New Brunswick, NJ: Rutgers University Press, 1969.

Barta, Gábor, István Bóna, Béla Köpeczi, et al. *History of Transylvania.* Budapest: Akadémiai Kiadó, 1994.

Bentley, Jerry H. *Politics and Culture in Renaissance Naples.* Princeton: Princeton University Press, 1987.

Biographie Universelle. Paris: Michaud, 1811–28.

Birnbaum, Maria. "Humanism in Hungary." In *Renaissance Humanism*, edited by Albert R. Rabil, 293–334. Philadelphia: University of Pennsylvania Press, 1988, Vol. 2.

Bisaha, Nancy. *Creating East and West: Renaissance Humanists and the Ottoman Turks.* Philadelphia: University of Pennsylvania Press, 2004.

———. "'Discourses of Power and Desire': The Letters of Aeneas Silvius Piccolomini (1453)." In *Florence and Beyond: Culture, Society and Politics in Renaissance Italy*, edited by David Peterson and Daniel Bornstein, 121–34. Toronto: Centre for Reformation and Renaissance Studies, 2008.

———. "Pope Pius II's Letter to Sultan Mehmed II: A Reexamination." *Crusades* 1 (2002): 183–200.

Bispham, Edward, ed. *Roman Europe.* Oxford: Oxford University Press, 2008.

Bisson, Thomas N. *The Medieval Crown of Aragon: A Short History.* Oxford: Clarendon Press, 1986.

Bjørnstad, Hall, ed. *Borrowed Feathers: Plagiarism and the Limits of Imitation in Early Modern Europe.* Oslo: Unipub, 2008.

Black, Jane. *Absolutism in Renaissance Milan.* Oxford: Oxford University Press, 2009.

Black, Robert. *Benedetto Accolti and the Florentine Renaissance*. Cambridge: Cambridge University Press, 1985.

Blastenbrei, Peter. "The Soldier and His Cardinal: Francesco Sforza and Nicolò Acciapacci (1438–1444)." *Renaissance Studies* 3, no. 3 (1989): 290–302.

Blockmans, Wim, and Walter Prevenier. *The Promised Lands: The Low Countries under Burgundian Rule, 1369–1530*. Translated by Elizabeth Fackleman; translation revised and edited by Edward Peters. Philadelphia: University of Pennsylvania Press, 1999.

Boia, Lucian, ed. *Great Historians from Antiquity to 1800: An International Dictionary*. New York: Greenwood Press, 1989.

Bolens, Guillemette, and Lukas Erne, eds. *Medieval and Early Modern Authorship*. Tübingen: Narr Verlag, 2011.

Bonfante, Larissa, ed. *The Barbarians of Ancient Europe: Realities and Interactions*. Cambridge: Cambridge University Press, 2011.

Bonjour, E., H. S. Offler, and G. R. Potter. *A Short History of Switzerland*. Oxford: Clarendon Press, 1952.

Brady, Thomas A., Jr. *German Histories in the Age of Reformations, 1400–1650*. Cambridge: Cambridge University Press, 2009.

Bratchel, M. E. *Lucca 1430–1494*. Oxford: Clarendon Press, 1995.

Braund, David. *Georgia in Antiquity: A History of Colchis and Transcaucasian Iberia, 550 BC–AD 562*. Oxford: Clarendon Press, 1994.

Broomhall, Susan, and Stephanie Turbin, eds. *Women, Identities and Communities in Early Modern Europe*. Burlington, VT: Aldershot, 2008.

Buchanan, W. W. "Frostbite Arthritis Consequence of First Papal Visit to Scotland?" *Clinical Rheumatology* 6, no. 3 (1987): 436–38.

Bunson, Matthew. *Encyclopedia of the Roman Empire*. New York: Facts on File, 1994.

Butler, Alban. *Butler's Lives of the Saints*. Edited by Paul Burns. Collegeville, Minn: Liturgical Press, 2003.

Bynum, Caroline Walker. *Wonderful Blood: Theology and Practice in Late Medieval Northern Germany and Beyond*. Philadelphia: University of Pennsylvania Press, 2007.

Calzona, Arturo, et al., eds. *Il sogno di Pio II e il viaggio da Roma a Mantova*. Mantua: Leo S. Olschki, 2003.

Carlino, Andrea. "*Kunstbüchlein* and *Imagines Contrafactae*: A Challenge to the Notion of Plagiarism." In *Borrowed Feathers: Plagiarism and the Limits of Imitation in Early Modern Europe*, edited by Hall Bjørnstad, 87–108. Oslo: Unipub, 2008.

Casella, Nicola. "Pio II tra geografia e storia: la 'Cosmographia.'" *Archivio della Società romana di storia patria* 95 (1972): 35–112.

Cavazza, Silvano, ed. *Da Ottone III a Massimiliano I: Gorizia e i conti di Gorizia nel medioevo*. Gorizia: Edizioni della Laguna, 2004.

Bibliography

Chambers, D. S. *Popes, Cardinals and War.* London: I. B. Tauris & Co, 2006.

Christiansen, Eric. *The Northern Crusades.* London: Penguin Books, 1997. 1st edition published by Macmillan, 1980.

Cochrane, Eric. *Historians and Historiography in the Italian Renaissance.* Chicago: University of Chicago Press, 1981.

Cohen, Jeffrey Jerome, ed. *The Postcolonial Middle Ages.* New York: St. Martin's Press, 2000.

Cohn, Samuel K. *Popular Protest in Late Medieval Europe.* Manchester: Manchester University Press, 2004.

Collins, James. *From Tribes to Nation: The Making of France, 500–1799.* Canada: Wadsworth/Thomson, 2002.

Collins, Roger. *Early Medieval Europe 300–1000.* New York: St. Martin's Press, 1991.

Cosenza, Mario. *Biographical and Bibliographical Dictionary of the Italian Humanists and of the World of Classical Scholarship in Italy 1300–1800.* Boston: G. K. Hall, 1962–1967.

Coxe, William. *History of the House of Austria.* Vol. 1. London: Henry G. Bohn, 1847.

Cremona, Vicki Ann, et al., eds. *Theatrical Events: Borders, Dynamics, Frames.* New York: IFTR/FIRT: 2004.

Croce, Benedetto. *Storie e leggende napoletane.* Bari: Giuseppe Laterza e Figli, 1919.

Dale, Sharon, Alison Williams Lewin, and Duane Osheim, eds. *Chronicling History: Chroniclers and Historians in Medieval and Renaissance Italy.* University Park: Pennsylvania State University Press, 2007.

Daly, William. "Clovis: How Barbaric, How Pagan?" *Speculum* 69, no. 3 (1994): 619–64.

Darling, Linda. "Contested Territory: Ottoman Holy War in Comparative Context." *Studia Islamica* 91 (2000): 133–63.

Davies, Norman. *Europe: A History.* Oxford: Oxford University Press, 1996.

Delaney, John. *Dictionary of Saints.* 1980. Rev. ed. Random House, 2005.

Delanty, Gerard. *Inventing Europe: Idea, Identity, Reality.* London: Palgrave Macmillan, 1995.

D'Elia, Anthony F. "Stefano Porcari's Conspiracy against Pope Nicholas V in 1453 and Republican Culture in Papal Rome." *Journal of the History of Ideas* 68, no. 2 (2007): 207–31.

———. *A Sudden Terror: The Plot to Murder the Pope in Renaissance Rome.* Cambridge, Mass.: Harvard University Press, 2009.

Del Treppo, Mario. *Condottieri e uomini d'arme nell'Italia del Rinascimento.* Naples: Liguori, 2002.

De Sousa, Armindo. "Portugal." *The New Cambridge Medieval History.* Vol. 7. Edited by Christopher Allmand, 627–44. Cambridge: Cambridge University Press, 1998.

De Vries, Kelly. "The Lack of a Western European Military Response to the Ottoman Invasions of Eastern Europe from Nicopolis (1396) to Mohács (1526)." In *Guns and Men in Medieval Europe, 1200–1500*. Aldershot: Ashgate, 2002.

Dictionary of the Middle Ages. Edited by Joseph R. Strayer. New York: Scribner, 1982–.

Dizionario biografico degli italiani. Rome: Istituto della Enciclopedia Italiana, 1960–.

Dollinger, Philippe. *The German Hansa*. London: Routledge, 1999.

Droege, Georg. *Verfassung und Wirtschaft in Kurköln unter Dietrich von Moers*. Bonn: Ludwig Röhrscheid Verlag, 1957.

Du Boulay, F. R. H. *Germany in the Later Middle Ages*. New York: St. Martin's Press, 1983.

Edwards, John. "Reconquista and Crusade in Fifteenth-Century Spain." In *Crusading in the Fifteenth Century: Message and Impact*, edited by Norman Housley, 163–81. New York: Palgrave Macmillan, 2004.

Enciclopedia italiana di scienze, lettere ed arti. Rome: Treccani, 1929–39.

Encyclopedia Britannica. Multiple editions.

Engel, Pál. *Realm of St. Stephen: A History of Medieval Hungary 895–1526*. London: I. B. Taurus, 2005.

Epstein, Steven. *Genoa and the Genoese 958–1528*. Chapel Hill: University of North Carolina Press, 1996.

Eubel, Konrad. *Hierarchia Catholica medii et recentioris aevi; sive, Summorum pontificum, S. R. E. cardinalium, ecclesiarum antistitum*. Vols. 1 and 2. Padua, 1952.

Ferente, Serena. *La Sfortuna di Jacopo Piccinino: storia dei bracceschi in Italia 1423–1465*. Florence: Olschki Editore, 2005.

Fine, John V. A. *The Bosnian Church: A New Interpretation*. Boulder, Colo.: East European Quarterly, 1975.

———. *The Late Medieval Balkans*. Ann Arbor: University of Michigan Press, 1987.

Fletcher, Richard. *The Barbarian Conversion: From Paganism to Christianity*. New York: H. Holt, 1998.

Gaeta, Franco. "Sulla 'Lettera a Maometto II' di Pio II." *Bulletino dell'Istituto storico italiano per il medioevo e archivio muratoriano* 77 (1965): 127–227.

Galasso, Giuseppe. *Il Regno di Napoli (Storia d'Italia XV)*. Turin: Unione Tipografico-Editrice Torinese, 1992.

Garin, Eugenio. *Portraits from the Quattrocento*. New York: Harper and Row, 1963.

Geanakoplos, Deno John. *Constantinople and the West*. Madison: University of Wisconsin Press, 1989.

Genesin, Monica, Joachim Matzinger, Giancarlo Vallone, eds. *The Living Skanderbeg: The Albanian Hero between Myth and History*. Hamburg: Kovac, 2010.

Gensini, Sergio, ed. *Europa e Mediterraneo tra medioevo e prima età moderna: l'osservatorio italiano.* San Miniato: Pacini Editore, 1992.

Gill, Joseph. *The Council of Florence.* Cambridge: Cambridge University Press, 1959.

Gould, Evlyn, and George J. Sheridan Jr., eds. *Engaging Europe: Rethinking a Changing Continent.* New York: Rowman and Littlefield, 2005.

Grafton, Anthony. *The Footnote: A Curious History.* Cambridge, Mass.: Harvard University Press, 1997.

Grendler, Paul F., ed. *Encyclopedia of the Renaissance.* 6 vols. New York: Charles Scribner's Sons, 1999.

———. *Universities of the Italian Renaissance.* Baltimore: Johns Hopkins University Press, 2002.

Gundersheimer, Werner. *Ferrara: The Style of a Renaissance Despotism.* Princeton: Princeton University Press, 1973.

Guthmüller, Bodo, and Wilhelm Kühlmann, eds. *Europa und die Türken in der Renaissance.* Tübingen: Max Niemayer Verlag, 2000.

Guzman, Gregory. "Encyclopedias." In *Medieval Latin: An Introduction and Bibliographical Guide,* edited by F. A. C. Mantello and A. G. Rigg, 702–7. Washington: The Catholic University of America Press, 1996.

Hale, John. *The Civilization of Europe in the Renaissance.* New York: Atheneum, 1994.

Halecki, Oskar. *Borderlands of Western Civilization: A History of East Central Europe.* New York: The Ronald Press Company, 1952.

Harris, Jonathan. *Constantinople: Capital of Byzantium.* London and New York: Hambledon Continuum, 2007.

Hay, Denis. *Europe: The Emergence of an Idea.* Edinburgh: Edinburgh University Press, 1957.

Hay, Denis, and John Law. *Italy in the Age of the Renaissance.* London and New York: Longman, 1989; Second impression, 1990.

Heath, Michael J. "Renaissance Scholars and the Origins of the Turks." *Bibliothèque d'humanisme et renaissance* 41 (1979): 453–71.

Hefernan, Thomas, and Thomas Burman, eds. *Scripture and Pluralism: Reading the Bible in the Religiously Plural Worlds of the Middle Ages.* Leiden: Brill, 2005.

Heinig, Paul-Joachim, ed. *Kaiser Friedrich III (1440–1493) in Seiner Zeit.* Cologne: Bohlau Verlag, 1993.

Held, Joseph. *Hunyadi: Legend and Reality.* Boulder, Colo.: East European Monographs, 1985.

Helle, Knut, ed. *The Cambridge History of Scandinavia.* Vol. 1. Cambridge: Cambridge University Press, 2003.

Helmrath, Johannes. "The German *Reichstage* and the Crusade." In *Crusading in the Fifteenth Century: Message and Impact,* edited by Norman Housley, 53–69. New York: Palgrave Macmillan, 2004.

———. "Pius II und die Türken." In *Europa und die Türken in der Renaissance,* edited by Bodo Guthmüller and Wilhelm Kühlmann, 79–137. Tübingen: Max Niemayer Verlag, 2000.

Holmes, George. *The Later Middle Ages (A History of England, part 3)*. New York: W. W. Norton and Company, 1962.

Housley, Norman. *The Later Crusades: From Lyons to Alcazar, 1274–1580*. Oxford: Oxford University Press, 1992.

———. "Capistrano and the Crusade of 1456." In *Crusading in the Fifteenth Century: Message and Impact*, edited by Norman Housley, 94–115. New York: Palgrave Macmillan, 2004.

———, ed. *Crusading in the Fifteenth Century: Message and Impact*. New York: Palgrave Macmillan, 2004.

———. "Pope Pius II and Crusading." *Crusades* 11 (2012): 209–47.

Hyland, William. "John-Jerome of Prague (1368–1440): A Norbertine Missionary in Lithuania." *Analecta Praemonstratensia* 78 (2002): 228–54.

Ianziti, Gary. "Challenging Chronicles: Leonardo Bruni's *History of the Florentine People*." In *Chronicling History*, edited by Sharon Dale, Alison Williams Lewin, and Duane Osheim, 249–72. University Park: Pennsylvania State Press, 2007.

———. *Writing History in Renaissance Italy: Leonardo Bruni and the Uses of the Past*. Cambridge, Mass.: Harvard University Press, 2012.

Imber, Colin. *The Ottoman Empire, 1300–1650: The Structure of Power*. Hampshire: Palgrave Macmillan, 2002.

Inalcik, Halil. *The Ottoman Empire*. Translated by Norman Itzkowitz and Colin Imber. London: Weidenfeld and Nicolson, 1973.

International Dictionary of Historic Places. Edited by Trudy Ring. Chicago: Fitzroy-Dearborn Publishers, 1995–96, vol 3.

Itzkowitz, Norman. *Ottoman Empire and Islamic Tradition*. Chicago: University of Chicago Press, 1972.

Izbicki, Thomas M. "'Reject Aeneas!' Pius II on the Errors of his Youth." In *Pius II, 'El Più Expeditivo Pontifice': Selected Studies on Aeneas Silvius Piccolomini*, edited by Zweder von Martels and Arjo Vanderjagt, 187–204. Leiden: Brill, 2003.

Jestice, Phyllis. *Holy People of the World: A Cross-Cultural Encyclopedia*. Santa Barbara, Calif: ABC Clio, 2004.

Jordan, William C. "'Europe' in the Middle Ages." In *The Idea of Europe from Antiquity to the European Union*, edited by Anthony Pagden, 72–90. Cambridge: Cambridge University Press, 2002.

Kaminsky, Howard. "Pius Aeneas among the Taborites." *Church History* 28, no. 3 (1959): 281–309.

Kendall, Paul M. *Louis XI, The Universal Spider*. New York: W. W. Norton, 1970.

Keyser, Paul T. "Greek Geography of the Western Barbarians." In *The Barbarians of Ancient Europe: Realities and Interactions*, edited by Larissa Bonfante, 37–70. Cambridge: Cambridge University Press, 2011.

Bibliography

Khan, H. A., ed. *The Birth of the European Identity: The Europe-Asia Contrast in Greek Thought, 490–322 B.C.* Vol. 2. Nottingham: Nottingham Classical Literature Studies, 1993.

Kirschbaum, Stanislav J. *History of Slovakia: The Struggle for Survival.* New York: St. Martin's Press, 1995.

Kitchin, G. W. *A History of France; Vol. I (B.C. 58–A.D. 1453).* Oxford: Clarendon Press, 1899.

Klassen, John Martin. "Hus, the Hussites, and Bohemia." In *The New Cambridge Medieval History*, vol. 7, edited by Christopher Allmand, 367–391. Cambridge: Cambridge University Press, 1998.

———. *The Nobility and the Making of the Hussite Revolution.* New York: Columbia University Press, 1978.

Koller, Heinrich. *Kaiser Friedrich III.* Darmstadt: Wissenschaftliche Buchgesellschaft, 2005.

Kotte, Andreas. "The Transformation of a Ceremony of Penance into a Play." In *Theatrical Events: Borders, Dynamics, Frames*, edited by Vicki Ann Cremona et al., 53–68. New York: IFTR/FIRT, 2004.

Kristeller, Paul Oskar. "The Humanist Bartolomeo Facio and His Unknown Correspondence." In *Studies in Renaissance Thought and Letters II*, 265–80. Rome: Edizioni di Storia e Letteratura, 1985.

Kunzle, Paul. "Enea Silvio Piccolominis Fortsetzung zum Liber Augustalis von Benvenuto Rambaldi aus Imola und ein ähnlicher zeitgenössicher Aufholversuch." *La Bibliofilia* 60 (1958): 166–79.

Lambert, Malcolm. *Medieval Heresy: Popular Movements from Bogomil to Hus.* London: E. Arnold, 1977.

Lane, Frederic C. *Venice, a Maritime Republic.* Baltimore: Johns Hopkins University Press, 1973.

Law, John. "Giovanni Vitelleschi: prelate guerriero." *Renaissance Studies* 12 (1998): 40–66.

Leeper, A. W. A. *A History of Medieval Austria.* Oxford: Oxford University Press, 1941.

Leuschner, Joachim. *Germany in the Late Middle Ages.* Translated by Sabine MacCormack. Amsterdam: North-Holland Publishing Company, 1980.

Lexikon des Mittelalters. Munich: Artemis Verlag, 1977–.

Lock, Peter. *The Franks in the Aegean 1204–1500.* London: Longman, 1995.

Lukowski, Jerzy, and Hubert Zawadski. *A Concise History of Poland.* Cambridge: Cambridge University Press, 2001.

Maffei, Domenico, ed. *Enea Silvio Piccolomini Papa Pio II.* Siena: Varese, 1968.

Mallett, Michael E. *The Borgias: The Rise and Fall of a Renaissance Dynasty.* New York: Barnes and Noble, 1969.

———. *Mercenaries and Their Masters: Warfare in Renaissance Italy.* Totowa, N.J.: Rowman and Littlefield, 1974.

Mantello, F. A. C., and A. G. Rigg, eds. *Medieval Latin: An Introduction and Bibliographical Guide*. Washington: The Catholic University of America Press, 1996.
Martines, Lauro. *Power and Imagination: City-States in Renaissance Italy*. 1979. Reprint. Baltimore: Johns Hopkins University Press, 1988.
Mattingly, Garrett. *Renaissance Diplomacy*. 1955. Reprint. New York: Dover Publications, 1988.
McGinn, Bernard. *Visions of the End: Apocalyptic Traditions of the Middle Ages*. New York: Columbia University Press, 1979.
McManamon, John M. *Pierpaolo Vergerio the Elder: The Humanist as Orator*. Tempe, Ariz.: Medieval and Renaissance Texts and Studies, 1996.
Medieval Germany, an Encyclopedia. Edited by John M. Jeep. New York: Garland Press, 2001.
Merriam-Webster Geographical Dictionary. Third edition. Springfield, Mass: Merriam-Webster, 1997.
Meserve, Margaret. "From Samarkand to Scythia: Reinventions of Asia in Renaissance Geography and Political Thought." In *Pius II, 'El Più Expeditivo Pontifice': Selected Studies on Aeneas Silvius Piccolomini*, edited by Zweder von Martels and Arjo Vanderjagt, 13–40. Leiden: Brill, 2003.
———. *Empires of Islam in Renaissance Historical Thought*. Cambridge, Mass.: Harvard University Press, 2008.
Milanesi, Marcia. "La rinàscita della geografia dell'Europa. 1350–1480." In *Europa e Mediterraneo tra medioevo e prima età moderna: l'osservatorio italiano*, edited by Sergio Gensini, 35–59. San Miniato: Pacini Editore, 1992.
Milham, Mary Ella. "Pomponius Mela." In *Catologus Translationum*, edited by Paul Oskar Kristeller. Vol. 5. Washington: The Catholic University of America Press, 1984.
Mitchell, R. J. *The Laurels and the Tiara: Pope Pius II 1458–64*. London: Harvill Press, 1962.
Mitterauer, Michael. *Why Europe? The Medieval Origins of Its Special Path*. Translated by Gerard Chappel. Chicago: University of Chicago Press, 2010. Originally published in German in 2003.
Monfasani, John. *Byzantine Scholars in Renaissance Italy: Cardinal Bessarion and Other Emigrés*. Aldershot: Variorum, 1995.
Montecalvo, Rolando. "The New *Landesgeschichte*: Aeneas Silvius on Austria and Bohemia." In *Pius II, 'El Più Expeditivo Pontifice': Selected Studies on Aeneas Silvius Piccolomini*, edited by Zweder von Martels and Arjo Vanderjagt, 55–86. Leiden: Brill, 2003.
Najemy, John M. *A History of Florence, 1200–1575*. Malden, Mass.: Blackwell Publishing, 2006.
Neillands, Robin. *The Hundred Years War*. London: Routledge, 1990.
Neue deutsche Biographie. Berlin: Dunker and Humblot, 1956–.

Bibliography 329

Nevola, Fabrizio, ed. *Pio II Piccolomini: il Papa del Rinascimento a Siena*. Siena: Protagon Editore, 2009.

The New Cambridge Medieval History. Vol. 6. Edited by Michael Jones. Cambridge: Cambridge University Press, 2000.

The New Cambridge Medieval History. Vol. 7. Edited by Christopher Allmand. Cambridge: Cambridge University Press, 1998.

New Catholic Encyclopedia. Detroit: Thomson Gale, 2003.

Nicholas, David. *The Northern Lands: Germanic Europe, c. 1270–1500*. Malden, Mass.: Wiley Blackwell, 2009.

Nicol, Donald. *The Immortal Emperor: The Life and Legend of Constantine Palaiologos, Last Emperor of the Romans*. Cambridge: Cambridge University Press, 1992.

———. *The Last Centuries of Byzantium, 1261–1453*. Cambridge: Cambridge University Press, 1993.

Norwich, John Julius. *A History of Venice*. New York: Vintage Books, 1989.

Nouvelle Biographie Générale. Paris: Firmin Didot Frères, 1853–66.

O'Brien, Emily. "The Anatomy of an Apology: The War against Conciliarism and the Politicization of Papal Authority in the *Commentarii* of Pope Pius II (1458–64)." Ph.D. diss., Brown University, 2005.

———. "Arms and Letters: Julius Caesar, the *Commentaries* of Pope Pius II, and the Politicization of Papal Imagery." *Renaissance Quarterly* 62, no. 4 (Winter 2009): 1080–89.

Oliva, Anna Maria. "Orazio Romano." *Roma nel Rinascimento* (1994): 23–29.

Ostrogorsky, George. *History of the Byzantine State*. Translated by Joan Hussey. New Brunswick, NJ: Rutgers University Press. Revised edition, 1969.

Oxford Classical Dictionary. Edited by Simon Hornblower and Anthony Spawforth. 4th ed. Oxford: Oxford University Press, 2012.

Oxford Latin Dictionary. Edited by P. G. W. Glare. Oxford: Clarendon Press, 1982.

Pagden, Anthony. "Europe: Conceptualizing a Continent." In *The Idea of Europe from Antiquity to the European Union*, edited by Anthony Pagden, 33–42. Cambridge: Cambridge University Press, 2002.

———, ed. *The Idea of Europe from Antiquity to the European Union*. Cambridge: Cambridge University Press, 2002.

Pánek, Jaroslav, Tůma Oldřich, et al. *A History of the Czech Lands*. Prague: Karolinum Press, 2009.

Paparelli, Giacchino. *Enea Silvio Piccolomini: L'Umanesimo sul Soglio di Pietro*. Ravenna: Longo, 1978.

Pastor, Ludwig. *The History of the Popes from the Close of the Middle Ages*. Vols. 1 and 2. London: Kegan Paul, Trench, Trübner & Co., 1899.

Paviot, Jacques. "Burgundy and the Crusade." In *Crusading in the Fifteenth Century*, edited by Norman Housley, 70–80. New York: Palgrave Macmillan, 2004.

Pellegrino, Nicoletta. "From the Roman Empire to Christian Imperialism: The Work of Flavio Biondo." In *Chronicling History: Chroniclers and Historians in Medieval and Renaissance Italy*, edited by Sharon Dale, Alison Williams Lewin, and Duane Osheim, 273–98. University Park: Pennsylvania State Press, 2007.

Peterson, David, and Daniel Bornstein, eds. *Florence and Beyond: Culture, Society and Politics in Renaissance Italy*. Toronto: Centre for Reformation and Renaissance Studies, 2008.

Philippides, Marios. "The Fall of Constantinople 1453: Bishop Leonardo Giustiniani and His Italian Followers." *Viator* 29 (1998): 189–225.

Phillips, Mark. "Machiavelli, Guicciardini, and the Tradition of Vernacular Historiography in Florence." *American Historical Review* 84 (1979): 86–105.

Plakans, Andrejs. *Concise History of the Baltic States*. Cambridge: Cambridge University Press, 2011.

Pollard, A. J. *John Talbot and the War in France: 1427–1453*. London: Royal Historical Society, 1983.

Pontieri, Ernesto. *Alfonso il Magnanimo, re di Napoli*. Naples: Edizione Scientifiche Italiane, 1975.

Rabil, Albert, Jr., ed. *Renaissance Humanism: Foundations, Forms and Legacy*. 3 vols. Philadelphia: University of Pennsylvania Press, 1988.

Ranković, Slavica, ed. *Modes of Authorship in the Middle Ages*. Toronto: Pontifical Institute of Medieval Studies, 2012.

Rietbergen, Peter. *Europe: A Cultural History*. London: Routledge, 1998.

Riis, Thomas. "The States of Scandinavia, c. 1390–c. 1536." In *The New Cambridge Medieval History*, vol. 7, edited by Christopher Allmand, 671–706. Cambridge: Cambridge University Press, 1998.

Riley-Smith, Jonathan. *The Crusades: A Short History*, 2nd ed. New Haven, Conn.: Yale Nota Bene Press, 2005.

Robin, Diana. *Filelfo in Milan*. Princeton, N.J.: Princeton University Press, 1991.

Rogers, Francis. *The Quest for Eastern Christians: Travels and Rumor in the Age of Discovery*. Minneapolis: University of Minnesota Press, 1962.

Romano, Dennis. *The Likeness of Venice: A Life of Doge Francesco Foscari 1373–1457*. New Haven, Conn.: Yale University Press, 2007.

Roper, Lyndal. "Gorgon of Augsburg." In *Women, Identities and Communities in Early Modern Europe*, edited by Susan Broomhall and Stephanie Turbin, 113–36. Burlington, Vt.: Ashgate, 2008.

Rörig, Fritz. *The Medieval Town*. Berkeley: University of California Press, 1967.

Rowell, Stephen C. "Bears and Traitors, or: Political Tensions in the Grand Duchy ca. 1440–1481." *Lithuanian Historical Studies* 2 (1997): 28–55.

Runciman, Steven. *The Eastern Schism*. Oxford: Clarendon Press, 1955.

———. *The Fall of Constantinople 1453*. Cambridge: Cambridge University Press, 1965.

———. *The Great Church in Captivity: A Study of the Patriarchate of Constantinople*

Bibliography 331

from the Eve of the Turkish Conquest to the Greek War of Independence. London: Cambridge University Press, 1968.

Ryder, Alan. *The Kingdom of Naples under Alfonso the Magnanimous.* Oxford: Clarendon Press, 1976.

———. *Alfonso the Magnanimous, King of Aragon, Naples and Sicily, 1396–1458.* Oxford: Clarendon Press, 1990.

Sablonier, Roger. "The Swiss Confederation." In *The New Cambridge Medieval History*, vol. 7, edited by Christopher Allmand, 645–70. Cambridge: Cambridge University Press, 1998.

Salway, Benet. "The Roman Empire from Augustus to Diocletian." In *Roman Europe*, edited by Edward Bispham, 69–108. Oxford: Oxford University Press, 2008.

Schmieder, Felicitas. "Der mongolische Augenblick in der Weltgeschichte oder: Als Europa aus der Wiege wuchs." *Produktive Kulturkonflikte*, edited by Felicitas Schmieder. Das Mittelalter 10, no. 2. Berlin: Akademie Verlag, 2005: 63–73.

———, ed. *Produktive Kulturkonflikte.* Das Mittelalter 10, no. 2. Berlin: Akademie Verlag, 2005.

Schwoebel, Robert. *The Shadow of the Crescent: The Renaissance Image of the Turk (1453–1517).* New York: St. Martin's Press, 1967.

———. *Renaissance Men and Ideas.* New York: St. Martin's Press, 1971.

Scott, Tom. "Germany and the Empire." In *The New Cambridge Medieval History*, vol. 7, edited by Christopher Allmand, 337–66. Cambridge: Cambridge University Press, 1998.

Seigel, Jerrold. *Rhetoric and Philosophy in Renaissance Humanism.* Princeton, N.J.: Princeton University Press, 1968.

Senatore, Francesco. "Pontano e la Guerra di Napoli." In *Condottieri e uomini d'arme nell'Italia del Rinascimento.* Edited by Mario Del Treppo. Naples: Liguori, 2002.

Seton-Watson, R. W. *A History of the Czechs and Slovaks.* New York: Hutchinson and Co., 1943.

Setton, Kenneth. *The Papacy and the Levant (1205–1571).* Vol. 2. Philadelphia: American Philosophical Society, 1978.

Simon, Kate. *Renaissance Tapestry: The Gonzaga of Mantua.* New York: Harper and Row, 1988.

Simonetta, Marcello. "Pius II and Francesco Sforza. The History of Two Allies." In *Pius II, 'El Più Expeditivo Pontefice': Selected Studies on Aeneas Silvius Piccolomini*, edited by Zweder von Martels and Arjo Vanderjagt, 147–70. Leiden: Brill, 2003.

———. *Rinascimento segreto: il mondo del segretario da Petrarca a Machiavelli.* Milan: F. Angeli, 2004.

Smith, L. F. "Pope Pius II's Use of Turkish Atrocities." *Southwestern Social Science Quarterly* 46 (1966): 408–15.

Smith, Sir William. *A Classical Dictionary of Greek and Roman Biography, Mythology and Geography*. Revised and in part rewritten by G. E. Marindin. London: John Murray. 1st ed., 1848; 4th ed. (revised), 1894; 23rd impression, 1925.

Sodi, Manlio, and Arianna Antoniutti, eds. *Enea Silvio Piccolomini, Pius Secundus Poeta Laureatus Pontifex Maximus*. Rome: Libreria Editrice Vaticana, 2007.

Sønnesyn, Sigbjørn Olsen. "Obedient Creativity and Idiosyncratic Copying: Tradition and Individuality in the Works of William of Malmesbury and John of Salisbury." In *Modes of Authorship in the Middle Ages*, edited by Slavica Ranković, 113–32. Toronto: Pontifical Institute of Medieval Studies, 2012.

Špiesz, Anton, and Dušan Čaplovic. *Illustrated Slovak History*, edited by Ladislaus J. Bolchazy, et al. Wauconda, Ill.: Bolchazy-Carducci, 2006.

Stieber, Joachim W. *Pope Eugenius IV: The Council of Basel and the Secular and Ecclesiastical Authorities in the Empire*. Leiden: Brill, 1978.

Stinger, Charles L. *The Renaissance in Rome*. Bloomington: Indiana University Press, 1985.

Storia di Milano. Milan: Fondazione Treccani degli Alfieri per la storia di Milano, 1953–66. Vols. 6–7.

Sugar, Peter F., and Péter Hanák, eds. *A History of Hungary*. Bloomington: Indiana University Press, 1990.

Tanner, Marcus. *The Raven King: Matthew Corvinus and the Fate of His Lost Library*. New Haven, Conn.: Yale University Press, 2008.

Tarugi, Luisa Rotondi Secchi, ed. *Pio II e la cultura del suo tempo*. Milan: Guerini e Associati, 1991.

Trease, Geoffrey. *The Condottieri: Soldiers of Fortune*. New York: Holt, Rinehart and Winston, 1971.

Turnbull, Stephen. *Crusader Castles of the Teutonic Knights, AD 1230–1466*. Oxford: Osprey, 2003.

Ullman, B. L. *The Public Library of Renaissance Florence: Niccolò Niccoli, Cosimo de' Medici, and the Library of San Marco*. Padua: Editrice Antenore, 1972.

Urban, Willam L. "Renaissance Humanism in Prussia." *Journal of Baltic History* 22 (1991): 29–73.

———. *Tannenberg and After: Lithuania, Poland, and the Teutonic Order in Search of Immortality*. Chicago: Lithuanian Research and Studies Center, 1999.

———. *Teutonic Knights: A Military History*. London: Greenhill, 2003.

Vékony, Gábor. *Dacians-Romans-Romanians*. Budapest: Matthias Corvinus Publishing, 2000.

Voigt, Georg. *Enea Silvio de' Piccolomini als Papst Pius II und sein Zeitalter*. 3 vols. Berlin: De Gruyter, 1856–63.

Vollman, Benedikt Konrad. "Aeneas Silvius Piccolomini as a Historiographer: Asia." In *Pius II, 'El Più Expeditivo Pontifice': Selected Studies on Aeneas Silvius Piccolomini*, edited by Zweder von Martels and Arjo Vanderjagt, 41–54. Leiden: Brill, 2003.

———. "*Enkyklios Paideia* in the Work of Aeneas Silvius Piccolomini." In *Pius II, 'El Più Expeditivo Pontifice': Selected Studies on Aeneas Silvius Piccolomini*, edited by Zweder von Martels and Arjo Vanderjagt, 1–12. Leiden: Brill, 2003.

von Martels, Zweder, and Vanderjagt Arjo, eds. *Pius II, 'El Più Expeditivo Pontifice', Selected Studies on Aeneas Silvius Piccolomini*. Leiden: Brill, 2003.

Wagner, John A. *Encyclopedia of the Hundred Years War*. Westport, Conn.: Greenwood Press, 2006.

Wakounig, Marija. "Una duplice dipendenza. I conti di Gorizia, Venezia e il Sacro Romano Impero (1350–1500)." In *Da Ottone III a Massimiliano I: Gorizia e i conti di Gorizia ne medioevo*, edited by Silvano Cavazza, 339–64. Gorizia: Edizioni della Laguna, 2004.

Walsh, Katherine. "Deutschsprachige Korrispondenz der Kaiserin Leonora." In *Kaiser Friedrich III (1440–1493) in seiner Zeit*, edited by Paul-Joachim Heinig, 339–445. Cologne: Böhlau Verlag, 1993.

Waugh, W. T. *A History of Europe From 1378–1494*. New York: Putnam and Sons, 1932.

Widmer, Berthe. *Enea Silvio Piccolomini, Papst Pius II*. Basel: Benno Schwabe and Co., 1960.

Wolf, Anne Marie. "Precedents and Paradigms: Juan de Segovia on the Bible, the Church and the Ottoman Threat." In *Scripture and Pluralism: Reading the Bible in the Religiously Plural Worlds of the Middle Ages*, edited by Thomas J. Heffernan and Thomas E. Burman, 143–60. Leiden: Brill, 2005.

Woolf, D. R., ed. *A Global Encyclopedia of Historical Writing*. 2 vols. New York: Garland Publishing, Inc., 1998.

Wormald, Jenny. "Scotland: 1406–1513." In *The New Cambridge Medieval History*, vol. 7, edited by Christopher Allmand, 514–31. Cambridge: Cambridge University Press, 1998.

Ziolkowski, Jan. "National and Other Contrasts in the Athenian Funeral Orations." In *The Birth of the European Identity: The Europe-Asia Contrast in Greek Thought, 490–322 B.C.*, edited by H. A. Khan, 1–35. Vol. 2. Nottingham: Nottingham Classical Literature Studies, 1993.

Zöllner, Erich. *Geschichte Österreichs: von den Anfängen bis zur Gegenwart*. Munich: R. Oldenbourg, 1970.

Zophy, Jonathan W., ed. *The Holy Roman Empire: A Dictionary Handbook*. Westport, Conn.: Greenwood Press, 1980.

WEB SOURCES

Cardinals of the Holy Roman Church, created by Salvador Miranda and hosted at Florida International University: http://www2.fiu.edu/~mirandas/cardinals.htm.

Condottieri di Ventura, created by Roberto Damiani: http://www.condottieridiventura.it/.

INDEX

Aachen, 119, 185
Abd al-Aziz II, ruler of Tunisia, 306
Abruzzi, Abruzzesi, 245n678, 256n718, 293
Acarnania, Acarnanians, 110–11, 113
Acciaiuoli, Franco, 107n207
Acciapacci, Niccolò, 260
Accumoli, 300
Acerra, 292, 294
Achaea, Achaeans, 105n198, 106, 108–10, 112, 180
Achelous River, 110, 112
Acquaviva, 245, 247
Acre, 149
Acroceraunian Mountains, 111, 113
Acte, 107
Actium, 112
Adam of Bremen, 159n361
Adamites, 170
Adda River, 221, 246
Adorno, Barnabò, doge of Genoa, 218
Adorno, Raffaele, doge of Genoa, 217–18, 300
Adorno family, 303n900
Adrianople. *See* Edirne
Adriatic Sea, 51, 103, 110, 113, 115, 117–18, 180
Aeacidae, 112
Aegean Sea, 69, 103, 108, 110
Aemilius Paulus, 112
Aeneas, 180
Aethicus, 72–73
Aetolia, 77–78, 110–11

Afonso V, king of Portugal, 215–16, 271n772
Africa, 4, 36, 306
Agamemnon, 70
Aganippe, 106
Agincourt, 208n535
Agios, 69
Agrippina, 183
Ahmed Celebi, 92
Aiton, 201n510
Aksamit, Peter, 63–64
Alans, 149, 181
Alaric, 183
Albania, Albanians, 30, 104–5, 109, 113–15, 271, 306
Albans, 180
Albe, 291
Albergati, Niccolò, cardinal, 7
Albert II, emperor, 49n5, 54–57, 60, 66n64, 127, 128n278, 134, 135, 140, 171, 193, 209n537
Albert III "Achilles," duke of Anspach, elector of Brandenburg, 129–30, 189–91
Albert V, duke of Austria. See Albert II, emperor
Albert VI, duke of Austria, 40n90, 119, 131–34, 195
Albert III, duke of Bavaria, 140, 194, 200
Albert III, elector of Saxony, 163
Albert of Bamberg, 187–88
Albert of Mainz. *See* Boniface

Index

Albert of Mecklenburg, king of Sweden, 167–68
Alberti, Leon Battista, 235n642, 265
Albia, 117
Albion, 209
Albizzi, Rinaldo degli, 242n663
Albornoz, Cardinal Gil, 274n790
Alciati, Opicino, 217
Aleman, Louis d', archbishop of Arles, 201
Alemannians, 183
Alençon, 202
Alessandria, Alessandrians, 223–24, 226, 229
Alexander VI, pope. *See* Borgia, Cardinal Rodrigo
Alexander the Great, 12n20, 66–67, 73n92, 104
Alexander "the bastard" of Bourbon, 202–3
Alexander of Roes, 11n18
Alfedena, 281
Alfonso, king of Aragon and Naples, 20, 28, 32, 34, 40n90, 49n1, 111n222, 113n232, 114, 199, 213n551, 215, 217n562, 219–23, 229, 230n617, 242–47, 251–52, 254n710, 256–58, 260, 268–70, 274–77, 280–83, 286–307
Alpheida, 184
Alps, mountain range, 51, 120, 191, 221, 224
Alsace, 197–98
Altenburg castle, 163
Álvaro de Luna, 213–14
Amantians, 52
Amatrice, 300
Amaxobians, 149
Ambracian Gulf, 111–12
Ambrose of Milan, St., 104
Amedeo VIII, duke of Savoy. *See* Felix V, pope
Amelia, 274
Americas, 4
Anatolia, 14, 74n96, 77n112
Ancona, 10, 92n161, 271n774, 275n792
Anello, 296
Anghiari, 242

Anghiari, Baldaccio d', 248n690
Angri, 292
Anjou, 202, 289n841
Ankara, 76n107
Anna (Habsburg), wife of Wilhelm III of Saxony, 127n276, 137n303
Anna of Brunswick, 194n485
Anobian Mountains, 176
Ansegisil, 184
Antenor, 117, 180–81
Antony, Mark, 112
Apennines, 143, 247
Apollo, 69, 113
Apollonia, 104, 113
Appiano, Emanuele d' 257–58
Appiano, Jacopo II d', 255
Appiano, Jacopo III d', 258
Apulia, 258, 294–95, 299, 301
Aquila, 287–88
Aquileia, 118. *See also* Trevisan, Ludovico
Aquino, Francesco d', 295
Aquitania, 182–83
Aragon, Aragonese, 212–13, 215, 217n562, 219, 247n687, 256n718, 280, 281n811, 300n887, 305, 307
Aragonnais, François l', 203
Arbogast, 181n441
Arcadia, 109
Arethusa, 106
Arezzo, 242, 246, 249, 265
Argolid, 108
Ariano, 295, 305
Aristotle, 34, 236, 249n694, 264n749
Arles, 197–201
Armenia, 105, 262
Arnulph, 122
Arpaia, 292
Arrian, 66
Arta, 111n222, 113
Artemidorus, 108
Arthur III, duke of Brittany, 208
Ascoli Piceno, 283–84
Asia, Asians, 4, 11–12, 13n21, 29, 31, 70, 72, 74, 76–77, 83–84, 88–89, 92, 105. *See also* Piccolomini: Writings
Assisi, 274

Asti, 223
Athens, 106–7, 109
Attendolo, Micheletto (da Cotignola), 220
Attica, 75, 107–111
Aufida, 281n814
Augustine, St., 268
Augustus, emperor, 52, 73, 104, 112–13, 176, 296
Aurelian, emperor, 52
Aurispa, Giovanni, 6, 236
Ausonian Sea, 112–13
Austria, Austrians, 7, 17, 51, 54, 59–61, 79, 116, 118–19, 120, 124, 126–36, 139, 190–91, 194, 198
Avars, 73
Aversa, 290–91, 294
Avignon, 13, 274n790
Azov Sea, 166, 180

Bactrians, 105
Baden, 129, 195–96
Bad Wilsnack, 165n381
Bagno, 247n689
Baldassino, Galeotto, 40n90, 256–57
Balkan Mountains, 69n76, 82n133
Balkans, 14, 29, 75n101, 76n105
Baltic Sea, 52, 136, 148–49, 156, 161n366, 167, 273
Balzo, 290n850
Bamberg, 187–89
Barbara of Cilli, 53–54
Barbaro, Francesco, 34, 232
Barbo, Pietro. See Paul II, pope
Bari, 256n718, 289n845, 294n867, 299n883
Basel, 6–7, 197–200, 211n546
Basel, Council of, 6–7, 62n52, 143–44, 174, 179, 195n489, 201, 215n556, 241n660, 262–63, 269n762, 274, 300
Bato, 52
Bavaria, Bavarians, 129, 132, 140, 156, 168, 182, 186, 189, 191–94, 200
Bayezid I, Ottoman sultan, 75–77, 114
Bayezid II, Ottoman ruler, 81n127
Bayezid Osman, 92n161
Beaufort, Edmund, earl of Somerset, 204, 210–11

Beaufort, Joan, 211n547
Beccadelli, Antonio, 303n901
Belgium, 240
Belgrade, 15, 30, 60–62, 79–80, 101–3, 272
Belisarius, 298
Benedict XIII, pope, 240
Benevento, 294n867, 295
Bengtsson, Jöns, 169
Bentivoglio, Annibale, 237–38
Bentivoglio, Ercole, 238
Bentivoglio, Sante, 238
Bentivoglio family, 237
Benzi, Ugo (da Siena), 34, 235–36
Berardi, Cardinal Giovanni, 295
Berengar, 187
Bergamo, 230, 232
Berlin, 158
Bernard, duke of Brunswick, 164
Bernardino of Siena, St., 8, 264, 287–88
Bernauer, Agnes, 194n484
Berta, 185
Bertrada, 185n458
Bessarion, cardinal, 238, 242, 264n749
Beszterce, 65, 129
Biccari, 295
Biondo, Flavio, 19–20, 42, 265–66
Bisina, 182
Bisinus, 182
Bithynia, 74, 92
Blanca of Navarre, 213n551
Boeotia, 75, 106–7, 109–11
Boffa, Marino, 292
Bohemia, Bohemians, 7, 17, 32, 53–57, 58, 61–63, 84, 90, 102, 125–31, 135–37, 140, 143, 153n344, 156, 161–63, 170–71, 186, 190–91
Boians, 192
Boioaria, 192
Boleslaw, duke of Opole, 137
Bologna, 6, 179, 220, 237–40, 262–63, 266–67, 271
Bolomier, Guillaume, 200
Bonde, Karl Knutsson. See Karl, king of Sweden
Boniface, St., 172n409
Bordeaux, 205–7

Borgia, Rodrigo, cardinal, 8, 270n771, 271, 284
Borja, Pedro de, 271
Bosnia, the Bosnians, 30, 43, 51, 75n104, 103n190, 115–16, 143
Boso, 186
Bosphorus, 84–85, 93, 166
Bossi, Giacomino, 34, 226–27
Bossi, Teodoro, 227
Bourbon, 202
Boyl, Ramón, 282
Brabant, 209
Bracceschi, 225, 228, 274n791
Bracciolini, Poggio, 249
Brandenburg, Brandenburgers, 54, 121n257, 129–30, 140, 156, 158, 165, 188–90, 195
Branković, Cantacuzina, 81
Branković, George, despot of Serbia, 30, 78–81, 83n135, 88n149, 90
Branković, Gregory, 78n118, 81
Branković, Lazarus, 81
Branković, Mara, 78n117, 81
Branković, Stephen, 78n118
Bremen, 158–59
Brescia, 225, 230, 232
Breslau, 136–37
Brethren, mercenary companies, 63
Brielle, 175
Britain, 209, 212
British Sea, 148
Brittany, 203–5, 207–8
Brno, 136
Brothers of St. Mary. *See* Teutonic Knights
Bructerians, 176
Bruni, Leonardo, 22n50, 25–26, 66n62, 249, 298n878
Brunoro, Pietro, 276, 280
Brunswick, 158, 160–64, 178, 194
Buda, 55–56, 58, 60–61, 65–66, 81
Bulgaria, Bulgarians, 69, 84n140, 143
Bura, 110
Burgundians, 182–83
Bursa, 74n98, 92
Bussatorians, 176

Byron, George Gordon, Lord, 231n624
Byzantium, Byzantines, 69–70, 71n83, 75n101, 77n114, 78n115, 83n136, 84, 93n164, 97n174, 98, 99n179, 100, 233n632, 298n878. *See also* Greece, Greeks

Cabanyells, Garcia de, 281n811
Caen, 210n543
Caesarea, 201
Caiazzo, 295
Caimi, Francesco, 226
Caimi, Giovanni, 226
Caivana, Giacomo da, 282–83
Caivano, 293
Calabria, 246n682, 301n894
Calandrini, Filippo, 264
Caldora, Antonio, 256, 294–96, 299
Caldora, Jacopo, 287n835, 289–91, 293–94
Caldora, Raimondo, 295
Caligula (Gaius), emperor, 108
Calixtus III, pope, 9, 15, 33, 40, 92, 101, 110, 114, 150, 175, 215n555, 239n654, 253, 258, 265n750, 266n752, 269–73
Calixtus Ottomanus. *See* Bayezid Osman
Camaldoli, 143n321
Cambrai, 182
Camerino, 259
Camerino, Fra Simonetto da, 230n616, 268
Cammin, 121n257, 157
Campania, 290
Campidoglio, 268
Campiglia, 244–45
Candians, 136
Canetoli, Battista, 237
Canetoli family, 237, 238n652
Cantacuzenus, Manuel, 109n216
Cantacuzina. *See* Branković
Cape Sounion, 110
Capistrano, Giovanni da, 79–80, 101–3, 135
Capodistria, 65, 117
Cappadocia, 73–74, 105
Capponi family, 248n690

Capranica, Domenico, cardinal, 6, 21n44, 144n324, 269
Capri, 296
Capua, 260, 289–91
Caravaggio, 224–25
Carda, Bernardo della, 284–85
Caria, 74
Carinthia, 40n88, 120–24, 133n290
Carl of Baden, 196
Carlinga, 184
Carlos of Viana, 215n557
Carmagnola, Francesco (Bussone), 232
Carmelites, 129, 292
Carnians, 115, 119, 124, 143
Carniola, 119–20
Carpathians, 163n375
Carpenone, 299
Carrara, Marsilio da, 232–33
Carrara, Ubertino da, 233n631
Carsians, 119
Carthusians, 144
Carvajal, Juan, cardinal of St. Angelo, 62, 81, 101, 115, 261n731
Casalmaggiore, 220, 228n605, 282
Casciano, 40n89, 250
Caserta, 292
Casimir IV, king of Poland, 57n29, 140–42, 151, 154–55
Cassope, 113
Castellammare, 290
Castellana, 266n754
Castellazzo, 281n815
Castelleone, 281n815
Castellina, 247
Castello Sforzesco, 231n619
Castelnuovo, 243, 298n879, 304
Castel San Pietro, Simonetto da, 244–46
Castel Sant'Angelo, 259, 267
Castelvecchio, 291–92
Castiglione della Pescaia, 244–45, 253
Castile, 212–16
Castillon, 206–7
Castriot, George "Skanderbeg," 114, 271
Castriot, Hamza, 114n237
Castriot, John, 114n235
Catalonia, 307

Catanzaro, 301
Catherine of Cilli, 125n271
Catulus, 166n384
Caucasus, 73n93, 105
Caudina Valley, 292, 294
Celano, 291
Centelles, Antonio, 301
Cerda, Cardinal Antonio de la (Lérida), 16, 49, 245, 264
Cerknica, Lake, 118n251
Cervantes, Juan, bishop of Ostia, 215
Cesarini, Giuliano, cardinal, 30, 42, 58–59, 82–84, 88, 109, 143–44
Chalcedon, 70
Chalcondyles, Demetrius, 264n749
Chaonians, 112
Charlemagne, emperor, 121, 157, 159, 176–77, 184–85
Charles the Fat, emperor, 122n261
Charles IV, emperor, 49, 52, 61, 251n700
Charles V, emperor, 28
Charles VI, king of France, 193n481
Charles VII, king of France, 63n54, 199–204, 209, 215n557, 219, 230n612, 303n900
Charles of Anjou, 202
Charles Martel, 184
Charles I, duke of Bourbon, 202
Charles II, duke of Lorraine, 289n842
Charles, duke of Orléans, 208, 222–23
Charles, margave of Baden, 129
Charlotte of Savoy, 209n538
Chelmno, 150
Chersonese, 75
Chiavelli family, 287n833
Chichester, 210n544
Chieti, 295
Childebert III, king of Francia, 184n452
Childeric, Merovingian ruler, 182
Childeric III, king of Francia, 184
Chios, 97, 302
Chojnice, 155
Christendom, concepts of, 4, 11, 13, 32
Christoph, son of Frederick III, 130n285
Christopher, king of Denmark, Sweden, Norway, 168

Chrysoloras, Manuel, 66n63
Chrysostom, John, St., 264n749
Ciccarella, 296n876
Cicero, 38–39, 188n468, 249
Cilicia, 74
Cilli, 61, 124, 125
Cimbrians, 166–67, 192
Cimmerians, 166
Cingoli, 276, 281
Cisalpine Gaul, 228n607
Cithaeron, 106
Claudius, emperor, 183
Cleopatra, 112
Clermont, 11
Cleves, 173
Clodius, 181–82
Clodoveus, 182
Clothild, 183
Clovis, king of the Franks, 31, 182–83
Coburg, 162
Coëtivy, Alain de, cardinal, 270
Coeur, Jacques, 209n538
Colchis, 113
Colle, 293n864
Colleoni, Bartolomeo, 224n592
Cologne, 173–74, 178–79, 182–83, 261
Colonna, Caterina, 284n822
Colonna, Paola, 255n714,
Colonna, Prospero, cardinal, 272
Colonna family, 272, 284
Como, 223, 227, 229
Condulmer, Cardinal Francesco, 84n138, 88
Condulmer, Gabriele. *See* Eugenius IV, pope
Conflans, 223
Conrad "the Old," 187
Conrad, duke of Masovia, 150
Constance, Lake, 192
Constance, Council of, 6, 54, 170
Constantine the Great, emperor, 70
Constantine XI Paleologus, emperor, 71, 101, 109
Constantinople, 9, 14, 17, 29, 40n89, 69–72, 75–76, 79, 92–100, 104, 109, 114, 147n328, 230n614, 236n646, 241, 268

Corcyreans, 104
Corinth, 107–8, 110
Correggio, Giberto da, 252–53
Correr, Angelo. *See* Gregory XII, pope
Correr, Antonio, 262
Corsignano, 5
Cortona, 246
Councils. *See* Basel; Constance; Florence
Crema, 223, 228n605
Cremona, 96n169, 233
Crete, 72, 231n624, 232
Crisa, Gulf of, 106
Crivelli, Leodrisio, 231
Croatia, Croatians, 43, 66n66, 78n116, 115–17, 124, 128n277, 143
Crotone, 301
Crusades, 11n18, 150n337. *See also* Belgrade; Nicopolis; Varna
Cullenborch, Bishop Desiderius von, 174
Curtius, Quintus, 85n143
Czechs. *See* Bohemia, Bohemians

Dacia, Dacians, 51–52, 64–65, 67, 192
Dacia (Denmark), 166–67
Dagobert III, king of Francia, 184
Dalmatia, the Dalmatians, 51–52, 97, 115–17, 143
Damascus, 76
Dania, 166n383
Danube River, 51–52, 60, 62–64, 67–69, 77, 80, 83n135, 84, 102, 117–18, 120, 124, 131, 135–36, 166n383, 189, 191–94
Dardanians, 69
Darius, king of the Persians, 67, 76
David of Burgundy, bishop of Utrecht, 173n413, 175n421
Decembrio, Pier Candido, 222n581, 264
Delebrio, 220n578
Denmark, Danes, 33, 148, 156, 159, 161, 165–70
Despuig, Luis, 215n557
Dionysus, 105n196. *See also* Liber
Dirce, 106
Djerba, 306
Długosz, Jan, 87n147, 88n150, 137n302, 140n313, 141n318

Dniester River, 67
Dodona, 112
Dominique. *See* Pierre II, duke of Brittany
Don River, 52, 138n304
Donato, Andrea, 231–32
Donato, Ermolao, 232
Dordrecht, 175
Doria family, 218
Doukas, 97n173, 100n181
Drakul, Vlad, ruler of Valachia, 79n121, 88n149
Drava River, 52, 120, 124
Drusus Germanicus (Nero Claudius), 176
Dubrovnik, 43. *See also* Ragusa
Dyrrachium, 103–4, 113

Edirne, 89, 91n156, 114n235
Edward IV, king of England, 210n542
Egidius Romanus, 182
Egypt, 105, 112, 233, 261
Ekkehard of Aura, 24, 181n438, 182n442
Elba, 255
Elbe River, 158
Elbe Sandstone Mountains, 164n375
Eleonora, empress, 130, 214, 232n628, 264, 302, 304n902
Elizabeth, queen of Hungary, 54, 57–58, 59n38, 140n315
Elizabeth (Habsburg), sister of Ladislas Postumus, 141n316
Elizabeth of Cilli, 123n263
Elizabeth of Frankopan, 124n267
Elizabeth of Pilcza, 137n302
Emathia, 68
Emathio, 68
Emilia, 68, 285
Emmerberg, Frederick von, archbishop of Salzburg, 194n486
Ems River, 176
Enetians, 180
England, English, 7, 18, 28, 34, 42, 49n1, 54, 168, 170, 202–12, 271
Enns River, 191
Enrique IV, king of Castile-León, 214–15
Enrique of Aragon, 213–14, 220n575
Epidamnus, 104

Épinal, 203
Epirus, the Epirotes, 77–78, 103, 110–13
Erbach, Dietrich von, 194–95
Erfurt, 158
Eric of Brunswick, 194n485
Erik, king of Denmark, Norway, Sweden, 168–69
Ernst, duke of Bavaria, 194
Ernst of Saxony, 163
Este, Borso, marquis of, 235
Este, Leonello, marquis of, 235, 246, 302
Este, Niccolò, marquis of, 235–36
Este, Ugo d', 235
Estouteville, Cardinal Guillaume d', 273
Esztergom, 56, 58, 66
Ethiopia, 271
Etsch, 132, 196
Euboean Sea, 106
Eugenius III, pope, 261
Eugenius IV, pope, 6–7, 40n90, 52n10, 54, 58, 71, 82–84, 174, 199–200, 233n635, 235, 238–39, 241–42, 259–63, 265n751, 266n752, 269, 273–76, 280–82, 285n827, 290–91, 295, 299–300, 306
Europe, concepts of, 3–4, 10–16
Eusebius, 264n749
Everso of Anguillara, 246, 272
Eytzing, Ulrich, 128–32

Fabriano, 286–87
Facio, Bartolomeo, 20–22, 27, 42–43, 242n666, 243n670, 245n678, 256n718, n719, 277n801, 278nn802–3, 280n809, 281n811, 287n834, 292n857, 293n860, n861, 295n871, 299n881, 301n892, 303n901, 306n910
Faenza, 246
Fano, 277, 279, 285n827
Faramundus, 181
Fausto da Longiano, Sebastiano, 36
Feltre, Vittorino da, 226n599
Felix V, pope, 6–7, 138n305, 198–201, 261–63, 300
Ferdinand I, king of Aragon, 213n551, 305, 307
Ferdinand II, king of Aragon, 215n555

342 Index

Fermo, 144, 275n792, 280, 282–83
Ferrandez, Juan, 215
Ferrante, duke of Calabria, king of Naples, 244n672, 246–47, 252, 256n718, 300, 302, 304n903
Ferrara, 6, 235–36, 288. *See also* Florence, Council of
Ferrer, Vincent, 271
Fieschi, Gianantonio, 217–18
Fieschi, Giovanni Filippo, 302
Fieschi family, 302
Fiesole, 241, 248
Filelfo, Francesco, 6, 34, 224n591, 231
Flaccia, 67
Flaminia, 68
Flanders, 208–9
Floquet, captain of Evreux, 203–4
Florence, the Florentines, 6, 12, 25, 33, 54, 66n63, 71–72, 107, 220, 228–30, 231n620, 236n646, 237n647, 238, 241–57, 259n726, 260–61, 265, 267n755, 268n761, 276, 281n815, 282, 286, 299, 301n895, 302, 306
Florence, Council of, 34, 71–72, 235–36, 241–42, 262n739
Florentinus, St., 159
Fogliano, Rinaldo da, 283n820
Foiano, 246–47
Foligno, 259, 274
Fons Populi, 301
Forchheim, 189
Fortiguerri, Niccolò, 239
Foscari, Camilla, 232n625
Foscari, Francesco, doge of Venice, 40n90, 231–33, 262
Foscari, Jacopo, 231
Fougères, 203
France, French, 7, 10, 13, 33, 36, 54, 173, 183, 193, 197–210, 211n546, 215, 219, 223–24, 230, 257, 270, 273, 299, 303n900, 306
Francia, Franks, 73, 157, 180–86
Franciscans, 207, 288
François I, duke of Brittany, 204, 207–8
Franconia, the Franconians, 156, 162, 164, 179–80, 186–91

Frankopan family, 124nn267–68
Frederick I Barbarossa, emperor, 73, 159n363
Frederick II, emperor, 149–50
Frederick III, emperor, 7, 9, 14, 16–18, 28–29, 35, 40n90, 50–51, 58–60, 63n53, n56, 82, 119, 123, 125–29, 131–34, 140, 153–54, 159, 164, 168, 179n436, 193–96, 198–200, 209, 218n571, 222, 226n602, 232, 235, 261, 264, 302–4
Frederick, count of Cilli, 124
Frederick I, count palatine of the Rhine, 195
Frederick II, elector of Saxony, 161–63
Frederick IV, lord of Tyrol, 132n289
Frederick I, margrave of Brandenburg, 54, 140, 189
Frederick II, margrave of Brandenburg, 189–90, 195
Fregoso, Battista, 217
Fregoso, Giano, doge of Genoa, 218
Fregoso, Ludovico, doge of Genoa, 218
Fregoso, Niccolò, 218
Fregoso, Piero, doge of Genoa, 218–19, 302n898
Fregoso, Tommaso, doge of Genoa, 217
Freiburg, 134n294, 198
Frisia, 171–73, 175–76
Friuli, 120
Fulda, 171–72
Furlano, Taliano, 281–83
Fuxanus (de Foxa or Fossano), Antonio, 256

Gaeta, 220n575, 254n712, 269, 289, 303n901, 306
Galata. *See* Pera
Galatia, 74
Gallienus, emperor, 52
Gallipoli, 75
Gambacorta, Gherardo, 247
Garai, Katerina, 123
Garai, Ladislas, count palatine, 53
Gardelegen, 158
Gascony, 205
Gatti, Guglielmo, 258

Index 343

Gatti, Princivalle, lord of Viterbo, 258
Gaudina, 184
Gaul, 166, 176n426, 182–85, 228n607
Gavere, 208n536
Gaza, Theodore, 235n642
Gdańsk, 149
Geneva, 199–200
Genoa, Genoese, 30, 84, 96, 100, 217–20, 237, 269n763, 288–89, 293n862, 296, 298, 300–303, 306
Geofroy de Tory, 36
George of Trebizond, 264, 303n901
Georgia, 73n91
Gepids, 51, 63
Gerace, 111n222
Germany, Germans, 7, 12n20, 13–14, 17, 28, 29n69, 36, 49, 51–55, 64–66, 82, 101–2, 119, 124, 136–40, 147–52, 155–61, 165–67, 171–73, 175–79, 181–82, 184–87, 189–94, 196–98, 200, 261, 263, 270. *See also* Holy Roman Empire
Gesatans, 192
Getes, 52, 67
Ghent, 208
Gherardesca, 244
Ghibellines, 226n601, 274
Gidelli, Yça, 201n510
Giglio, 245
Gilles, 207
Giosia d'Acquaviva, 283–84, 295
Giovanni, count of Tagliacozzo, 243
Giovanni II, lord of Bologna, 238n650
Giugliano, 290
Giustiniani, Bishop Leonard of Chios, 94n166, 97n173, 99n180, 100n181
Giustiniani-Longo, Giovanni, 96–97
Głogów, 137
Golden Bull, 187n463
Golem, Moses (Musa) Komninos, 113–14
Golubac, 83n135
Gomphi, 105
Gonzaga, Carlo, 225–28, 234
Gonzaga, Gianfrancesco, marquis of Mantua, 226n599
Gonzaga, Ludovico, marquis of Mantua, 226n599, 234

Gorizia, 120–21
Goslar, 33, 164
Goths, 52, 149, 166, 170, 181, 183, 213, 298, 307
Gotland, 168–70
Gradara, 283
Graeca, 99
Graecus, 29n70, 106
Granada, 212, 214
Greece, Greeks, 11–12, 14, 17, 29–30, 34, 65–66, 69, 70, 71–72, 74–77, 84, 87–88, 93–99, 102, 104–10, 113, 143, 148, 156, 181, 185, 226, 231n620, n624, 235–36, 237n647, 238, 241–42, 249, 262, 264, 271, 307. *See also* Byzantium, Byzantines
Gregory III, patriarch of Constantinople, 71
Gregory XII, pope, 240, 262
Gregory of Tours, 183n449
Greifswald, 157
Grimoald, 184
Guarco, Isnardo, 217
Guarini, Guarino (da Verona), 6, 23n54, 66, 235n642, 236
Guelderland, 173
Guelphs, 226n601, 274
Guglielmo, lord of Monferrato, 226, 229–30
Guicciardini, Francesco, 22n50, 24n57
Günz, 59
Gurk, 126n272
Gythonians, 149n333

Haakon, king of Norway and Sweden, 167
Habsburg, Katherina, 196n492
Habsburgs, 54n21, 58n34, 92n161, 119n255, 140
Haemus, Mount, 69
Halberstadt, 158–60
Halil Pasha, 89–92, 101
Hannibal, 188
Hanseatic League, 161n366
Havelberg, 158, 165
Helen, 106
Helena, 110

Helene, 56
Helenus, 106
Helice, 110
Helicon, 106
Hellas, 12, 107
Hellenes, 11, 29, 106
Hellespont, 69, 75, 83
Helvetia, Helvetians, 192, 197
Henry II, emperor, 164n377, 187
Henry III, emperor, 164n377
Henry IV, king of England, 168n395, 204n522
Henry V, king of England, 204n522
Henry VI, king of England, 42, 203, 204n522, 207n533, 209, 210n543, 211n547
Henry the Fowler, king of Germany, 164n377, 186n461
Henry, count of Gorizia, 34, 40n90, 123–24
Henry, duke of Bavaria-Landshut, 193
Hercegovina, 116n243
Hercules, 105–6
Hercynian Forest, 163, 192–93
Herman, count of Cilli, 53, 124
Herodotus, 11, 264n749
Hesse, Hessians, 176, 179–80
Hildesheim, 158–59
Hinnenberger, Ulrich, bishop of Gurk, 126
Holland, 172–75
Holtemme River, 159
Holy Roman Empire, 7, 13, 16–17, 49–50, 52–53, 55, 129, 135, 149, 157, 164, 185, 222n584. *See also* Germany, Germans; *and emperors by name*
Homer, 29n70, 105–7, 265
Horace, 229n609
Hum, 116n243
Hundred Years War, 7, 203–7, 211n546
Hungary, Hungarians, 15, 28, 30, 34, 51–69, 73, 77–79, 81–92, 101–2, 109, 123, 127–29, 135–38, 139n306, 140, 149, 190, 232, 270, 272
Huns, 52, 166
Hunyadi, John, 25, 30, 42, 59–62, 65–68, 78–79, 82, 84–88, 90–92, 102–3, 127–29
Hunyadi, László, 61–62, 65, 81n126

Hunyadi, Matthias. *See* Matthias Corvinus, king of Hungary
Hus, Jan, 136n300, 165n381, 170–71
Huska, Martin, 170n401
Hussites, 32, 55n24, 57n29, 59n38, 63, 79n122, 135–37, 143, 170–71, 203n516
Hystaspes, 67

Iadera, 117
Iapidians, 119
Iberia, 105
Ibrahim Beg, 83n134
Iliad, 265
Illyria, Illyrians, 43, 51, 75, 78, 103, 113, 115–17, 166, 180
Imola, 220
Imola, Benvenuto da, 16–17, 49
India, 105
Ingo, 121
Innocent IV, pope, 249
Inn River, 51, 191, 196
Insubria, 68, 192
Ionia, Ionians, 74, 107
Ionian Sea, 108, 112–13
Ireland, 49n1, 212
Isa, Ottoman prince, 76n109
Isabella of Anjou and Naples, 289–91
Isabella I, queen of Castile, 214n555
Isabella, queen of France, 193n481
Isabella of Portugal, 213n552
Isabelle of Armaganac, 201n512
Isfendiyaroglu, 92
Isidore of Kiev, cardinal, 71–72, 100, 147, 242
Isidore of Seville, 24n58, 68n74, 108
Ismenus River, 106
Ister (Danube) River, 117–18
Istria, Istrians, 115, 117–19
Istula River. *See* Vistula
Italy, Italians, 7, 9–10, 13–14, 17–20, 23n52, 24, 28, 30, 32–34, 36, 43, 51, 54, 65–66, 67, 72, 102, 113–15, 117–19, 128, 148, 166, 180, 181, 185n459, 187, 216–307
Iustinopolis, 117
Iustula River, 149. *See also* Vistula
Iuvavia, 193

Jacobellus of Mies, 170–71
Jadwiga, queen of Poland, 139
Jaime of Portugal, 270–71
Jakob of Baden, 195–196
Jakob I of Sierk, elector and archbishop of Trier, 195, 261
Jakub, Ottoman prince, 75n102
James I, king of Scotland, 7, 211
James II, king of Scotland, 211
Jean II, count of Alençon, 202,
Jean V, count of Armagnac, 201
Jean, count of Clermont, 205
Jean, count of Nevers and Étampes, 205
Jean V, duke of Brittany, 207
Jean, duke of Cleves, 178
Jean le Jeune, bishop of Conserans, 174
Jeanne d'Arc, St., 33, 202, 210n541
Jerome of Prague, 170
Jesi, 275n792, 276, 277n798, 283n819
Jews, 193
Jiškra, Jan, 58–59
Joanna II, queen of Naples, 288n839, 289n845, 305–6
Jobst, emperor, 49n5
Johann of Brandenburg, 189
Johann of Reisberg, 194n486
John XXIII, pope, 179
John V Paleologus, emperor, 75n101
John VI Cantacuzenus, emperor, 75n101, 109n216
John VIII Paleologus, emperor, 71, 104
John, duke of Burgundy, 77, 202n514, 240
John of Bavaria, 240n658
John of Gorizia, 123n263
John Jerome of Prague, 21, 32, 143–46, 170n403
John Paul II, pope, 170n403
Jordanes, 149, 166n387, 213
Joseph II, patriarch of Constantinople, 71, 242
Juan II, king of Castile-León, 213–14
Juan, king of Navarre and Aragon, 213–14, 220n575, 306
Juana of Portugal, 214n555
Julian, friar, 52n10
Julius Caesar, 21n43, 39, 108
Jungingen, Ulrich von, 151n342

Justin, 73n93, 123n262
Justinian, emperor, 98

Kalmar, 168n394
Kalocsa, 66
Karaman, 77n112
Karl, king of Sweden, 168–69
Kaufungen, Conrad von, 40n89, 162
Kempe, Margery, 165n381
Klagenfurt, 122
Komarno, 57n31
Koper, 117n248
Koranda, Václav, 170–71
Kosača, Stefan Vukčič, ruler of Hum, 116
Kosovo, 76n, 78n119, 79n121, 90–92
Kottaner, Helene, 56n27
Kraków, 34, 138
Kritoboulos, 100n181, 101n183
Krujë, 114
Kuhschmalz, Francis, bishop of Warmia, 150

Laconia, 108
Ladislas Postumus, king of Hungary and Bohemia, 57–61, 63n54, 64–65, 79, 126n272, 127–31, 137, 140–41, 161n368, 171, 193, 208, 232, 304n902
Lago di Vico, 258
Lagonissa, Jacopo, 293–94
Lampugnano, Giorgio, 226–27
Langobards, 176
Lapiths, 105
Lapps. *See* Sami
Latins, 14, 34, 71–72, 94, 100, 102, 107–8, 236, 241
Lebus, 158
Lech River, 191
Leibnitz, 162
Leitha River, 51
Leo III, pope, 185n459
Leonard of Chios. *See* Giustiniani, Bishop Leonard
Leonard of Gorizia, 123n263
Leonidas, 106n201
Leonine, 33, 270
Liber, Father (Dionysus), 105–6
Liburnia, 117, 180

Liège, 240
Liguria, Ligurians, 96, 217, 303
Lippe River, 176
Lithuania, Lithuanians, 27, 31–33, 54, 138–47, 151–53
Livonia, 31, 147–48, 151
Livorno, 247n687
Ljubljana, 119
Ljubljanica River, 118–119
Lodi, 223–25, 228, 230, 242, 254n710
Lodi, Peace of, 14, 30, 32, 230, 247, 252, 253n707, 268, 286
Loire River, 182, 184
Lolli, Gregorio, 254
Lollius, Marcus, 176n426
Lombardy, Lombards, 52, 68, 185, 187n465, 220n576, 223, 243, 283n819
London, 210–211
Lorraine, 173n414, 198n497, 202–3, 289
Lothar, 187n465
Lotharingia, 173
Louis the German, emperor, 122
Louis III "the Child," emperor, 186
Louis, dauphin of Vienne (Louis XI of France), 197–198, 201n512, 202–3, 209
Louis IV, king of Germany, 187
Louis, king of Hungary and Poland, 53, 139
Louis III, duke of Anjou (king of Naples), 195, 288n839, 305
Louis I, duke of Savoy, 198–199, 223
Louis of Gorizia, 123n263
Lübeck, 158, 161
Lubiana, 119
Lucan, 133n291
Lucania, 292–93
Lucca, 250
Lucera, 292, 295
Ludwig IV, count palatine of the Rhine, 194–95
Ludwig VII, duke of Bavaria, 193
Ludwig VIII, duke of Bavaria, 193
Ludwig IX, duke of Bavaria, 129, 132, 193
Ludwig I, landgrave of Hesse, 179–80
Lugeum, 118–19
Luis Juan del Mila, cardinal, 239, 270–71

Lüneburg, 33, 158, 164
Lusatia, 156, 164
Luther, Martin, 28
Lutinianus, Bartholomaus, 144
Luxembourg, 53n11, 161n367, 208–9
Lysimachus, 67

Macedon, 12
Macedonia, Macedonians, 67n70, 68–69, 75, 103–6, 108n211, 110, 112–13, 117, 156, 166
Macerata, 276
Machiavelli, Niccolò, 22n50, 24n57, 247n688, 248n690
Maddaloni, 292n857
Maddaloni, Santo di, 294
Madeleine, French princess, 63n54
Maeotic Marsh, 166n386
Magdeburg, 158–59
Magnesia, 103, 105, 110
Magnus Eriksson, king of Sweden and Norway, 167
Maguntia, 186
Magyars, 55n23
Mahmud Pasha, 83n135
Main River, 186
Mainz, 40n89, 157–58, 171, 172n409, 182, 184, 186–88, 194–95
Majorca, 264
Malatesta, Carlo, lord of Rimini, 66, 285n827
Malatesta, Pandolfo, lord of Fano, 285n827
Malatesta, Parasina, 235n640
Malatesta, Sigismondo, lord of Rimini, 244, 246, 252, 277n799, 283, 285–86
Malipiero, Pasquale, doge of Venice, 233
Malorix, 172
Manetti, Giannozzo, 303n901
Manfredi, Astorre, 246–47, 286
Manfredi, Guidantonio, 286
Manfredonia, 295, 299
Manichees, 115–16, 143
Manisa, 89n151
Mantegna, Andrea, 235n642
Mantua, 9, 66, 226n599, 234

Index

Manuel II Paleologus, emperor, 104, 108n212
Marca, Jacopo della, 55–56
Marches, 223, 260, 271, 274–83, 285, 291, 295, 300, 306
Marcomannians, 136
Marcomer, 181
Margaret of Anjou, 203n517
Margaret of Austria, 193n482
Margaret, queen of Denmark, Sweden, Norway, 33 167–68
Margaret of Savoy, 195n490
Maria, queen of Aragon, 215
Maria, queen of Hungary, 53
Maria of Savoy, 219n574
Marie of Anjou, queen of France, 202n515
Marienburg, 151, 153, 155n352
Marius of Arpinum, 166, 274
Mars, 158n358
Marseilles, 306
Marsians, the Marsica, 287, 299, 300
Marsuppini, Carlo, 249n694
Martial, 265n751, 274n789
Martin, St., 158n358, 183
Martin V, pope, 54n15, 174, 255, 272, 284n822, 287
Martinengo, Cesare, 295
Martini, 256n719
Martinopolis, 158
Martorell, Francesc, 252
Masovia, 149–150
Massagetans, 148n331
Massa Marittima, 287–88
Matthias Corvinus, king of Hungary, 59n38, 61–63, 65, 66n64
Maurice, St., 159
Medes, 105
Medici, Cosimo de', 33, 231n620, 238n649, 248, 250
Medici, Lorenzo de', 248n691
Megara, 70, 107
Megarid, 107
Mehmed I, Ottoman sultan, 76n109, 77, 114n238
Mehmed II, Ottoman sultan, 10, 15, 21n46, 72, 81, 89, 91–94, 95n168, 96, 99n178, 100–103, 105n198, 107, 109–10, 231n624, 233n632
Meissen, Meisseners, 156, 158, 163–64
Mella, Juan de, bishop of Zamora, 271
Melo, 176
Merovech, 182n442
Meroveus. *See* Merovech
Merovingians, 182–83
Merseburg, 158
Messenia, 108
Metauro River, 277
Metz, 198n497, 203
Michelozzo (di Bartolomeo), 248n691
Milan, Milanese, 26–27, 34, 104, 144, 199, 208, 217, 219–32, 234, 242–43, 245–46, 249–50, 260, 264n749, 268, 276, 279, 281, 283n819, 285n826, 289, 300n889, 302, 306
Modena, 235
Modon, 231n624
Moers, Dietrich von, elector and archbishop of Cologne, 174n418, 178–79, 261
Moers, Henry von, 178n432, 179
Moers, Johann von, 179
Moers, Walram von, 174–75, 178, 179
Moesia, 67n71
Moganus River, 186
Mojmir II, king of Moravia, 135n298
Moleyns, Adam de, bishop of Chichester, 34, 210
Molossians, 112
Monferrato, 226, 229–30
Mongols, 11, 76n108
Montalto, 282
Montecastello, 243
Montechiaro, Riccio da, 295
Monte Circeo, 302
Montefabbri, 282
Montefeltro, 273
Montefeltro, Federico da, lord of Urbino, 244, 246, 282, 285–86
Montefeltro, Guidantonio da, duke of Urbino, 284–85
Montefeltro, Oddantonio da, duke of Urbino, 284

Montefóscolo, 290
Monte Garulo, Nerio de, bishop of Siena, 239–40
Monteloro, 279–80, 283
Montemilone, 282
Montepulciano, 247
Montesa, 215
Montesanto, 282
Montolmo, 281
Montone, Braccio da, 225n596, 235n642, 274, 278–79, 287, 293
Monza, 225, 227
Moors, 300
Morava River, 131
Moravia, Moravians, 54, 56, 57n29, 135–36, 143
Morea, 105n198, 108–109
Mugello, 242
Muhammad, the Prophet, 78, 113, 201
Münster, 174n418, 176, 178–79
Murad I, Ottoman ruler, 75
Murad II, Ottoman sultan, 30, 56n28, 59, 77–79, 81, 83–93, 101, 104, 109, 114
Mur River, 124
Mursia River, 118
Musa, Ottoman prince, 76n109, 77
Muses, 106
Mustafa, Ottoman prince, 77
Myrmidons, 29n70, 106
Mysia, the Mysians, 51, 69, 75, 84, 117, 166

Nagykanizsa, 66
Naples, Neapolitans, 10, 20–21, 28, 32, 34, 40n89, 111n222, 113n232, 114n237, 203n517, 204n523, 215n557, 220n575, 244–48, 251n699, 254, 269, 276, 282, 286–307
Narni, 274
Naumburg, 158
Nauportus River, 118–19
Navarre, 212–15, 220, 306
Nepi, 266n754, 281n811
Nepos, 117
Nero, emperor, 108, 172
Neszmély, 56
Neustrians, 184n454

Nevers, 202, 205n527
Nicaea, 75n98
Nicholas V, pope, 9, 40n90, 49n1, 71, 115n240, 128, 138n305, 154, 164, 173n413, 179, 194–95, 200–201, 238, 258, 261n731, 261n733, 263–69, 271, 275n793
Nicholas of Cusa, 14n26, 165n381
Nicomedia, 75n98
Nicopolis, 14, 77n110, 112–13
Noce, Giovanni della, 301
Noceto, Pietro da, 144
Nola, 290, 292, 294
Norcia, 274
Noricum, Noricans, 51, 120n256, 189, 191–92
Normandy, 203–5, 210
North Pole, 167
Norway, Norwegians, 33, 148, 165–70
Notaras, Lucas, 100
Novara, 223, 226, 275
Novello, Francesco, lord of Padua, 233n631
Novgorod, 147
Nuremberg, 54, 188–90

Olesnicki, Cardinal Zbigniew, 38–39, 138
Oquenians, 176
Orkneys, 33
Orléans, 182, 208, 222–23
Ornos, Jordi de, 300n887
Orsini, Aldobrandino, 252
Orsini, Caterina of Piombino, 255–57
Orsini, Giovanni Antonio (del Balzo), 290–91, 299n883
Orsini, Latino, cardinal, 272
Orsini, Napoleone, 246
Orsini, Orso, 281
Orsini, Raimondo, 290
Orsini, Rinaldo, 255–57
Orsini family, 272
Ország, Michael, 66
Osman, Ottoman ruler, 14, 74
Ossa, mountain, 105
Otón de Moncado de Luna, 300n887
Otto, bishop of Mainz, 187–88

Otto of Freising, 24, 73, 171, 181n438, n440, 187n467
Ottoman Empire, Ottomans, 4, 9–10, 14–15, 28–30, 33, 35, 52–53, 55–56, 59–62, 65, 67–69, 71n83, 72–79, 81–87, 89–90, 92–106, 108–11, 114–16, 129, 140, 202n512, 216, 230, 233, 253n708, 268, 270–72, 300, 306
Otvos, John, 55n23

Paderborn, 176
Padua, 6, 180, 232–33, 237n647
Padula, 295
Paeonia, 69, 103–4
Palatinate, 194–95
Paleologus, Andronicus, 104
Paleologus, Demetrius, 109
Paleologus, Helen, 81n129
Paleologus, Theophilus, 97
Paleologus, Thomas, 109–10
Palermo, 300n887
Palocz, George de, bishop of Esztergom, 56
Pamphylia, 74
Pancrace of Liptov, 66
Pandolfo, 285
Pannonia, the Pannonians, 51–52, 69, 115, 117, 120, 124, 166, 185, 192
Pannonius, John, 66
Panormita (Antonio Beccadelli), 295n871, 303n901
Papal States, 9, 237n648. See also Rome
Paphlagonia, 103
Parentucelli, Tommaso. See Nicholas V, pope
Paris, 186
Parma, 223, 227, 229, 252n706
Parthians, 70
Paschal III, pope, 159
Patrizi, Francesco, 254
Paul, St., 104, 288
Paul II, pope, 92n161, 273n784
Pausanias, 69
Pavia, 223–24, 242n662
Payne, Peter, 170–71
Pedro, infante of Portugal, 215–16

Pedro of Aragon, 289, 292–93
Pegnitz River, 187, 189
Pelagonia, 103n189
Pelignians, Peligna, 245, 292–93, 299
Pelitza, 91n157
Pellene, 110n221
Peloponnese, 107–11, 231
Peneus River, 105–6
Pepin the Short, king of Francia, 73, 183–85
Pepin II (the Fat) of Heristal, 184
Pera, 75, 94, 96–97, 100
Perotti, Niccolò, 265
Perseus, 112
Persia, Persians, 11, 12, 29n70, 69n78, 105–6, 271
Perugia, 287
Perwez, Theodore de, 240n658
Pesaro, 246n684, 283n818
Pest, 60–61
Petrarch, Francesco, 14n25, 23n52
Peuce, 68
Pherae, 110n221
Philip, king of Macedon, 104
Philip, count of Geneva, 199
Philip III, duke of Burgundy, 14, 83, 172–75, 202, 208–9, 289
Philip, elector and count palatine of the Rhine, 195n490
Philippa, 168
Phocis, 75, 110
Phrygia, 74
Piacenza, 223–24, 226
Piadena, 281n815
Piasio, Battista, 233
Piccinino, Francesco, 228, 281
Piccinino, Jacopo, 225, 228, 251n699, 253–54, 270, 286
Piccinino, Niccolò, 40n90, 220, 225, 242, 260, 270, 274–82, 300n889
Piccolomini, Aeneas Silvius, 4–45, 49–50, 74, 92n161, 110n218, 118, 123, 138, 144, 150, 201n512, 210–11, 215, 226, 231n621, 251, 262–63, 265n750, 266n752, 269, 271, 273
Piccolomini, writings of: letters, 10; *Asia*, 10, 23n55, 28n68, 35, 36, 44n92;

Piccolomini, writings of: (cont.)
   Chrysis, 8; Commentaries, 10, 18;
   Europe, 4, 7, 9, 15–45; Execrabilis, 9;
   Germania, 17; History of Austria, 127;
   History of Bohemia, 15n28, 17, 102,
   135, 171; Miseries of Courtiers, 8;
   Origins and Authority of the Roman
   Empire, 17; Tale of Two Lovers, 8,
   254n713
Picenum, 223n588, 274. See also Marches
Pienza, 5
Pierian Olympus, mountain, 105
Pierre II, duke of Brittany, 207–8
Pindus, 105
Pio, Manfredo, 284
Piombino, 244–45, 255–58
Pisa, 247
Pisa, Antonio da, 259
Pisanello, Antonio, 235n642
Pisidia, 74
Pistoia, 239
Pius II, pope. See Piccolomini, Aeneas
   Silvius
Pizzighettone, 281n815
Pizzolpasso, Francesco, bishop of Milan,
   144n323
Plataea, 69n78
Plato, 34, 236, 264n749
Pliny, 11, 23, 28n68, 68n74, 69, 103n189,
   104–5, 106n199, 108, 110, 112, 117,
   118n252
Plzen, 171n404
Po River, 118, 192, 220, 282
Podiebrad, George, king of Bohemia,
   57n29, 61, 63n55, 137, 162, 171
Podiebrad, Katerina, 63n55
Poitiers, 184n456
Pola, 117
Poland, Poles, 30–31, 34, 51, 53n12, 54,
   56–59, 83–84, 87–88, 137–41, 143,
   148–49, 150n337, 151–55, 190
Pole, William de la, duke of Suffolk, 210
Poliorcetes, Demetrius, 108
Polybius, 108, 112, 265
Pomarance, 243
Pomerania, 156–58, 168–69

Pomesania, 150
Pompeius Trogus, 73n93, 123n262
Pompey, 172
Pomponius Flaccus, 67n71
Pomponius Mela, 23, 117
Pont-de-l'Arche, 204
Pontedera, Antonio da, 259n725
Pontevico, 230n613
Pontifical, use of term, 121n257
Pontius Pilate, 189
Pontus, 73–74
Ponza, 217n562, 220n575, 289n840,
   302n899
Populino, 255
Populonia, 244, 255
Porcari, Stefano, 266–67
Portovenere, 289
Portugal, 18, 212–16, 232n628, 270–71
Posidonius, 166
Pozzuoli, 296
Prague, 21, 32, 61, 133, 137n301, 143–44,
   170, 171n404, 172n409, 194n485
"La Praguerie," 203n516
Priam, 70, 180–81
Prignitz, 158
Primis, Giovanni de, 261n731
Procopius, 298n878
Prokop Holý, 170
Propontis, 69, 84
Protasius of Czernahora, 135
Provence, 289n841, 299n880, 306
Prussia, Prussians, 54, 138–39, 141, 148–
   56, 172n409, 176, 190
Prutenians, 176
Ptolemy, 23, 110–12, 117, 136, 149, 176,
   186, 264n749
Ptolomea of Siena, 235
Puglia, 295
Pula, 117
Pyrenees, 185
Pyrrichean Mountains, 73

Quadians, 136n299
Quintilian, 38, 249
Qur'an, 201

Ragusa, 43, 116
Rammelsberg Mountain, 164n377
Rampini, Enrico, 261n731
Rascians, 52, 69
Reformation, Protestant, 4
Regensburg, 9
Reggio, 235
Reims, 182
Remigius, St., 182
Rencine, 247
Rende, 301n894
René of Anjou, king of Naples, 203, 204, 229–30, 256n718, 288–95, 297–99, 306
Rhaetians, 192
Rhine River, 144, 156, 163n375, 172n411, 173, 175–76, 178–79, 181n441,182, 185–86, 194–95
Rhone River, 182
Richard, duke of York, 210
Ricimer, 182n444
Rido, Antonio, 259n726
Rieti, 274
Rimini, 150n337, 244n673, 285–86
Ripaille, 199n501
Ripley, Sir John, 207n531
Roccacontrada, 277, 282–83
Roccaguglielma, 295–96
Rokycana, Jan, 170–71
Romagna, 68
Romania, 65n59, 69–72, 84
Romano, Orazio, 265
Rome, Romans, 7, 11, 12, 14, 21n44, 33, 50, 52, 54, 64–65, 67, 69n77, 70, 73, 104n191, 112, 116, 124–25, 162, 166, 172, 176, 180–83, 185, 187–88, 192–93, 205, 213n549, 218n571, 220, 232, 235, 254, 258–73, 274n788, 284, 291, 300n888, 304n902. *See also* Holy Roman Empire
Rossano, Bona Caterina da, 277n798
Rossano, Troilo da, 276–77, 280
Rostock, 157
Rotenham, Anthony von, bishop of Bamberg, 187
Rothenburg, 195
Rouen, 204, 210n543, 272

Roxanians, 67, 147
Roxolanians, 147n327
Rožmberk, Henry, 128
Rudolph, duke of Żagań, 155
Rudolph of Diepholt, bishop of Utrecht, 174–75
Rupert, emperor, 49n5
Russians, 72n86, 167n388
Ruthenians, 67, 71, 143, 147, 167, 242

Saal, 121
Sabines, 243, 245n678
Sagundino, Niccolò, 21, 74–75, 241
Salernitans, 293
Sallust, 40
Salona, 117
Salutati, Coluccio, 66n62, 249
Salzburg, 122, 193–94
Salzwedel, 158
Sambia, 150
Sami, 148 n330
Samogitia, 148, 153n345
Sannio. *See* Pelignians, Peligna
Sanseverino, 276
Santiago de Compostela, 213–14, 220
Saracens, 184
Sardanapalus, 123n262
Sardinia, 245n676
Sarmatia, Sarmatians, 138, 148–49, 273
Sarno River, 290
Sarzana, 217n565, 263
Sassoferato, Bartolo da, 249
Satriano, 295n874
Saturnalia, 73
Sava River, 51–52, 69, 101–2, 118–20
Savoy, 6, 195n490, 197–200, 209n538, 219, 223, 263, 300
Saxon Brother War, 161
Saxony, Saxons, 31, 33, 64, 127, 129, 137, 148–49, 156–58, 161–65, 170–71, 177n430, 178, 186–87, 193, 208
Scafati, 290–291
Scandia, 166n387
Scandinavia, 33, 149, 159n361, 166
Scarampo. *See* Trevisan, Ludovico
Schedel, Hartmann, 36

Schism, Papal, 6, 13, 32, 54, 71, 262
Sciarra, Battista, 267
Sclavus, John, 97
Scotland, 7–8, 18, 28, 32–33, 40n89, 49nn1–2, 211–12
Scythia, Scythians, 29, 52, 67, 72, 73n93, 76, 113, 180–81, 185, 271
Segovia, Juan de, 200–201, 300n887
Seine, 184, 204
Senonians, 192
Sepusium, 63
Serbia, Serbians, 30, 55, 60, 62n51, 69, 75n103, 78– 81, 83, 88, 90, 101n184
Sertorius, Quintus, 274
Seville, 215n556
Sforza, Alessandro, 246, 280, 282–83, 295
Sforza, Bianca Maria Visconti, 222n586, 226, 275
Sforza, Drusiana, 225n597
Sforza, Francesco, duke of Milan, 25, 40nn89–90, 220n579, 222–31, 232n625, 234, 242n664, 245–46, 253, 260, 268, 274–83, 285, 287n835, 295–96, 300, 302, 306
Sforza, Muzio Attendolo, 278
Sforza, Polidoro, 275n793
Sforza, Polissena, 285n827
Shakespeare, William, 206n529
Sibenik, 65
Sicambrians, 176, 180–81
Sicily, Sicilians, 111, 195, 203, 215, 219, 236, 245n676, 256, 281n811, 289, 307
Siena, Sienese, 5–6, 8, 34–35, 49, 144n324, 235–36, 239, 240n657, 250–55, 262, 264, 269–70, 287–88
Sigismund, emperor, 49n1, 52–54, 59n38, 66, 77, 124n268, 131, 134–37, 142, 153, 161, 170n403, 171, 189, 216, 220, 262
Sigismund (Zygimantas), duke of Lithuania, 142n319
Sigismund, lord of Tyrol, 132, 133, 196
Silesia, Silesians, 57n29, 136–38, 155–56, 164, 190
Sinop, 92
Siponto, 265n751
Sitonians, 149

Skanderbeg. *See* Castriot, George
Slavonia, 124n267, 128n277
Slavs, 51, 115, 118–20, 124, 143
Slovakia, Slovaks, 57n31, 59n38, 63n56
Slovenia, 118n251
Smederevo, 56, 78, 83n135
Soest, 178
Sofia, 79, 82, 91
Soissons, 182
Sophia of Kiev, 140n310
Sorel, Agnes, 209
Sozzini, Mariano, 254
Spain, Spanish, 18, 28, 49n1, 54, 166, 200, 201, 212–16, 269, 271, 274n788, 289n840, 305–7
Spano, Pippo, 54
Spartans, 69, 106n201
Spinola, Francesco, 217
Spinola family, 218, 303n900
Spoleto, 266n754, 274
Spree River, 158
Squarciafico, Uberto, 302n898
Sredna, 66n64
Stades, modern equivalent, 84n141
Stefan Tomas, king of Bosnia, 115
Stendal, 158
Stensson, Knut, 168–69
Stephen, St., 57n31, 63n53
Stettin, 157
Stewart, Walter, earl of Atholl, 211
St. Jakob an der Sihl, 197n495
Stockholm, 169
Strabo, 11, 23, 28n68, 43, 69–70, 104, 106n199, 107n204–5, 108n208, 110, 111n223, 112–13, 115, 118, 147, 166, 176, 192–93, 264n749
Stralsund, 157
Strasbourg, 200
Stratonice, 108
Straubing, 194
Strymon River, 69
St. Veit an der Glan, 118, 120, 123n264
Styria, 40n89, 51, 58–59, 120, 124–26, 128
Subequana Valley, 291
Sudinians, 136
Suevians, 176n427

Suffolk, 210
Suleyman, 75–77
Sulla, Lucius, 124
Sullaceum, 124
Sulmona, 291
Suno, 181
Surienne, François de, 203–4
Svatopluk, king of Moravia, 135
Švitrigaila, duke of Lithuania, 142
Swabia, Swabians, 183, 186, 191–95
Sweden, Swedes, 33, 165–70
Switzerland, the Swiss, 6–7, 196–99, 203, 220
Syagrius, 182–83
Sygambrians, 176
Syria, 76, 105, 149
Szécsi, Dénes, cardinal and archbishop of Esztergom, 58, 66
Székelys, 64
Székesfehervár, 55, 57, 58, 63n53
Szilágyi, László, 80
Szilágyi, Michael, 61–62, 65, 67, 80–81
Szumborski, Bernard, 155n351

Taborites, 170
Tacitus, 96n169, 98n175, 172
Tagliacozzo, Giovanni, count of, 272
Talbot, Henry, 207n531
Talbot, John, earl of Shrewsbury, 204–207
Talbot, John, viscount of Lisle, 206n529, 207
Tamerlane (Timur Lenk), 76
Tannenberg, 40n89, 54n17, 152–53
Taracontan islands, 73
Taranto, 290, 295, 299n883
Tartars, 67, 139, 147, 151–53
Tauriscans, 192
Taurus, 52, 105
Teano, 301
Tebaldi, Giacomo, bishop of Montefeltro, 273
Tebaldi, Simone, 273
Teramo, Teramitans, 280, 283
Terracina, 300
Teutonic Knights, 54, 141, 147–56
Thames River, 210

Thebes, 106
Theodosius I, emperor, 104
Theodosius II, emperor, 70n81
Theopompus of Chios, 112
Thermopylae, 29n70, 106
Thérouanne, 174
Thessalonica, 74n95, 77, 78n115, 104, 109
Thessaly, Thessalians, 29n70, 75, 103–6, 110
Thorn, 150n336, 151n339, 153n345, 155n352
Thrace, 67–72, 75–77, 101, 103, 105
Thucydides, 264n749
Thuringia, Thuringians, 127n276, 156–60, 161n367, 162, 164, 179, 181–82, 186
Tiber River, 33, 158, 243, 259, 270
Tiberius, emperor, 176n424, 296
Tifernate, Gregorio, 23n54, 264
Tifernate, Niccolò, 144
Timavo, 115, 119
Tisza River, 56, 118
Tivoli, 243, 260
Tocco, Carlo, lord of Arta, 22n51, 111n222
Tocco, Leonardo, 111n222
Todi, 260
Toggenburg, 197n494
Tolentino, 276
Tomoritsa, 114n237
Torquemada, Juan de, 21n46
Torre del Greco, 296
Torre di Palme, 280
Tortona, 223, 226, 228n605
Torún, 149, 150n336
Toscanella, Giovanni, 218n571
Toscano, Galeotto, 227
Toul, 198n497, 203
Tournai, 182
Tours, 184
Tragurium, 117
Trajan, emperor, 52
Trani, 256n718, 291
Transylvania, 52, 59n39, 64–68
Trapani, 302n899
Trastevere, 259
Trent, 196

Trevisan, Ludovico Scarampo, cardinal,
   242, 259, 281, 300
Triballians, 51, 69, 75
Trier, 182, 195, 261
Trieste, 8, 119, 263, 269
Trinci, Corrado, ruler of Foligno, 259
Trivento, 299n883
Troad, 70
Troia, 258, 281n811, 295
Troy, Trojans, 72, 180
Tudeschi, Niccolò de, archbishop of
   Palermo, 300n887
Tuditanus, Gaius Sempronius, 118
Tunisia, 306n910
Turbin, 194
Turkey, modern, 3
Turks. See Ottoman Empire, Ottomans
Tuscany, Tuscans, 243–44, 251, 253–56,
   259, 261, 263, 286, 301–2
Tyrol, 132, 133n290, 134n293, 196

Ujlaki, Nicholas, voivode of Transylvania,
   66
Ukrainians, 147n326, 167n388
Ulm, 195
Ulmerigans, 149
Ulrich, count of Cilli, 34, 58, 60–61, 81,
   119, 123, 124n267, 125, 126n272, 128–30
Umbria, Umbrians, 259n726, 264n749,
   274–82
Ungnad, John, 126
Ungnad, George, 126
Uppsala, 169
Urban II, pope, 11n18
Urbino, 244, 246, 282, 284–86, 288
Urbisaglia, 281n815
Urrea, Lope Ximénez de, 281
Utraquists, 171n405
Utrecht, 171, 172n410, 173–76, 179

Vada, 247
Valachia, Vlachs, 52, 59, 64–65, 67–69, 77,
   79n121, 84
Valdemar IV Atterdag, king of Denmark,
   167
Val di Bagno, 247n689

Valence, 223
Valencia, 215, 269, 280, 307
Valentinian, emperor, 157, 181
Valeria, 51, 124
Valla, Lorenzo, 249n693, 264, 303n901
Valtellina, 220n578
Várad, 54, 66
Varano, Piergentile, 259n725
Varese, Perpetua da, 275
Varna, 9n11, 14, 25, 29–30, 40n89, 79–91,
   109, 140n312
Vatican Library, 266n753
Vegio, Maffeo, 242
Venedians, 149
Venice, Venetians, 34, 54, 74n95, 77,
   78n115, 83, 84n138, 88, 92, 95n168,
   100, 104, 113, 118, 180, 220–21, 223–25,
   228–34, 237n647, 242–43, 245, 246,
   252–53, 260–62, 267n756, 268–69, 273,
   276, 281n815, 282–83, 285, 301–2
Venier, Leonardo, 228–29
Ventimiglia, Giovanni, marquis of Gerace,
   22n51, 111, 281–82, 290, 294
Ventimiglia family, 301
Vercellae, 166n384
Verden, 158
Verdun, 198n497
Vergerio, Pier Paolo, 65–66
Verme, Luigi dal, 225
Verona, 6, 66, 69, 112, 236
Veronica (of Cilli), 124
Vienna, 55–56, 65, 128–33
Vienne, 197, 202, 209
Vilamari, Bernat, 113, 303n900
Vincent of Beauvais, 24n58
Vindelicans, 192
Virgil, 66, 96n171, 117n245, 122, 180n437,
   215n558, 263n743
Virgin Mary, 8, 159
Virunum, 120n256
Visconti, Filippo Maria, duke of Milan, 27,
   40n90, 199, 208, 217–24, 227, 231n620,
   232, 242–43, 250, 261, 274–76, 281–83,
   289, 306–7
Visconti, Giangaleazzo, duke of Milan,
   249, 251n700

Visconti, Valentina, 208n535
Visigoths, 183n447, 307n912
Visso, 276
Vistula River, 138n304, 148–50, 170
Visurgis River, 175
Vitelleschi, Giovanni, patriarch of Alexandria, 22n51, 259, 274n274, 290–91, 306
Viterbo, 265n750
Vitéz, John, bishop of Varád, 66
Vitovec, John, 125
Vitus, St., 61
Viztum, Apel, 161–62
Vladislas IV of Hungary. *See* Wladyslaw III, king of Poland and Hungary
Vlorë, 114
Vogelsang, 151n339
Vogtland, 197–200
Volkertsdorf, Sigismund of, archbishop of Salzburg, 194
Volterra, 243, 247
Vytautus, duke of Lithuania, 54, 141–43, 146, 151

Wallsee, 118
Warmia, 150, 273
Wars of the Roses, 34, 211n545
Wenceslas, emperor and king of Bohemia, 49–50, 54, 136, 171
Weser River, 156, 175

Westphalia, 171, 173–79
Wiener-Neudstadt, 9, 128, 130–32
Wilhelm, duke of Austria, 139
Wilhelm III, duke of Saxony, 127, 129, 137, 161–62, 209n537
William of Malmesbury, 11n18, 22n48
Wismar, 157
Witold. *See* Vytautus
Wittenberg, 164
Wladyslaw II Jagiello, king of Poland, 31, 139–41, 143, 151–52
Wladyslaw III, king of Poland and Hungary, 30, 57–60, 66n68, 83–85, 87, 89n151, 140
Würzburg, 187–88

Xàtiva, 280
Xerxes, 29n70, 76, 106

York, 210–11

Zacharias, pope, 184n451
Zambeccari family, 237, 238n652
Zamora, 271
Žižka, Jan, 170
Zlatitsa Pass, 82n133
Znojmo, 54, 136
Zürich, 197–98
Zygimantas. *See* Sigismund, duke of Lithuania

Europe was designed in Dante and composed by Kachergis Book Design of Pittsboro, North Carolina. It was printed on 60-pound House Natural Smooth and bound by Sheridan Books of Ann Arbor, Michigan.

www.ingramcontent.com/pod-product-compliance
Lightning Source LLC
Chambersburg PA
CBHW031404290426
44110CB00011B/250